TV'S BIGGEST HITS

TV'S BIGGEST HITS

The Story of Television Themes from
"Dragnet" to "Friends"

Jon Burlingame

SCHIRMER BOOKS
An Imprint of Simon & Schuster Macmillan
New York
Prentice Hall International
London   Mexico City   New Dehli   Singapore   Sydney   Toronto

Permission to quote the following lyrics is gratefully acknowledged:

"Car 54 Where Are You": Lyrics by Nat Hiken, music by John Strauss, Jonalion Music, Ltd. (ASCAP). Copyright 1961, renewed 1989.

"The Ballad of Jed Clampett": Music and lyrics by Paul Henning. © 1962 Carolintone Music Company, Inc.

Schirmer Books
An Imprint of Simon & Schuster Macmillan
1633 Broadway
New York, NY 10019

Library of Congress Catalog Card Number: 96-13289

Printed in the United States of America

Printing Number
1 2 3 4 5 6 7 8 9 10

Library of Congress Cataloging-in-Publication Data

Burlingame, Jon.
    TV's biggest hits : the story of television themes from Dragnet to
Friends / Jon Burlingame.
        p.   cm.
    Includes bibliographical references and index.
    ISBN 0-02-870324-3 (alk. paper)
    1. Television music—History and criticism.   I. Title.
ML2080.B87   1996   96-13289
781.5′46′09—dc20   CIP
                                              MN

This paper meets the requirements of ANSI/NISO Z39.48-1992 (Permanence of Paper).

To the memory of David Kraft (1957–1993)

Table of Contents

Acknowledgments

First, I offer heartfelt thanks to all of the composers, producers, music editors, and other professionals who agreed to be interviewed for this book (and, in a few special cases, lent me tapes of their original scores). It is their work that inspired this chronicle.

Many people, both inside and outside of the television business, contributed time, information, and guidance. I owe an enormous debt to James DiPasquale and David Raksin, who opened the files of the now-defunct Composers and Lyricists Guild of America, where I discovered a wealth of information and literally hundreds of obscure television credits (particularly for now-stellar film composers).

Richard Carlin, my long-suffering editor, and composer Fred Karlin (the author of two Schirmer books on film music) were supportive of this project from the start. I am grateful to both.

Similarly, a nod of thanks to my friends at ASCAP and BMI, where I began my research: at BMI, Michael McGehee, Doreen Ringer-Ross, and Dave Sanjek; at ASCAP, Nancy Knutsen, Jamie Richardson, Kim Dankner, and Pam Allen. Friends on the business side of music-making in Los Angeles were also of great help, notably Dennis Dreith of the Recording Musicians Association and Bill Peterson of Local 47, American Federation of Musicians.

Three colleagues read the manuscript and acted as early editors of the material: Craig Henderson, editor of the media quarterly *For Your Eyes Only,* whose detailed knowledge of the history of television is unparalleled in my experience; D. L. Fuller, to whom I regularly turned for background on many of the composers discussed herein; and Nick Redman, whose literary and musical insights enabled me to find the right balance of fact and anecdote.

I am especially grateful to my musical mentors Bruce Babcock, Richard Bellis, and Larry Blank, who helped me to locate any number of composers and musicians that I might never have tracked down otherwise, and offered frequent advice on musical matters. Tony Thomas, Jeannie Pool, Randall Larson, Fred Steiner, Pam Gates, Lois Carruth, Arthur Hamilton, David Schecter, Clifford McCarty, Susanna Moross Tarjan, D. J. Olsen, Lori Barth, Andy Edelstein, Michael O'Hara, Mauro Bruno, Gene Walsh, David Walstad, Ted Richichi, John W. Waxman, Ronny Schiff, Dennis Spiegel, Vic Ghidalia, and Ford A. Thaxton have proven to be special friends whose knowledge, business contacts, and advice were equally important.

Friends in the TV business who helped—often with huge favors involving programs in their archives and tape libraries—include Frank Annino at Universal, Donna Dees and Tom Goodman at CBS News, Eileen Kurtz and Dan Doran at ABC, Lucy Kraus at ABC News, Kevin McDonald at CBS, Brian Robinette at NBC, Robyn Burt and Susan Baerwald at NBC Productions, Earl Weirich and Ann Abrahams at cable's Family Channel, Zenon Dmytryk and Jim Weiss at TNT, Brian Donlon at Lifetime, David Stapf at Lorimar/Warner Bros., Kathleen Nitting at fX, Carla Princi of Disney TV, Ellen Stanley and Anne Marie Hammers of the National Geographic Society, Chris Creed and Pete Sauerbrey at the Sci-Fi Channel, Mark Ringwald at Nostalgia Television, and Shirley Powell at the Cartoon Network.

Assisting me with the research for this book were a number of professionals who not only were interested in the subject but went out of their way to help me find otherwise unattainable material. Among them were Ned Comstock of the cinema-TV library at the University of Southern California; Stephen Fry and Timothy Edwards at the music library of the University of California at Los Angeles; Stuart Ng at the Warner Bros. archives at USC; Warren Sherk, Stacey Behlmer, and Howard Prouty at the Margaret Herrick Library of the Academy of Motion Picture Arts and Sciences; James D'Arc of Brigham Young University; Dave Smith of the Walt Disney Studio Archives; Hank Rieger and Charles Phillips of the Academy of Television Arts and Sciences; and Gina Handy and Ann Gunning at TV Data Technologies in Queensbury, New York.

I am also grateful, for myriad favors, to music contractor Sandy DeCrescent, Scott Perry at Turner Entertainment, Julian Bratalyubov at the Universal music library, Joel Franklin at the Warner Bros. music library, Bob Krueger in the Paramount Television music department, and John Williams of the British publication *Music from the Movies*.

Dave Mitchell, film-score archivist extraordinaire, and Steve Harris, whose own books have covered the world of movie and TV scores on record more thoroughly and with greater accuracy than anyone to date, supplied amazingly obscure audio and video recordings. Henry Adams, Brad Arrington, Larry Blamire, Jim Doherty, Irving Jacobs, John King, and Sal Mauriello permitted me access to their video collections; and Donovan and Heidi Brandt helped me to locate dozens of long-forgotten shows.

Several colleagues graciously gave me permission to quote from their interviews: John Caps (Jerome Moross), D. L. Fuller (Gerald Fried, Stan Margulies), Ron Miller of the *San Jose Mercury News* (Henry Mancini), Gary Crowdus of *Cineaste* (Ennio Morricone), and David Kraft (John Addison).

Experts who offered help on specific composers include Nick Redman (Jerry Fielding), Steven C. Smith (Bernard Herrmann), Bobbie Fromberg (Victor Young), Bill Halvorsen (Percy Faith), Phil Lehman (John Addison), Linda Danly (Hugo Friedhofer), Steven Lasker (Duke Ellington), John W. Morgan (Max Steiner), Preston Neal Jones (Hans J. Salter, Walter Schumann),

John Fitzpatrick (Miklós Rózsa), Bart Andrews (Eliot Daniel), and Jim DiGiovanni (Michel Legrand).

The tireless Lenore Coffman transcribed many of the interviews that are excerpted throughout this book.

Finally, and most important, my grateful thanks and personal gratitude to three close friends who believed in this project and encouraged me when few others did: Nick Redman, Steven Smith, and the late David Kraft.

Jon Burlingame
1995

Introduction

Television music, someone once said, is "the soundtrack of our lives." For the postwar "baby boom" generation and beyond, that is unquestionably true. We grew up in front of the set. The music that accompanied those images became—for better or worse—indelibly stamped on our minds. Kids of the fifties don't think of the *William Tell* overture as the start of a Rossini opera: to them it's the "Lone Ranger" theme. Children of the sixties can sing "a horse is a horse, of course, of course"; "now sit right back and you'll hear a tale, a tale of a fateful trip"; and "they're creepy and they're kooky, mysterious and spooky"—all instantly recognizable as the title songs for "Mister Ed," "Gilligan's Island," and "The Addams Family," respectively.

Instrumental music, too, became as familiar as the pop tunes we were hearing on the radio. Any boomer can hum the opening notes of the "Dragnet," "Twilight Zone," and "Hawaii Five-0" themes. Kids who grew up still later are equally conversant with the music of "The Brady Bunch," "The Mary Tyler Moore Show," "Dynasty," and "Hill Street Blues."

But the story of this unique subgenre of American popular music extends well beyond the simple creation of catchy tunes or clever lyrics. Virtually all of the most successful film composers of the 1960s, 1970s, and 1980s—including Jerry Goldsmith, John Williams, Henry Mancini, and Lalo Schifrin—enjoyed their first taste of success in television. They learned and honed their craft toiling on weekly series.

For veteran film composers, the sixties and seventies marked a downturn in their motion-picture fortunes, especially as the movies increasingly shunned the traditional film score in favor of pop songs. So men like Alex North, Bronislau Kaper, Bernard Herrmann, George Duning, Franz Waxman, and Hugo Friedhofer turned to the small screen for work, while others including Earle Hagen, Arthur Morton, and Alexander Courage (who had worked on major films in better times) not only found steady employment in TV, but enjoyed bigger success in the new medium than they ever found in the old one.

And their work wasn't all for silly sitcoms, clichéd westerns, or turgid drama shows. Some of the century's most celebrated composers created music for television, often in the documentary field: Richard Rodgers on "Victory at Sea," Norman Dello Joio for "Air Power," Darius Milhaud on "The Twentieth Century," and Morton Gould with "World War I." Even the great Aaron Copland composed the theme for "CBS Playhouse."

In the seventies and eighties, as the made-for-TV movie matured into a forum for important social discourse and the miniseries tackled subjects on a grand scale—from "Roots" to "War and Remembrance," "Shogun" to "Lonesome Dove"—the medium lost much of its stigma, as front-rank film composers such as Elmer Bernstein, David Raksin, John Barry, Michel Legrand, and Ennio Morricone wrote television scores that lingered in the memory just as their greatest music for films always has.

Music for television is often dismissed as lacking the quality or lasting impact of feature film scores. This is the argument made by arrogant, elitist, and largely ignorant observers who consider the medium as a whole beneath serious consideration. Television scoring—just like its better-paid cousin, music for movies—is written to exacting specifications, under pressure of impending airdates and impatient producers, and is designed to meet specific dramatic needs. The difference is that the small screen demands more music, more quickly, and, these days, more cheaply.

To relegate all TV music to the junk pile is myopic. The fact is that not all film scores are great, just as not all television scores are memorable. Both are commercial endeavors, combining art and business for the sake of profit (and sometimes entertainment, education, or edification). Even Mozart didn't write *Così Fan Tutte* as high art; he was trying to pay his bills.

What follows is a survey of music for American television, from its earliest days, when very little of the music was original, to the present. The focus is on music specifically created for the medium, although there is (in Chapter 1) a discussion of the extensive use of library music for "tracking" into various shows. Three areas of television music are outside the scope of this study: daytime (mostly soap operas and game shows); public television (most of whose dramas have been British imports); and the realm of musicals and operas (which deserves a detailed study of its own).

This book is the product of several years' research, including nearly two hundred interviews with composers, producers, orchestrators, and music editors; a thorough review of what little previous literature exists in the field; and viewings of countless series episodes, documentaries, telefilms, and miniseries with a critical eye toward the scores as they were heard by the millions of viewers at home over the past forty-odd years.

I make no pretense of musicological analysis. While I hope that musicians and other industry professionals will find this work informative, my intent was always to reach a more general readership: viewers who remember, with some fondness, the themes and music they grew up with. I hope this book will be both nostalgic and enlightening, gently prodding readers to listen just a little more closely the next time they turn on the set.

Hi-yo, Silver!
The Birth of TV Music

Many of television's earliest series simply moved over from radio, in some cases taking the same scripts and committing them to film (or restaging them live). Making the transition were many of the same actors and producers—and, often, the music.

Television adopted the commonplace radio strategy of using "canned" music in the vast majority of shows. Only in the rarest instances were early television programs actually graced with original music. The term "canned music" applied to prerecorded selections, usually chosen for specific purposes (whether "source" music, meaning originating on a radio, record player, or other obvious source; or as dramatic cues, designed to evoke suspense, create romantic moods, bridge disparate scenes, or otherwise enhance the on-screen action).

The classic example of a popular radio hero adapted for the new medium—along with his highly identifiable theme music—was "The Lone Ranger" (1949–57, ABC). A radio favorite since 1933, the masked avenger of the western plains was heralded by the finale of the overture to Gioacchino Rossini's 1829 opera *William Tell.*

The opening trumpet notes, and the narrator intoning, "A fiery horse with the speed of light, a cloud of dust and a hearty hi-yo Silver!" made the transition to the small screen intact. As in radio, the drama was heightened by additional excerpts of classical music drawn from the works of composers such as Tchaikovsky and Liszt, plus music originally written for the "Lone Ranger" movie serials and other Republic westerns.

In fact, the performances themselves were identical. "We had all of the music which had been recorded in Chicago by George W. Trendle, who owned the Lone Ranger," music editor Byron Chudnow recalled. "All those pieces, that familiar classical stuff that was on the radio. They sent the records out to us, and I had the records transferred to film. We'd never even heard of tape."

Chudnow, who had long studied the violin, was the only musician at Apex Films, where "The Lone Ranger" was being edited. So the job of putting music to the adventures of Clayton Moore and Jay Silverheels fell to him. "Most of [the cues] were bridges from one scene to another; sometimes you had a horse chase," he said. In all, he estimated, the entire music library consisted of only a few dozen cues (all "badly recorded, with a small orchestra," Chudnow remembered). "People didn't expect anything else."

The entire "Lone Ranger" music library amounted to twenty-five single-sided, twelve-inch, 33 1/3 rpm transcription records (plus the *William Tell* overture on a 78 rpm disc); sixty-seven of its eighty-nine cuts were classical music excerpts, the remainder rescored pieces of compositions by Republic composers William Lava, Alberto Colombo, Karl Hajos, and Cy Feuer. The music was recorded in Mexico around 1940.

The use of previously written and recorded music was known, as it was in radio, as a "needle-drop." In radio, an engineer literally cued up a record and lowered the needle onto the spinning platter at the appropriate moment during the action. In television, it was technically more complex: music was committed to film as a carefully synchronized element of the sight-and-sound presentation. But the object of the score—increasing the tension, propelling the chases, emphasizing emotional moments—and the nature of the music itself, remained the same.

The vast majority of filmed television shows utilized canned music for a simple reason: it was cheaper than recording new scores. James C. Petrillo, the iron-fisted president of the American Federation of Musicians, had long fought against the "mechanized" use of music in film, phonograph records, and radio (because it supposedly discouraged the employment of musicians for live performances). In 1950, Petrillo demanded that producers pay a 5 percent tax on the cost of every show that used union musicians to record a score, with the surcharge payable to the union's already-rich Performance Trust Fund. The networks agreed to Petrillo's demand in 1951, but members of AFM locals 47 (Los Angeles) and 802 (New York) fought the controversial union boss on the issue, correctly believing that the demand had cost them considerable work—because producers balked at such payments and skipped hiring "live" musicians altogether.

CBS West Coast music director Lud Gluskin, during testimony at a House subcommittee hearing in May 1956, blamed AFM policies for the fact that an average show using ten musicians cost $2,000 in salaries and another $1,500 in Trust Fund payments. Because of this, he routinely went abroad to record music for CBS television and radio broadcasts (and was expelled from the

Lud Gluskin. Courtesy Hearst Newspaper Collection, USC Library.

union for doing so). An attorney for an association of TV producers testified at the same hearing that "90 percent of the television film now being produced is made with canned music."

Producers avoided much of the expense associated with recording music in Hollywood by privately licensing canned music that had been recorded outside the United States, often in Europe or Mexico. A number of entrepreneurs—some of them composers, some just shrewd music "packagers"—shopped these "libraries" of dramatic cues around town, particularly to independent producers who were anxious to provide stations with much-needed product for the burgeoning medium.

"The Adventures of Superman" (1952–57), one of television's first, and most successful, syndicated series, was typical of the programs that utilized music libraries. For the first season of this enduring adaptation of the DC Comics hero ("fighting a never-ending battle for truth, justice, and the American way!"), producer Robert Maxwell contracted with music packager David Chudnow (the father of "Lone Ranger" music editor Byron).

Chudnow (b. 1902) pioneered the music-library business in television. A former studio pianist, he eventually became an independent music supervisor for dozens of mostly low-budget films throughout the 1940s, hiring composers, overseeing recording sessions, and handling the music budget. In 1950, he created the Mutel (Music for Television) music service. "Lucky Strike Theater," later known as "Robert Montgomery Presents" (1950–57, NBC), became his first client; "Superman" quickly followed.

Chudnow approached talented composers eager for work and paid them a flat fee to write music that could fit a variety of dramatic situations. He then took the music overseas for recording, committed it to film, and created a series of discs that could be played for producers and music editors for auditioning purposes.

Three of his earliest composers were Herschel Burke Gilbert, Joseph Mullendore, and Herb Taylor (each of whom would go on to later fame with the themes for such fondly remembered shows as "The Rifleman," "Honey West," and "Death Valley Days," respectively). Gilbert recalled: "Chudnow came to us and said, 'Look, I need music for television. You guys write me two hours of music.' I don't remember if he gave us a thousand dollars apiece. We wrote two or three chases; two or three mysteriosos, you know, the sneak-alongs; some comedy music, [and] love themes. And we'd write them so they could be longer or shorter, and with long tails so that they could be edited. By then, we really knew what we were doing from a craftsman's point of view."

As written, most of the "cues" (individual pieces of music) were rather long—a minute and a half, two minutes—and played by an approximately forty-piece orchestra, conducted by an anonymous Frenchman. Because this was an operation effectively designed to circumvent union regulations, the composers adopted pseudonyms for purposes of royalty payments by the music-licensing organizations (in this case, ASCAP, the American Society of Composers, Authors and Publishers; and BMI, Broadcast Music Incorporated, which later represented many film and TV writers). "But we still got the credit," Gilbert pointed out, "because we sent ASCAP a list of our pseudonyms. That's why we wrote the music, to get the ASCAP credit, and it's made some of us fairly rich today. So it was no joke."

Their music was "tracked" into dozens of fifties series, besides "Superman": "Annie Oakley" (1952–56, syndicated), "Broken Arrow" (1956–58, ABC), "Captain Midnight" (1954–56, CBS), "China Smith" (1953, syndicated), "Duffy's Tavern" (1954, syndicated), "Man with a Camera" (1958–60, ABC), "Racket Squad" (1951–53, CBS), "Ramar of the Jungle" (1952–53, syndicated), "Sky King" (1951–54, NBC, ABC), "Topper" (1953–55, CBS), and many others. In subsequent seasons of "Superman," the Mutel music was supplanted by music from British mood libraries.

Another aspect of the music of "Superman" that typified fifties TV scores was the commission of an original series theme: music written and recorded specifically for the opening main-title sequence, the end-credit roll, and, sometimes, interludes during the body of the program itself. For this, the producers turned to composer Leon Klatzkin (1914–92), who had written music for Hal

Roach films (including *Tales of Robin Hood,* 1951), and would later go on to score CBS westerns such as "Gunsmoke" and "Cimarron Strip."

Just as much of the visual main-title sequence for "Superman" mirrored the opening of the Max Fleischer cartoons of the 1940s, Klatzkin's heroic theme—familiar to generations of wide-eyed young superhero fans—was actually inspired by the fanfare composed by Sammy Timberg for the animated Fleischer series. (Both would later be echoed in John Williams's far more memorable symphonic score for the first of the big-budget Christopher Reeve *Superman* movies in 1978.) Klatzkin also supplied library music to the fledgling television operation at Twentieth Century-Fox, beginning with "My Friend Flicka" (1956–57, CBS), "Broken Arrow," and "How to Marry a Millionaire" (1958–59, syndicated).

Another prominent figure was Alexander Laszlo (1895–1970), a Hungarian-born composer who emigrated to the United States in 1938 and became active in film work during the 1940s. Laszlo supplied music to the Roland Reed filmed-television operation, which produced such shows as the sitcom "My Little Margie" (1952–55, CBS/NBC), the drama "Waterfront" (1954–56, syndicated), and the early science-fiction serial "Rocky Jones, Space Ranger" (1954, syndicated). "He had recorded [the music] in Europe, or Mexico, or in his garage," music editor Robert Raff quipped. "I think he wrote most, if not all, of it, because his style was quite distinctive.

"I really started working with him on what the cues should be, and what music should sound like for television," Raff said. "I found most of the music to be like underscore for motion pictures. He was a fine musician, but he had not been trained in the intricacies of television. We had long discussions, and he started coming up with music cues that were more in keeping for TV. If I was stuck [without music for a scene], I would call him and he would manufacture, somehow or other, the particular cue."

Composer Albert Glasser (b. 1916), who later became famous for scoring such drive-in movie classics as *The Amazing Colossal Man* (1957) and *Teenage Caveman* (1958), was responsible for the music of "The Cisco Kid" (1950–55, syndicated) and "Big Town" (1950–56, CBS/NBC). Both series employed libraries of music, but unlike many series, all of the music was clearly Glasser's and a substantial portion was original to television.

Producer Phil Krasne, who made low-budget *Cisco Kid* movies in the late 1940s, had struck a deal with independent television producer Fred Ziv to create a "Cisco Kid" series for syndication. The TV programs were to retain two key elements from the films: actors Duncan Renaldo and Leo Carillo as Cisco and his sidekick Pancho, and the flavorful, Mexican-style music written by Glasser for the original films.

Glasser gathered up the scores, sent them to a colleague in Tokyo for rerecording, and delivered the finished tracks to a music editor at Ziv's for tracking purposes. "The Cisco Kid," filmed in color, became another favorite with

Albert Glasser. Courtesy Screen Archives.

the younger set, and Glasser's rousing score accompanied all 155 episodes. (Glasser, despite being paid only $3,000, including all orchestra costs, achieved an authentic sound on the old film scores by spending time researching Mexican music of the period.)

While "Cisco Kid" simply reused the music from the *Cisco* movies, Glasser's "Big Town" was one of the first scores specifically conceived as a library of original music for one series. Another adaptation of a popular radio show, "Big Town" was a half-hour newspaper drama featuring Patrick McVey as crusading crime reporter Steve Wilson and Mary K. Wells as society columnist Lorelei Kilbourne. Explained Glasser: "I would compose a ton of music for all the scenes in the series, including the cues for into-commercial, out-of-commercial, fights, love scenes, driving around town, chasing the crooks, in the police station, etc., etc. Then I would orchestrate the whole mess and send it in a big bundle to [another overseas friend] in Paris. There he would get the music copied out—it was much cheaper there—get the musicians and record everything on quarter-inch tape."

Glasser conceptualized his music based on scripts. ("Big Town" debuted as a live series in New York in 1950 but moved to Hollywood as a filmed series in 1952, and it was for those shows that Glasser's music was designed.) For his main theme, the composer went the Gershwin route of *An American in Paris*, attempting, in the composer's words, to portray "the exciting rhythms of traffic in the big city, with a sweeping melodic line."

In 1954, the series switched networks and was recast with Mark Stevens (formerly "Martin Kane, Private Eye") and Trudy Wroe. And, recalled Glasser, the sponsors demanded new music as well: specifically, something along the lines of the then-popular "Dragnet" theme. Glasser ultimately came up with a five-note phrase (instead of the familiar "Dragnet" four-note motif) and wrote "a ton of material, all based on those five notes." It was all scored for eight French horns and two percussionists (the latter playing not only timpani but also snare drums, vibes, cymbals, and more). "Some of the tricks I had to devise to get various flavors and sounds out of this combination started to become very sneaky," he said.

Although Glasser had planned a Paris recording session, as he had done for the orchestral "Big Town" score, he ended up literally recording the music in his own living room in Los Angeles. Two horn players and one percussionist, using overdubs, recorded the entire score. Although this was technically a violation of union regulations then in force, Glasser was proud that the $3,500 he had to record the score went to three local musicians and a sound engineer, and not overseas to anonymous French performers.

Raoul Kraushaar (b. 1908), a music director at Republic Pictures, frequently enlisted composers to write music for films, often without screen credit. Much of the music written under Kraushaar's aegis wound up in his own music service. The original "Lassie" (1954–71, CBS), starring Tommy Rettig, was among the first series to utilize the Kraushaar library for tracking purposes. The earliest MGM TV shows, including "The Thin Man" (1957–59, NBC) and "Northwest Passage" (1958–59, NBC), were also scored with music from the Kraushaar library.

Composer Dave Kahn (b. 1910) was one of Kraushaar's "ghost" writers. He wrote some of the library music heard in the "Hopalong Cassidy" episodes specifically made for syndication (1952–54), a business relationship that had resulted from Kahn's work as an orchestrator on Republic westerns. Kahn's anonymity stretched into the 1960s (when he became a screen-credited music editor at Filmways), but his music—mostly written for track libraries—was everywhere on television in the late 1950s. The fame he never enjoyed should have begun with his music for "Alfred Hitchcock Presents" (1955–62, CBS/NBC), the half-hour suspense anthology hosted in droll fashion, and occasionally directed, by the master filmmaker.

Kahn created one of the early orchestral arrangements of Charles Gounod's *Funeral March of a Marionette,* which served as the main-title music introducing Hitchcock as he "stepped into" his trademark caricature on-screen to introduce the program ("Good eeeveninnnnng . . ."). Hitchcock reportedly borrowed the idea from a screening of F. W. Murnau's 1927 film *Sunrise,* during which the Gounod snippet was used as underscore. The music, almost overnight, was inextricably linked with Hitchcock and became, like the Rossini overture for "The Lone Ranger," better known for its television associations than as a piece of classical music.

Kahn's frequent employer during the late 1950s was David M. Gordon (1907–83), a music publisher who had contracted with MCA-owned Revue Studios (later Universal) to provide music for their new television series. Unlike many earlier series, which used music on a more or less generic basis (comedy, dramatic, or suspense cues, often interchangeable between series), Revue commissioned music for specific shows without actually scoring individual episodes.

Kahn not only arranged the Gounod theme, he composed a library of music specifically for "Alfred Hitchcock Presents." Kahn also composed the themes and, as with "Hitchcock," wrote a substantial library suitable for tracking as underscore for the John Payne western "The Restless Gun" (1957–59, NBC), the family comedy "Leave It to Beaver" (1957–63, CBS/ABC), and the original Mickey Spillane tough-guy detective series "Mike Hammer." In each case, despite Kahn's role as the undisputed sole composer, the music was often cocredited to Kahn and Melvyn Lenard (the first and middle names of Gordon's son, enabling the publisher to participate directly in the royalties).

The "Beaver" theme, a playful tune with a hint of mischief, later gained a lyric and an unrelated title, "The Toy Parade" (a further division of royalties occurred, because lyricist Mort Greene was entitled to a third of the proceeds). Kahn wrote the "Beaver" theme without ever seeing the pilot. "I was just told it was a kids' show and, basically, what it was all about," he said. Like the music for "Hitchcock" and the other shows, it was written in Los Angeles but taken to Munich, Germany, for recording in order to skirt AFM regulations and penalties.

Kahn contributed several other themes to fifties television, including the suspense anthology "Suspicion" (1957–58, NBC), the detective show "21 Beacon Street" (1959–60, NBC/ABC), and the William Bendix western "Overland Trail" (1960, NBC). He went on to become music editor for many of the Filmways comedies of the 1960s, starting with "Mister Ed"—for which he composed a library of music, also recorded overseas—and several other series for which he did not write, including "The Beverly Hillbillies" and "Green Acres."

The issue of ghosting and awarding proper credit to the composer was a serious problem in those early days. Screen credits were rare and cue sheets—listing each composition and its timing for royalty credit with ASCAP or BMI—even when filed, did not always reflect the truth. Ziv, a major supplier of syndicated programming in the fifties, almost never gave screen credit, and its own music editors professed ignorance as to the actual origin of the music they tracked into their shows, much less the identities of the composers.

David Rose, the composer of "Holiday for Strings" and "The Stripper," is widely believed to have written the themes for Ziv's "Highway Patrol" (1955–59) and "Sea Hunt" (1958–61), yet both are officially credited to one Ray Llewelyn—a name that no one connected with Ziv during that period could recall. If Llewelyn existed, he never joined BMI or ASCAP, and therefore never received any royalties for the thousands of plays of his music over the years.

The grim martial rhythms of the Broderick Crawford police drama ("Ten-four!") and the melodramatic opening for the Lloyd Bridges skin-diving adventure became as well known as any themes of the era. No one received screen credit for the music in either case; the underscores were drawn from established music libraries, according to Ziv supervising music editor Milton Lustig. Rose (who also wrote music for Ziv radio shows in the early 1950s) later composed, and received credit for, the themes for Ziv's "Men into Space" (1959–60, CBS) with William Lundigan and "The Case of the Dangerous Robin" (1960, syndicated) with Rick Jason.

Many of the individual music libraries eventually were supplanted by a highly organized new library created in the mid-1950s by Capitol Records. Composer William G. Loose (1911–91), with the title of "western studio representative" at Capitol, oversaw this operation and, as a result, became the supplier of several memorable themes including "The Donna Reed Show" (1958–66, ABC), "Dennis the Menace" (1959–63, CBS), and "The Texan" (1958–60, CBS), all officially credited to Loose and Capitol executive John Seely.

William Loose. Courtesy BMI Archives.

Jack Cookerly (b. 1926), who worked closely with Loose and wrote hours of music that was licensed through the Capitol library, explained the beginnings of the operation: "Bill Loose had written five hours of music for Capitol, without any reference to any films. They were [scoring] industrial films and in-house films, so Bill set up some categories: dramatic, melodic, light activity, mechanical, this and that. So you could come in for any film and find some music for it. It wasn't tailored for television at all."

When Screen Gems began production on "The Donna Reed Show," executives "came over looking for a theme," Cookerly recalled. "Bill had written a real nice, pleasant little melody which we eventually called 'Music to Wash Windows By,' because it's so insipid. They picked that piece of music for the 'Donna Reed' theme. [The studio] made a request that that theme be restricted—because you didn't want to find it on an Ajax commercial, which happened a couple of times—so that theme was locked into the show." Loose wrote the "Dennis the Menace" theme specifically for that series. Often, producers would request a "theme set," essentially a small library of cues based on an original theme that Loose, Cookerly, or both might compose; this was the case with "Donna Reed," "Dennis," and others.

Among the major users of the Capitol library was Desilu. Music editor Robert Raff, who joined Desilu about 1958, recalled that "99 percent of the track was out of Capitol" in those days. Shows such as "The Real McCoys," though not owned by Desilu, utilized the studio's production facilities. "They had a theme written for them, but beyond maybe half a dozen cues based on the main title, the rest was track," Raff said.

The anthology "Desilu Playhouse" (1958–60, CBS), which boasted an original theme by longtime MGM musical director Johnny Green *(Raintree County)*, utilized no original dramatic underscore. Some of those first-season shows that Raff tracked with previously recorded Capitol music were "The Time Element," a Rod Serling fantasy that served as the basis for his "Twilight Zone"; and the two-part "The Untouchables," the ambitious Eliot Ness story that became the pilot for the famed crime series.

Raff, in consultation with Loose, chose the cues to score the various films. The Capitol music proved so useful that "we actually physically moved the entire library into the studio," Raff recalled. "They made duplicates of everything. I had two or three file cabinets full of records, just from the material that I liked." Capitol's so-called "Hi-Q" library encompassed several hundred hours of commercially available music by the mid-1960s.

The vast majority of prime-time programs during the fifties were tracked with library music. But there were a few notable exceptions, all attributable to producers who understood the value of original scoring to create moods and enhance atmosphere—and agreed to pay the high premium demanded by the AFM in order to achieve this.

One of the earliest, and at the same time the most innovative, was

Tony Mottola (with guitar, seated) with Yul Brynner, rehearsing for an episode of "Danger." Courtesy the composer.

"Danger" (1950–55, CBS), a live suspense anthology based in New York City. Guitarist Tony Mottola (b. 1918), a highly respected musician on staff at CBS, had been doing a nightly fifteen-minute music show, "Face the Music" (1948–49), with vocalists such as Johnny Desmond, when he heard from a young director named Yul Brynner (later the noted stage actor). According to Mottola, Brynner had been assigned "Danger," a new half-hour show designed to follow "Suspense" (1949–54, CBS) on Tuesday nights. In another holdover from radio, a number of studio shows, including "Suspense," featured an organist playing live background music.

"Yul wanted to do something different," Mottola recalled. At the time, the postwar drama *The Third Man* (1949) was doing well at the box office and its score, played entirely on a single instrument—the zither—had become something of a sensation. "So Yul asked me if I would be interested in coming up with a theme."

Brynner described the opening visuals he had in mind: The camera pans along a fence at night. Suddenly, a dagger is thrown and sticks in the fence. A flashlight illuminates the still-quivering weapon and the graffitilike scrawl on the boards: "Danger" and the names of the evening's stars. Mottola's concept—for electric guitar alone—was both simple and undeniably effective: the insistent rhythm of a single repeated low note, interrupted at the point of the dagger flying into the fence by a single, ominous chord. Musicians began referring to it as "the 'Danger' chord," or "the Tony Mottola chord," although in fact the entire theme was quite haunting and Mottola's work involved more than just a signature tune for the opening and closing of the show. Brynner insisted, as did his successor, Sidney Lumet, on an original score each week.

Mottola explained: "I would attend readings and rehearsals during the week. Then I would see a run-through a couple of days before [air], and I would have a meeting with Yul, and later Sidney. We would discuss the various moods that we felt were needed, where music was needed, and so forth. And I would proceed to write to the script. Then, the day of the show, we would have a run-through and I would play, although it was difficult for me [in terms of] timing, because it was stop-and-go, stop-and-start. And then airtime, you got a cue and away you went."

Mottola was located in a booth next to the control room. He could see the stage action via a monitor, and the director in the control room before him; his headphones gave him the dialogue and sound effects in one ear and instructions from the director in the other. Mottola's biggest problem was having only two hands. "I had to practically memorize those areas of the script that I was underscoring," he said, "as I couldn't turn pages and play the guitar at the same time."

The subject matter was often quite dark, and murder was never far away. But the source material was frequently impeccable: adaptations of stories by Ambrose Bierce, Agatha Christie, Edgar Wallace, Daphne du Maurier, and, for a particularly grisly episode about a malevolent child, Saki. The performers, as was typical for high-profile network dramas in that era, were stellar indeed: Grace Kelly, Paul Newman, Jack Lemmon, Basil Rathbone, Charlton Heston, and many others.

Mottola himself appeared in a 1953 show about a singer controlled by the mob. His fellow CBS star Johnny Desmond was cast in the lead; Mottola did double duty by playing the bandleader and, between nightclub scenes, racing back to his guitar to play the underscore.

In an effort to vary the sound from week to week, Mottola often tried out fresh ideas for performance. For "The Killer Scarf," a circus-themed show televised live from Madison Square Garden in 1951, Mottola stroked the guitar strings with a pocket comb to imitate a hurdy-gurdy. Just as often, the scripts would dictate a musical approach: a folk-style melody for a western episode, Latin tempos for another set in a tropical port, an Irish reel for a show with J. Pat O'Malley, and a mock nursery rhyme for the murderous little girl in the Saki story "Sredni Vashtar." For the first episode, 1950's "August Heat" with Alfred Ryder, Mottola created an ambitious study in triplets: light, rapid music to depict "nervous excitement, fear, trepidation, flight."

The music of "Danger" proved so popular that, in 1951, Mottola published a thirty-one-page folio for guitar players, and recorded several suites from the series' first-season scores on a ten-inch LP. It was television's first soundtrack album. Not one to hoard his hard-won secrets of scoring for the medium, the guitarist filled his folio with explanations about creating bridges, curtains, stings, and other dramatic musical effects. Despite other work on "The Perry Como Show" (1950–55, CBS) and various studio commitments, Mottola found time to score other television shows including "Crime Photographer" (1951–52, CBS) and the soap opera "Portia Faces Life" (1954–55, CBS).

Meanwhile, on the West Coast, radio star Jack Webb had been successful in translating his popular police show to television, complete with music. The filmed "Dragnet" (1951–59, NBC) became the definitive fifties cop show, its stilted dialogue, the detectives' humorless demeanor ("just the facts, ma'am"), and the emphasis on investigative technique setting the stage for dozens of police procedurals to follow in the fifties, sixties, and beyond. Webb, a jazz aficionado who owned ultra-high-end stereo equipment with gigantic speakers, demanded original scoring for the television "Dragnet" just as he had the radio show (which continued until 1956).

Walter Schumann (1913–58) joined Webb's "Dragnet" team shortly after its 1949 debut on NBC radio. He composed the "dum-de-dum-dum" theme that millions associated with "Dragnet" on both radio and television. The decisive and melodramatic four-note phrase—which became a kind of American musical code for "you're in trouble now"—accompanied the opening shot of Sgt. Joe Friday's badge number 714, as narrator George Fenneman solemnly intoned: "The story you are about to see is true. The names have been changed to protect the innocent." The introductory four-note theme, coupled with Schumann's "Dragnet" march (used over the remainder of the main title and the end titles) was carried over intact from radio. During the drama itself, Schumann's music was used largely as a transitional device and for dramatic emphasis at the end of many scenes.

Schumann consistently used Nathan Scott (b. 1915) as his orchestrator. The two had met before World War II, and Scott had often arranged for Schumann. After the war, Scott went to Republic as a composer-orchestrator on the studio's many westerns. But soon after "Dragnet" went to television, Schumann contacted Scott again about orchestrating. The two went on to do both radio and TV versions for the remainder of their run during the 1950s—Schumann as composer, Scott as orchestrator and sometime composer of the underscore. They also collaborated on other projects, notably a series of highly successful choral albums featuring "The Voices of Walter Schumann."

Webb was so keen on the importance of original scoring that he gave Schumann's name prime placement during the end credits: an entire card just before Webb's own as producer-director. In addition, Scott received screen credit as orchestrator, an unprecedented move (and one that would rarely be repeated in series TV).

According to Scott, the "Dragnet" orchestra consisted of fourteen players (three trombones, a trumpet, four woodwinds, two violas, two celli, string bass,

Walter Schumann. Courtesy Academy of Motion Picture Arts and Sciences.

and keyboard). "The theme was kind of martial," Scott recalled, "and the police dialogue was very rigid, clipped, and kind of militaristic in a sense. It seemed to fit, and so we stuck with it. Walter wrote nearly every theme, three or four notes for each episode. I would build on those themes, if he was ill or unable to do it for whatever reason. I would often take a theme from some past show and do it my way for this new show." Scott also conducted about a third of the scores overall.

Bandleader Ray Anthony's jazz arrangement of the "Dragnet" theme became a top-10 hit in 1953, the first television theme to crack the record charts. When Webb made the cover of *Time* in March 1954, the four famous notes appeared on a staff behind the image of Webb's face, with bullets replacing the notes. Schumann also won the first Emmy ever given to a composer for original music for television (in 1954, beating Bernard Herrmann, Victor Young, and Gian-Carlo Menotti).

This popular and critical success also resulted in the first major lawsuit charging musical plagiarism in television. Robbins Music Corp., a music publisher for Universal, formally accused Schumann of infringement, charging that the "Dragnet" motif actually originated in Miklós Rózsa's score for *The Killers* (1946). The Hungarian-born Rózsa won Academy Awards for scoring *Spellbound* (1945) and *A Double Life* (1947), and would go on to even greater success with such biblical epics as *Ben-Hur* (1959, another Oscar winner) and *King of Kings* (1961).

In *The Killers,* based on an Ernest Hemingway story, those four insistent notes served as the underpinning of the main title, then resurfaced periodically as a leitmotif, or recurring theme, to characterize the cold-blooded murderers of the film's title (played by William Conrad and Charles McGraw). As harmonized, the motif was actually more sinister and menacing in *The Killers* than ever heard on "Dragnet." But the association of that music with a crime drama might well have led one to the conclusion that a musical borrowing had taken place.

Rózsa's attention was first called to the matter by a September 1953 *Life* magazine article that celebrated "Dragnet"'s top-10 status and Anthony's hit record. According to Rózsa, Schumann's lawyers made musical comparisons to similar motifs in the Dvorak cello concerto and one of Brahms's *Hungarian Dances,* but were unable to find "the ominous tritone" of the *Killers* motif in either.

Scott contended that any plagiarism, if it occurred, was unintentional. Schumann happened to be at Universal during the scoring of *The Killers,* working as musical director on Abbott and Costello films. Scott said that Schumann did not recall the film or the music, although Rózsa believed that Schumann was present for the scoring sessions. "But because Walter worked there [at Universal] at the time, Rózsa contended that he had stolen this dum-de-dum-dum from him," Scott said. "Walter was devastated by that. Because if he did it, it was not conscious. He was a very moral guy." An out-of-court settlement of $100,000 and a fifty-fifty split of all future royalties between Rózsa and Schumann was negotiated, although Rózsa never received screen credit on "Dragnet," either the fifties or sixties version.

At the time, Schumann's health was failing. He suffered from a rare and complicated heart ailment, and died after heart surgery at the University of Minnesota in August 1958, not long after scoring the pilot for the series "Steve Canyon" (1958–59, NBC), based on the Milton Caniff comic strip. (Scott took over the series scoring chores, but in tribute to the late composer, the credit read "music by Walter Schumann, conducted and orchestrated by Nathan Scott.") After Schumann's death, Webb said of the composer: "He was as much a part of 'Dragnet' as I am." Rózsa never wrote for television.

Webb's strong feelings about original music rubbed off on one of his writers. James Moser left "Dragnet" to create "Medic" (1954–56, NBC), a pioneering medical drama whose realistic approach to such hitherto undramatized subjects as manic depression, open-heart surgery, and the likely aftereffects of a hydrogen bomb explosion, helped to expand the storytelling potential of the medium. The half-hour medical anthology was introduced and

Victor Young.

often narrated by Richard Boone (in his first starring role) as Dr. Konrad Styner. The style of "Medic" was more documentary than drama, the result of Moser's journalism background and his firsthand research at Los Angeles-area hospitals.

"Medic" was also a breakthrough for original music in television. For the first time, a major film composer was signed to compose weekly scores for a filmed series: Victor Young (1900–56), whose facility with a melody was legendary (he had written standards such as "Stella by Starlight" and "Sweet Sue"), and whose scores for such films as *For Whom the Bell Tolls* (1943) and *Shane* (1953) contributed to their status as classics. Young's theme—music of great dignity—which went on to become a top-40 hit in a vocal version as "Blue Star" (sung by Felicia Sanders), opened each episode, as a narrator defined the physician as "guardian of birth, healer of the sick, comforter of the aged." The end-title music, spectacularly beautiful for television in that era, was an expansive piano solo against strings.

The composer approached this assignment no differently than he would one of his features. "Victor's sketches were immaculate," recalled orchestrator Sidney Fine. "There was no distinction between what he sketched for this TV show and its small orchestra, as opposed to what he did for his films with a large orchestra. He wrote the same way."

Young wrote thirty-two original scores between mid-1954 and early 1956, about twelve minutes of music per show, for an orchestra that averaged twenty-six players (including seventeen strings). Fine, who went on to orchestrate parts of Young's music for *Around the World in 80 Days* (1956), believed that Young was "compulsive" as a composer—considering the fact that, during the two-year period of "Medic," he also wrote more than a dozen film scores. Yet his scores were "always melodic, and dramatic," Fine said. "What he did was so right." Fine's orchestrations were so rich that, although he never received screen credit, his work was recognized with a 1956 Emmy nomination. (Young himself was nominated in 1954 as composer of "Medic," but won in a separate category as musical director for the four-network simulcast of the "Diamond Jubilee of Light" special.)

Also in 1954, the Walt Disney studio was preparing to plunge into television with "Disneyland" (1954–58, ABC), a show that would later be known as "Walt Disney Presents" (1958–61, ABC), "Walt Disney's Wonderful World of Color" (1961–69, NBC), "The Wonderful World of Disney" (1969–79, NBC), "Disney's Wonderful World" (1979–81, NBC), and "Walt Disney" (1981–83, CBS). The series was a convenient way to plug Disney's grand new California theme park as well as serving to showcase the studio's film releases, cartoons, documentaries, and original programming.

Disney's musical staff expanded to handle the television work. George

George Bruns (left) and Tom Blackburn working on "Davy Crockett." Courtesy Stephanie Blackburn.

Bruns (1914–83) had joined the Disney operation in 1953 when planning began to turn Tchaikovsky's *Sleeping Beauty* ballet into an animated feature (finally released in 1959, bringing Bruns an Academy Award nomination for his faithful adaptation). Bruns was not only working on "Disneyland," but also helping plan the upcoming, five-day-a-week afternoon children's show "The Mickey Mouse Club" (1955–59, ABC).

Like Webb on "Dragnet" and Moser on "Medic," Walt Disney was one of a few producers who understood the value of original music. In fact, he insisted on "live" scoring, not tracking of previously written music, on all of his television shows. "We scored everything, but we didn't have to," Bruns noted in a 1968 interview. "We could have saved a lot of money, but Walt wanted the music right. He was not budget-conscious when it came to music. He'd say, 'Well, if you need that many men, use them.'"

One of Bruns's first assignments was the theme and underscore for a three-part historical adventure to air during the "Frontierland" portion of "Disneyland": the story of American frontier hero Davy Crockett, starring Fess Parker. According to Bruns, Disney asked for "a little throwaway melody . . . a little ditty or something" that could be used to link sequences from different times in the life of Crockett, as a means of avoiding excess narration. Screenwriter Tom Blackburn "gave me a bunch of lines," Bruns said. "He wasn't a lyric writer. I just picked his lines and put them together, made a verse out of them. Then he took that and wrote a lot more."

Bruns started at 7:00 A.M.; two hours later, he had finished the tune. Disney heard and approved it by noon the same day. "The Ballad of Davy Crockett" (". . . Davy, Davy Crockett, king of the wild frontier") was first heard in "Davy Crockett, Indian Fighter" in December 1954. Bill Hayes was the first to record it and wound up with the biggest hit, including five weeks at Number 1 and twenty weeks on the charts overall. Parker himself recorded one of twenty cover versions which sold about seven million copies over six months in 1955.

Bruns, in 1978, attributed the tune's blockbuster success to its simplicity and honest, folklike quality that seemed to have come out of the time and place: "There's nothing to it. Funny thing was, we never had a lawsuit on that song, because everybody thought it was P.D. [public domain]. It wasn't." Blackburn ultimately wrote twenty six-line stanzas to the song, covering Crockett's entire life from Indian scout to member of Congress to Alamo freedom fighter. For the final program of the initial Crockett trilogy, "Davy Crockett at the Alamo," Bruns set to music a poem found in Crockett's own journal; it was called "Farewell."

Bruns scored again with the title song for "Zorro" (1957–59, ABC), Disney's half-hour adventure series with Guy Williams as the masked avenger of Spanish California in the 1820s. Williams played the swashbuckling, black-clad night rider El Zorro ("the fox") and his foppish civilian alter ego Don Diego de la Vega. The dramatic opening began with lightning striking in the form of a *Z* and the silhouette of Zorro astride his speedy horse, Toronado. A male chorus sang the lyrics (by series writer-director Norman Foster): "Out of the night, when the full moon is bright, comes the horseman known as Zorro. . . ."

Other memorable themes for the Disney series followed, including "The Swamp Fox" (1959), a lively ditty for Leslie Nielsen as a Revolutionary War hero of the Southeast, written by Buddy Baker and Lew Foster; and "The Scarecrow of Romney Marsh" (1964), an exciting, filmed-in-England trilogy with Patrick McGoohan as a Scarlet Pimpernel-style character of the late eighteenth century, accompanied by the tune of a ballad by singer-songwriter Terry Gilkyson.

In 1961, Walt Disney made a momentous musical decision: he hired Richard M. Sherman and Robert B. Sherman as staff songwriters. The brothers had created pop hits for ex-Disney Mouseketeer Annette Funicello (including "Tall Paul" in 1958), and, as freelancers, had written songs for "Zorro" and other Disney TV programs. Although they were hired for features as well as TV, it was on the small screen that they first made their mark. Disney moved his weekly series to NBC in the fall of 1961, and the all-color telecasts demanded a new name ("The Wonderful World of Color").

Richard Sherman recalled: "We were doing comedy numbers for this [animated] character Ludwig von Drake, who was a brand-new but very understandable sort of Dutch comedian, voiced by Paul Frees. We did two rather phonetic songs: 'The Spectrum Song' and 'The Green with Envy Blues,' to illustrate how color is used musically. Then Walt came to us and said, 'At a certain point, when Ludwig von Drake finally turns on the knob, we want to have something really beautiful, totally different.' Not a von Drake crazy song, but a real pretty song that would indicate that the world is full of gorgeous visual color."

The Sherman brothers' tune—which began "The world is a carousel of color . . ."—set against kaleidoscopic shots and lovely images of nature ranging from rainbows to autumn leaves to flowers (and Buddy Baker's arrangement, which caught the action as well as showcased the song), introduced the Disney series for the entire 1960s. The vocal group The Wellingtons, who sang the "Wonderful World of Color" main title, would go on to even greater fame by performing the title ballad of "Gilligan's Island."

The Sherman brothers contributed songs to a parade of fondly remembered "Wonderful World of Color" programs, including three starring, and with songs performed by, Annette: "The Horsemasters" (1961); "The Golden Horseshoe Revue" (1962); and "Escapade in Florence" (1962). Still later came their title themes for "The Mooncussers" (1962), the Civil War story "Johnny Shiloh" (1963), "The Ballad of Hector, the Stowaway Dog" (1964), and "Gallegher" (1965). Their greatest fame, of course, came with their Oscar-winning score for Disney's musical classic *Mary Poppins* (1964).

Baker (b. 1918), meanwhile, was musical director for nearly the entire run of "The Mickey Mouse Club," whose theme song ("Who's the leader of the club that's made for you and me?") was written by host Jimmie Dodd (an actor and songwriter who penned many of the child-friendly tunes heard on the series). After the "Club" ended in 1959, Baker went on to compose the scores for many of the fine nature documentaries that aired on "The Wonderful World of Color," including "One Day at Teton Marsh" (1964). Among his notable theatrical films for Disney were the Oscar-nominated score for *Napoleon and Samantha* (1972) and the music for the animated *Fox and the Hound* (1981).

Disney may have been the first motion picture studio to sign on with the new medium, but soon after the Disney deal with ABC, Warner Bros. followed suit. As with Disney, there was a strong promotional angle involved: a ten-minute "Behind the Cameras" featurette, promoting an upcoming Warner feature film, in every hour of programming. But viewers weren't interested in the promos, which were eventually dropped. The programs were what counted. For its first season on the air, "Warner Bros. Presents" (1955–56) was the umbrella title for three rotating series, all based on Warner movies of the 1940s: *Casablanca, Kings Row,* and *Cheyenne.* Ironically, the least known of the titles, the Clint Walker western "Cheyenne," was the sole survivor of the trio and went on to become a long-running ABC hit.

"Casablanca" starred Charles McGraw in the Humphrey Bogart role of saloon owner Rick Blaine, while "Kings Row" had Jack Kelly and Robert Horton in key roles. Both were equally uninspired adaptations; "Casablanca" lasted ten episodes, "Kings Row" just seven, before the ax fell. Viewer interest in "Cheyenne" led ABC to order more of the Old West wanderings of Cheyenne Bodie, for a total of sixteen shows. Rounding out the network's thirty-nine-episode order were six stand-alone anthology shows, essentially pilots for unsold series.

Like Disney, Warner Bros. insisted on original music for their shows. Every episode of the 1955–56 season was scored—a surprising development, and one that would only rarely be repeated until musicians' union rules mandated it more than twenty years later. The "Warner Bros. Presents" main title was borrowed from Max Steiner's score for *The Fountainhead* (1949), but each series had its own musical signature.

For "Cheyenne" (1955–62, ABC), William Lava (1911–71) was signed. He scored ten of the first sixteen episodes, with Leith Stevens (1909–70) filling in on the remaining six. Lava was an old hand at western music, having labored on dozens of Republic serials and B westerns such as *The Painted Stallion* (1937) with Ray Corrigan and Hoot Gibson and *Overland Stage Raiders* (1938) with John Wayne. He became a Warner Bros. fixture in the late forties and early fifties, scoring films like *Colt .45* (1950).

Songwriters Jerry Livingston and Mack David contributed a "Cheyenne" song heard, in instrumental form, over that first season's end titles. Lava's familiar loping theme, called "Bodie," however, formed the basis for the underscore, and it won out as the series' theme during the second season and beyond. Country songwriter Stan Jones (1914–63), who wrote the classic "(Ghost) Riders in the Sky" and acted in John Ford films such as *Rio Grande* (1950), provided a lyric ("lonely man, Cheyenne . . .") that was heard starting with the second episode of the 1956–57 season.

David Buttolph (1902–83) scored "Casablanca," "Kings Row," and the anthology series, although "Casablanca" naturally used the song "As Time Goes By" as its theme and "Kings Row" drew on a Max Steiner tune from *Saratoga Trunk* (1945) for its end-title theme. Buttolph had spent the war years at Twentieth Century-Fox, scoring a number of notable pictures including *Guadalcanal Diary* (1943) before moving to Warners for most of the fifties, scoring films such as *Montana* (1950) and *House of Wax* (1953). Buttolph and Lava divided scoring chores for the second season of Warner Bros. shows on ABC (1956–57): Lava did all of the "Cheyenne" episodes and Buttolph composed the theme and scored all nineteen hours of "Conflict," a dramatic anthology.

However, live scoring abruptly ended at Warner Bros. after "Conflict." In the summer of 1957, Warners contracted with David Chudnow's Mutel service to supply "canned" music for all its series, both continuing and new. Themes and short cues based on those themes would continue to be commissioned, but scoring of individual episodes would not return to Warner Bros. television until 1963.

A handful of other programs utilized original music on a regular basis. Harry Lubin (1906–77) served as composer-conductor for several seasons on "The Loretta Young Show" (1953–61, NBC), originally "Letter to Loretta," a half-hour filmed dramatic anthology hosted by and often starring the actress. Young made her entrance every week in a stylish new gown to Lubin's sweeping, lilting theme. "Every single week we had a scoring date," remembered Byron Chudnow, who served as music editor on this series as well. "[Lubin] did eight or nine minutes of music every week.

"The guy was incredible," Chudnow said. "He had a head full of melody. He wrote like nobody I ever heard. What was so astonishing was, he would come to the dubbing sessions; he wanted to be on the dubbing stage so that he could see how his music was being laid down. I used to set up a table for him with a lamp, over on the side. He would sit and orchestrate while the bloody picture was going—he was listening to his cue and orchestrating next week's show at the same time. I've never seen anybody write music that fast."

Lubin also wrote music for later seasons of "Fireside Theatre," later "Jane Wyman Theater" (1949–58, NBC), Dick Powell's "Zane Grey Theater" (1956–62, CBS), and, most audibly, "Alcoa Presents," better known as "One Step Beyond" (1959–61, ABC). Lubin's use of electronic keyboard instruments such as the novachord and trautonium, and a coloratura soprano voice, in conjunction with traditional orchestral elements, lent an appropriately eerie tone to the stories of psychic phenomena.

In live television, Russian emigré Wladimir Selinsky (1910–84) scored many episodes of the "Kraft Television Theatre" (1947–58, NBC/ABC) throughout the middle 1950s. A violin soloist in Europe, he moved to America in 1925 and formed a string quartet that played popular music. He had his own radio show, "Strings in Swingtime," and composed for radio drama before moving into live TV in New York. "Mr. Selinsky never puts a note on paper till he has seen one of the final rehearsals, a bare three days before show time," the liner notes for an album of Selinsky's "Kraft" compositions pointed out. He scored original plays by the likes of Rod Serling, Paddy Chayefsky, Reginald Rose, and Tad Mosel, which were directed by live-TV stalwarts such as John Frankenheimer, George Roy Hill, and Fielder Cook.

Selinsky used a boys' choir and chamber orchestra for the Stephen Vincent Benet story "A Child Is Born" with Mildred Dunnock and Harry Townes in December 1954, and researched the music actually played on the *Titanic* for the award-winning "A Night to Remember" with Claude Rains and a cast of one hundred in March 1956. He also contributed music to "Lux Video Theatre" (1950–57, CBS/NBC) and the "U.S. Steel Hour" (1953–63, ABC/CBS).

Perhaps most notable during this period was an original score by Aaron Copland for a drama based on Ernest Hemingway stories for John Houseman's Sunday-afternoon cultural series "The Seven Lively Arts" (1957–58, CBS). CBS music director Alfredo Antonini conducted Copland's score for "The World of Nick Adams" in November 1957. It was the composer's only complete dramatic score for the medium.

Of course, original music remained the exception rather than the rule. A 1954 *New York Times* survey of anthology shows found excerpts from all of the following works on "Studio One" (1948–58, CBS) within a single month: Prokofiev's *Cinderella* and *Romeo and Juliet,* Coleridge-Taylor's *Petite Suite de Concert,* Kabalevsky's *The Comedians,* Thomson's *The Plow That Broke the Plains,* Charpentier's *Impressions d'Italie,* Sinigaglia's *Danza Piemontese,* Respighi's *Pines of Rome* and *Feste Romane,* Saint-Saëns's *Carnival of the Animals,* Berlioz's *Roman Carnival Overture,* Bartók's *Concerto for Orchestra,* and Poulenc's *Les Biches.*

On the West Coast, CBS maintained a balance between tracking and live scoring. Almost from the beginning of television activity there, music director Lud Gluskin began to create a music library that was exclusive to CBS: music that would serve a variety of dramatic needs for both radio and television programs originating in Hollywood.

Gluskin was a former dance-band leader and confirmed Francophile who visited the Continent every year, often recording music for the CBS library and bringing it back to Los Angeles (thus avoiding the use of the more expensive local musicians and incurring the wrath of the AFM). Two of his French colleagues, René Garriguenc and Lucien Moraweck, came to the United States and became staff composers at the network. Gluskin was reputed to be a friend of CBS founder William S. Paley and was universally acknowledged as a power to be reckoned with in all matters of music at the network.

According to Don B. Ray, who started at CBS as a "cue selector" in 1954, oversaw the development of the CBS music library during the late 1950s, and went on to become an Emmy-nominated composer (on "Hawaii Five-0"), Gluskin would frequently recruit foreign composers to write original music for the CBS library. At the same time, Gluskin would also bring scores of music that had already been written and recorded for specific shows in New York or Los Angeles, such as music written for CBS radio programs by Bernard Herrmann, and rerecord them abroad to avoid paying a reuse fee to the musicians' union.

As late as 1962, Gluskin continued to defend the use of library music for tracking. Citing time and financial pressures as adverse to writing good scores tailored to individual series episodes, Gluskin said: "Music for TV has become a mass production off the assembly line. Like a piece of scenery, one is not conscious of good mood music, but he misses it if it isn't there. In [feature] pictures you can't compose music factory-style. Canned music is best because it is created by the best composers under normal conditions."

Still, during the heyday of live drama—which moved from New York to Hollywood in the mid-1950s—live music often accompanied live shows, usually at the insistence of the producer. The most distinguished figure to emerge from this pressure-cooker world was Jerry Goldsmith.

Born in 1929, Goldsmith attended Los Angeles City College, studied piano with Jakob Gimpel and composition with Mario Castelnuovo-Tedesco, before landing a job, in 1951, at CBS—as a script typist. Eventually, he convinced Gluskin to give him some radio assignments (on shows including "Frontier Gentleman," "Suspense," and the "CBS Radio Workshop"), and he was signed to a seven-year contract with the network. Goldsmith moved into live television starting in 1955 with scores for the anthology series "Climax" (1954–58), the first live drama to originate on the West Coast. Scores for live productions on "General Electric Theatre" (1953–62), "Studio One in Hollywood" (1958), and "Playhouse 90" (1956–60) followed.

When he started on "Climax," Goldsmith recalled, his job was primarily that of cue selector: choosing appropriate cues from prerecorded music in the CBS library and editing them into a coherent score. As time went on, he convinced the producers to let him add an instrument or two, then to compose original scores. "I'd get to hire three instruments and I would play the piano, organ, and novachord," he said. The scores themselves, perhaps twenty-five minutes of music or more, would often be written in as short a span as three days and nights.

"It was a wonderful training ground," Goldsmith said. "Not just for me, for everybody: directors, actors, writers. None of us knew what we were doing. That's why we were doing it," he laughed. "It was the blind leading the blind."

For $175 a week, the composer was expected to come up with as much music as was demanded, for however many shows were assigned: sometimes a "Climax" and a "G.E. Theatre" in the same week and, toward the end of his CBS tenure, a "Gunsmoke," a "Twilight Zone," and a "Playhouse 90."

The original, New York-based "Studio One," for the most part, had been tracked with previously recorded music. Producer Norman Felton, who came out from New York to produce the new Los Angeles-based "Studio One in Hollywood," insisted upon original scores. "I had quite a set-to with CBS over it," Felton later recalled. "I finally did get Jerry, who was quite young, to do the music with a small group for the 'Studio One' shows that I did out here."

On one occasion, Felton called Goldsmith in after a run-through of the music, which the producer would hear for the first time about two hours before air. "I need music from here to there," Felton said, indicating a portion of the script. Goldsmith, puzzled, pointed out that no music had been written for that sequence and that, dramatically speaking, none was needed. "Oh, yes, it is," Felton replied. "I've got to have music to cover the noise of moving the cameras around!" It was a lesson in the practical side of music-making for television, especially in that early era.

Goldsmith also credited producer Herbert Brodkin, who oversaw "Playhouse 90," with stressing the importance of original music. But "Playhouse 90"—so called because it was a ninety-minute, weekly showcase for original scripts by writers such as Rod Serling, Reginald Rose, and JP Miller—would sometimes require as much as forty minutes of music for an orchestra of up to eighteen players.

For "Playhouse 90," the musicians would be assembled in a studio next to the stage where the performance would take place. (Sometimes, on a "Climax" or a "Studio One," Goldsmith and a small ensemble would even be in a corner of the same soundstage where the actors were located.) With a headset and a monitor, Goldsmith would cue the musicians. "From a technical point of view, you never knew what was going to happen," the composer said. "Writing the music was one thing. The timings were only a guess." Using a stopwatch to time an actor's movement across a stage when the props hadn't been placed yet was just one of many dicey elements.

"It all changed when you went on the air," he continued. "It picked up, or it slowed down, or [the actors] would forget their lines. You had to devise means of getting in, cutting. . . . It was really up to me to make it work." Goldsmith had already had a firm foundation in harmony, counterpoint, orchestration, and composition. "And when I got into [television], I found I didn't know a thing. It was like starting all over again," he said.

He and his fellow craftsmen had no idea that they were in the midst of television's Golden Age. "We were just struggling to get from one week to the next. The big hope was that we could finish one show without getting a camera in the shot, without getting a microphone in the shot, without having an actor blow a line, or catching a stage manager running from set to set. We just wanted to get on and off the air on time."

It was on these shows that Goldsmith met many of the directors with whom he would later collaborate on big-screen films, including John Frankenheimer (*Seconds*), Franklin J. Schaffner (*Planet of the Apes*), Jack Smight (*The Illustrated Man*), Robert Mulligan (*The Spiral Road*), Delbert Mann (*A Gathering of Eagles*), Ralph Nelson (*Lilies of the Field*), and Arthur Hiller (*The Lonely Guy*).

As live television waned and a growing number of the anthology series, including "Playhouse 90," were produced on videotape, "there was a whole energy drop," Goldsmith said. "You felt it among everybody. There was something about counting off and going on the air live to a zillion people. I never experienced that energy again."

2

Crime to a Beat

Cop and Detective Shows

In the fall of 1958, members of the AFM's Los Angeles local, angry over union president James C. Petrillo's intransigence on the "live" scoring issue, formed their own union. Petrillo, whose financial demands upon producers caused most to avoid using original music in their shows, stepped down. His successors dropped the union's claim to a percentage payment for every show with new music.

MCA-owned Revue Studios, which had become one of the leading suppliers of original programming to the networks, instituted a policy of scoring many episodes of its higher-profile series, including "Wagon Train" and "General Electric Theater." But one independent production in particular brought original scoring for television to widespread attention for the first time. The series was "Peter Gunn," and the composer was Henry Mancini.

"Peter Gunn" (1958–61, NBC/ABC) was the brainchild of filmmaker Blake Edwards, who had created "Richard Diamond" for radio and gone on to write and direct several feature films (notably *Mister Cory,* 1957). Gunn (Craig Stevens) was an unflappable private detective who hung out at a nightclub called Mother's, dated torch singer Edie Hart (Lola Albright), and enjoyed a friendship with a sour police lieutenant named Jacoby (Herschel Bernardi). With Edwards as producer and sometime writer-director of individual episodes, "Gunn" offered a sophistication rarely glimpsed in the medium to that time.

Mancini was born in 1924. A flute player during his youth in the steel town

Henry Mancini with Craig Stevens and Lola Albright. Courtesy Hearst Newspaper Collection, USC Library.

of West Aliquippa, Pennsylvania, he studied with arranger Max Adkins in Pittsburgh and became pianist-arranger with the Glenn Miller-Tex Beneke Orchestra (which was where he met his future wife, vocalist Ginny O'Connor, one of the original members of Mel Tormé's Mel-Tones singing group) after the war. Mancini spent six years under contract at Universal, where he composed and orchestrated dozens of pictures that ranged from such high points as *The Glenn Miller Story* (1954, for which he received his first Academy Award nomination) and Orson Welles's *Touch of Evil* (1958) to such low points as cocomposer on B science-fiction flicks like *The Creature from the Black Lagoon* (1954) and *It Came from Outer Space* (1953). While at Universal, he cowrote parts of scores for three of Edwards's pictures.

Mancini happened to be getting a haircut on the Universal lot when he ran into Edwards, who was then planning "Peter Gunn." Edwards casually asked if the out-of-work composer might be interested in writing the score. His positive response altered the direction of television scoring practically overnight. "Peter Gunn" was an entirely jazz-based score. Reflecting later on the choice, Mancini said: "It was an idea that, I think, was obvious. Blake had set it in a jazz club. The minute that hit, the rest of it all fell into place. I could think of nothing else to put in there. I certainly didn't want to use any strings."

As a film background, it wasn't particularly innovative. Jazz had been an integral element of several widely admired film scores earlier in the decade, notably Alex North's *A Streetcar Named Desire* (1951), Leith Stevens's *The Wild One* (1954), and especially Elmer Bernstein's *The Man with the Golden Arm* (1955). But prior to 1958, jazz was rarely heard in a television score except as source music from an occasional radio, record player, or jukebox.

"Peter Gunn" gained immediate attention for three musical reasons: the nightclub setting was an obvious showcase for popular music; Mancini's fresh-sounding underscore consistently utilized jazz in dramatic, and occasionally comedic, contexts; and every episode featured an original score, not one tracked from a library of related cues that were recorded overseas. This was "cool" jazz of the West Coast style, written by an arranger from the big-band era and played by some of the top soloists in the field.

Although "Peter Gunn" was just a half-hour show, there was often as much as fifteen minutes of music per episode. Mother's had a resident five-man combo, often seen in the background or featured as backing behind Edie's vocals. Mancini augmented the core rhythm group with a trumpet, four trombones, and four woodwinds for the dramatic cues. "It had some unique sounds that people are still using," Mancini later acknowledged. "Unique kinds of playing techniques: fall-offs on the end of notes and things like that, that were used dramatically; the use of bass flutes and alto flutes, for dramatic uses, and to take the place of a string section."

Prerecording was necessary when Lola Albright sang a number in the club, or when jazz soloists were seen performing on-screen (drummer Shelly Manne, trumpeters Shorty Rogers and Pete Candoli, and guitarist Laurindo Almeida were among those who played themselves). All of the underscore, and much of the source music, was actually recorded after each show had been filmed and edited. "There were many times when the band was playing and they were way off," Mancini admitted. "But they were hardly seen. They would have a temp track—slow, medium, fast—and [the on-screen performers] would just mime while the dialogue was going on. I would replace it later."

Mancini considered Albright the ideal Edie Hart. "She had an off-the-cuff kind of jazz delivery that was very hard to find. Just enough to believe that she'd be singing in that club and that she shouldn't be on Broadway or doing movies. That's not in any way disparaging; it just was perfect casting."

Every episode opened with a teaser underscored by a closely miked walking bass. As fully developed later for the "Peter Gunn" soundtrack album, the piece was called "Fallout!," but for the series, it would often go in a variety of different musical directions depending on the scene being scored. The title theme actually underscored one of the least interesting main-title sequences in television history. A mere twenty seconds long (in black-and-white, like the rest of the show), the visuals simply identified the show and named star Craig

Stevens and creator-producer Blake Edwards against a bland background and crudely flashing bullet-striation patterns.

The familiar "Gunn" theme—still one of the most famous pieces of music ever written for television—was built on an ostinato, a piano-guitar unison combination that the composer found "sinister," with a melody consisting of what he later described as "shouting brass" and "frightened saxophone sounds." Because the series main title was so short, viewers only heard the first nine bars and the last four bars of the theme; the entire piece, never used during the show itself, was finally heard during the fifty-second end-credit sequence. "Fallout!" and "Peter Gunn" were the only recurring themes in the show. The original album consisted largely of source-music pieces written for the first few episodes, although the sensuous "Dreamsville" became something of a love theme for Pete and Edie.

The "Gunn" album was another unique, even visionary, aspect of the Mancini score that altered not only the way that the public perceived TV music but, perhaps more important, the way network and record-label executives viewed musical scores created for the medium. Alan Livingston, then vice president in charge of television programming at NBC and prior to that vice president of artists and repertoire at Capitol Records, saw the commercial potential of the "Gunn" score. "He saw the pilot," Mancini recalled, "and being a music guy himself—an A and R guy responsible in a great way for bringing over the Beatles—he heard it, called RCA, and said, 'You guys ought to listen to this.'"

The album was recorded in August and September 1958, the last session just a week after the show first went on the air. In fact, some of the tunes (among them "The Floater" and "The Brothers Go to Mothers") were written for the LP and later used as source pieces in the show itself. "And then I made a whole piece out of 'Fallout!,' the opening walking-bass theme," Mancini said. "It was just my instinct, that the tunes were there. That was the main thing. I felt that they should be handled for records, not just as throwaway pieces in a TV episode." Mancini's instincts were unfailing. By early 1959, *The Music from "Peter Gunn"* had reached Number 1 on the *Billboard* popular-album charts, spending 10 weeks at the top and 117 weeks on the chart overall. Although nominated for an Emmy, the music found greater success at the very first Grammy awards, where Mancini won his first two of twenty Grammys during his lifetime: one, the coveted "Album of the Year" award, the other for his arrangements on the LP.

Mancini, previously a virtually anonymous "background score" composer, became a household name. "It was a very exciting period," the composer later recalled. "People knew about it. The musicians were all very up for it; they enjoyed coming in to play. And the mail was completely surprising. I got letters from all over the place concerning the music, which was something that had never really happened to a composer before. It was almost like the music became one of the stars of the show." And, of course, it was. Press coverage of

Mancini's contribution began within a month after the debut of "Gunn." By December 1958, *Newsweek* reported that Mancini was receiving a third of all the show's fan mail. By February, the band was back in the studios recording a second album for RCA. *More Music from "Peter Gunn,"* based on other themes from that first season, went to Number 7 on the *Billboard* charts and received six Grammy nominations.

The success of "Gunn," a top-20 show in its first season, led to a second Edwards-Mancini collaboration in television. "Mr. Lucky" (1959–60, CBS), based on the 1943 Cary Grant movie, starred John Vivyan as the suave owner of a floating gambling casino anchored just off the California coast. Ross Martin (later Artemus Gordon in "The Wild, Wild West") played his colorful sidekick Andamo, a fugitive from an unidentified Latin American country where he had been involved in revolutionary activities.

Mancini consciously moved in a new direction with "Mr. Lucky." The main title sequence was, again, just twenty seconds, but unlike "Gunn," this one was animated and classy: a floating roulette wheel and tumbling dice in space, shifting to the shadow of a cat appearing over the dice (a seven, naturally) and a series of cards that formed themselves into the words "Mr. Lucky," as the cat winked its single open eye.

"It was a different approach," Mancini said. "I really couldn't use the flutes like I had on 'Peter Gunn.' It had to be a turnaround, stylistically. That's why I did the theme with strings, and added the Hammond organ over." The music was a statement of elegance, with the organ solo providing a jazzy element of intrigue.

Also unlike "Gunn," the theme worked its way into the episodic under-scores. Whenever it was opened, Lucky's pocket watch played, like a music box, the first five notes of the theme; it was also heard as source music aboard the ship *Fortuna.* On the other hand, "Lucky" emulated "Gunn" in its consistent use of a familiar opening motif: sparse, suspenseful Latin-styled percussion (called "Floating Pad" on the soundtrack album).

The *"Mr. Lucky"* LP went to Number 2 on the *Billboard* charts in 1960 and won two more Grammys for Mancini (for orchestral album and arrangements). Andamo's background, the southern California setting, and the need for almost constant source music aboard the *Fortuna* meant an abundance of Latin tunes in the score. They spawned a second LP, *"Mr. Lucky" Goes Latin,* which was actually released after the show's cancellation.

The 1959–60 season may have been the busiest in Mancini's career. "We recorded 'Lucky' on Tuesday nights and 'Gunn' on Wednesday nights," he recalled. He would "spot" (decide where music was appropriate) the next "Lucky" on Tuesday afternoon, then record the music for the show he had just written on Tuesday night. On Wednesday afternoon, he would spot the next "Gunn," then record the show that he had just completed writing on Wednesday night. In all, Mancini composed original scores for 114 "Gunns" and 34 "Luckys." After the cancellation of "Gunn" in the spring of 1961, Mancini concentrated on his film career, almost immediately winning Academy Awards for the song "Moon River" and the score for *Breakfast at Tiffany's* (1961) and for the title song of *Days of Wine and Roses* (1962). Apart from two themes—for the London-based "Man of the World" with Craig Stevens (1962, syndicated) and the dramatic anthology "The Richard Boone Show" (1963–64, NBC)—and the score for a United Nations-produced television film, "Carol for Another Christmas" (1964, NBC), Mancini wrote no more television music until 1971.

Almost lost in the hullabaloo surrounding the jazz score for "Peter Gunn" was the fact that, three nights before "Gunn" debuted, another series went on the air with the same idea: "M Squad" (1957–60, NBC), sporting a new musical signature by the legendary Count Basie. "M Squad" was a violent melodrama set in the crime-ridden streets of Chicago, with Lee Marvin portraying Sgt. Frank Ballinger, a member of a special investigative unit of the Chicago police department. The first season of "M Squad" featured an appropriately grim opening and a martial end-title theme (composed by Stanley Wilson, then musical director of Revue). The underscore, as with most series at that time, was drawn from library music commissioned, or acquired, by Wilson at Revue.

In the fall of 1958, however, Revue's new policy of "live" scoring began, and "M Squad" was one of the shows that benefited. "When I first got this notion I approached Basie," Wilson told *TV Guide* in 1959. "He made the recording that opens the show every week. But it was too large a sound to carry through the rest of the show. That's when I looked up two really top jazzmen, Benny Carter and Johnny Williams.

"The three of us now do the writing and scoring. We record with a band heavy on brass—four trombones, two trumpets—[plus] rhythm section and two soloists: Carter, one of the best-known in the business, and Williams." Benny Carter was a veteran alto sax player and composer of note in the jazz world; Williams was a session pianist and up-and-coming composer-arranger for television and movies. (He would later change his billing to John Williams and, with Oscars for such films as *Jaws, Star Wars,* and *E.T. the Extra-Terrestrial,* become the world's best-known film composer.)

So who first came up with the idea of jazz scoring for TV: Mancini or Wilson? As the anonymous *TV Guide* writer put it: "As nearly as can be determined, the decision to try jazz was reached by the two independently of each other."

The Basie theme was a characteristically brassy number with piano solo, and the tune was often interpolated into the episodic underscores, usually as an identifying motif for Ballinger puffing on a cigarette while giving his hard-boiled first-person narration and walking the streets of Chicago.

Wilson actually experimented with a number of composers before he settled on Carter and Williams. Ernest Gold (b. 1921), two years before he would write his Oscar-winning score for *Exodus* (1960), contributed the first score and a subsequent one, but they were more in the metropolitan-jazz realm than the swinging Basie-Carter-Williams mode that would become the norm for "M Squad."

Benny Carter recalled: "I did a date that John Williams was scoring. I was just a musician on the date, the soloist. That was the first time I met Stanley Wilson. And after the thing was over, he said to me, 'Would you like to do a show or two for us?' And I said, 'Indeed I would, thanks for the opportunity.' It started there. After I did one or two they offered me a contract."

Of that season's thirty-nine episodes, Williams and Carter scored twenty-four. Williams, who was under contract to Revue, moved on to other series, while Carter stayed on to score all thirty-nine half hours of the third and final season. Much of their best work from the second season of "M Squad," including some of the tunes contributed by Wilson (who routinely eschewed screen credit, except as musical supervisor), was preserved in the "M Squad" soundtrack, recorded in March 1959 for RCA. It received two Grammy nominations, as the year's outstanding orchestra album and as top film or TV soundtrack.

Wilson's hiring of Benny Carter may have seemed casual. Perhaps it was. But it broke precedent, because Benny Carter became the first black composer to receive screen credit in prime time. Carter (b. 1907) had been active in the film studios throughout the forties and fifties, working on such classics as *Stormy Weather* (1943) and *The Snows of Kilimanjaro* (1952), sometimes even appearing on-screen as in *Thousands Cheer* (1943). Carter also successfully led the fight to merge the segregated musicians' union's locals in Los Angeles. Yet Carter remembered no instances of racial prejudice while he worked in television, which extended into the sixties and seventies with more than a dozen episodes of "Chrysler Theatre," a handful of "Ironside" hours, and several made-for-TV movies.

The success of "Peter Gunn" and "M Squad" had immediate, and far-reaching, consequences, not only for private-eye shows but throughout the medium. A particularly odd case was "Richard Diamond, Private Detective" (1957–60, CBS/NBC), which had one of the strangest musical histories of any show in television.

"Richard Diamond" was David Janssen's first starring role in series television. The character had originated on radio, with Dick Powell in the title role, in 1949; it was Powell's Four Star Productions that made the television series. Diamond was a former New York City police officer who went into business as a private eye; Regis Toomey played his old friend, a gruff lieutenant on the force.

"Diamond" began as a summer replacement series, in July 1957, with a theme by Frank DeVol (the ex-bandleader who would go on to sitcom success with "My Three Sons" and "The Brady Bunch") and the usual tracked underscore utilizing library music. DeVol's theme could barely be heard in the thirty-second main title (because of an announcer prattling on about the sponsor, then slowly reading the title of the show and the name of the star), which underscored an atmospheric shot of a fedora-topped Janssen walking down a dark alley, his face only illuminated when he lit a cigarette. DeVol's end-credit arrangement had an almost military feel, with its clipped brass under strings. It returned, along with the tracked score, when "Richard Diamond" came back as a mid-season replacement in January 1958.

All that was jettisoned when "Peter Gunn" became the talk of the business. When "Richard Diamond" returned for a third season in February 1959, not only was the format altered (the New York locale was dumped for the sunnier climes of southern California): the show had flashy new main- and end-title credit sequences and an outstanding jazz score by Pete Rugolo (b. 1915).

Title designer Maurice Binder, in one of his most distinctive jobs before gaining fame with the James Bond movie credits, created an animated opening in which white bars moved across the screen (first horizontally, then diagonally) and tiny silhouetted figures ran and climbed within them. A vertical bar appeared and widened as the silhouetted Janssen walked toward the camera, finally coming into view as he lit another of those cigarettes. The end titles, in an echo of the earlier "Diamond" credits, had the silhouetted Janssen, still smoking, walking into the distance at the right side of the screen while the credits occupied the left two thirds.

Rugolo created a dual-purpose theme: the bass line served as a convenient villain motif in the underscore, while the brassy primary melody stood for Diamond. He also wrote several secondary themes, most of which got a weekly workout: a traveling motif for Diamond; a love theme for his sometime girlfriend Karen Wells (Barbara Bain); a Latin feel for the show's teaser, a quiet melody for "Sam" (Diamond's telephone answering-service girl, never fully seen and played early on by Mary Tyler Moore); and plenty of jazz for any nightclub into which Diamond might venture.

Born in Sicily, Rugolo moved to the United States in 1921 and studied with composer Darius Milhaud before becoming famous in the jazz world as a composer and arranger for Stan Kenton's postwar band. He spent most of the fifties working as an arranger and orchestrator at MGM, breaking into television in 1958. Rugolo's first assignment was to compose a new theme for "The Thin Man" (1957–59, NBC), the lighthearted TV adaptation of the classic film series, with Peter Lawford and Phyllis Kirk in the William Powell and Myrna Loy roles; longtime MGM musical director Johnny Green had written the original series theme. But "Richard Diamond" put Rugolo on the television-scoring map. Rugolo, who was also West Coast musical director for Mercury Records, turned the "Richard Diamond" score into a jazz album to rival the "Gunn" records in both performance and sound quality (with liner notes by ex-bandleader Dick Powell).

Hiring Rugolo to score "Richard Diamond" was, surprisingly, Janssen's idea. "I was a bachelor then," Rugolo said, "and we went to ball games together. We were buddies, and besides, he liked my work. He had all my albums; he was a big jazz lover." Rugolo used an average of twelve musicians on "Richard Diamond," including, like Mancini on "Gunn," some of the West Coast's finest jazz soloists. Unlike "Gunn," however, Rugolo took offbeat chances with an occasional cello or oboe solo.

Unfortunately, it didn't last. As "Richard Diamond" entered its fourth season of production, Four Star, in a cost-cutting move, chose to create new library music for all of its shows and record it overseas. Rugolo's publishing partner, songwriter Jimmy McHugh ("I'm in the Mood for Love"), owned all rights to the Rugolo score, which was recorded in Los Angeles. The two factions could not come to terms on future uses of the Rugolo music, so when "Richard Diamond" returned with new episodes for the 1959–60 season, the animated titles remained but Rugolo's music was gone.

In its place was a theme that Richard Shores (b. 1917) had written for the Four Star library, a staccato piece—aptly titled "Nervous"—for percussion and brass, followed by a tenor sax solo. The same music would later become the teaser theme for the dramatic anthology "The Dick Powell Show" (1961–63, NBC). Out of sixty-four episodes of "Richard Diamond, Private Detective," only eighteen featured Rugolo scores. Yet it's Rugolo's music that fans associate with the series, and rightly so.

Back at Revue, the jazz trend continued with "Staccato" (1959–60, NBC), starring actor-director John Cassavetes in the unlikely role of Johnny Staccato, jazz pianist-turned-private eye. Between assignments, Staccato hung out at Waldo's, a Greenwich Village club where he often sat in with the house band. As he explained in the pilot: "I put my musicians' union card in mothballs five years ago, when it dawned on me that my talent was an octave lower than my ambition. So while my heart is still on the bandstand, I pay for the groceries away from the piano."

Music was such an integral part of the series that composer Elmer Bernstein (b. 1922) was involved from the beginning. Bernstein was a natural for "Staccato," having drawn wide attention to the dramatic possibilities of jazz with his innovative score for the movie *The Man with the Golden Arm* and followed it up with another jazz score for *Sweet Smell of Success* (1957). In fact, Bernstein had written a jazz theme for an unsuccessful pilot, "Take Five," in 1956. But "Staccato" became Bernstein's contribution to the trend in television and, like its predecessors, spawned an outstanding album of music from the series.

Bernstein's approach to "Staccato" was more orchestral in nature, employing (mostly for dramatic cues) a big band of up to twenty-five players: six saxophones, four trumpets, four trombones, two flutes, two French horns, and a tuba; plus a large rhythm section including two percussionists, two guitarists, bass, and piano. For the source music involving the band at Waldo's, of course, he retreated to a more standard small combo of rhythm with vibes and trumpet.

The original main-title sequence involved animation of crudely drawn piano keys, with Cassavetes's face appearing in the framework to Bernstein's swinging saxophones and screaming trumpets. Low ratings, however, led the producers to retitle the series "Johnny Staccato" and replace it with action-oriented visuals of Cassavetes punching his fist through glass and firing his revolver at the camera to the tune of a fast-moving piano figure. One of the few unique aspects of "Staccato" was on-screen billing for the musicians who both played on the score and were sometimes seen at Waldo's. "M Squad"'s Johnny Williams, on piano, was featured in the pilot.

The same Johnny Williams was responsible for another of the era's great private-eye jazz scores: "Checkmate" (1960–62, CBS). "Checkmate" was a one-hour detective series, also from Revue, created by crime novelist Eric Ambler. Anthony George, Doug McClure, and Sebastian Cabot played the principals at the San Francisco agency of Checkmate Inc., in Ambler's words "the men who do the peculiar work of manipulation necessary for the prevention of death by violence." Atmospheric and often intriguing, "Checkmate" was the class of the genre at that time, and it gave Williams his first opportunity to musically carry an entire series by himself.

John Towner Williams was born in New York in 1932. He moved with his family to California in 1948, although he went back to New York for studies at Juilliard after serving in the air force. Later he studied at UCLA and with private teachers such as Mario Castelnuovo-Tedesco. His father, Johnny Williams Sr., was a well-known drummer who was part of Raymond Scott's famous quintet in the 1930s. Williams began his studio work, about 1956, as a pianist, both for composer Alfred Newman at Twentieth Century-Fox and later on staff in the Columbia Pictures orchestra, doing occasional orchestration for composers Morris Stoloff, Dimitri Tiomkin, and Adolph Deutsch. From 1958, he was under contract as a composer at Revue, where his earliest assignments had been "M Squad" and various episodes of "Wagon Train," "Tales of Wells Fargo," and "General Electric Theatre." "Checkmate," however, "was my first responsibility as a show," Williams recalled, and was Wilson's "expression of confidence in me."

"It meant that I had to produce a lot more music than I had been used to doing, and had to be on the [scoring] stage every week. Maybe he thought I would be most comfortable with that, because it was a kind of jazz-oriented score," Williams said.

In fact, Williams's main-title theme for "Checkmate" was arguably the most arresting of the period. Set against a striking visual pattern of swirling liquid shapes and shades, the theme's blaring brass over a driving ostinato for electric guitar, bass, and percussion set the viewer on edge from the start. "The band on the main-title session was probably eight brass with some winds, maybe as many as twenty musicians," Williams recalled. "But the episodes were done with a small group; I think I had two flutes, two horns and two trombones, percussion and keyboard, [an average of] six or eight musicians. Shelly Manne was the percussionist, and he could always be relied upon for imaginative sounds." Williams even convinced Wilson to record the format music (main and end titles and short "bumpers" for pre- and postcommercial show identifications) at Western Studios in Hollywood, which Williams felt "would give us the brilliant jazz sound that we needed."

Williams individually scored every one of that first season's thirty-six hour-long episodes (plus three in the second season). He developed some of his first-season themes into a Columbia soundtrack album; its superb big-band charts and dreamy dance music resulted in a Grammy nomination as outstanding film or TV score of 1961. Several months later, drummer Manne even did his own small-combo *"Checkmate"* LP consisting of extended jazz improvisations on seven of Williams's original themes.

The record albums multiplied during this period. Nelson Riddle created only the theme and a handful of highly dramatic cues for "The Untouchables" (1959–63, ABC), yet he cleverly wrote an entire album when the series became a hit. Riddle's music for producer Quinn Martin's ultraviolent drama about G-man Eliot Ness (played by Robert Stack), and his Walter Winchell-narrated, Depression-era battle against organized crime in Chicago, relied on dark brass colors. As played over the end-credit roll—a drawing of desperate-looking characters against a cityscape backdrop—it was almost dirgelike, as if Ness was leading the gangsters to the death house.

In fact, recalled Desilu music supervisor Jack Hunsaker, "there was a tremendous amount of track music in those first few years [of the series]. We relied on Capitol Records almost exclusively for a great deal of the underscore." Most of it was actually written for the series by Capitol library stalwarts William Loose and Jack Cookerly. "Bill and I wrote a lot of packages specifically for 'The Untouchables,'" Cookerly said, including Dixie tunes for the speakeasies and stark, dramatic music for the score: "timpani rolls, low trombones, and forget the melody except for certain cues. Really slam-bang."

Dave Kahn, who had created the early library for "Alfred Hitchcock Presents," went on to compose the theme for the original TV version of "Mickey Spillane's Mike Hammer" (1958–59, syndicated) starring Darren McGavin. As before, it was commissioned by entrepreneur Dave Gordon and recorded in Munich. But the success of private-eye jazz scores led to a quick deal for an RCA album, which Kahn wrote and Skip Martin arranged into a first-rate big-band "soundtrack." The music was never heard in the series. (Wrote Spillane in his liner notes: "These sounds of violence fit Mike just like his all-seasonal trenchcoat: crisp, strong and pulsating, yet with an underlying streak of sentiment.")

Warner Bros., meanwhile, took a very different tack. "Cool" was the byword, with the success of "77 Sunset Strip" (1958–64, ABC) and its several companion series: "Hawaiian Eye" (1959–63, ABC); "Bourbon Street Beat" (1959–60, ABC); "Surfside 6" (1960–62, ABC); and "The Roaring Twenties" (1960–62, ABC).

"77 Sunset Strip" starred Efrem Zimbalist Jr. and Roger Smith as Hollywood private eyes Stu Bailey and Jeff Spencer, whose tony offices were located on, in the words of the Jerry Livingston-Mack David theme, "the street that wears the fancy label, that's glorified in song and fable." Also in the cast was Edd Byrnes as Kookie, the parking-lot attendant at the nightclub next door. Long-haired, ever-primping hepcat Kookie's popularity with the teenage crowd resulted in his joining the firm the next season.

In "Hawaiian Eye," set in Honolulu but filmed on the Warners backlot, Anthony Eisley and Robert Conrad were the detectives, with Connie Stevens as a lounge singer and Poncie Ponce as a cabbie; Grant Williams later joined the cast. "Bourbon Street Beat" was set in New Orleans with Richard Long and Andrew Duggan as the investigators, while Miami Beach was the setting for "Surfside 6," with Troy Donahue, Van Williams, Lee Patterson, and Diane McBain in the leading roles. Only "The Roaring Twenties" tried something different, with a setting of New York City during the Prohibition era (but even that was obviously the result of the success of "The Untouchables"), with Dorothy Provine as a singer and Donald May and Rex Reason as newspaper reporters.

All five shows prominently featured theme songs written by composer Jerry Livingston (1909–87) and lyricist Mack David (1912–94). The two had won

Mack David (left) and Jerry Livingston. Courtesy Mack David collection, USC Performing Arts Archives.

acclaim, and an Academy Award nomination, for the songs of Walt Disney's *Cinderella* (1950), including "A Dream Is a Wish Your Heart Makes" and "Bibbidy-Bobbidi-Boo," and would continue to collaborate, again receiving an Oscar nomination for their ballad in *Cat Ballou* (1965). Separately, Livingston had a giant hit with "Mairzy Doats" in the 1940s, and David later penned the words to Vikki Carr's late-1960s hit "It Must Be Him."

"77 Sunset Strip" was their longest-running prime-time series. Performed by a small chorus and punctuated by finger-snapping—an aural hint that these dapper young men were "with it"—the boogie-woogie piano and jazzy brass sounds were heard not just in the main and end titles, but often several times during the hour.

For "Hawaiian Eye," Livingston and David reminded viewers that "the soft island breeze brings you strange melodies . . . exotic mysteries" (against a hilariously improbable visual backdrop of Eisley, Conrad, and company "surf-ing" off Waikiki). "Bourbon Street Beat" had a blues-rock feel, while "Surfside 6" was a cha-cha, and you could dance the Charleston to "The Roaring Twenties." All were memorable, all were right for their shows, and four of the five spawned record albums ("Surfside 6" being the exception, although there was a single). Jack Halloran was credited with the arrangements for television.

Warner Bros. bucked the trend, however, in its indifference to the growing number of original scores for episodic television. For the first two seasons of the studio's venture into television (1955–57), original music was consistently written and recorded for series such as "Cheyenne" and "Conflict." But for six seasons starting in the fall of 1957—which encompassed the entire runs of most of its popular shows, both westerns and private-eye series, until the final year of "77 Sunset Strip"—Warners primarily relied on library music acquired from outside sources or scores from earlier Warner productions. The main themes and a series of cues (act opens and closers, mostly) based on those themes were newly recorded for each show, but the majority of dramatic underscore was supplied by composers Paul Sawtell (1906–71) and Bert Shefter (b. 1904) for three seasons beginning in 1958–59. As the company Music Scores Inc., they were given "musical supervision" screen credit and supplied libraries of cues for tracking by music editors.

Supervising music editor Erma Levin used material that Sawtell and Shefter had composed (sometimes specifically for the shows, sometimes from old movies) and tracked it into the series wherever possible. However, for unusual situations, as well as to meet musicians-union regulations about scoring a specific number of hours for each series, Los Angeles recording sessions were also held for music written by a trio of Warner regulars. Levin explained the process: "I would read a batch of scripts and get a generic idea of what they felt like. And then do what I call prototype timing: descriptions of scenes as if they had come off film, with intervals for throwing a punch, and landing a punch . . . I would hand them out to all the composers: Frank Perkins, Michael

Heindorf, Howard Jackson, you name them. All of them would be given the same piece, the same timings, and each one would write his mental creation [based on the written descriptions]. And we would have them performed." That material, too, would go into the library.

The exceptions generally involved the use of visible source music, such as the Frankie Ortega Trio at Dino's in "77 Sunset Strip," The Baron's piano in "Bourbon Street Beat," the standards sung by Connie Stevens in "Hawaiian Eye," and the Pinky & the Playboys music performed by Dorothy Provine and company for "The Roaring Twenties." They were all prerecorded; Livingston and David supplied occasional incidental songs for the routines.

The Sawtell-Shefter agreement expired in the fall of 1961, but the Warners series continued with virtually no original music on a weekly basis. "77 Sunset Strip," for example, was tracked from a variety of sources within the Warner music catalog. Cues from old Max Steiner scores like *Angels with Dirty Faces* (1938) and *The Big Sleep* (1946) often surfaced, as did excerpts from Alex North's *A Streetcar Named Desire* (1951) and bits from David Buttolph's original scores for the "Conflict" and anthology series of the 1955–57 seasons.

There was one notable exception, and that was "Hawaiian Eye." The leg-

Max Steiner.

endary Max Steiner (1888–1971)—composer of literally hundreds of film scores including such classics as *Gone with the Wind, King Kong,* and *Casablanca*—wrote a small library of music for this grade-B private-eye series. Steiner cues appeared with surprising regularity throughout the 1961–62 season, bearing such generic titles as "Hawaii #12," "Hawaii #19," "Love Scene #1," "Misterioso #10," "Fight #2," "Oriental," "Tiptoe," and "Murder."

Steiner discussed the experience with characteristic humor: "One day I received a cue sheet which said, 'The *Lurline* enters Honolulu. We would like to have a majestic approach to this arrival. Try and give us some Hawaiian flavor and at the same time make it very majestic.' The length of the sequence was five and a half seconds. The orchestra was as follows: one trumpet, one trombone, one horn, one piano, two violins, one cello, one drummer, four woodwinds, four saxes, and we doubled other instruments. How you can create a majestic arrival with an orchestra like that and give it Hawaiian flavor, all in five and a half seconds, I wouldn't know." That may explain why he wrote a library of longer cues and left it up to the music editors to track such sequences.

After Count Basie wrote the "M Squad" theme in 1958, the race was on to sign other outstanding jazz artists to compose television scores. MGM may have scored the greatest coup of all when Duke Ellington committed to compose the music for the pilot of "The Asphalt Jungle" (1961, ABC). Ellington (1899–1974) had dabbled in movie scores, writing *Anatomy of a Murder* (1959) and receiving an Oscar nomination for *Paris Blues* (1961). "The Asphalt Jungle," a cop-show retooling of the 1950 film classic, was Ellington's only foray into writing for dramatic television. Jack Warden, Arch Johnson, and Bill Smith starred in this adaptation, codeveloped by W. R. Burnett (who wrote the original novel), which ran for just thirteen episodes.

Ellington wrote fifteen minutes of music for the one-hour pilot, which was recorded with his own seventeen-piece ensemble. The band came in (from Las Vegas, where Ellington was performing) for a single recording date at MGM on April 25, 1960. Experienced film composers normally record a quarter hour of music in one three-hour session; Ellington and the band, apparently accustomed to more leisurely record dates, took eleven hours and went into the early morning of the next day.

MGM music supervisor Harry Lojewski recalled: "Frankly, there were a lot of problems with Duke's score. They were very disorganized. They finally had to lock the doors of the scoring stage because every time they'd call a 'ten' [the ten-minute break required for every hour of recording by union musicians], the band would go to the bar next door. Finally some of them came in and set up a little bar behind their music stands. Many cues were done, but Duke didn't understand what the timing was all about. So during the final dubbing of the pilot, there had to be a lot of editing."

Less than eleven minutes of the Ellington score survived in the final version, and only his theme was retained when the series went into production. Calvin Jackson, a black composer who had worked with MGM composer Georgie Stoll and was a fine jazz pianist, wrote five original scores. The remainder of the series was tracked with the earlier Jackson music and various cues from earlier MGM productions and the Capitol music library.

Regardless of the problems associated with the pilot, Ellington's music was the single most interesting element of the entire show, which went on the air a year later as a summer replacement series. The main-title sequence consisted of helicopter shots of a big city at night, gradually panning down to the words "The Asphalt Jungle" painted on a well-lit rooftop. Ellington's own distinctive piano could be heard over the main and end titles, and the unmistakable solo sounds of Johnny Hodges on alto saxophone, Harry Carney on baritone, and Jimmy Hamilton on clarinet were audible throughout the pilot score.

For two memorable seasons, a police captain regularly rolled up to a murder scene in his chauffeur-driven Rolls-Royce to a sexy alto saxophone and a breathy female voice whispering, "it's 'Burke's Law' . . . " The lighthearted series (1963–65, ABC) starred Gene Barry as the wealthy homicide detective, whose cases routinely involved an all-star cast of suspects. The theme was by Herschel Burke Gilbert, who was then supervising the music of all of Dick Powell's Four Star productions, including "Burke's Law." Gilbert also wrote the theme for Robert Taylor's "The Detectives" (1959–62, ABC/NBC).

Many episodes of "Burke's Law" were scored by Gilbert's former orchestrator Joseph Mullendore (1914–90), who had written the "Racket Squad" theme many years earlier. Mullendore got his own show when "Burke's Law" spun off "Honey West" (1965–66, ABC), a half hour starring Anne Francis as a private detective. Mullendore's brassy, jazzy theme was set to a screen filled with beehive-style hexagonal portraits of Francis, which then cut to a series of action and glamour shots of the elegant private eye, her pet ocelot, and sidekick Sam (John Ericson). Mullendore's *"Honey West"* LP was one of the best big-band television soundtracks of the period.

"Mr. Broadway" (1964, CBS) was not, strictly speaking, a cop show. But its star, former "Peter Gunn" actor Craig Stevens, played sophisticated Manhattan press agent Mike Bell, who regularly became involved with investigations involving shady schemes and underworld types. Jazz great Dave Brubeck musically enhanced this short-lived creation of writer Garson Kanin. Brubeck (b. 1920), whose unusual time signatures and sophisticated harmonics had made his Dave Brubeck Quartet a favorite of record buyers (particularly with the popular hit "Take Five" in 1960), was an early collaborator in the development of "Mr. Broadway," starting work in the spring of 1964, more than half a year before the series debut.

"I was reluctant to become involved in a medium unfamiliar to me," wrote

Brubeck in the liner notes to his 1965 LP *Jazz Impressions of New York,* which consisted entirely of music written for "Mr. Broadway." "I did not want to write fragmented themes and hours of cues which did not develop into tunes. Musical producer Robert Israel assured me . . . that I should feel free to write full-length tunes from which cues and other background material could be developed," Brubeck wrote. "My assignment, basically, was to capture the rhythm and atmosphere of New York City."

Israel ran the music operation for producer David Susskind's Talent Associates, which made "Mr. Broadway." So it fell to him not only to sign Brubeck but, since the composer had not previously written for film, to find a way to make it work. First came the raw material: "He was like a little boy with a balloon toy," Israel recalled. "He got involved to the point where I couldn't stop him from writing melodies. I spent many hours with him going over sketches, a lot of which I knew would be inappropriate, but you couldn't dampen his enthusiasm. The great inspiration was signing Oliver Nelson to the project."

Nelson (1932–75) was the brilliant jazz saxophonist who became, in the early 1960s, a well-known composer-arranger. His "Stolen Moments" is a jazz standard and his large-scale orchestral works, including *Afro-American Sketches* (1961), *The Kennedy Dream* (1967), and *Jazzhattan Suite* (1967), incorporated

Dave Brubeck (left) and Oliver Nelson in the studio during the recording of "Mr. Broadway." Photo by Sheldon Secunda, courtesy R. A. Israel Collection.

both jazz and concert-music influences. "It was a chance to get my feet wet in TV," Nelson said in 1968, "and actually it involved some challenging work. They would give me a melodic line written by Brubeck and ask me to construct and orchestrate a love song or some other kind of theme out of it."

Explained Israel: "Dave wrote his material in song form, which would then be fragmented, inverted, the harmonies changed or altered to suit adaptation into cues, transitions, and background [by Nelson]. We drilled Oliver in terms of procedures and lengths. A lot of the stuff was improvised, in terms of timings, in the control room. I would say, 'Listen, cut this off at bar twenty-four and give me a button at the end.' And I would know that that would be a thirty-second cue which otherwise I couldn't edit out because it wasn't designed that way."

Brubeck noted that "music for the television series ran the gamut of emotions and moods from 'horror' to 'flippant,' 'romantic' to 'violent,' and are so described on studio worksheets. The locale assignments ranged from nightclubs to churches, Greenwich Village to Harlem, Japanese to Latin. Ideas came easily from every source—words, situations, places, characters—all stamped with the personality of the city itself."

Brubeck's involvement was deemed so important that he received main-title credit: "original music by Dave Brubeck." (The end titles further explained that the score had been "orchestrated and conducted by Oliver Nelson.") The theme, with melody played by alto saxophonist Paul Desmond, was unmistakably Brubeck, and was set to silhouettes of the Manhattan skyline.

"I decided on a basic polyrhythmic approach to [the theme] because the Quartet has been long identified with the jazz waltz and unusual time signatures," Brubeck explained. "Also, inherent in multiple rhythms is an inner pull which creates conflict and dramatic excitement on a sophisticated level. Once settled upon this polyrhythmic approach . . . I wrote four different countermelodies related to it: an eerie twelve-tone melody, two blues themes, and a lighthearted baroque melody. These countermelodies, played either alone or simultaneously with the original theme, are the backbone of the television score." For Mike Bell's Japanese assistant Toki (Lani Miyazaki), Brubeck wrote a colorful theme that combined "Western beat and pseudo-Oriental sounds."

Brubeck's quartet could regularly be heard performing the source-music jazz in various episodes. According to Israel, Brubeck did not play on the larger orchestral sessions but was present to supervise the recording.

Quincy Jones burst onto the scene in 1967 with his brash pilot score, and subsequent series work, on "Ironside" (1967–75, NBC). He had started in TV in the previous season, with lively, funny scores for the Will Hutchins sitcom "Hey Landlord" (1966–67, NBC), but it was on "Ironside" that his reputation, particularly for writing jazz in a dramatic context, was cemented.

Jones (b. 1933) was born in Chicago but grew up in Seattle. A trumpeter

Quincy Jones. Photo by George Fields.

who toured with the Lionel Hampton band, he began arranging in the mid-1950s, studied in Paris with classical theorist Nadia Boulanger, and by 1964 had become the first black vice president of a major record label (Mercury). Well known as an arranger-conductor for artists such as Frank Sinatra and Ella Fitzgerald, he began a move into films with an acclaimed score for *The Pawnbroker* (1965) and an Oscar-nominated one for the chilling *In Cold Blood* (1967).

"Ironside"'s two-hour TV-movie pilot established the premise: San Francisco's outspoken chief of detectives Robert Ironside (Raymond Burr), paralyzed by a sniper's bullet, survived to find his would-be assassin and returned, wheelchair bound, to work with a special team including a former juvenile delinquent, a detective sergeant, and a well-to-do policewoman. Recalled Jones in 1972: "I played straight off the title. He was a rough dude, a metallic, strong-principled cat. I just went straight with the emotional image." So metallic was this image, in fact, that the composer used a cymbalum, whose sharp, percussive sound is the result of metal striking metal.

The score was heavily jazz-influenced and highly dramatic, setting the stage for the series that would debut that fall. Jones, who had initially planned to score the entire series, wrote two full scores, two songs for subsequent first-season episodes (one with Bob Russell, the other with Alan and Marilyn Bergman), and turned over the remainder to other writers. "It was just too hard, it was too much music every week," Jones said later. "I was going for the throat. We had forty-four musicians and you scored on a Thursday; on Friday you were spotting the next one for the next week."

Although Jones continued to use a cymbalum in his episode scores, he drew far more attention with the brand-new sound that he introduced in his forty-second main-title theme: "Ironside" was the first series to use a Moog synthesizer. The composer, searching for a tone that would imitate a police siren, had been introduced to the Moog by early electronic-music expert Paul Beaver and found it useful for the opening seconds of his series main title. There was little resistance to this innovation, he recalled, because executives "didn't know what the hell it was."

The composer even made his acting debut in one of his two early episodes, "Eat, Drink and Be Buried," playing a hip jazz-club owner. Guest star Lee Grant could be heard, in the teaser, remarking to a cocktail-party guest that "Quincy Jones really turns me on" while the composer's Oscar-nominated song from *Banning* (1967) played in the background.

Jones's multifaceted "Ironside" signature melody—to which the main-title visuals, all in shades of red, black, and white that first year, were edited—exemplified his philosophy of writing television themes. "You need a variety of elements," he said in 1972. "I try to get a bass pattern that will work collectively or individually, also two or three accompaniment figures that are highly distinguishable. It's designed so you can put all the elements together. You've got all different parts that are musically related in some way from an interval standpoint, and then the intervals have a relationship, so the material is organic."

Jones, initially warned by some anonymous executive against writing "too much street music" for the series, "tamed down" his theme for the TV version, but included a powerful, straight-ahead jazz arrangement of "Ironside" on his Grammy-winning 1971 LP *Smackwater Jack*. Universal acquired the rights to the newly recorded tune and adopted an abbreviated version that fall, and in subsequent seasons, for the series main title.

Apart from Jones, the first season of "Ironside" included scores by Oliver Nelson (who had recently moved to Los Angeles to pursue studio work) and fellow jazz greats Benny Carter and Benny Golson. Beginning with the second season, Nelson became the primary composer, with Marty Paich (1925–95) taking over the series for the sixth and seventh seasons, and Nelson returning for the eighth.

Paich, a highly respected West Coast arranger and bandleader, recalled being given complete freedom by producer Cy Chermak. "He loved the sound of the dectet, which was a sound that I had used behind Mel [Tormé] plus several other [singers]: a few horns—a trumpet, an alto, a trombone—and then maybe four or five rhythm players. That gave me the jazz feeling; I didn't want to go into strings and legitimate woodwinds because that wasn't the kind of score it was."

In addition, Paich collaborated with his son David Paich (later a member of the rock group Toto) on a number of original songs that often opened episodes and became the basis for the dramatic underscore, a practice that was highly unusual for television at that time. Marty Paich received the series' only two Emmy nominations for music: one, for his scoring of the 1972–73 season; and a second, which he won with David, for the song "Light the Way," composed for an episode in the 1973–74 season.

"Hawaii Five-0" (1968–80, CBS) went in a completely different direction. Composer Morton Stevens (1929–91) had written a memorable theme for the police drama "87th Precinct" (1961–62, NBC) but created an entirely new sound for "Hawaii Five-0."

"Five-0" concerned a special investigative unit based in Honolulu and headed by tough, single-minded Steve McGarrett (Jack Lord), who reported only to the governor of Hawaii. Rather than tackling routine crimes, McGarrett and his team were called in only on the most baffling, politically sensitive, or logistically complicated cases. The result was a highly contemporary, rarely routine hour that was filmed entirely on location in the fiftieth state and became the longest-running police show in the history of television. Some of its phraseology even entered the American lexicon, such as "Book 'em, Dan-O," McGarrett's barked order to his second-in-command (James MacArthur), and Lord's voiceover after the weekly preview of next week's show: "Be there. Aloha."

Stevens, a Juilliard graduate who spent much of the 1950s as musical director for Sammy Davis Jr., was a television-scoring veteran, having worked on

Morton Stevens. Courtesy Annie Stevens.

"Thriller," "The Man from U.N.C.L.E.," and many other series at Revue and MGM. He also happened to be a card-playing buddy of "Five-0" creator Leonard Freeman, and, since 1965, had been director of music for CBS West Coast operations. He was therefore in the ideal position to score the pilot (since it was not only Freeman's production but was partly financed by CBS Entertainment).

The composer recalled that Freeman originally described the show to him this way: "It's about a guy who's as hard as a rock. And he's living on a rock. And he's hard." Stevens interpreted Freeman's rather crude sexual parallel to mean that he wanted the music to suggest a "macho strength," and, after one false start (nixed by his favorite sounding board, his wife Annie, a former singer with bandleaders such as Claude Thornhill), came up with the forceful theme that the popular instrumental group The Ventures subsequently turned into a top-10 hit and a gold album in 1969.

"It took eleven minutes to get the basics down," Stevens said. "The simplicity of it, and the driving force of instruments rather than simply the drums, made it into a popular rhythmic entity. With two trumpets playing the melody, and two trumpets playing the same melody an octave lower, it sounded like a blunderbuss coming at you."

Freeman, in his liner notes for Stevens's own Capitol LP of first-season "Five-0" music, said he insisted on "no ukeleles or steel guitars or falsetto singers or overused bongos," a demand that Stevens later confirmed. "He didn't want the typical Hawaiian sound," the composer said, "so I found a new Hawaiian sound that Hawaii didn't know it had."

The final triumph was the fusion of the music with editor Reza S. Badiyi's main-title visuals, a montage that is still one of television's most impressive. The teaser smash-cut to a giant wave rolling in to the sound of Stevens's drumbeat. Scenes of the surf, the Honolulu setting, and the Hawaiian people were cut in precise time to the beat; a spectacular sunset and the gyrating hips of a hula dancer were superbly matched to the rhythm of the theme.

The "Five-0" pilot featured four trumpets, four trombones, four French horns, six woodwinds, six celli, and four percussion, for a total of twenty-eight players. The average episode was scored with eighteen to twenty musicians, Stevens said.

While still juggling his administrative duties as head of CBS music (producing other composers' recording sessions, and assigning composers to various in-house productions), Stevens managed to score six episodes of the first season of "Five-0" and three dozen more over the course of the next eleven seasons. Literally dozens of others were tracked with music Stevens had written for earlier episodes. Jack Lord, who effectively assumed the reins of the show after Freeman's death in 1973, demanded and got the composer's commitment to score at least a few shows every year.

Three of Stevens's nine Emmy nominations were for "Hawaii Five-0," and he won two of those. The first nod was for the two-hour 1968 pilot; the winners were for "A Thousand Pardons, You're Dead," the opening installment of the second season, and what may be Stevens's masterpiece, the sixth-season opener, "Hookman," in 1973. (In an instance that has never been repeated in the history of the Emmys for music, all three nominees for the 1973–74 season were "Hawaii Five-0" episodes, including one each for Stevens's fellow composers Bruce Broughton and Don B. Ray.)

Stevens even appeared, as a heroin-addicted musician, in a third-season episode, "Trouble in Mind," with singer Nancy Wilson. And when CBS decided that Khigh Dhiegh, who played McGarrett's nemesis Wo Fat on "Five-0," was popular enough to merit his own series (as a private eye in San Francisco's Chinatown), Stevens again came up with a memorable theme, deploying Oriental instruments in a Western musical context. The theme for "Khan!" (1975, CBS) had an aura of mystery but a highly contemporary sound, with a rock 'n' roll beat.

Stevens's other great cop-show theme was for "Police Woman" (1974–78, NBC), which starred Angie Dickinson as Sgt. Pepper Anderson, an undercover detective for the Los Angeles police department's criminal conspiracy division. For this one, Stevens opened with a downward-spiraling synthesizer sound, simulating a police siren (although quite different from Jones's use of the same instrument on "Ironside") into what the composer described as a "heavy Brazilian beat." And, in an in-joke probably noticed only by composers in the business, Stevens took his friend Jerry Goldsmith's theme for the film *Our Man Flint* (1966) and "turned it upside down and backwards" to create the primary melody.

One of the most distinguished composers in films made a brief sojourn into television that produced two of the finest themes ever written for the medium, both of them for the law-and-order field. Bronislau Kaper (1902–83) established the musical formats for "Arrest and Trial" (1963–64, ABC) and "The FBI" (1965–74, ABC).

Kaper spent twenty-eight years at MGM, scoring such pictures as *Green Dolphin Street* (1947), *The Red Badge of Courage* (1951), and *Mutiny on the Bounty* (1962), winning an Academy Award for the score of *Lili* (1953). He was also a brilliant pianist, which may partially explain his Rachmaninoff-concerto-style theme, with its beautiful piano solo, for "Arrest and Trial."

Revue had made a success of its ninety-minute western "The Virginian," and so tried a similar-length show about the criminal justice system. The first forty-five minutes of "Arrest and Trial" focused on the crime and the investigation (with Ben Gazzara as the police detective), while the second forty-five involved the accused's day in court (with Chuck Connors as a public defender). The prestige that Revue attached to this series was especially evident in its musical treatment. Not only did Kaper compose the theme and score two episodes, but the equally gifted film composer Franz Waxman (1906–67) contributed three more, all in the fall of 1963.

Waxman saw television less as a creative challenge than as an economic necessity. Waxman founded, and personally underwrote, the Los Angeles International Music Festival, which annually presented the best of contemporary concert music on the West Coast. "The income that he derived from working in television went to pay for the music festival," explained the composer's son, John W. Waxman.

"Arrest and Trial" (the progenitor of the nineties hit "Law & Order") was short-lived. But Kaper enjoyed a long-running hit series in "The FBI." Quinn Martin, who had turned "The Untouchables" into a hit, by now had his own production company and a solid ABC series in "The Fugitive." For "The FBI," Quinn Martin music supervisor John Elizalde approached his old friend Kaper, whom he had known during the fifties at MGM.

"Bronny always had a way of doing really high-quality, institutional sorts of things, which is exactly what 'The FBI' was," Elizalde said. "That show seemed made to order for the Ford Motor Company. At that time, they were looking for an institutional icon that would destroy the Tin Lizzie concept. They wanted something really solid."

That was evident in the opening titles, a series of shots of Washington, D.C., landmarks including the Capitol, the Washington Monument, and finally the Federal Bureau of Investigation. Kaper composed a theme of great grandeur and dignity, befitting these symbols of United States government. He scored three episodes at the start of the first season; veteran studio orchestrator Leo Arnaud wrote two more. Dominic Frontiere, an old Elizalde friend and colleague, conducted all of these scores with an orchestra of as large as forty-two pieces.

Quinn Martin stayed in the cop-show business throughout the seventies. First came "Dan August" (1970–71, ABC) with Burt Reynolds as a young California cop, which had a jazz theme by Dave Grusin. Noted Elizalde: "Dave was right for the picture. There's a freewheeling quality to his music." Grusin added color with a buzz kalimba, an African percussion instrument.

Things heated up considerably with Pat Williams's music for Quinn Martin's "The Streets of San Francisco" (1972–77, ABC), an hour-long drama shot on location in the California city with Karl Malden and Michael Douglas as police partners. Williams was inspired by the frenetic main-title visuals of San Francisco exteriors, according to Elizalde.

"It was pretty hip for its time," Williams admitted. "I took a sound that I had used in some of the brass albums I had made in New York. To play the melody, there was a unison between the trumpets in the medium register and the trombones in a high register. The trombones being that high added this intensity. It had this real hot quality to it. The band loved to play it." Twenty years later, "The Streets of San Francisco" main title remains one of the most exciting themes ever written for television. Its electric harpsichord, wild rhythm guitar, and tenor saxophone solo made the music of "Streets" frequently more interesting than the show itself.

One of the longest-running of the Quinn Martin shows was the unlikely "Barnaby Jones" (1973–80, CBS), which cast Buddy Ebsen as a private eye who came out of retirement to solve his son's murder and remained in business, with Lee Meriwether as his daughter-in-law and assistant. Equally unlikely was Elizalde's choice of composer: Jerry Goldsmith, who hadn't done a police procedural since "The Lineup" expanded to an hour (1958–59, CBS) and "Cain's Hundred" (1961–62, NBC) fought crime with syndicate lawyer-turned-prosecutor Mark Richman.

Goldsmith's "Barnaby Jones" music almost didn't happen. The offer coincided with a fallow period in the composer's career when, despite five Academy Award nominations for his scores for films such as *The Sand Pebbles* and *Patton*, he was receiving few motion-picture assignments. So he agreed to attend a screening of the pilot. "I got out of there, and I called my agent," Goldsmith later related. "And I said, 'Marc, please get me out of this. This [show] is horrible.' And he said, 'Do it. You can do it in five days.'" So Goldsmith sat down, composed the theme and pilot score, and—in time—walked away with the BMI royalties for a long-running hit on network television.

Goldsmith's theme accompanied a graphic main-title sequence in which the name "Barnaby Jones" pieced itself together, jigsaw-puzzle style. Blaring French horns gave way to a theme for alto flutes and very prominent bass, over a fast-moving rhythm section: music that, in one minute, conveyed more energy than the elderly detective displayed in eight seasons. (Goldsmith also wrote a very contemporary theme for the acclaimed anthology "Police Story" [1973–77, NBC].)

Elizalde matched composer to show time and again: John Parker, whose tuba theme for "Cannon" (1971–76, CBS) annoyed the overweight star William Conrad; Johnny Mandel, whose vintage 1930s sound, complete with swinging clarinet solo, perfectly complemented the period private-eye series "Banyon" (1972–73, NBC) starring Robert Forster; and Nelson Riddle, whose vaguely Latin beat for "Caribe" (1975, ABC) was appropriate for Miami-based police lieutenant Stacy Keach.

By the 1970s, crime shows had achieved a new sophistication. In the fall of 1971, one network began rotating three different ninety-minute detective series under a single umbrella: the "NBC Mystery Movie" (1971–77). Each had its own distinctive musical style, but all three were introduced by the same main-title sequence—one that marked the return to television of Henry Mancini.

Mancini's "Mystery Movie" theme marked the start of the composer's fascination with offbeat electronic sounds: a whistlelike tone (made by the Yamaha YC-30 combo organ) over strings and rhythm. (Mancini also employed unusual electronic sounds on two other cop-show themes of that period: "Cade's County" [1971–72, CBS] with Glenn Ford and "The Blue Knight" [1975–76, CBS] with George Kennedy.)

"Columbo" (1971–78, NBC; 1989–, ABC) started out as a one-shot World Premiere movie, "Prescription: Murder" (1968). Peter Falk played the rumpled, seemingly confused Los Angeles police lieutenant to a jazzy score by Dave Grusin. But it was a second TV movie, "Ransom for a Dead Man" (1971), that sold the series. It was scored by Billy Goldenberg (b. 1936), who had become a fixture at Universal.

The Brooklyn-born Goldenberg began his career as a rehearsal pianist for the Broadway theater. He wrote an original musical based on Ray Bradbury's *Dandelion Wine* (which had a brief run in New York) and dance music for TV's "Hullabaloo" before working as musical director on several TV specials starring Petula Clark, Ann-Margret, and Elvis Presley. In late 1968, he became assistant to Universal music chief Stanley Wilson, scoring episodes of "It Takes a Thief" and "The Name of the Game" and landing several major TV-movie assignments.

For "Ransom for a Dead Man," Goldenberg set out to write "a dark, madly passionate and beautiful theme" for murderess Lee Grant. Goldenberg's approach set the style for the "Columbo" series to follow; he scored three of the first-season episodes, including the first, "Murder by the Book," which was directed by Steven Spielberg, and featured typewriter sounds integrated into the score; and "Lady in Waiting," for which he received an Emmy nomination.

Billy Goldenberg, 1973. Photo by Andy Sackheim, courtesy BMI Archives.

Neither Goldenberg's rich, haunting "Ransom" score nor his scores for the "Columbo" series featured a theme for the disheveled detective. "There are characters in films that you do not musicalize," said the composer. "They do it all for themselves. You can't musicalize an investigation. You can't make Columbo funny because [Falk] is doing it already in the acting. There's too much of the intellectual in 'Columbo' to write music. He is his own music."

Yet when Universal received requests for a "Columbo" theme and recording artists expressed interest in detective-theme compilations, music executives chose a jazzy 6/4 tune that Goldenberg had written as Columbo's introduction in "Ransom" and published it as the "Columbo" theme (even though Gil Mellé had written his own signature motif and used it in four first-season scores). After that, "Columbo" episodes were treated as individual mysteries, each as a separate musical entity. In the 1973 episode "Any Old Port in a Storm," the character was heard to hum the children's tune "This Old Man" ("knick-knack-paddy-whack . . .") and, because of Falk's fondness for the song, it began to recur even in the scores themselves, becoming a kind of unofficial "Columbo" theme (especially in the two-hour ABC movies of the nineties).

Goldenberg went on to write three more memorable seventies detective-show themes: "Banacek" (1972–74, NBC), with George Peppard as a high-priced Boston insurance investigator; "Harry O" (1974–76, ABC), the well-liked David Janssen series about a world-weary San Diego private detective; and "Kojak" (1973–78, CBS), which brought Telly Savalas to series television as a lollipop-sucking New York City police lieutenant. "Harry O" was an outgrowth of the TV movie "Smile Jenny, You're Dead" (1974), while "Kojak" was a spinoff of the acclaimed three-hour docudrama "The Marcus-Nelson Murders" (1973), which won Goldenberg another Emmy nomination (for a song he had written with lyricist Bob Russell). Goldenberg's original "Kojak" theme was succeeded by a new one written by regular "Kojak" composer John Cacavas during its final season.

The second of the rotating series was "McMillan and Wife" (1971–77, NBC), a lighthearted mystery with Rock Hudson as the San Francisco police commissioner and Susan Saint James as his curious wife. The theme and most of the scores over the six seasons were written by Jerry Fielding (1922–80), an outspoken and immensely talented composer who never received his due from Hollywood.

Fielding, like Mancini, began his studies with Max Adkins in Pittsburgh and went into radio as arranger for "Kay Kyser's Kollege of Musical Knowledge" in the 1940s. He was Groucho Marx's original bandleader on "You Bet Your Life" (1950–61, NBC), but, because he took the Fifth Amendment before the House Un-American Activities Committee in 1953, he was blacklisted for much of the fifties. Betty Hutton insisted upon hiring Fielding as musical director of her "Betty Hutton Show" (1959–60, CBS), and he went on to such prestige pictures as *Advise and Consent* (1962) and the first of three Oscar nominations for *The Wild Bunch* (1969).

Fielding's approach to "McMillan," beginning with the pilot film "Once upon a Dead Man" (1971), was one of musical sophistication: a jazzy, upbeat theme for Mac and Sally, and much more dark textures for the inevitable murder scenes—some of which would hint at the grim, often dissonant music he would be called upon to write later in the seventies for filmmakers Sam Peckinpah (*Straw Dogs*), Michael Winner (*The Mechanic*), and Clint Eastwood (*The Outlaw Josey Wales*).

The third element in the "Mystery Movie" wheel was "McCloud" (1970–77, NBC), which began the season before as an element of another rotating Wednesday-night series, "Four-in-One." For this reworking of Universal's movie *Coogan's Bluff* (1968), Dennis Weaver starred as a Taos, New Mexico, marshal studying criminal-investigation techniques with the New York City police department. David Shire scored the first season of "McCloud," including a lively, country-flavored theme. Producer Glen A. Larson eventually wrote his own "McCloud" theme which was first heard in late 1973.

Shire (b. 1937), who had been writing off-Broadway musicals, worked as a rehearsal pianist in the New York theater. His work on Stephen Sondheim's original television musical "Evening Primrose" (in November 1966, on "ABC Stage '67") led to an offer from its director, Paul Bogart, to score some of the prestige dramas on "CBS Playhouse" the following season. Old friend Goldenberg introduced him to Stanley Wilson at Universal, and Shire joined the ranks of composers working in television. He went on to score many acclaimed films, including *The Conversation* (1974) and *All the President's Men*

David Shire. Courtesy BMI Archives.

(1976), win an Academy Award for *Norma Rae* (1979), and a Grammy for the *Saturday Night Fever* soundtrack (1978).

The success of the "NBC Mystery Movie" led the network to program two nights the following season. "Columbo," "McCloud," and "McMillan" moved to Sundays, along with the Mancini theme, while the new "Wednesday Mystery Movie" (1972–74, NBC) boasted a rousing big-band signature by Quincy Jones.

ABC, meanwhile, tried its own rotating series, called "The Men" (1972–73), and commissioned an umbrella theme from Isaac Hayes. Hayes (b. 1938), who a few months earlier had won a Best Song Oscar for his theme from *Shaft* (1971), wrote a four-minute tune that made the top-40 charts as a single. Heard strictly on television, however, his "Hot Buttered Soul"-style strings, brass, and rhythm—with reverbed female voices repeatedly cooing, "the mennnn . . ."—was butchered into a forty-second main-title sequence designed to introduce "Assignment: Vienna" with Robert Conrad, "The Delphi Bureau" with Laurence Luckinbill, and "Jigsaw" with James Wainwright. Hayes's only other work for television was a theme for his recurring character of Gandy on "The Rockford Files" in 1976; his "Shaft" theme was arranged for Richard Roundtree's TV spinoff (1973–74, CBS) by Johnny Pate.

"The Mod Squad" (1968–73, ABC) broke new ground in the genre, both in terms of concept and music. Michael Cole, Peggy Lipton, and Clarence Williams III played three young people who worked under cover for the Los Angeles police. Their music was the work of one of the legendary figures of American television scoring: Earle Hagen.

Hagen (b. 1919) came out of the big-band era, playing for Benny Goodman and Tommy Dorsey. In 1939, while playing first trombone and arranging for bandleader Ray Noble, he composed "Harlem Nocturne," which became not only a jazz standard but also, nearly half a century later, the theme for "Mickey Spillane's Mike Hammer" (1984–87, CBS) starring Stacy Keach. In 1946, he began a seven-year stint as a contract arranger and orchestrator at Twentieth Century-Fox. He and fellow orchestrator Herbert W. Spencer worked almost exclusively on musicals; two of their films, *Mother Wore Tights* (1947) and *Call Me Madam* (1953), won Oscars for musical direction. In 1953, they left Fox and formed a partnership to provide music for the burgeoning new medium of television, initially for "The Danny Thomas Show." Later, on his own, Hagen scored such TV classics as "The Andy Griffith Show," "The Dick Van Dyke Show," "I Spy," and "That Girl."

Hagen's theme for "The Mod Squad" was one of the most dynamic ever. Written specifically for the already-shot main-title visuals of Cole, Lipton, and Williams running down a darkened, rain-soaked alleyway, its pounding beat, gutsy brass, and jazzy organ solo immediately told viewers that this was an action show.

"We used rock 'n' roll in the open spots: chases, fights, and things like that," Hagen recalled. "But rock 'n' roll doesn't have any harmonic drive to it; it's rhythmic drive, which doesn't work well under dialogue. So when we got into scoring, especially scoring that had any tension to it, we went to twelve-tone," an advanced form of composition that was developed by twentieth-century composer Arnold Schoenberg. "With the exception of a theme that Shorty Rogers wrote [for the pilot] that we used for an association with the kids—that we used to finish the shows with, very melodic—the rest of the scoring was always pretty tense. Twelve-tone [composition] creates a lot of tension," Hagen explained. Fellow big-band arranger Billy May also wrote many "Mod Squad" episodes.

Aaron Spelling, who produced "The Mod Squad" in association with Danny Thomas, subsequently went into business with former ABC executive Leonard Goldberg. Elmer Bernstein composed the theme for their young-cop series "The Rookies" (1972–76, ABC), with Michael Ontkean, Georg Stanford Brown, and Kate Jackson, and Barry DeVorzon created a pop hit with his theme for "S.W.A.T." (1975–76, ABC).

"S.W.A.T.," which was widely criticized for its violence, starred Steve Forrest as the head of a police Special Weapons and Tactics unit called in whenever big firepower was necessary. DeVorzon's ultracontemporary theme, in a disco version by Rhythm Heritage, became the first single from a prime-time series to hit Number 1 on the *Billboard* pop charts since "The Ballad of Davy Crockett" twenty years earlier. (DeVorzon would have an even more enduring hit in "Nadia's Theme," a cut from his and partner Perry Botkin Jr.'s soundtrack from the 1972 film *Bless the Beasts and Children.* It became the theme for the daytime soap "The Young and the Restless," and an international success after Romanian gymnast Nadia Comaneci used it to accompany her 1976 Olympics routine.)

Then, in 1976, a new Spelling-Goldberg show opened with this introduction: "Once upon a time there were three little girls who went to the Police Academy. And they were each assigned very hazardous duties. But I took them away from all that, and now they work for me. My name is Charlie." The voice belonged to John Forsythe, but the faces were far more memorable: Kate Jackson, Farrah Fawcett-Majors, and Jaclyn Smith as "Charlie's Angels" (1976–81, ABC), the private-eye series that redefined the term "jiggle" and immediately shot to the top of the ratings (it was in the top five during its first two years, and in the top 20 for four of its five seasons on the air).

Charlie was the never-seen boss of an agency whose operatives were intelligent, attractive women (in succeeding seasons, Cheryl Ladd, Shelley Hack, and Tanya Roberts); their liaison was played by David Doyle. To Jack Elliott and Allyn Ferguson fell the task of setting their adventures to music.

Elliott (b. 1927) studied with contemporary classical composer Lukas Foss but came to Hollywood via the Broadway theater. He became a popular dance arranger on variety shows headlined by Judy Garland and Andy Williams; by 1971 he was music director of the annual Grammy Awards program and had scored films such as *Where's Poppa?* (1970) and *T. R. Baskin* (1971). Ferguson (b. 1924) studied with Aaron Copland, Nadia Boulanger, and Ernst Toch. He created a chamber jazz group in the late 1950s, arranged and conducted for Johnny Mathis, and joined his old friend Elliott (whom he had met while studying at Tanglewood in the 1950s) in a television-scoring partnership in 1968. In a solo capacity, he went on to score many of producer Norman Rosemont's television remakes of literary classics, notably "Les Miserables" (1978), "Ivanhoe" (1982), and his Emmy-winning "Camille" (1984).

The Elliott-Ferguson team provided the underscores for many action shows of the seventies, including "The Rookies," "Starsky and Hutch," "Get Christie Love," and "Police Story." The ninety-minute "Charlie's Angels" pilot initially had a score by another composer; Elliott and Ferguson were called in with just four or five days to create a new one. They demanded and won the right to compose a new theme (because they hadn't written the main title for either "Rookies" or "Starsky," both Spelling-Goldberg shows), gaining a long-running hit.

The "Charlie's Angels" scores were actually assembled by committee. The Elliott-Ferguson company was handling the music for so many shows that the work was divided up among several composers. One of the principals would spot the show and write the thematic material, which would then be developed and orchestrated by members of their team, usually including veteran orchestrators Greig McRitchie and Jack Smalley. Some of the episodes had as much as thirty-eight minutes of music per week. "Inevitably, there would be the car chase, or one of the Angels was in trouble and she'd have to get away," laughed Scott Smalley, who joined the orchestration team with his father Jack. "So we'd crank up the rhythm section and have a big band screaming through it. With the big band, we could give it an element of fun, even though they were being chased by some serial killer or drug lord that they were going to arrest."

Elliott and Ferguson also wrote the small-combo, urban-jazz theme for "Barney Miller" (1975–82, ABC). In 1978, they created the Foundation for New American Music and its performing arm The Orchestra, which commissioned new concert works (often merging jazz and classical influences) from many established film and television composers. Their partnership broke up shortly thereafter.

"Don't do the crime if you can't do the time. . . . Keep your eye on the sparrow when the going gets narrow" went the theme for "Baretta" (1975–78, ABC), which starred Robert Blake as an unorthodox cop with a cockatoo named Fred.

Composer Dave Grusin (b. 1934) was already an old hand at television, having composed the "Name of the Game," "It Takes a Thief," and "Maude" themes, scoring everything from "Gidget" to "The Virginian," and working as musical director on Andy Williams's variety show. He had also begun a promising career in feature films with scores such as *Divorce American Style*

(1967), *The Heart Is a Lonely Hunter* (1968), and *Winning* (1969), and continued to work in the recording field as an arranger and jazz artist.

Blake had asked his friend, lyricist Morgan Ames, to write a song for the series; Ames enlisted frequent collaborator Grusin to write the music. According to Ames, both had been extremely busy on various projects, and, on the day the instrumental track for the main title was to be recorded, "We hadn't written anything. I was writing this other song, a gospel [flavored] song called 'Keep Your Eye on the Sparrow,' taking off on that old spiritual," Ames said. Working with Grusin at another session the same day, she told him as he was preparing to leave for the "Baretta" rhythm date: "Here's the chorus: 'Keep your eye on the sparrow when the going gets narrow.'"

"As I recall, he passed out blank paper to the band, which [included drummer] Harvey Mason and [guitarist] Lee Ritenour. And David went to the piano and started doing his magic. I know he did write it in his head driving to Universal. Fortunately, we didn't have to do the lyric that day. I wrote that driving to the session a couple of days later."

Observed Grusin: "We were trying to get a street feel for the show." So he and Ames hired black vocalist Jim Gilstrap to record the song, and a trio of women (including Ames) to sing backup. "Actually, David thought of 'don't do the crime if you can't do the time,'" Ames admitted, "and I did 'don't go to bed with no price on your head.' And 'don't do it,'" she laughed, referring to the line interjected by the trio in response to the lead.

Later, word came back that Universal executives had rejected the vocal for the series. "The reason was, they said, you can't open a white show with a black singer," Ames said. "That was the tenor of the times. So the first season of the show was an instrumental theme with no vocal. We were really disappointed." Ames got a letter from producer Jo Swerling Jr. that spoke of his "shock" and "heartbreak" at the decision by his superiors, adding that "I am hoping that if 'Baretta' is a hit we'll be able to convince our colleagues to reconsider their decision and allow us to use what is probably the best damn main-title theme ever created."

"Baretta" was a hit, and nobody says no to the star of a hit show. Blake got his song for the second season, with Sammy Davis Jr. recording the vocal. Grusin scored just two episodes.

Two composers revolutionized the sound of television scoring, both, initially, for cop and detective shows: Mike Post, starting with "The Rockford Files" (1974–80, NBC); and later, Jan Hammer, with "Miami Vice" (1984–89, NBC). Post was the first major composer to bring a pop music sensibility into weekly television, while Hammer's all-electronic approach was hailed as a stylistic breakthrough at the time.

Post (b. 1944) was a rock 'n' roll musician with little formal musical education. He played guitar on Sonny and Cher's hit "I Got You Babe," produced The First Edition with a then-unknown vocalist named Kenny Rogers, and won a Grammy for arranging Mason Williams's 1968 hit "Classical Gas." In 1969, he became the youngest musical director in TV history on "The Andy Williams Show."

Two chance meetings changed Post's life, and ultimately the sound of television music. The first was on a southern California beach during the summer of 1968, when he nearly came to blows with fledgling TV scriptwriter Stephen J. Cannell over squatting rights for a choice spot on the sand. The second was at a golf tournament where he met trombonist-arranger Pete Carpenter (1914–87), another avid golfer who had been impressed by the unique sound of "Classical Gas." Post and Carpenter became friends, and soon partners. Cannell, who befriended Post after the near-fight on the beach, became a producer for Universal, and hired them to score his first series, "Toma" (1973–74, ABC), with Tony Musante as a New Jersey undercover cop. The breakthrough came the following year, on "Rockford," with a Post-Carpenter theme for the James Garner character that combined harmonica, synthesizer, electric guitar, and a pounding beat in a way that had never been heard before.

"The whole story of that is Garner," Post explained. "This great character, and the perfect casting. He's Oklahoman—a little southern, but not completely—so a harmonica makes sense. I had just gotten a mini-Moog [synthesizer] with that sassy sort of weep, 'nya-nya,' to it. And I'm very guitar-oriented, and nobody had done it on TV.

"'Rockford Files' isn't real rock 'n' roll, but it's close," Post added. "We got calls from the dubbing stage [saying] 'What is this?' What it was, was our turn: guys who were raised on Chuck Berry, Bo Diddley, and the Rolling Stones." Post remembered thinking at the time: "It's going to be thundering guitars

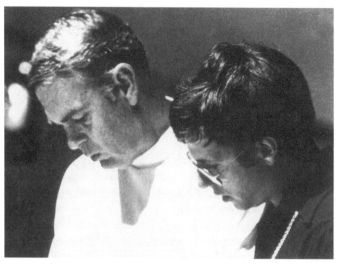

Pete Carpenter (left) and Mike Post. Courtesy Maybeth Carpenter.

now, guys. That's all there is. It isn't five saxophones anymore: it's thundering guitars." Post had to fight to get a record out, but his extended version of the "Rockford Files" theme became a top-10 hit in 1975, winning a Grammy for Post and Carpenter for Best Instrumental Arrangement.

The Cannell connection led to several other hits for Post and Carpenter, including "Magnum, p.i." (1980–88, CBS), from former Cannell producer Donald Bellisario. Post, who coincidentally had gone to high school with "Magnum" star Tom Selleck, came up with a rhythmically aggressive theme that again spotlighted rock guitar. ("Look, they put him in a red Ferrari, so it's Testosterone City, right?" Post said.) The lighter moments of the theme were meant to underscore Magnum's sense of humor, while the strings were inspired by the pastoral shots of the series' Hawaiian locations.

Later came "The A Team" (1983–86, NBC), about the adventures of a team of Vietnam veterans (played by George Peppard, Mr. T, Dirk Benedict, and Dwight Schultz) whose services were available for the right price. Post and Carpenter emphasized their service-unit style with militaristic percussion and their Vietnam backgrounds with a Cream-like guitar solo out of the late sixties.

Post and Carpenter worked together on literally dozens of series, pilots, and TV movies—an estimated 1,800 hours of television before Carpenter's death from cancer in 1987. Along the way there were military scores for the Robert Conrad wartime drama "Baa Baa Black Sheep" (1976–78, NBC); Beach Boys-style high-vocal harmonies for "Richie Brockelman, Private Eye" (1978, NBC); a top-10 hit in their song from "The Greatest American Hero" (1981–83, ABC), "Believe It or Not," sung by Joey Scarbury; and an in-your-face theme for keyboards and guitars for the Fred Dryer police series "Hunter" (1984–91, NBC). Cannell so valued their contributions that he began giving them main-title screen credit on several of his shows.

Musically speaking, it was a surprising but fruitful partnership. The middle-aged Carpenter came from a big-band background and understood the technical aspects of scoring for dramatic television, while the young, hip Post knew contemporary music and the record business, and had an undeniable facility with a catchy tune. Recalled Post: "All of his friends thought, 'Oh, poor Pete, he's hooked up with this hotshot business guy, this hummer who really doesn't know anything. Pete's carrying the kid.' And all of my friends were going, 'Oh, man, what is Mike doing? He's hooked up with this old guy who couldn't hit a groove if he had to. Mike's just getting ripped off.'

"The truth of the matter," said Post, "is that nobody got ripped off. It was a real partnership. We never missed a deadline. We never had a contract. We never had a handshake. We split fifty-fifty on everything and neither of us could remember who had written what. For the vast majority of the eighteen years [we were together], we wrote in the same room at the same time. He'd play, I'd orchestrate. I'd play, he'd orchestrate. And we never had an argument. Not one unkind word between us in eighteen years. If he was here today, I'd still have a partner."

Mike Post.

Post occasionally worked alone, most notably on "Hill Street Blues" (1981–87, NBC). With a simple series of solo piano chords, followed by synthesizer, strings, and rhythm-section backing, Post created a gentle counterpoint to the main-title visuals of police cars careening around corners and down mean city streets. It became a top-10 hit and won two Grammys, for Best Pop Instrumental Performance and Best Instrumental Composition.

Series cocreator Steven Bochco recalled asking for "a piece of music that completely contradicts the film . . . sweet and sad and lyrical and melodic. The script was hard and bleak and urban and gritty, and I didn't want to do the obvious musical interpretation of that." Post said that he wanted to write "something poignant, that really had some heart to it," and that he spent just half an hour on it before calling Bochco with the basic thematic material. Post's solo piano set the tone—sometimes light, often melancholy—for many episodes of the acclaimed, Emmy-winning ensemble drama about life in and around a big-city police precinct (with Daniel J. Travanti, Veronica Hamel, and Michael Conrad in the cast).

Post went in an entirely different direction with "NYPD Blue" (1993–, ABC), Bochco's controversial, often graphic police drama with Dennis Franz, David Caruso, and (starting in the second season) Jimmy Smits. According to Post, Bochco suggested "serious power percussion," while pilot director Gregory Hoblit said he had been thinking of subway sounds. At first puzzled, then inspired, Post came up with slam-bang percussion that receded into a low-key synthesizer theme before returning to those powerful drum sounds, all set to a rapidly moving succession of images of New York City that begin and end with a subway train. The scores themselves became an eclectic mixture of percussion, synthesized and sampled sounds, hip-hop, Irish influences, and more, all realized by Post on a weekly basis.

Post's other credits included the dark, low-brass sounds of the Ken Wahl undercover-agent melodrama "Wiseguy" (1987–90, CBS); his Emmy-nominated theme for "Unsub" (1989, NBC), which featured the strange Australian wind instrument didjeridu (a long, hollowed-out wooden tube that produces a haunting, breathy sound); and the Dire Straits-style guitar that he himself played in the main title of the acclaimed contemporary crime drama "Law & Order" (1990–, NBC). Post also supervised all of the music for Bochco's daring but short-lived musical crime drama "Cop Rock" (1990, ABC), for which Randy Newman won a songwriting Emmy.

"Miami Vice" was something else entirely. By 1984, MTV was a potent force in television, and music videos had become more than just a novelty: their quick-cut, often impressionistic method of musical storytelling had become the ultimate sales tool for popular music. The idea started with NBC boss Brandon Tartikoff, whose scribbled "MTV cops" memo became legend in the annals of network program concepts. Executive producer Michael Mann ran with the notion, signing former "Hill Street" writer Anthony Yerkovich to create a series that would look and sound like no previous police drama in TV history.

"Miami Vice" was, in essence, just another buddy-cop show, with Don Johnson as a white Miami vice detective and Philip Michael Thomas as a black New York City officer who originally came to Florida to avenge the murder of his partner. Edward James Olmos played their ultraserious superior. The difference was in the execution. The pastel-colored look, MTV-style editing, the hip attitudes of the cops, and the then-hot topic of drug use made "Vice" a very big hit, particularly with the desirable demographic of younger audiences.

Musically speaking, "Vice" broke new ground for network television. Built into each episode were montages set to current, or recent, rock 'n' roll songs or those of up-and-coming artists. Several of the tunes heard on "Vice" went on to hit status, notably two by Glenn Frey: "Smuggler's Blues" and "You Belong to the City."

Mann went outside of the usual ranks of Hollywood composers for his series composer. He turned to Czech-born artist Jan Hammer (b. 1948), who had played keyboards in the popular Mahavishnu Orchestra fusion group of the early 1970s. He later performed with guitarist Jeff Beck and enjoyed success with his own group before plunging into the world of film and television scoring.

"We discussed different styles, basically modern, hip, progressive rock-pop music," Hammer recalled. "I happened to have some sketches that I carried

Jan Hammer. Courtesy Elliott Sears Management.

around on cassette, music that I was working on. And I played them—Michael, and Thomas Carter, the director of the pilot—one thing. And they really loved it. And the piece of music that I played them was the 'Miami Vice' theme." Actually, Hammer later auditioned five other themes as possible musical signatures, but they always returned to the original. "People ask me, 'Did you go to Miami, look at palm trees, absorb the flavor and the locale and all that?' And I say, 'No, I wrote this during the winter here in the hills north of New York City,'" the composer laughed. The series main title, in fact, was built around Hammer's music: a series of shots of south Florida, including bikinied women, pink flamingos, the beaches, and the surf, played against Hammer's highly contemporary theme.

After the success of the two-hour pilot—which was handled conventionally, with Mann, Carter, and Hammer spotting the music and, as a committee, choosing the sounds—Hammer enjoyed unprecedented freedom in scoring the series. "What kind of music, and where it would go," Hammer said, was entirely in the hands of the composer, a rarity on a weekly series. "It was a challenge," Hammer said. "I had to come up with something fresh week after week. It was like making a one-hour movie as opposed to recycling thematic material, which is how 99 percent of TV shows are done.

"It was radically different from week one to week ten. There would be a show that was based totally on Jamaican reggae, and a show that would be balls-to-the-wall rock 'n' roll. Then you would have voodoo zombies walking around, so there was a Haitian percussion approach, and so on. Some shows were almost musique concrète, very strange, eerie electronic things."

Hammer worked entirely at his Red Gate studios in upstate New York. Each week, the videotape would arrive and Hammer would go to work. Rarely was there less than twenty minutes of music per week, and on the average Hammer had just four days to write and perform the score. "Most of it was done with keyboards," Hammer said—Fairlight, Memory Moog, Prophet, DX-7—although "there were some occasions where I played some rhythm guitar."

The keyboard approach involved "lots of acoustic samples," Hammer explained. The score often included various congas, log drums, and as many different percussion sounds as Hammer could achieve in his studio. "The first two years went by like a blur, a total creative high," Hammer said. He also scored all of the third season, but that "wasn't so much fun." For the fourth year, he scored the opening six and final three episodes, supervising the music for the remainder. Hammer actually appeared in two episodes, notably as a musician at the wedding of Johnson's character to a rock star played by Sheena Easton in November 1987.

The first "Miami Vice" album was the first television score since "Peter Gunn" to reach Number 1 on the *Billboard* album charts; it stayed there for twelve weeks, and Hammer's theme went to Number 1 as a single. He won two 1985 Grammys, for Best Pop Instrumental and Best Instrumental Composition, and was nominated for Emmys for his work on the first and second seasons of the series. A second "Miami Vice" album and Hammer's own *Escape from Television* disc contained still more music from the series, both hugely successful on a worldwide basis.

In the wake of the success of "Miami Vice," cop-show producers began lining up around the block for all-electronic scores. Tangerine Dream, the German group that had won fans with its synthesizer scores for *Sorcerer* (1977) and *Thief* (1981), provided the music for "Street Hawk" (1985, ABC) with Rex Smith on a high-powered motorcycle. Stewart Copeland, drummer for The Police, took a highly percussive techno-pop approach to the urban-paranoia look of the main titles of "The Equalizer" (1985–89, CBS), with Edward Woodward as an ex-intelligence agent helping New Yorkers in distress.

Bucking the trend was "Remington Steele" (1982–87, NBC), the creators of which astutely sought out Henry Mancini for its sophisticated title music, the title itself a takeoff on "Peter Gunn." Mancini actually wrote two themes: an optimistic motif for the mysterious con artist (Pierce Brosnan) who adopted the persona of the fictional detective-agency head, and a romantic theme for Laura (Stephanie Zimbalist) that was heard over the end titles.

The familiar theme for "Cagney & Lacey" (1982–88, CBS) was actually the series' second. Bill Conti was signed to create a new theme when the series was recast (with Sharon Gless replacing Meg Foster as Chris Cagney; Tyne Daly remained as Mary Beth Lacey) and rescheduled from Thursday to Monday nights. "Cagney & Lacey" was unusual for its focus on two female New York City cops, covering their personal lives as well as their profession as detectives.

Recalling his initial meeting with one of the producers, Conti said: "Barney Rosenzweig said two things to me: We follow a comedy; we want to hold that audience. And don't advertise that it's a cop show." So Conti conceived of a theme with "a light element," starting with two alto saxophones playing in thirds (Ernie Watts and Ray Pizzi performed the original).

"When it went into the tune, it didn't sound like 'Magnum p.i.,' or other [cop shows] that might have been on at the time," Conti said, although it did sport a strong beat. "It's a happy tune. It has nothing to do with the show. When you think about it, this could be 'Laverne & Shirley.' The music doesn't advertise that this is a serious cop show; it made you smile."

How do you set to music the character of a sweet little old lady who writes best-selling murder mysteries while also helping the police to solve real-life crimes? That was the challenge for John Addison in creating the theme for the long-running Angela Lansbury series "Murder, She Wrote" (1984–, CBS).

Addison (b. 1920) moved to the United States in 1975. Born in Surrey, England, he had won an Oscar and a Grammy for his charming score for *Tom Jones* (1963), another Oscar nomination for his classically styled *Sleuth* (1972), and two Emmy nominations for his music for the Richard Chamberlain production of "Hamlet" (1970). His seventy other films include *Torn Curtain* (1966), *The Seven-Per-Cent Solution* (1976), and *A Bridge Too Far* (1977), and he scored all twenty-six hours of the miniseries "Centennial" (1978–79, NBC). Addison sought, in his words, "to express the character of Jessica Fletcher" in all its facets: the writer, the sleuth, the intellectual, the friendly lady—in the space of a minute.

"For instance," he explained, "you see a lot of shots of her at the typewriter. So that gave me the idea of doing that piano accompaniment figure" (the solo piano that begins the piece). "Then over it, I came up with a rising theme—which is often heard on violins—which I thought expressed her warmness and out-of-doors and nice-person element, which people respond to. That rising phrase is then heard with trombones and bass instruments in a different variation, a little bit tongue-in-cheek, which is her sleuthing side. And there is a middle section, for the piano and other instruments, which has a baroque feeling, that conveyed her intellectual side."

Addison's "Murder, She Wrote" theme, with its warmth and lighthearted tone, was delightfully appropriate for both Jessica Fletcher and the series. He won an Emmy for his score for the two-hour pilot, "The Murder of Sherlock

Holmes." Also in the detective genre, he composed a jazzy theme for "The Eddie Capra Mysteries" (1978–79, NBC), and a classically styled one for William Conrad as "Nero Wolfe" (1981, NBC).

In later seasons, as Mrs. Fletcher's murder investigations took her to exotic locales, the producers often turned to composer Bruce Babcock (b. 1951) for appropriate musical backdrops. He contributed authentic-sounding Irish, Chinese, Russian, African, English, Italian, and other ethnic music, earning multiple Emmy nominations for his work.

In terms of music schedules, "Moonlighting" (1985–89, ABC) went from the sublime to the ridiculous. Writer-producer Glenn Gordon Caron's witty, often outrageous series about a wisecracking private detective (Bruce Willis) and his icy, ex-model partner (Cybill Shepherd) became almost as famous for its production problems and behind-the-scenes battles as for its sophisticated banter and well-played sexual tension between the characters.

Caron brought in composer Lee Holdridge at a surprisingly early stage. "Before he shot the film, he wanted me to write a theme, which is unusual," Holdridge recalled, "just based on the script, what my impressions would be." Holdridge's most astute move may have been to ask Caron to name his favorite singer. It was Al Jarreau. The composer listened to several of Jarreau's albums; what he heard was "this very sophisticated, jazz-oriented singer with these wonderful striking rhythmic tracks." He was inspired to write "something that's elegant on top but streetwise on the bottom, because that's what I saw with the two characters."

Holdridge wrote five proposed themes, which he then auditioned for Caron with a thirty-five-piece orchestra (while the pilot was still shooting). The producer chose the third of five—the one that Holdridge happened to write the night before the date. "The character in the script had said that he played the harmonica," the composer remembered. "I used the harmonica with string orchestra and sax, and I had this great rhythm section playing underneath it." The theme set, Holdridge wrote the pilot score; Jarreau was subsequently signed to write the lyric and sing the theme over the end titles of the two-hour movie. "That tune really became a signature for the show," Holdridge said. It was also Emmy-nominated and later received two Grammy nominations.

Alf Clausen (b. 1941) orchestrated most of the pilot and worked, with Holdridge, on the initial five episodes; he soon became the series' regular composer. Clausen grew up in North Dakota. A former French horn and bass player, he graduated from and taught at Boston's Berklee College before moving to Los Angeles, where he eventually became musical director on the "Donny and Marie" variety show in the late seventies.

The complexities of shooting "Moonlighting"—tons of dialogue, offbeat filming techniques, the backstage controversies—not only kept the series constantly behind schedule, it tightened the scoring process (one of the last elements of production, and the one that usually gets squeezed when a show is late) almost to the breaking point. "When I started," Clausen said, "I would spot on Tuesday and score on Friday—usually Friday at four or seven o'clock so that I would have the bulk of Friday to finish. As the series went on and the time crunch got to be more ridiculous, we would spot on Wednesday morning and score on Friday. There was actually an episode where I had sixteen hours to write the score. Somehow it all got done."

Clausen recalled frequent phone calls to Caron begging for "another six hours" to write. Yet, Clausen insisted, the last-minute demands were worth the trouble. "To me, at the time, it was probably the most adventurous piece of episodic on television. It was groundbreaking in many ways. The creative juices that were flowing in the entire company were really something to behold. And you don't come upon those very often."

In one case, for example, it was Caron who suggested that Clausen write an entire score for solo tenor saxophone (for the 1986 "Big Man on Mulberry Street," which featured Sandahl Bergman dancing an impressionistic production number, directed by Stanley Donen, to the Billy Joel tune). Clausen was most proud of his Emmy-nominated work on "The Dream Sequence Always Rings Twice," the 1985 black-and-white episode in which David and Maddie imagined themselves as a trumpeter and a torch singer in a 1940s Hollywood nightclub. Before shooting, Clausen wrote arrangements for Shepherd's two songs (Rodgers and Hart's "Blue Moon" and Herb Ellis's "I Told Ya I Love Ya, Now Get Out") and three originals in the same forties big-band style. After shooting—and with all of six days to write—Clausen wrote the underscore, also in the style of the period.

Beyond that, however, Clausen went to enormous lengths to ensure musical accuracy in Willis's on-screen horn playing. "Bill Berry was hired to coach Bruce, on the set, in the art of playing trumpet. So for the postscore I got Bill back. Frame by frame, I took down every one of [Willis's] fingerings, and I made a chart for myself of every possible note that could be played with every one of those fingerings. And then I composed my blues melody based on what I had in that combination of notes-versus-fingerings. I made sure everything was in synch, and then we went back in and recorded with Bill Berry. We got it really close."

The following season, Clausen was nominated for his Elizabethan-style music for the 1986 episode "Atomic Shakespeare," an often hilarious adaptation of *The Taming of the Shrew* with David and Maddie as Petruchio and Kate. "That was one of the legendary 'Moonlighting' episodes that was only two-thirds finished when I scored it," the composer recalled. His orchestra included such period instruments as lutes and viola da gamba; the tongue-in-cheek nature of the show required Clausen to arrange the Carpenters hit "Close to You" for recorder and harpsichord. (As Willis strolled through the courtyard hearing this, he remarked: "I loveth a band that playeth the oldies.")

Clausen received four more Emmy nominations for his work on "Moon-lighting." Surprisingly, at the same time, he was also writing weekly scores for the sitcom "ALF" (1986–90, NBC), about a fur-covered, smart-aleck alien who becomes part of a suburban family. Asked about the coincidence in names, Clausen often replied: "No, they didn't name the series after me, but I granted them the rights to use my face as a likeness."

Head 'Em Up!
Move 'Em Out!

The Westerns

esterns, mostly low-budget affairs, were a television staple almost from the beginning: "The Lone Ranger," "The Cisco Kid," "The Roy Rogers Show" (1951–57, NBC), "The Gene Autry Show" (1950–56, CBS), and others were favorites, mostly with younger viewers. Every kid in America could sing such familiar themes as Dale Evans's "Happy Trails to You" and Autry's "Back in the Saddle Again." Most of these shows were tracked with library music for their underscore.

The fall of 1955 marked the beginning of the "adult western" on network television, with the debuts of "Gunsmoke" (1955–75, CBS), "The Life and Legend of Wyatt Earp" (1955–61, ABC), and "Cheyenne" (1955–63, ABC). "Gunsmoke" was an adaptation of the CBS radio series that was then being scored by Rex Koury (b. 1911), and the television series naturally adopted his theme (although Koury never received screen credit, as was the practice of the time).

Koury's loping, "On the Trail"-style theme was used under the end titles; a variation on it was heard during the dramatic opening scenes, as Marshal Matt Dillon (James Arness) gunned down an outlaw in the streets of Dodge City, Kansas; and it was, on rare occasions, alluded to in the underscores. Fred Steiner and Morton Stevens created the most dramatic versions of Koury's original tune in various arrangements during the fifties and sixties.

Apart from the theme, all of the music during the early years of "Gunsmoke," as well as in such later CBS-owned westerns as "Have Gun—

Will Travel" and "Rawhide," was drawn from the CBS music library. The network's West Coast music director, Lud Gluskin, regularly commissioned music from various composers specifically for tracking into CBS series. By the end of the 1950s, the CBS library included literally hundreds of hours of generic western music written by composers both famous and unknown, all of which was logged (by composer, timing, and nature of cue) for easy reference. The unknowns included René Garriguenc and Lucien Moraweck, two French composers whom Gluskin had known for years and who emigrated to the United States to become staff writers at CBS. Garriguenc and Moraweck wrote considerable material for the library but only received screen credit much later when they composed scores for specific episodes of the CBS westerns.

The more famous included William Grant Still (1895–1978), the esteemed concert composer who may have been the first black to write for American television. His ten-minute "Laredo" suite, which contained such cues as "Cowpoke Visits Mexico," "Frontier Fort," and "Lonesome Cowboy," was tracked into many episodes. Even more western music, however, was contributed by Bernard Herrmann (1911–75), whose relationship with Gluskin dated back to the days of Herrmann's work for CBS radio in New York during the late 1930s.

Herrmann's first film score happened to be for a picture that many critics still consider the finest ever made: *Citizen Kane* (1941). He won an Academy Award for *The Devil and Daniel Webster* (also 1941), and wrote colorful and distinctive scores for diverse films such as *Jane Eyre* (1943), *The Ghost and Mrs. Muir* (1947), and *The Day the Earth Stood Still* (1951). During the period of his writing for the CBS library, he had just embarked on a ten-year relationship with director Alfred Hitchcock that would produce such classics as *Psycho* (1960).

Herrmann wrote only two film scores with western themes: *Garden of Evil* (1954) and *The Kentuckian* (1955). But he wrote several hours of western-flavored music for television, beginning with two television pilots and four suites of music specifically composed for the library at CBS. Herrmann's "Western Suite," which Gluskin recorded in Paris in July 1957, was written for woodwinds and percussion and consisted largely of suspense cues bearing such generic titles as "Tranquil Landscape" and "Gunfight."

Herrmann composed and orchestrated three other suites for brass and percussion, including "Western Saga," recorded by Gluskin in London during the same month. This music was more recognizably "western" in tone, and met myriad scoring needs as indicated by such cue titles as "Street Music," "Open Spaces," and "The Hunt." Also written for brass and percussion were the shorter "Desert Suite" and "Indian Suite." All were imaginative in their use of limited orchestral resources to produce a variety of unique sounds and dramatic effects.

Also for CBS, Herrmann scored the unsold pilot "Ethan Allen" (which went into the library) and, more significant, the pilot for "Have Gun—Will Travel" (1957–63, CBS). Richard Boone starred in this half-hour series as Paladin, a thoughtful and highly educated gunfighter-for-hire whose home base was the Hotel Carlton in San Francisco. He was frequently attired in all black and his business card bore the symbol of a chess knight. This was no

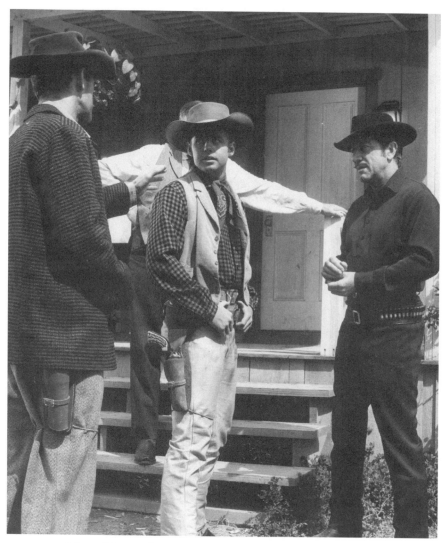

Johnny Western (middle) and Richard Boone filming Western's
episode of "Have Gun—Will Travel," 1958. Courtesy Johnny Western.

singing cowboy; Paladin could shoot a villain and recite a Shakespeare solilo-
quy over the corpse. Herrmann responded with an atmospheric score, again
for brass and percussion, that included a decisive series of descending two-,
three-, and four-note phrases that opened each episode as Paladin drew his
long-barreled revolver and aimed at the camera. His title music also accompanied the first season's end credits.

That changed at the start of the second season, the result of an incredibly
lucky break for a young singer-actor named Johnny Western (b. 1934).
Western had performed with Gene Autry during 1956 and 1957 and went on
to live his dream as a TV cowboy with a number of guest shots and a continuing role on the syndicated "Boots and Saddles" (1957). The interiors for that
show were shot on the same studio lot where Boone was filming "Have Gun—
Will Travel," and Western, a Boone admirer, wrangled a role as an overconfi-
dent young gunfighter on the new CBS series.

While shooting the episode "The Return of Dr. Thackeray" in March 1958,
Western came up with a lyric that he liked: "Paladin, Paladin, where do you
roam/Paladin, Paladin, far, far from home." His wife was expecting their second child, and he happened to be on location with the show on the day his
daughter was born. Nervous and unable to be with his family, he recalled: "I
picked up my guitar for something to do, and started playing and singing
'Ghost Riders in the Sky.' And this 'Paladin, Paladin, where do you roam'
starting coming out, to exactly the same beat as 'Ghost Riders.' So I sat down
with a yellow legal tablet and I wrote it down just as fast as I could. It all just
fell into place. I wrote the whole thing in about twenty minutes."

Before the end of the day, Western had returned to Hollywood and cut a
demo at a friend's studio. He delivered copies to series producer/cocreator
Sam Rolfe and star Boone. "I had nothing in mind at all, except to say, here's
a musical thank-you card for having me on the show," Western explained.
Within just days, the songwriter heard from Rolfe, who had discussed the tune
with Boone and decided to make it a theme; subsequent negotiation with the
top brass of CBS resulted in a firm deal, including ownership of the song,
screen credit, and a recording contract with Columbia Records. "The Ballad
of Paladin" would become the series' new end-title theme.

According to Western, the song's authorship is also credited to Boone and
Rolfe because, in the recording studio, Boone suggested a more driving
rhythm and Rolfe modified one line to read ". . . his fast gun for hire heeds the
calling wind." But even if neither had contributed, Western said, "it would
have been worth it to me to have given them each a third of the song, because
both of these guys had gone to CBS without my knowledge and said, 'We want
this for the theme song on the show.'"

The theme, as heard in the series, was actually recorded by Gluskin in
England (with three guitars and a bass) with Western adding his vocal later in
the states. Over the years, Western recorded five different versions for various

album projects, although it was guitarist Duane Eddy who achieved the biggest popular success with his version (a top-40 hit in 1962).

The earliest occasion of a major Hollywood songwriter contributing a theme to a television western came in 1955, when Harry Warren (1893–1981) wrote, with lyricist Harold Adamson, the title song for "The Life and Legend of Wyatt Earp" (1955–61, ABC). Hugh O'Brian rose to stardom in the title role of this semiserialized tale of the famous Old West marshal, his friendships with Bat Masterson and Doc Holliday, and his stints as a lawman in Dodge City, Kansas, and Tombstone, Arizona.

Warren's amazing output included movie hits such as "We're in the Money" from *The Gold Diggers of 1933* (1933), "I Only Have Eyes for You" from *Dames* (1934), "Jeepers Creepers" from *Going Places* (1938), "You Must Have Been a Beautiful Baby" from *Hard to Get* (1938), "Chattanooga Choo Choo" from *Sun Valley Serenade* (1941) and "The More I See You" from *Billy Rose's Diamond Horseshoe* (1945). He won Oscars for "Lullaby of Broadway" from *Gold Diggers of 1935* (1935), "You'll Never Know" from *Hello, Frisco, Hello* (1943), and "On the Atchison, Topeka and Santa Fe" from *The Harvey Girls* (1946).

Warren got the "Wyatt Earp" job thanks to executive producer Louis F. Edelman. The two had been good friends for many years, their association dating back to the producer's involvement with the *Gold Diggers* series and

Harry Warren. Courtesy Four Jays Music.

many other films at Warner Bros. The Warren-Adamson collaboration produced the first memorable western tune specifically written for television. Robustly sung by an all-male chorus led by Ken Darby, the song painted a heroic picture of the title character: "Wyatt Earp, Wyatt Earp, brave, courageous and bold/Long live his fame and long live his glory and long may his story be told. . . ."

Perhaps the most unusual aspect of the music of "Wyatt Earp" was the fact that most of the score, like the title song, was performed a cappella by Darby's quartet. Darby (1909–92), a veteran vocal arranger and associate of longtime Twentieth Century-Fox music director Alfred Newman, arranged the bridges and transitional cues for his singers (although, in a token nod to traditional western scoring, library music was also heard occasionally). "Using only singers gives [us] something new and different in the way of background music, but it costs us about a third of what live music would cost," Edelman told *TV Guide* in 1958. Added Darby: "We can hum [to sound like] banjos, jew's-harps, drums, three trombones, and a trumpet."

Warren went on to write two other themes for television, both westerns: "The Californians" (1957–59, NBC), another song with Harold Adamson lyrics for the Adam Kennedy-Sean McClory half hour about San Francisco in the 1850s; and an instrumental theme for "Tales of Wells Fargo" (1957–62, NBC) when it expanded to an hour in the fall of 1961.

Darby also scored "The Californians" with his quartet, The King's Men, as well as another Louis Edelman production, "The Adventures of Jim Bowie" (1956–58, ABC) with Jim Forbes as the knife-wielding title character. For "Bowie," Darby himself wrote the title song, "Jim Bowie, Adventurin' Man." Darby later wrote the familiar words to Lionel Newman's theme for the long-running "Daniel Boone" (1964–70, NBC), the Fess Parker series about the Kentucky folk hero, although screen credit went to Darby's wife, Vera Matson.

With the success of "Cheyenne," another fall 1955 entry, Warner Bros. attempted to capitalize on the national mania for TV westerns with six more westerns over the next four seasons. Warner's initial habit of creating weekly original scores, however, would last for only the first two seasons of "Cheyenne."

Debuting in the fall of 1957 were "Sugarfoot" (1957–60, ABC), with Will Hutchins as a gentle cowpoke studying the law by correspondence course; "Colt .45" (1957–60, ABC), with Wayde Preston as a government agent who posed as a gun salesman; and "Maverick" (1957–62, ABC) with James Garner and Jack Kelly as gambler brothers and good-natured con artists Bret and Bart Maverick.

For "Sugarfoot," the producers reached back to the music that Max Steiner had written for the 1951 film with Randolph Scott, with an added bridge by Warner music director Ray Heindorf; Paul Francis Webster (1907–84) added lyrics for a vocal version in the fall of 1958. Composers Paul Sawtell and Bert Shefter, whose own western library (courtesy of the Mutel music service) was being used to score most of the Warner westerns, composed the "Colt .45" theme, which was replaced halfway through the first season when a new title song was written by composer Hal Hopper (1912–70) and writer-producer Douglas Heyes.

For "Maverick," the studio again turned to David Buttolph, who had written so much music for "Conflict" and the Warner anthology series during the two years that the studio commissioned original scores. Buttolph's jaunty tune would be accompanied, starting in the second season, by another Paul Francis Webster lyric (". . . Natchez to New Orleans, livin' on jacks and queens, Maverick is a legend of the West . . ."). According to Warner music department correspondence of the time, these themes and cues based on them were "recorded abroad, [to be used] as signature music and also for scoring whenever possible." The remainder of the scoring was provided by Mutel, mostly the music of Sawtell and Shefter. During the 1958–59 season and for the next two seasons, Warners would contract directly with Sawtell and Shefter (as Music Scores Inc.) for the underscores.

"Bronco" (1958–60, ABC), with Ty Hardin as a drifter in post-Civil War Texas, featured a song by Jerry Livingston and Mack David, originally sung by Hal Hopper, later by arranger Jack Halloran's vocal group. Livingston and David also wrote "Gold Fever" as the theme for "The Alaskans" (1959–60, ABC), which starred Roger Moore, Dorothy Provine, and Jeff York as fortune hunters during the Gold Rush of 1898.

Over at Revue, library music was still the order of the day. At first, "Tales of Wells Fargo" (1957–62, NBC), with Dale Robertson, and then "Wagon Train" (1957–65, NBC/ABC), with Ward Bond and Robert Horton, were tracked with library music commissioned by Revue musical director Stanley Wilson and usually supplied by music publisher David Gordon. Wilson (1917–70) was a veteran western composer, having spent seven years at Republic where he worked on more than one hundred films ranging from the serial *Commando Cody* to B features with titles like *Vigilante Hideout* and *Leadville Gunslinger*. Originally a trumpet player from New York, he became an arranger for Freddie Martin's band in the 1940s and an orchestrator at MGM, before joining Republic in 1947 (where, with Leo Shuken, he orchestrated Victor Young's 1952 classic *The Quiet Man*).

Wilson went to Revue in 1954 and oversaw the scoring of the then-fledgling studio's early television output, supervising the tracking for various series and often composing the themes himself. His own themes included "Cimarron City" (1958–59, NBC), "Buckskin" (1958–59, NBC), and the original theme for "Tales of Wells Fargo." In 1958, original scores became the rule rather than the exception at Revue.

On no series was this more apparent than "Wagon Train." The story of a Missouri-to-California trek, "Wagon Train" started out in the fall of 1957 with a theme by composer Henri René (1906–93) with a never-heard lyric by Bob Russell. It was replaced the following season by a new theme by songwriters Sammy Fain (1902–89, who had won Oscars for "Love Is a Many-Splendored

Stanley Wilson conducting at Universal. Courtesy Phyllis Paul.

Thing" and "Secret Love") and Jack Brooks (1912–71, who had Oscar nominations for "Ole Buttermilk Sky" and "That's Amore"), and again in 1959 with a theme by Jerome Moross (1913–83), which became its best-known theme, and remained with the series until its cancellation. Wilson himself wrote the theme for "Major Adams, Trailmaster," the new title for "Wagon Train" episodes in syndication.

Wilson commissioned original scores for the series every week, many from major Hollywood film composers. During the 1958–59 season alone, the roster of composers working on "Wagon Train" included Roy Webb (*Notorious*), David Raksin (*Laura*), Ernest Gold (*Exodus*), Daniele Amfitheatrof (*Lassie Come Home*), Cyril Mockridge (*Miracle on 34th Street*), David Buttolph (*Guadalcanal Diary*), Conrad Salinger (*The Last Time I Saw Paris*), Laurindo Almeida (the world-renowned guitarist), and Heinz Roemheld (*The Lady from Shanghai*), several of whom scored more than one episode.

Wilson's genius was in signing Jerome Moross to score a second-season episode that guest-starred Brian Donlevy. Moross, who divided his time between the theater, concert music, and Hollywood (having orchestrated Aaron Copland's *Our Town*, 1940, and Hugo Friedhofer's *The Best Years of Our Lives*, 1946), composed the quintessential western film score in *The Big*

Country (1958). His grasp of musical idioms that were uniquely American in character was, at that time, matched only by Copland's concert music.

Moross was subsequently commissioned to compose the new "Wagon Train" theme, also known as "Wagons Ho!" (Ward Bond's signal to move the wagon train forward). Moross's "Wagon Train" main-title theme—like his Oscar-nominated *Big Country* score, music that speaks of wide-open spaces and the American West—accompanied drawings of Bond, Horton, and the covered wagons they led. Unfortunately, he had used it once before, as a minor motif in a 1959 Jeff Chandler film titled *The Jayhawkers.*

"I wrote that theme, which is very unimportant in *The Jayhawkers,* and I forgot about it," Moross later explained. "They [Revue] hired me to write a new theme for 'Wagon Train,' and without thinking of it, this theme was in my mind and I wrote it down for 'Wagon Train.'" Paramount, which released *The Jayhawkers,* complained (considering "Wagon Train" was then the second most popular series on television). "They brought the matter to me," Moross recalled, "and I said, 'it can't be.' Sure enough, it was." According to Moross, however, Paramount "let it pass" and did not pursue legal action over the theme. "It was unimportant in the film and, after all, I suppose Paramount felt they might have to ask a similar favor of Universal some day."

Jerome Moross. Courtesy Screen Archives.

In all, Moross scored six "Wagon Train" episodes during the 1959–60 and 1960–61 seasons but, although asked, declined to stay with the series. He did, however, compose two short scores for CBS westerns (for 1961 episodes of "Have Gun—Will Travel" and "Gunsmoke") and, much later, the theme for the series "Lancer" (1968–70, CBS), a family western set in California during the 1870s that starred Andrew Duggan, James Stacy, and Wayne Maunder. All were examples of the distinctive western flavor and momentum that made *The Big Country* such a groundbreaking score.

CBS, meanwhile, was launching a new western of its own and moving in a different musical direction. The show was "Rawhide" (1959–66), and Dimitri Tiomkin had agreed to compose the theme for this ambitious hour created by Charles Marquis Warren and starring Eric Fleming and Clint Eastwood as trail boss and ramrod, respectively, of a Texas-to-Kansas cattle drive.

Tiomkin (1894–1979) was a film composer of note, a Russian who took naturally to westerns as heard in his scores for *Duel in the Sun* (1946) and *Red River* (1948). It was his music for *High Noon* (1952), however, that significantly altered the way that many westerns were scored: he used a simple, folk-style tune, "Do Not Forsake Me, Oh My Darlin'" (with lyrics by Ned Washington), throughout the film, winning Academy Awards for Best Song and Best Score for his efforts. Although Tex Ritter sang it in the movie, it was Frankie Laine who had the hit record with *High Noon*. So when the commercially minded Tiomkin scored *Gunfight at the O.K. Corral* (1957), again with Washington and again using a ballad throughout the film, Laine got the call to perform it on the soundtrack. And, in early 1958, when Tiomkin and Washington agreed to collaborate on a theme for "Rawhide," Laine once more was signed to sing.

Legend has it that the famous, high-priced Tiomkin agreed to write a TV theme as the result of a colossal misunderstanding. When initially approached, the composer reportedly asked who was starring in the series. Told over the phone that it was Eric Fleming, Tiomkin is said to have replied: "Good. If Errol Flynn is the star, I'll write the music." Tiomkin is also said to have had difficulty understanding the dialogue and nature of the "Rawhide" pilot, and that as a result the initial "Rawhide" song had to be considerably modified. The original music and lyrics on file at CBS, in fact, were marked "revised, June 28, 1958."

The "Rawhide" theme was one of the earliest examples of commercial considerations dictating a musical approach for television. According to Laine, CBS wanted a single released at least eight weeks before the series was to debut (originally, in the fall of 1958); and the plan was to use the record, in part, as the actual series main title. CBS-owned Columbia Records executive Mitch Miller, who had produced Laine's similarly outdoorsy "Mule Train" hit eight years earlier, arranged "Rawhide" for Laine, a twelve-voice male chorus, guitars, bass, and accordion (punctuated by whip cracks à la "Mule Train"). The driving, country-flavored tune made the charts, effectively preselling the series—which had by now been delayed until midseason.

Ned Washington (left) and Dimitri Tiomkin around the time they composed the theme for "Rawhide." Courtesy Dimitri Tiomkin collection, USC Performing Arts Archives.

"Keep rollin', rollin', rollin'/Tho' the streams are swollen/Keep them dogies rollin', Rawhide! . . ." went the colorful Washington lyrics. Laine's rendition proved so popular that the "Rawhide" producers wrote him and his actress wife Nan Grey into a third-season episode, 1960s "Incident on the Road to Yesterday."

Tiomkin wrote only the theme, although several cues based on it were arranged and recorded later. The original music package for "Rawhide" was composed by Russell Garcia (b. 1916), the veteran composer-arranger who would later score *The Time Machine* (1960) and the theme and many scores for the comic western "Laredo" (1965–67, NBC). CBS music head Lud Gluskin asked him for "some wide-open-spaces music, some chases, some fights, all sorts of music" for a new western series, Garcia recalled (in all, thirty or forty minutes of music, all recorded in Europe prior to Tiomkin's involvement). Garcia's own "Rawhide" theme, frequently heard in the underscore, finally achieved prominence as the end-credit music for the series' final season.

The vast majority of "Rawhide" episodes were tracked from stock music in the CBS library; in fact, of the first one hundred episodes only four benefited from original scores. Most were written by TV veterans Fred Steiner, Leon Klatzkin, and Rudy Schrager; the final season boasted original scores by film greats such as Bernard Herrmann, Hugo Friedhofer, and Johnny Green.

Two other Tiomkin themes graced the CBS airwaves for "Hotel De Paree" (1959–60) and "Gunslinger" (1961). Tiomkin composed his only original television score for the pilot of "Hotel," about a Colorado adventurer named Sundance, played by Earl Holliman. With a lyric by Paul Francis Webster, the melody was used for a song called "Sundance" over the end credits. For "Gunslinger," a short-lived series starring Tony Young, Tiomkin reteamed with Washington and Laine for another great song in the service of a hopeless show. "Gunslinger," at least, was released as a single. Laine, parodying his own western-theme reputation (à la *Blazing Saddles*), later sang the title songs for the comedy westerns "Rango" (1967, ABC) and "Lobo" (1979–81, NBC).

Meanwhile, "The Rifleman" (1958–63, ABC) took a new approach to the traditional western by concentrating to a greater degree on family matters. Chuck Connors played Lucas McCain, a widower who ran a ranch near North Fork, New Mexico, with his young son Mark (Johnny Crawford). Every

Herschel Burke Gilbert. Photo by George Fields.

episode began with a determined-looking McCain firing his .44 Winchester at some unseen outlaw on the streets of North Fork, accompanied by the strains of Herschel Burke Gilbert's memorable theme.

Gilbert (b. 1918) was a Juilliard-trained violist who had become an arranger for the Harry James band during the mid-1940s. He went to Columbia as an orchestrator in 1946, working on pictures such as *Rogues of Sherwood Forest* and *The Fuller Brush Man*. He also orchestrated for Dimitri Tiomkin on films including *Duel in the Sun* and *It's a Wonderful Life* before becoming a full-time composer in the early 1950s. He received consecutive Oscar nominations for his score for *The Thief* (1952), the title song of *The Moon Is Blue* (1953), and musical direction on *Carmen Jones* (1954). Gilbert's past experience on films for producers Jules Levy and Arthur Gardner and director Arnold Laven (including 1952's *Without Warning*) led them to call him for the pilot of "The Rifleman." And, because it was always a strong series possibility, Gilbert not only scored the pilot, he wrote an entire library of music (an hour and a half) for the series to come. It was all recorded in Munich with a sixty-piece symphony orchestra, and the same library served the series for its entire five-year run.

"The Rifleman" theme was "my idea of a western melody," Gilbert said later. "I wrote about four themes: a very pretty one for the boy [Crawford], a couple for heavies, any crook." (At one point, Gilbert recalled, the music "got more fan mail than Chuck Connors.") Gilbert's "Rifleman" score was so successful that Dick Powell, whose fledgling Four Star Television operation had bought the series, offered the composer the post of music director. For five years, Gilbert oversaw the music of all Four Star series, writing some of it, assigning composers to write others, and conducting the annual library sessions in Germany.

Gilbert's associates at Four Star included Joseph Mullendore, who wrote the theme for the western anthology "Zane Grey Theatre" (1956–62, CBS), and Rudy Schrager (1900–83), who scored "Wanted—Dead or Alive" (1958–61, CBS) with Steve McQueen as bounty hunter Josh Randall. Gilbert himself scored the Robert Taylor crime drama "The Detectives" and episodes of the dramatic anthology "The Dick Powell Show" (1961–63, NBC).

For every series, a library of music was created that was designed to meet every possible scoring need. "Every picture has a chase of some kind," Gilbert explained. "Most of them, especially in series, have a love scene of some kind. Almost every picture has a happy ending. It's a framework within which you can write classical music and be right most of the time. Plus, when you're dealing with drama, you can really write contemporary music. You can get away with all kinds of dissonance."

One of the Four Star westerns was "Black Saddle" (1959–60, NBC/ABC), whose unusual musical history began with Jerry Goldsmith. Goldsmith had scored the radio western "Frontier Gentleman" for producer Antony Ellis. When Ellis moved into television with "Black Saddle," starring Peter Breck as a gunfighter-turned-lawyer, he asked Goldsmith to write the theme. Because the composer was still under contract to CBS at the time, he penned it under a pseudonym (that of his then-brother-in-law, J. Michael Hennagin) and never received screen credit for his fast, rhythmically exciting theme for guitars, brass, and percussion. Arthur Morton (b. 1908), who several years later became Goldsmith's regular orchestrator, wrote a library of Coplandesque music for the series.

The fall of 1959 also saw the debuts of two important new series that involved top musical talent: "Bonanza" (1959–73, NBC) and "Riverboat" (1959–61, NBC). "Bonanza," the first television western to be broadcast in color, was the story of a gigantic Nevada ranch and the family that owned it: strong-willed patriarch Ben Cartwright (Lorne Greene) and his three sons (Pernell Roberts, Dan Blocker, and Michael Landon), all by different mothers. Alan Livingston, at the time vice president of television programming at NBC (which owned "Bonanza"), asked his brother Jay Livingston—who with

Jay Livingston (left) and Ray Evans. Courtesy Hearst
Newspaper Collection, USC Library.

his partner Ray Evans formed one of the all-time great Hollywood songwriting teams—to pen a theme for this new series.

Livingston (b. 1915) and Evans (b. 1915) had, at that time, been nominated six times for the Best Song Oscar, and won three of those, for "Buttons and Bows" from *The Paleface* (1948), "Mona Lisa" from *Captain Carey, USA* (1950), and "Que Sera, Sera" from *The Man Who Knew Too Much* (1956). They also wrote the Bob Hope standard "Silver Bells" as well as the song score for one of TV's first "spectaculars," "Satins and Spurs" (1954), which marked Betty Hutton's small-screen debut. The team agreed to write a song for $750, with another $750 payment if the series sold. (The back-end money was what counted: Livingston and Evans would publish the song themselves, which turned out to be a bonanza of its own.) Recalled Evans: "The only guidelines they gave us were, it can't be long, it's got to sound triumphant, it's got to sound western and be like a march, that sort of thing."

"The title didn't make any sense," Livingston pointed out. "They talked about changing it but they liked the sound of it. There's no reason for 'Bonanza,' when you think about it. The ranch is called Ponderosa." Added Evans: "We had a hell of a time trying to write lyrics to make 'Bonanza' make sense." Nonetheless, Livingston and Evans wrote a song that became one of television's best-known themes—at least, as played instrumentally. The finale of the pilot script called for the Cartwrights to ride out of Virginia City singing the title song, and although the scene was filmed, the episode as aired used an alternate take without the tune. The lyrics—"we've got a right to pick a little fight, Bonanza! . . ."—were first widely heard on an album sung by star Lorne Greene in 1964.

Creator-producer David Dortort was unhappy with the lyrics, but agreed to use the Livingston-Evans song, instrumentally, over the main and end titles, so long as his composer of choice—David Rose—did not have to interpolate the song into the weekly dramatic underscores. Rose (1910–90) had been a pianist and arranger for NBC Radio in Chicago and Mutual Radio in Los Angeles in the 1930s and 1940s. He became the musical director for comedian Red Skelton's radio program in 1947 and made the transition to television with Skelton's variety show in 1951 (an association that lasted throughout Skelton's twenty-year TV career). As a film composer, he received Oscar nominations for his scoring of *The Princess and the Pirate* (1944) and the song "So in Love" from *Wonder Man* (1945). His active recording career throughout the fifties and sixties included such hits as "Holiday for Strings" and "The Stripper," and he won his first Emmy for musical direction on "An Evening with Fred Astaire" (1958).

Dortort was a believer in the power of music in film. He not only gave Rose an orchestra of as many as thirty-five musicians, he also insisted upon scoring every episode (despite union regulations that, at the time, permitted extensive tracking). The result was one of the richest-sounding series of the era, often comparable to the lush sounds of Rose's concert albums. In 1962, Rose called

David Rose. Photo by George Fields.

the series "the best thing I've done musically, principally because I'm given such broad latitude. My concept of TV music involves thinking of various instruments in terms of colors, and then fitting the colors to the mood and action on the screen."

Rose scored the vast majority of the 430 episodes, often orchestrating his own scores despite his myriad other commitments, including the Skelton show and several other television series. His stately "Ponderosa" theme opened act one of every episode. Highlights of his work during the first two seasons appeared on an MGM album, including a tender waltz for "Silent Thunder," a 1960 episode in which Little Joe (Landon) fell in love with a blind girl played by Stella Stevens; the dramatic score for the 1961 episode "Sam Hill"; and tasteful, reverent music for the 1960 episode "The Hopefuls," about a religious sect en route to California. He was especially proud of his heroic score for the two-part "Ride the Wind," a story of the early days of the Pony Express that aired in early 1966; he won an Emmy for "The Love Child" episode in 1970.

The Livingston-Evans song, freshly arranged every year, lasted twelve seasons, until Dortort asked Rose to write his own, new "Bonanza" theme for the 1971–72 season. Viewer demand for the familiar original Livingston-Evans tune led to its reinstatement for the fourteenth and final season in 1972.

Rose also scored the two-hour pilot for Dortort's second successful western series, "The High Chaparral" (1967–71, NBC). This too was the story of a powerful landowner, rancher Big John Cannon (Leif Erickson), his marriage to Mexican heiress Victoria Montoya (Linda Cristal), and their struggle to forge an empire in the Arizona Territory during the 1870s. The score was one of Rose's finest, including a noble main theme with strummed guitars that helped to establish the southwestern locale. All ninety-five subsequent episodes were scored by Harry Sukman (1912–84), who occasionally filled in for Rose on "Bonanza" (including the entire eleventh season), and who had won an Academy Award for adapting the music of Franz Liszt for *Song Without End* (1960). Sukman would later arrange John Williams's film theme for Dortort's TV spinoff of "The Cowboys" (1974, ABC) and score that series as well.

Rose's longtime association with the "Bonanza" company led Michael Landon to choose Rose as his primary composer for three Landon-produced series that followed: "Little House on the Prairie" (1974–83, NBC), based on the Laura Ingalls Wilder books about growing up in Minnesota in the 1870s, starring Landon, Karen Grassle, Melissa Gilbert, and Melissa Sue Anderson; "Father Murphy" (1981–82, NBC), with Merlin Olsen as a kindly orphanage keeper in the Dakota Territory; and "Highway to Heaven" (1984–89, NBC), with Landon as an angel helping people on earth, and Victor French as his human guide and companion. Landon preferred stories filled with sentiment, and Rose's music helped him to achieve his weekly goal of moving the audience emotionally. About "Little House," Rose explained in 1974: "It has nothing to do with western music. It's dramatic, contemporary music done in a legitimate scoring fashion, which is almost a disappearing art." Rose received four more Emmy nominations for "Little House," winning two, as well as a final nomination for "Father Murphy." Both Dortort and Landon gave Rose full publishing rights to his scores, something that few composers would ever achieve in television.

Rose's other television credits included two more westerns, "The Monroes" (1966–67, ABC) with a young Barbara Hershey, and "Dundee and the Culhane" (1967, CBS) with John Mills; plus the backstage-Hollywood series "Bracken's World" (1969–70, NBC) with Eleanor Parker; and the sitcom "Mr. Adams and Eve" (1957–58, CBS) with Howard Duff and Ida Lupino.

For "Riverboat," also an hour-long period drama, Revue musical director Wilson wisely turned to Elmer Bernstein. "Riverboat" starred Darren McGavin as the colorful captain of the *Enterprise,* a stern-wheeler that plied the Mississippi, Missouri, and Ohio rivers during the 1840s; Burt Reynolds played his pilot. Bernstein scored this adventure in a distinctly Americana idiom, clearly folk-influenced yet big and bold in a grand orchestral manner. The rhythms and colors heard throughout the pilot, and fourteen subsequent Bernstein-scored episodes that first season, presaged the famous score that he would compose the following year for *The Magnificent Seven.*

Bernstein had always been interested in American folk music and, having studied with Aaron Copland—"Aaron kind of invented American music," he

Elmer Bernstein.

pointed out—he had "always been looking for some opportunity to use it. Until the time of 'Riverboat,' I never had a real chance. I had a sense of it in a picture I did very early on, called *The Tin Star* [1957] with Henry Fonda. But 'Riverboat' was the first chance, really, to go all out with that kind of material." The series was considered so important by the executives at Revue that, Bernstein recalled, the pilot score boasted more than fifty musicians and "the orchestras on all the 'Riverboats' were always around forty," an unheard-of ensemble for episodic television. "It's kind of hindsight," he added, "but I realize now that *The Magnificent Seven* was a logical outgrowth of 'Riverboat.'"

By utilizing the services of veteran orchestrators Leo Shuken (1906–76) and Jack Hayes (b. 1919)—the team that would orchestrate all of Bernstein's sixties westerns, including *The Magnificent Seven, The Hallelujah Trail,* and *The Sons of Katie Elder*—the composer was able to write not only all those "Riverboat" episodes the first year but also the jazz scores on "Johnny Staccato" at the same time. Shuken and Hayes also wrote their own "Riverboat" scores, as did other veteran orchestrators such as Al Sendrey (b. 1922) and Al Woodbury (1909–89).

For the second season, the Bernstein theme was replaced by a new one written by Gerald Fried (b. 1928), who took over the weekly scoring chores.

His "Riverboat" theme had a distinctly southern feel, with the banjo prominently featured (and which hinted at some of the down-home sound that would later win him an Emmy for "Roots"). "I thought the five-string banjos were the most exciting instruments that man ever made," Fried said. "You had the most American sound possible, a five-string banjo twanging along. The producer just didn't like it [so] they took out some of the banjo tunes."

Fried endured a certain amount of criticism for his earlier series at Revue, the jazz score for "Shotgun Slade" (1959–60, syndicated), a western with Scott Brady as a frontier detective with a unique firearm (its lower barrel fired a twelve-gauge shell, the upper barrel a .32 caliber bullet). The small-combo jazz approach (prominently featuring electric guitar and harpsichord) seemed hopelessly anachronistic for a sagebrush saga. In his liner notes for the LP, Wilson admitted: "The idea of writing a musical score with a jazz feeling for a western TV series is something that was joked about, but never taken seriously, until we started the 'Slade' series."

A former oboist with the Dallas and Pittsburgh symphonies, Fried was a Juilliard-trained composer who scored some of his boyhood friend Stanley Kubrick's earliest films, including *The Killing* (1956) and *Paths of Glory* (1957). A prolific composer for television, his later credits included the comedy "Gilligan's Island," the adventure series "The Man from U.N.C.L.E.," and both "Roots" miniseries.

Revue was churning out westerns left and right throughout this period. Englishman Cyril J. Mockridge (1896–1979) wrote the rich, full-blooded theme and nearly two dozen scores, over the first two seasons, for "Laramie" (1959–63, NBC), which starred John Smith and Robert Fuller as Wyoming ranchers. "The Deputy" (1959–61, NBC), with Henry Fonda as the marshal of an Arizona town, was scored by veteran studio guitarist Jack Marshall (1921–73). "The Tall Man" (1960–62, NBC), with Barry Sullivan as Pat Garrett and Clu Gulager as Billy the Kid, was scored by Juan Esquivel (b. 1918), who had achieved success in the recording field with mood-music albums featuring unorthodox orchestrations. His "Tall Man" music was an equally strange mixture of jazzy sounds and western styles. (Esquivel and Stanley Wilson were cocredited with the Revue/Universal emblem fanfare that followed every end-credit roll from the studio for many years.)

Two more greats of the silver screen toiled briefly in the realm of the TV western, both at virtually the same time: Hans J. Salter (1896–1994), who wrote "Wichita Town" (1959–60, NBC), and Hugo Friedhofer (1901–81), who scored the majority of "Outlaws" (1960–62, NBC).

Salter was known as "the master of terror and suspense" for his superb scores for the Universal horror films of the 1940s and 1950s. His music for movies such as *The Wolf Man* (1941), *The Ghost of Frankenstein* (1942), and *The Creature from the Black Lagoon* (1954) frightened filmgoers as much as the imagery in those black-and-white classics. Born in Vienna, Salter conducted in opera houses, studied composition with modern composer Alban Berg, and wrote music for early talkies at Berlin's famous UFA studios, until the rise of Hitler brought him to America in 1937. In the United States, he worked on more than two hundred films over a thirty-year period and received six Academy Award nominations. Salter had scored several Joel McCrea westerns, including *Wichita* (1955) and *The Oklahoman* (1957), so when McCrea prepared to go into TV with a series called "Wichita Town," loosely based on the feature, Salter was signed to provide the music. The half-hour series cast McCrea as the marshal of Wichita, Kansas, and the actor's son Jody McCrea as his deputy.

"There wasn't even one script ready when I was engaged," Salter recalled, "so I had to visualize what kind of music I would need. I had to write about an hour of music for different situations—for chases, stampedes, quiet prairie moods, and things like that." Salter composed and orchestrated an entire library of cues, which he recorded with a seventy-piece orchestra in Munich, giving "Wichita Town" a symphonic sound that was rare for television.

The music of "Wichita Town" was purposefully descriptive, with pastoral moments, melancholy moods, and uptempo hoedowns. The reason for the composer's facility within the genre stretched back to Salter's childhood in Vienna. "There was one movie house that specialized in westerns," the composer recalled. "I used to spend whole afternoons there, watching and observing the western flavor. So when I came to America, it was nothing new to me. I felt at home in this atmosphere and it inspired me; I think the opening and the exploring of the West is the most interesting part of American history." Salter, who was as talented at the oater genre as he was with horror scores, went on to compose scores for "Laramie," "Wagon Train," and "The Virginian," all for Wilson at Revue. He also wrote a library of exotic and dramatic music for the filmed-in-India adventure "Maya" (1967–68, NBC) with Jay North.

Friedhofer was one of the most revered composers in Hollywood. As legendary in musicians' circles for his dry wit as for his brilliance as an orchestrator and composer, he won an Academy Award for his score for *The Best Years of Our Lives* (1946), and was nominated for eight other films including *An Affair to Remember* (1957) and *The Young Lions* (1958). He also orchestrated fifteen of Erich Wolfgang Korngold's film scores, and scored other films, including *Vera Cruz* (1954) and Marlon Brando's *One-Eyed Jacks* (1961).

"Outlaws" was one of two western pilots that Friedhofer scored in 1960; both sold. The second one, a Civil War saga called "The Blue and the Grey," was retitled "The Americans" (1961, NBC) and became the midseason replacement for "Riverboat" with a new score by Bernard Herrmann. "Outlaws" starred Barton MacLane and Don Collier as lawmen in the Oklahoma Territory circa 1890, and the stories dealt more with the bad guys than the good. Friedhofer's theme actually was a song heard only in the initial episode ("Outlaws runnin' from the hang-rope, outlaws runnin' from the gun/ Outlaws stayin' on the back trails, hidin' from the sun . . ."), but it was still effective in instrumental form in succeeding hours.

Hugo Friedhofer. Courtesy Harold B. Lee Library, Brigham Young University.

"I composed, orchestrated, and conducted some thirty-four episodes, after which I bowed out," Friedhofer later recounted. "Trying to maintain a certain standard of quality while knocking out anywhere from fifteen to twenty-five minutes of music weekly well-nigh did me in. Bear in mind that not a single show was scored with track, and such material that was repeated was carefully tailored, and generally reorchestrated because—like an idiot—I wrote practically every episode for a different orchestral combination. It was fun, until my strength started to give out. It was also sheer idiocy, considering the fact that mass production is not, and never was, my forte."

Friedhofer scored the entire first season and the first several episodes of the second season. His later association with Earle Hagen led to cocomposer credit on "The Guns of Will Sonnett" (1967–69, ABC), including a wistful ballad sung over the titles by star Walter Brennan; he also wrote a 1965 "Rawhide" and three scores for "Lancer."

While "Wagon Train" was initially the leading western at Revue, for which Stanley Wilson recruited so many top composers, it was ultimately succeeded as the studio's "A" genre entry by "The Virginian" (1962–70, NBC). The ambitious "Virginian," based on the Owen Wister novel, was television's first ninety-minute film series, an expensive gamble by both the studio and network that viewers wanted a virtual western movie with the same cast every week. Initially produced by Charles Marquis Warren ("Rawhide"), the series was set on the Shiloh Ranch near Medicine Bow, Wyoming, and originally starred James Drury as the never-named title character, its foreman; Lee J. Cobb as Judge Garth, its owner; and Doug McClure as Trampas, a headstrong young cowhand.

The choice of composer for this prestige series was something of a surprise: Percy Faith (1908–76), the Canadian-born arranger-conductor whose appealing, often string-drenched, arrangements of popular music had become a staple of beautiful-music radio stations and a hit with adult record buyers throughout the fifties and sixties. Faith's involvement came about because of his friendship with Harry Garfield, Universal's recently named business head of the music department (Wilson remained the department's "creative" head). Despite his success as a Columbia Records artist, Faith was no stranger to film scoring, having received an Oscar nomination for the Doris Day film *Love Me or Leave Me* (1955) and scored *Tammy Tell Me True* (1961) for Ross Hunter at Universal; he later wrote an elegant score for the all-star turkey *The Oscar* (1966).

The scope of "The Virginian" attracted top guest stars (including Bette Davis, Robert Redford, and George C. Scott) and, in terms of script and direction, few concessions were made to the series' small-screen origins. Everyone treated "The Virginian" like a movie, and Faith was no different. His stirring theme—set to shots of Drury and friends galloping down dusty trails—was instantly memorable, and his three original scores (particularly for "The Executioners" in the first season and "No Tears for Savannah" in the second) featured multiple themes and displayed musical subtleties that were unusual for television.

For Stanley Wilson, however, the problem of "The Virginian" was one of logistics: how to create a full score, often at least forty minutes of music, on a weekly basis for this high-profile series. Wilson's solution was to commission some complete original scores, create some partial scores, divide others among several composers, and track the rest with music from earlier shows.

The list of composers who wrote for "The Virginian" was, like "Wagon Train," another who's-who from the feature-film side of the business: Paul J. Smith (1906–85), the Disney composer who won an Oscar for *Pinocchio,* scored one and part of a second; David Buttolph wrote three in the second season; Hans Salter wrote one complete score and part of another; Franz Waxman scored a fifth-season show; Leonard Rosenman did six; and Lyn Murray wrote three. Max Steiner, who had written classic big-screen westerns such as *Dodge City* (1939) and *The Searchers* (1956), was asked to score "The Virginian" but never did. The team of Leo Shuken and Jack Hayes, whose total grasp of American musical styles made them perfect as orchestrators for Elmer Bernstein's film and television scores, contributed ten originals themselves. Wilson and staff composer-orchestrator Sidney Fine also wrote large sections of "Virginian" scores, often without screen credit.

Bernard Herrmann wrote four complete scores between the summer of 1965 and the summer of 1968. Herrmann's final work for the medium, in fact, was on "The Virginian," an episode (telecast in January 1969) titled "Last Grave at Socorro Creek." Composer Patrick Williams, who attended the August 1968 sessions, recalled marveling at the makeup of the orchestra—thirty strings and an electric bass—and the sight of a cowering young producer who was awed by the great, and typically rude, Herrmann (who, during a break, gruffly and disdainfully asked, "How do you like your little *tune?*").

For the fall of 1970, Universal decided to revamp the series. The renamed "The Men from Shiloh" (1970–71, NBC) continued to star Drury and McClure but added Stewart Granger as the new owner of Shiloh and Lee Majors as a ranch hand. The Percy Faith theme was eliminated in favor of a new musical signature by Ennio Morricone—his only theme for American series television.

Morricone (b. 1928) was by then world-famous for his music for the witty, violent "spaghetti westerns" of Italian filmmaker Sergio Leone: *Fistful of Dollars* (1964), *For a Few Dollars More* (1966), and *The Good, the Bad and the Ugly* (1966), all starring Clint Eastwood. His unique musical approach, which included offbeat vocal effects and orchestrations that ranged from the bizarre to the traditionally symphonic, was as responsible for the success of those films as any single element. The television piece was conceived along similar musical lines.

For "The Men from Shiloh," Morricone created a one-minute theme that musically captured a day on the ranch, beginning quietly with strings, adding a duet for recorder and electric guitar, and moving into a galloping rhythm for strings and guitars, augmented by solo female voice and male chorus (with the brief addition of harmonica and occasional whip cracks). Edited precisely by designer Jack Cole to sepia-toned daguerreotypes of frontier life, excerpts from period advertisements ("revolver for only $2.50"), and similarly nineteenth-century-styled drawings of the four stars, "The Men from Shiloh" main title was the most atmospheric evocation of the Old West ever created for television.

Richard Markowitz (1926–94) contributed two classic themes to the medium, both for westerns: "The Rebel" (1959–61, ABC) and "The Wild Wild West" (1965–69, CBS). A California native, Markowitz studied in France with classical composer Arthur Honegger and wrote ballet music for modern-dance choreographer Katherine Dunham's company before breaking into movies with his jazz score for *Stakeout on Dope Street* (1958). Producer Andrew J. Fenady and director Irvin Kershner, who made *Stakeout,* came back to Markowitz when they joined forces with actor Nick Adams to bring "The Rebel" to television.

Adams, who received cocreator credit with writer Fenady, played Johnny Yuma, a Confederate soldier who, as the title song put it, "roamed through the West" during the years after the Civil War. Johnny Cash sang the song, while a branding iron in the shape of Adams's profile (Confederate cap and all) burned the image into a wooden fence during the main title. "My friend Johnny never did get the lyrics right," producer Fenady (who wrote the lyrics) recalled. "He couldn't keep his tenses straight. I'd say, 'Johnny, look, I don't care whether you say, "Johnny Yuma was a rebel, he roamed through the West," or "Johnny Yuma is a rebel, he roams through the West," please don't

Richard Markowitz. Photo by Michael Bentzen, courtesy Brenda and Kate Markowitz.

say, "Johnny Yuma was a rebel, he roams through the West."' He never did get it right the first time around. We went back and got it another time. But still, he made us rich." Cash's recording of "The Rebel" went to Number 24 on the *Billboard* country charts.

Markowitz scored the first season of "The Rebel" with a thirteen-piece band, including period-appropriate harmonica and guitar. For the second season, because a musicians' strike forced an overseas recording date, Markowitz reorchestrated many cues into a library of music for a thirty-five-piece orchestra. He oversaw the recording in Belgium, then returned to the United States and worked on a weekly basis with the music editor to track the second-season episodes.

While he was scoring the first season of "The Rebel," Markowitz was also writing weekly jazz scores for "Philip Marlowe" (1959–60, ABC) with Philip Carey as Raymond Chandler's famous private eye. Writing jazz for a crime drama and a western-style score for "The Rebel" at the same time proved to be good training for his biggest hit: "The Wild Wild West." Robert Conrad and Ross Martin starred in this fun series about James West and Artemus Gordon, a pair of resourceful Secret Service agents who reported directly to President Ulysses S. Grant. It was essentially "The Man from U.N.C.L.E." out West; they battled mad scientists and assorted megalomaniacs with the aid of various gadgets, operating out of their own private railroad car.

In fact, Markowitz almost didn't get to write the theme. CBS, in hopes of striking gold again with another "Rawhide," commissioned a title song from Dimitri Tiomkin and Paul Francis Webster. "The Ballad of Big Jim West," to which Tiomkin would have owned publishing rights (via his Erosa Music company, which owned "Rawhide"), was written and at least two different instrumental arrangements were recorded in December 1964 and January 1965. Herschel Burke Gilbert, who had left Four Star to become music director at CBS, conducted the sessions. He recalled that Tiomkin's song "was old-fashioned, and the picture was sort of update-western." Said Markowitz: "It just didn't have any of the fun in it." Tiomkin claimed at the time that network executives liked the melody but asked for a change of lyrics, which the composer said he refused. In any case, the song was ultimately rejected and Tiomkin was paid a hefty sum. Markowitz believed that, as part of Tiomkin's settlement with CBS, Markowitz was denied "theme by" credit during the entire run of the series (a highly unusual situation, since on-screen theme credit had by this time become routine).

As for his own, now-classic main title, "I conceived of the idea of going half traditional western and half jazz, kind of a sense of jazz," Markowitz explained. The "Wild Wild West" theme is in two parts: the "work" motif, played by Fender bass and brushes on the drums, for West "doing his schtick, getting out of a tight spot," and the "Big West" motif, a heroic orchestral signature for the good guys. Markowitz felt that "being quasi-serious with the big theme, and fun with the rhythmic theme," was the solution to the scoring dilemma posed by a show that had outrageous characters and plots yet played the danger and suspense for real.

The animated main title intertwined both. It consisted of five panels, with a drawing of West in the middle. First, West fells a bank robber with a karate chop in the lower left panel; then he draws his gun on a gambler about to pull an ace out of his boot at top right; then he disarms a man at top left; and finally he kisses a woman who pulls a blade from her hair, leaving her breathless (in the first season) or knocking her down (in subsequent years) as he walks away and the title "The Wild Wild West" appears. The same artwork appeared at each act break, freeze-framing the final scene of each act into a new drawing.

In all, Markowitz scored eleven episodes (six in the first season, four in the second, and one in the third), with many others being tracked with Markowitz's earlier music. It remained the project of which he was most proud. "I had done other westerns, movies of the week, and so forth," he said, "but I never came up with something quite as happily wedded to the material, for me, as that was." Markowitz wrote a secondary theme for Artemus Gordon—"a European feel, polite but quirky"—and, with colleague Robert Drasnin, a motif for recurring villain Dr. Miguelito Loveless (Michael Dunn), who first appeared in the Drasnin-scored 1965 episode, "The Night the Wizard Shook the Earth."

Markowitz also scored the western "Hondo" (1967, ABC), with Ralph Taeger as a cavalry scout in the Arizona Territory; and dozens of other television classics ranging from episodes of "Dr. Kildare" and "The FBI" to "Police Story" and "Murder, She Wrote." His last main-title theme was for "The Law and Harry McGraw" (1987–88, CBS) featuring Jerry Orbach as a Boston private eye and Barbara Babcock as a sophisticated lawyer.

George Duning's work on "The Big Valley" (1965–69, ABC) was perhaps the last great western score for American series television of the sixties. Another family-centered hour, this one was set on a ranch in the San Joaquin Valley of central California during the 1870s. Barbara Stanwyck starred as the widowed matriarch of the Barkley family, with Richard Long, Peter Breck, Lee Majors, and Linda Evans as members of her family.

Duning (b. 1919) had been a jazz trumpet player and an arranger for bands and radio, eventually serving as musical director on Kay Kyser's "Kollege of Musical Knowledge" for eight years. After World War II, he became a contract composer, arranger, and conductor for Columbia Pictures, where he

George Duning. Courtesy Society for the Preservation of Film Music.

stayed for seventeen years and received five Oscar nominations, including two for his classic scores for *From Here to Eternity* (1953) and *Picnic* (1955). He also scored *Bell, Book and Candle* (1958) and *The World of Suzie Wong* (1960); for the western genre, he wrote *3:10 to Yuma* (1957) with its Frankie Laine-performed title song, and *Cowboy* (1958). By the mid-1960s, Duning had become quite active in television, having written the themes for "Naked City," "Tightrope," and George Burns's "Wendy and Me," among others. After screening the "Big Valley" pilot, Duning decided "that it should have an Americana feeling, a wide-open sound.

"I treated it like I would have a theatrical motion picture. One thing that seems to have happened over the years, as television started getting big, a lot of motion-picture composers were treating it as sort of a stepchild. And frankly, I don't think they gave their best on some of the earlier TV shows. Also, they were fighting deadlines that were much worse than you ever had in motion-picture scoring. But I treated every show, no matter how small—a half-hour sitcom or a two-hour movie of the week—as if I was writing a major motion picture score."

That was immediately apparent on "The Big Valley." Duning's main theme had a grandeur unlike many of its small-screen counterparts. In addition to the main theme, he composed a theme for the Barkley family and individual motifs for Victoria (Stanwyck), characterized on Duning's original sketches as having a "quiet dignity"; music of turmoil for illegitimate son Heath (Majors); and a haunting melody for headstrong daughter Audra (Evans). "I used the tried-and-true leitmotif technique of setting an identifying theme for each of the major characters," Duning explained.

Duning scored the pilot, four first-season episodes, and a library for track-ing purposes. Later scores were written by Elmer Bernstein, Lalo Schifrin, and Joseph Mullendore. On "The Big Valley," Duning conducted an orchestra of forty musicians. The soundtrack LP, in contrast, featured an orchestra of eighty and—while drawn from those early scores—was reorchestrated by Duning into a complete concert work, developing and extending themes that he had written for the series into a virtual tone poem of the American West. Ray Heindorf conducted the music in Italy.

The year 1965 saw the start of two other notable westerns. "Branded" (1965–66, NBC) starred ex-"Rifleman" Chuck Connors as a disgraced cavalry officer who had been unjustly dismissed from the service for cowardice. "Branded: marked with a coward's shame/What do you do when you're branded? Will you fight for your name? . . ." Composer Dominic Frontiere (with lyricist Alan Alch) penned the song that quickly established the series premise.

Frontiere remembered immediately disliking the producer who engaged him: an individual who asked for "a song that sounds like a bugle call" with lyrics to explain the story. He called Alch, an old colleague with whom he once wrote comedy material. "We wrote this terrible piece of music. It was hysterical. We laughed all night," Frontiere recalled. "The next day, the producer came in with his entourage, and Alan stood in the crook of the piano, barely containing his laughter. We started to play this military song, and the god-damned producer says, 'I love it.' And for years, this worst piece of music was on the air," he laughed, "the theme for 'Branded.'"

For Rod Serling's short-lived and underrated "The Loner" (1965–66, CBS), about a disillusioned Union soldier (Lloyd Bridges) searching for life's mean-ings in the post–Civil War West, Jerry Goldsmith borrowed a countermelody from a theme in his score for the Kirk Douglas classic *Lonely Are the Brave* (1962) but imbued his theme and two "Loner" scores with the concertina-and-percussion, guitar-and-marimba flavor of his music for the more recent *Rio Conchos* (1964). (Dimitri Tiomkin, incidentally, was originally asked to supply the theme for "The Loner" but declined when Twentieth Century-Fox refused to give him publishing rights on the music.)

The granddaddy of them all, "Gunsmoke," remained on the air through 1975, and the increasing number of scoring hours required by the musicians' union led to an equivalent number of original scores, some by major com-posers. When Morton Stevens became CBS music director in 1965, he recruited several feature-film composers for the task. Among them were Franz Wax-man, whose two-part "The Raid" in 1966 bore similarities in sound and color to his Oscar-nominated score for *Taras Bulba* (1962); Goldsmith, who had written a handful of "Gunsmoke" half hours in 1960, returned to write a charm-ing score for "The Whispering Tree" in 1966; and Elmer Bernstein, who wrote a grim score for the 1972 episode "Hostage."

Many of those late sixties and early seventies scores were penned by CBS western workhorse Leon Klatzkin, plus John Parker and Jerrold Immel. Immel's later theme for "How the West Was Won" (1977–79, ABC), which also starred James Arness, was his finest work for television, a sweeping orchestral overture that played against spectacular footage of the unspoiled landscapes of the American West: forest-covered mountains, rushing rivers, colorful canyons, and buffalo grazing on the open plains. Equally impressive was his end-title arrangement, set entirely against paintings by western artist Charles M. Russell.

After "The Virginian" became a success at the ninety-minute length, two other series emulated the longer-is-better formula: "Wagon Train" expanded from an hour for one season starting in the fall of 1963, and "Cimarron Strip" (1967–68, CBS) tried the longer format, but lasted just a single season. "Cimarron" starred Stuart Whitman as a federal marshal in the Oklahoma ter-ritory of the late 1880s; Jill Townsend played a café owner, Randy Boone a photographer, and Percy Herbert a hard-drinking Scotsman.

Maurice Jarre, who was best known for his Oscar-winning music for the David Lean epics *Lawrence of Arabia* (1962) and *Doctor Zhivago* (1965), but who had also scored Richard Brooks's western *The Professionals* (1966), was signed to compose the theme and pilot score. Jarre's title music, set against a slowly retreating aerial shot of Whitman riding across the prairie, was impressive. CBS music director Stevens brought in several other veteran western composers to score individual "Cimarron" episodes including George Duning, Cyril Mockridge, and Richard Shores (who had scored many episodes of Audie Murphy's 1961 western "Whispering Smith" at Revue).

To no one's surprise, the most unusual score was contributed by Bernard Herrmann. For a 1968 episode titled "Knife in the Darkness," a Harlan Ellison script about a Jack the Ripper-style killer terrorizing the town, Herrmann created chilling music written entirely for the lowest woodwinds, double basses, harps, and timpani. Filled with growling bassoons and thumping percussion, it may have been the scariest western score ever written.

Bruce Broughton recalled the Herrmann sessions: "He was up there conducting, and he got the downbeat right, but when the piece was supposed to end, he was still conducting and the orchestra was still playing. So we racked [the film] up again. Second pass, same thing: he starts in the right place and the last streamer [a visual indicator on the film] comes and Herrmann's still emoting. He was way off." Stevens, who was supervising, gently suggested that Herrmann come into the booth to help balance the sound levels while Stevens conducted a cue or two.

"Herrmann turned to him and said, 'Are you worried because it isn't ending on time? It doesn't matter. It's all going to work anyway.' The point is that he was right," Broughton said. "The producers felt afterward that it was the best score they had all year—because it was not specific to the action, it was specific to the emotion. It didn't matter whether it went out when it was supposed to go, or it hit this nose twitch or this eye blink. Emotionally, it was right on the money."

"Kung Fu" (1972–75, ABC) may have been television's most unique western. Set in the nineteenth-century American West but regularly flashing back to the hero's youth in a Chinese monastery, it starred David Carradine as Kwai Chang Caine, a former Shaolin priest who was wanted for the murder of a member of the royal family.

It began as a ninety-minute movie but attracted so much attention that ABC ordered a series. The mysterious Caine was a man of few words and resorted to his considerable martial-arts skills only when threatened. He often reflected on the teachings of his Chinese masters (Keye Luke, Philip Ahn) in flashbacks filled with sometimes cryptic, sometimes profound sayings ("the dust of truth swirls and seeks its own cracks of entry") based on Eastern philosophies.

"We knew that we had to have [a composer] who was not necessarily Hollywood mainstream if we were going to make this an original television series," producer Alex Beaton recalled. He and his colleagues chose Jim Helms (1933–91) to score the film and subsequent series. Helms, a former studio guitarist and arranger for singer Rod McKuen, became the musical voice of Caine. His pilot score was filled with authentic-sounding Oriental instruments: flutes and considerable percussion, including bells, gongs, wind chimes, and wood blocks, with few hints of melody in the traditional Western sense.

For the series, Helms created one of the seventies' most memorable themes: graceful and gentle, with the flavor of the Orient—at least as perceived by Western ears—that musically described the soft-spoken, always peaceful character of Caine (seen walking through the desert at sunrise during the main title, at sunset during the end credits).

"I don't remember telling him to give us an Oriental theme," Beaton recalled. "What we wanted were suggestions, subtle references, the nuances of an Oriental overtone. That main title suggests something Western and Eastern. It actually defines the man," he added, referring not to Caine but to Helms: "really a very sensitive, quiet, and unassuming talent."

Helms's music was an important component of what Beaton referred to as "constant transitional challenges," moving back and forth between the West and old China without confusing viewers. Working with as few as twelve musicians, his choices were often unusual: sometimes scoring the slow-motion fight sequences, sometimes not; sometimes beginning act one or closing act four without music at all. In addition to his adroit use of percussion to imply the Orient and the mysticism associated with the character, he suggested the period in America with a harpsichord, and also created Caine's bamboo-flute melodies when the character began to play on camera during the first season. Like Caine himself, Helms's music exhibited a quiet power.

You Are Traveling Through Another Dimension

Fantasy and Sci-Fi

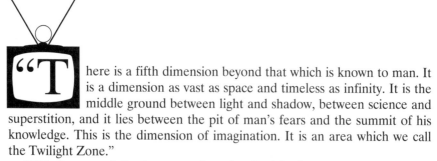

"There is a fifth dimension beyond that which is known to man. It is a dimension as vast as space and timeless as infinity. It is the middle ground between light and shadow, between science and superstition, and it lies between the pit of man's fears and the summit of his knowledge. This is the dimension of imagination. It is an area which we call the Twilight Zone."

With those carefully chosen words, writer Rod Serling ushered in a new era of fantasy and science fiction on television. It was his opening narration on the first episode of "The Twilight Zone" (1959–64, CBS), a weekly anthology of thought-provoking tales, often told with irony, sometimes with twist endings and nearly always with a serious point. Serling was one of the medium's most talented writers. His scripts for "Playhouse 90" and "Kraft Television Theatre" had won three Emmys (for "Patterns," "Requiem for a Heavyweight," and "The Comedian"), two Writers Guild Awards, and a Peabody. He saw "The Twilight Zone" as a vehicle for commentary on the human condition. His writing on "The Twilight Zone" would bring him two more Emmys during the seasons to come, and his on-screen role as narrator and host would make him a household name.

Music played an integral role in "The Twilight Zone," sometimes in establishing far-off locales, more often in setting the mood and creating the dramatic and emotional context in which the characters functioned. Lud Gluskin, then CBS West Coast music head, was credited with the choice of Bernard Herrmann to write the theme and score the pilot, a half-hour Serling script titled "Where Is Everybody?" Herrmann's "Twilight Zone" theme—played against images of moving webs, otherworldly landscapes, and a twinkling starfield—immediately established a sense of foreboding. Performed by a small ensemble of strings, brass, woodwinds, and harp, Herrmann's unresolved back-and-forth minor chords left the listener unsettled and in expectation; "slowly moving, subtle, and dreamy" was how fellow composer Fred Steiner described it. Herrmann's end-title theme, slightly shorter than the narrated main title, ultimately resolved to a major chord, allowing the listeners a final release from the tensions and enthralling storytelling they had just experienced.

Herrmann wrote seven scores for the series, including three of the earliest. For "Where Is Everybody?," with Earl Holliman as an apparent amnesiac wandering lost in a deserted town, Herrmann musically established the victim's confusion and growing paranoia with a frequently repeated three-note phrase. For "The Lonely," about a convict (Jack Warden) exiled to a deserted asteroid who falls in love with his robot companion (Jean Marsh), the composer impressionistically evoked both the solitude and the nighttime sky with vibraphone, harp, organ, and brass (similar to the Atlantis sequences in his *Journey to the Center of the Earth* score, also composed in 1959).

For Serling's moving script "Walking Distance," with Gig Young as a stressed-out executive who finds himself thrown back in time twenty-five years

Bernard Herrmann around the time he composed "The Twilight Zone." Courtesy Steven C. Smith.

to his happy childhood, Herrmann composed a haunting reverie to the nostalgia of the past. Written only for strings, harp, and celeste, it was alternately poignant and passionate, and, Herrmann's biographer suggested, may hint at the composer's own "longing for a similarly romanticized childhood." In tone and color, it presaged Herrmann's finale music for *Fahrenheit 451* (1966).

In the second season, Herrmann scored another classic episode, "Eye of the Beholder," in which plastic surgeons unsuccessfully attempt to alter a supposedly ugly woman's appearance. Because of the clever filming techniques used to shoot Serling's teleplay, only at the end did the viewer realize that the "deformed" woman was conventionally beautiful and that her hope was to become like the rest of her alien society, with monstrous porcine features. Later Herrmann scores included the 1962 "Little Girl Lost"—in which Herrmann's music merited an up-front title card along with the writer and director, a rare acknowledgment for a composer in television in that era—plus the 1963 episodes "Living Doll" and "Ninety Years Without Slumbering."

Herrmann returned to "Twilight Zone" after its first season despite a monumental slap in the face: the elimination of his original series theme in favor of a radically different musical approach, and then only after two other proposed new Herrmann themes had also been written and rejected. As the second season of "Twilight Zone" neared, a new, shorter main title was designed. The fuzzy images of webs remained, but a horizontal black bar now moved slowly across the screen from right to left, while a sun (or moon?) gradually disappeared beneath it, leaving a starfield and the sudden appearance of the show title.

In August 1960, Herrmann wrote his new themes for the series. One, marked "allegro maestoso," was a triumphant fanfare for brass, vibes, and harps (which bore stylistic similarities to the composer's theme for the 1951 science-fiction classic *The Day the Earth Stood Still*). A second, written for the same ensemble but with far more urgency, hinged on a series of sharp, repeated two-note phrases for muted brass. Both were recorded; a shorter version of the latter was ultimately used for an act-break "bumper."

Enter Marius Constant (b. 1925), a French avant-garde composer from whom Gluskin, on some of his many trips abroad, had commissioned original music for the CBS library. Constant was a pioneer in such twentieth-century musical forms as musique concrète, aleatory music, and improvisatory music for the concert hall; he also had written a number of widely performed ballets. Virtually all of the Constant music in the CBS library consisted of brief fragments, some no longer than five seconds, many scored for a strange ensemble including electric guitars, flute, tenor saxophone, and percussion including bongo drums.

For reasons that remain shrouded in mystery, the revised Herrmann themes were rejected, either by producers or executives at the network. "I'm sure the problem with Herrmann's version was, it was very 'down,'" recalled CBS music supervisor Don B. Ray. "And somebody decided it had to be more 'up.' I would say that Lud had no hand in causing this to happen, because when all was said and done, he was very loyal to Herrmann, the quality of his writing."

"Evidently they didn't like it," said Jerry Goldsmith, referring to the dark, original Herrmann motif. "So I wrote a theme they didn't like, and I think a couple of other people wrote themes that they didn't like. So, out of desperation, Lud said, well, here, let's try this."

"This" was Gluskin's assembly of two unrelated Marius Constant pieces that happened to be in the library. The brief "Etrange No. 3" and slightly longer "Milieu No. 2," taken together, were built into a new theme for "The Twilight Zone." The Constant music "was never intended to be used as a main title," Ray pointed out. In fact, "it was not really good for [tracking as] backgrounds. It was too fragmentary. It was marvelous if you had four seconds and then a dissolve," but otherwise the Constant music went largely unused in the library.

Producer Buck Houghton recalled: "We just wanted to make it different. That is about the only reason. The title background was different too. You see, 'Twilight Zone' was not a huge success while it was on the air. Everybody was reasonably content, but it was not a hit. So there was a motive behind everybody to say, 'Well, let's not let them think they're seeing a rerun. Let's jump off with new music, new title backgrounds, new approach.'"

The Constant music—written and recorded merely as two fragments for tracking into odd dramatic situations—went on the air at the start of the second season, in the fall of 1960. "We all thought [Gluskin] was out of his mind," Goldsmith laughed. "It was the most ridiculous theme I ever heard in my life. But it came back to haunt me, because when I did *Twilight Zone: The Movie* [1983], I had to rerecord it."

Marius Constant never received any screen credit for his surprising contribution to American pop culture; he wasn't even aware of what had been done with his music. At its core, his eerie, instantly recognizable "Twilight Zone" wasn't even a melody. It began with a series of repeated, intriguingly dissonant, four-note phrases played by two electric guitars. (Also in the band: a flute, piccolo, clarinet, tenor sax, three trombones, timpani, bongos, and harp.)

The majority of "Twilight Zone" episodes, like most other CBS-produced programming of the time, were tracked with music from the library. In addition to the Constant material, there was considerable Herrmann music available. Herrmann's "Outer Space Suite," composed for woodwinds and percussion in 1957, was used, as were Gluskin's overseas rerecordings of several Herrmann scores for CBS radio, including "The Hitchhiker" (1942) and "The Moat Farm Murder" (1944).

Still, Gluskin commissioned original scores when he felt the programs merited them, and often recruited top composers to write them. Early in the first season, Franz Waxman, who won an Oscar for his music for *Sunset Boulevard* (1950), scored the similarly themed "The Sixteen-Millimeter Shrine" with Ida Lupino; Leonard Rosenman, who won acclaim for his *East of Eden* music (1955), scored the men-into-space episode "And When the Sky Was Opened";

and Leith Stevens (1909–70), no stranger to end-of-the-world tales with his music for *When Worlds Collide* (1951) and *War of the Worlds* (1953), scored the classic "Time Enough at Last," with Burgess Meredith as a bookworm who survives a nuclear holocaust.

Fred Steiner (b. 1923) scored seven episodes. A veteran composer for radio and live TV (notably the early 1950s CBS comedies "Life with Luigi" and "My Friend Irma," and seven "Playhouse 90s" including the classic "The Miracle Worker"), Steiner was a versatile musician who had scored "Gunsmoke" and "Have Gun—Will Travel," and written the themes for "Perry Mason" and "Navy Log." Among his best scores were two 1961 half hours with nineteenth-century settings: harmonica-and-guitar folk melodies for "A Hundred Yards over the Rim," with Cliff Robertson as a pioneer who had somehow stumbled into a twentieth-century town; and music of profound sadness, for strings alone, for "The Passerby," about the aftermath of the Civil War, with Joanne Linville and James Gregory.

Steiner's hour-long shows, all from 1963, included "Mute," with a young Ann Jillian as a telepathic child, for which Steiner provided strange string effects; "Miniature," a charming story with Robert Duvall as an introvert who imagines life inside a dollhouse, scored with familiar silent-film-era music, played music-box style; and "The Bard," a comic episode with Jack Weston as a hack writer who magically summons William Shakespeare to help him pen a TV pilot.

"Lud was not exactly what one might call a thoroughly educated or accomplished musician," Steiner said, "but luckily for all concerned, he had the willingness and open-mindedness to not only hire the best composers available, but to allow them almost complete freedom in the music they wrote for these shows. In all the years that I worked for Gluskin at CBS, I cannot recall any instance of Lud interfering with me or insisting on changes in my music—which is not to say that he would not suggest a minor change or two, talking to me from his listening post in the control booth. The ensembles we used at CBS were always small, obviously for budgetary reasons. My ensembles on 'Twilight Zone' ranged in size from five players on 'Miniature' to fourteen on 'King Nine Will Not Return.'"

Nathan Van Cleave (1910–70) scored the most "Twilight Zone" episodes: a dozen in all. Frequently working in collaboration with his former radio colleague Fred Steiner (as they did on such films as 1958's *Colossus of New York* and 1964's *Robinson Crusoe on Mars*), Van Cleave's scores included the 1959 "Perchance to Dream," which marked an early and unusual use of electronic instruments in television. Later came his otherworldly music for the 1960 "Elegy," a coolly militaristic score for the Elizabeth Montgomery-Charles Bronson postapocalyptic tale "Two" (1961), and the lyrical music (for strings, winds, guitar, and novachord) for 1962's "I Sing the Body Electric," based on the Ray Bradbury story.

Some of the most striking scores for "The Twilight Zone" were penned by the versatile Jerry Goldsmith. For the first-season episode "The Big Tall Wish," about a boy who believes that his wish has helped a prizefighter (Ivan Dixon) win a bout, the music focuses on the child with variations on a melody played on the harmonica. For the second-season episode "Nervous Man in a Four-Dollar Room," Goldsmith wrote a jazz-oriented score utilizing electric guitar, bass, percussion, and flute to create an almost constant feeling of agitation.

Goldsmith's final three "Twilight Zone" scores (his final work as a contract composer for CBS) were heard in rapid succession in January 1961, yet they couldn't be less alike in style. For "Dust," about a nineteenth-century hanging averted, allegedly, by a bag of magic dirt, the composer played the Old West setting with guitars, harmonica, and pump organ. For "Back There," a time-travel story about a theoretician (Russell Johnson) who attempts to avert Lincoln's assassination, Goldsmith suggested the period with harpsichord and a small string ensemble.

What many consider Goldsmith's "Twilight Zone" masterpiece, "The Invaders," was a tour de force for Agnes Moorehead as a solitary farm woman besieged by tiny astronauts in a UFO. Filmed virtually without dialogue, the visual action, sound effects, and—most important—music, carry this Richard Matheson script. Goldsmith underscored the action with jagged, often frightening musical effects for strings, harp, and keyboards.

"The norm for an orchestra on 'Twilight Zone' was six men. Which is wonderful because it forces you to be very inventive," Goldsmith said. "It's easy to write for a sixty-five-piece orchestra." (When Joe Dante asked Goldsmith to score a half-hour "Amazing Stories" in 1985, the composer treated it as if it were a "Twilight Zone" episode, using six musicians. The "Amazing Stories" production staff had been prepared to give him forty-five players, which was not uncommon on that show.)

When Goldsmith left CBS, he went to Revue and steady employment on its horror series "Thriller" (1960–62, NBC). He composed sixteen original scores for the Boris Karloff-hosted anthology, which lasted only two seasons but remains a favorite of fantasy buffs despite only rare appearances in syndication.

"Thriller" actually began as a more sedate, mystery-oriented hour with few scares. Pete Rugolo started the series, writing the theme—which played against lines crisscrossing the screen and forming the title—and twenty of the initial thirty-seven episodes. Well known as a jazz composer (with "The Thin Man" and "Richard Diamond" already behind him), Rugolo might have been an ideal choice had the direction of the series not changed radically at midseason.

"It was very challenging," Rugolo recalled, "because we only had a budget for maybe eight to ten men. I would use very unusual combinations: a harp, flute, French horn, tuba, it all depended on the script. Each story was different. Sometimes I would just use strings alone; harpsichord, all different instruments that would make unusual sounds because [the stories] were a little strange." The time crunch, however, was nightmarish. "They would give it to us on a Friday and we'd have to score it on a Monday. And there would be a lot of music, twenty-five or thirty minutes of music," Rugolo said, "and so some weeks it was impossible." Rugolo's scores were often jazz-tinged but were more dramatic in nature than his "Richard Diamond" scores. As with "Richard Diamond," he arranged his best themes from the series into a first-rate album filled with the unusual orchestral colors and combinations that marked his writing for "Thriller."

The lack of true horror, however, worried the higher-ups. According to associate producer Douglas Benton, network executives—who had been expecting scary tales introduced by the veteran horror-film actor—were shocked to see film-noir stories, "something out of RKO, 1947," in Benton's words. Several key production personnel were let go, among them Rugolo. When Goldsmith was free of CBS, Revue music director Stanley Wilson immediately hired him for "Thriller." The hour-long "Thriller" proved to be a far better showcase for Goldsmith than the half-hour "Twilight Zone." As an anthology, it offered a smorgasbord of stories, both period and contemporary; with Wilson as a supportive boss, Goldsmith was offered the freedom to experiment with various musical styles and approaches. It brought him his first Emmy nomination (shared with Rugolo, for the series' 1960–61 season) and, more important, attention from Alfred Newman, the legendary music director at Twentieth Century-Fox. After hearing one of Goldsmith's "Thriller" scores, Newman called to praise his efforts and ultimately recommended him to the producers of *Lonely Are the Brave*, his first major picture.

"Being experimental was a matter of economics in television," Goldsmith said. "The numbers force you to be creative. If you're doing a show with three musicians, you have to be pretty imaginative to make it hold for an hour. When I was doing 'Thriller,' the wilder and more off-the-wall I could be, the happier the producer was. It wasn't being different just to be different—it was letting your imagination run rampant, as long as it was within the realm of the dramatic context."

Goldsmith's innovative work on "Thriller" (all of which aired in 1961) included an Old English-style folk tune for "Hay-Fork and Bill-Hook," a grim tale of ancient Druid rites in a Welsh village; a demented nineteenth-century music-hall waltz for alto saxophone to represent the title character in "Yours Truly, Jack the Ripper" (foreshadowing his theme for the 1963 film *The List of Adrian Messenger*); a charming lullaby for celeste and harp for the little girl in "Mr. George," about a child's imaginary friend (which presaged his approach to *Poltergeist,* 1982); a darkly whimsical salon valse for solo piano in "What Beckoning Ghost?," about a woman who thinks her husband is trying to murder her; and ethereal flute with modal writing for strings and brass in "God Grant That She Lye Stille," about the return of a three-hundred-year-old witch to her ancestral English home.

One of the most chilling—and musically interesting—of the "Thrillers" was the first-season "The Terror in Teakwood," with Guy Rolfe, Hazel Court, and Charles Aidman in a story of a concert pianist whose crazed ambition leads him to literally steal the hands of a more talented rival out of the dead performer's crypt. Goldsmith's orchestral score created the fright, but the lime-light belonged to two original pieces for piano written and played by Caesar Giovannini (b. 1925). Giovannini, a freelance studio musician, composed a Chopinesque nocturne and a flamboyant, virtuoso sonata—a key element in the script—for performance in a concert-hall setting. The notes for Stanley Wilson's 1963 Decca LP *Themes to Remember* (which consisted entirely of music from Revue shows) noted that the "Teakwood Nocturne" had "evoked more requests for a recording than any other theme in the Revue repertoire." Although written for "Thriller," Giovannini's "Teakwood" themes would often resurface in other Revue/Universal shows throughout the 1960s when classically styled solo piano pieces were needed.

The other composer on "Thriller" was Morton Stevens, who wrote an additional sixteen original scores. Stevens's output included virtually all of the series' black comedies, plus one particularly notable hour of terror: the 1961 "Pigeons from Hell," based on a story by famed fantasy writer Robert E. Howard, scored entirely for strings, percussion, and eerie solo voice.

One of the perks of scoring "Thriller" was the opportunity to write a short "overture" of the episode's score for the end titles, a departure from standard television practice of reprising the series theme. Although Rugolo often contributed fresh arrangements of his "Thriller" theme, Goldsmith and Stevens used the opportunity to showcase their own weekly scores. Sometimes the end titles on "Thriller" ran for a minute and forty seconds (a length rare for TV even then).

Benton attributed this degree of musical freedom to Wilson. "If anybody is responsible for the quality of television film scoring, it's Stanley Wilson," Benton said. "He had a tremendously high standard. If you weren't any good, you didn't last. But if you were, he would find the right spot for you. MCA [which owned Revue] was essentially a music outfit, and although they got everything out of the pig but the squeal, they did understand that musicians had to have something to work with. So as long as Stanley was alive, we had far and away the best television music in the business."

For its first seven seasons, "Alfred Hitchcock Presents" aired as a half-hour series and was tracked entirely with library music. For its expansion into "The Alfred Hitchcock Hour" (1962–65, CBS/NBC), executive producers Norman Lloyd and Joan Harrison, both longtime Hitchcock associates, began to commission original scores. The mainstays of the mystery series were two other Hitchcock associates: Lyn Murray (1909–89), who had scored *To Catch a Thief* (1955) for the director, and Bernard Herrmann, who was by now Hitchcock's most celebrated composer. Herrmann's scores for *Vertigo* (1958), *North by Northwest* (1959), and *Psycho* (1960) not only elevated those films into suspense masterpieces, they became textbook examples of the dramatic possibilities inherent in original film music.

Murray wrote twenty-three scores, eleven of them in the first season, including a new arrangement of the Gounod *Funeral March for a Marionette* as the series main title (set against creepy new visuals involving a castle under threatening skies, weird-looking eyes, and the famous Hitchcock caricature). Murray would go on to compose the themes—a main title and a rock 'n' roll tune called "Assembly Stomp" for the end credits—for "Mr. Novak" (1963–65, NBC) with James Franciscus as a high school English teacher; the music for "Sandburg's Lincoln" (1974–76, NBC), a prestigious series of six specials with Hal Holbrook as Abraham Lincoln; and the scores for a number of public television programs, including the controversial "Steambath" (1973) and his Emmy winner, the National Geographic special "Miraculous Machines" (1984).

Herrmann composed seventeen scores for the "Hitchcock Hour," all for the second and third seasons. It was the most music he would ever write for any television series, and in the most concentrated periods. He worked from August to November 1963 on six of his seven second-season scores, and from July through October 1964 on seven of his ten third-season scores. Between stints on the television series, the composer wrote the *Marnie* music (1964) for Hitchcock. He also rearranged the Gounod main title—solely for bassoons—for the series' final two seasons.

Herrmann's most compelling work nearly always involved surprising instrumental combinations and vivid musical colorations. The 1963–64 scores included "A Home Away from Home," a clever Robert Bloch story about the inmates literally taking over the asylum (scored for strings, harp, and vibes); "Terror at Northfield," an all-woodwind ensemble for an Ellery Queen tale about a father's vengeance for his son's murder; and "The Jar," in which a calliope and variations on the ancient "Dies Irae" theme underscored a bizarre Ray Bradbury story about the effect that the contents of a weird carnival sideshow artifact have on the residents of a tiny backwater town.

For the series' final season, Herrmann's contributions included "The Life Work of Juan Diaz," Ray Bradbury's macabre tale of a Mexican family victimized by a gravedigger, with a score based almost entirely on an habanera (and thus reminiscent of the nightmare sequence in *Vertigo*); Scottish reels for "The McGregor Affair," about a Scotsman's murder of his alcoholic wife; vibes and harps for "Consider Her Ways," a science-fiction story about a future Earth populated entirely by women; and a playful waltz for flute and harp for the imaginative child of "Where the Woodbine Twineth."

"There is nothing wrong with your television set. Do not attempt to adjust the picture. We are controlling transmission. . . ." So intoned the narrator at the start of "The Outer Limits" (1963–65, ABC), another innovative anthology and one that assumed monumental cult status over the years, based largely on a handful of thoughtful scripts penned by creator Leslie Stevens, producer Joseph Stefano (who scripted *Psycho*), and science-fiction author Harlan Ellison; on innovative direction by the likes of Byron Haskin (*War of the*

Dominic Frontiere. Photo by George Fields.

Worlds) and Gerd Oswald; and on creative cinematography by Conrad Hall (who would later become the Oscar-winning cameraman of *Butch Cassidy and the Sundance Kid* and *The Day of the Locust*).

The music for the first season of "The Outer Limits" was composed by Stevens's associate Dominic Frontiere (b. 1931), who also received "production executive" credit on the series as a principal in Stevens's Daystar Productions company. Prior to "The Outer Limits," the former accordionist and Twentieth Century-Fox arranger had written the theme for the cop show "The New Breed" (1961–62, ABC) and scored all of Stevens's "Stoney Burke" (1962–63, ABC), which starred Jack Lord as a rodeo performer. Later, he scored a hit with his music for the western *Hang 'Em High* (1968) and received an Oscar nomination for *The Stunt Man* (1980). Frontiere's "Outer Limits" theme began with an orchestral fanfare and segued to a strange, string-dominated sense of wonder. The main-title visuals, set to the famous narration, ranged from a sine-wave oscilloscope pattern to fuzzy images of a test pattern and the moon.

"The Outer Limits" was one of the first series to benefit from a "sound design" approach: one that integrated music and sound effects to create a unique overall sonic atmosphere. Daystar music supervisor John Elizalde worked closely with Frontiere on the series. "We made all kinds of crazy sound effects and musical things," Elizalde said. "We rigged up an oscillator, and Dominic would play it just by jiggling the knob. He has absolutely perfect pitch, and a huge physical facility. Somehow or other he could play that thing just like an instrument. We used to call it the Onafets, which is Stefano spelled backwards."

Elizalde, who not only had been a concert pianist and music editor but was also highly proficient in technical matters involving all kinds of sound reproduction, created many of the sound effects for the series, including alien voices and electronic tonalities as needed. He even reviewed scripts for proper terminology and often concocted scientific-sounding jargon for the dialogue. "It was all very primitive, but a lot of fun," he said.

Unlike the Revue series "Thriller" and "The Alfred Hitchcock Hour," "The Outer Limits" operated on budgetary restrictions that demanded a handful of original scores and extensive tracking of many episodes. As with "The Twilight Zone," however, Frontiere and Elizalde chose the key episodes for original music. The two largest sessions were in August 1963 (creating a massive library of music along with scores for early episodes such as "The Architects of Fear" and "The Human Factor"), when Frontiere conducted a forty-four-piece orchestra, and in February 1964, when he had forty-two players for "The Forms of Things Unknown" (a highly stylized hour that Stefano had designed as a pilot for a possible spinoff series). On other dates, Frontiere's orchestra would fluctuate from as few as five players to an average of twenty-nine.

The music of "The Outer Limits" may have been Frontiere's best work for television. His approaches ranged from a lyrical love theme for "The Man Who Was Never Born" to menacing Oriental sounds in "The Hundred Days of the Dragon" and early electronic music for the alien environment of "Nightmare." For the largest scores, Frontiere utilized the services of one of Hollywood's premier orchestrators, Edward B. Powell, who spent many years orchestrating the scores of Alfred Newman at Twentieth Century-Fox.

A falling-out with ABC management resulted in the ouster of most of the Daystar production group, including Stevens and Frontiere, for the second season of "The Outer Limits." Even Frontiere's theme was replaced with new music by composer Harry Lubin. It wasn't exactly new, however. Lubin simply wrote a variation of his "Fear" main title from "Alcoa Presents: One Step Beyond" (1959–61, ABC), the John Newland-hosted anthology of supposedly fact-based incidents involving the occult and the supernatural. Lubin's scores—which ranged from fully orchestral on "Soldier" to predominantly organ and percussion on "Demon with a Glass Hand"—were usually far less subtle than those of Frontiere. And, as on "One Step Beyond," Lubin frequently employed electronic instruments to stress the science-fiction elements of the stories.

Meanwhile, Frontiere scored the pilot and three episodes of "The Invaders" (1967–68, ABC), the Quinn Martin-produced paranoia exercise about the arrival of aliens on Earth and the odyssey of architect David Vincent (Roy Thinnes), who tried to convince everyone else that the visitors had taken human form and were out to colonize the planet. For the main title—a three-note motif denoting alarm, to visuals of multicolored elliptical lights illuminating the title—Frontiere drew from his "Outer Limits" score for "The Forms of

Things Unknown." The early "Invaders" scores consisted largely of suspense cues, action music for Vincent battling the aliens, and even themes borrowed from other "Outer Limits" shows (including, in the pilot, the love music from "The Man Who Was Never Born"); the series' end-title theme also originated in an "Outer Limits" score.

Frontiere later scored "The Immortal" (1970–71, ABC), a Christopher George series about a man whose blood made him immune to disease and the aging process. A terrific TV movie (1969) with a bittersweet Frontiere theme, the same premise turned out to be a colossal mistake as a series (with a man on the run storyline à la "The Fugitive").

Duane Tatro (b. 1927), a Stan Kenton band alumnus who had studied with Arthur Honegger in Paris, was hired to write several "Invaders" scores. His interest in modern compositional techniques, particularly the twelve-tone system, made him perfect for "The Invaders" and subsequent Quinn Martin series including "The FBI" and "Manhunter" (1974–75, CBS).

Twentieth Century-Fox was a consistent supplier of science fiction to sixties television, primarily due to one man: producer Irwin Allen, who had made the classic sci-fi films *The Lost World* (1960) and *Voyage to the Bottom of the Sea* (1961). He turned the latter into a television series (1964–68, ABC) starring Richard Basehart and David Hedison as the inventor and captain, respectively, of the highly advanced nuclear submarine *Seaview*.

As with most of Allen's shows, "Voyage" started on a somewhat serious premise but quickly degenerated into monster-of-the-week melodramatics. Paul Sawtell, who had scored the *Voyage* feature film, came back to score the pilot (including a new theme for the series) and five first-season episodes. A more intriguing choice for composer was Hugo Friedhofer, who scored four more 1964 episodes (two of them completed, because of Friedhofer's notoriously slow pace, by Alexander Courage), although Friedhofer later referred to his work on "Voyage" as "sheer torment." "The producer of this waterlogged epic is so sound-effects happy," Friedhofer wrote, "that the show might just as well be scored with an infinite series of variations on 'Asleep in the Deep' for all the difference it would make." A variety of other composers worked on the four seasons of "Voyage," including such sci-fi veterans as Leith Stevens, who wrote nine episodes.

Sawtell's original theme was briefly replaced, for exactly one episode. Jerry Goldsmith was hired to score the opening show of the second season, "Jonah and the Whale." He wrote a dark, brooding, Herrmannesque piece that was used over the main and end titles. Sawtell's brighter, more familiar theme returned the following week, and remained with the series until its cancellation in 1968.

"Lost in Space" (1965–68, CBS) was Allen's futuristic version of the classic *Swiss Family Robinson,* about an extended family of castaways on a far-off planet in 1997. John Williams (then still billed as "Johnny"), newly freed of his

Universal contract, first worked for Fox music director Lionel Newman on this show. The premise had husband-and-wife scientists (Guy Williams, June Lockhart), their three children (Marta Kristen, Angela Cartwright, Billy Mumy), their pilot (Mark Goddard), and an obnoxious stowaway named Dr. Smith (Jonathan Harris) enduring countless crises in space, including the usual quota of monsters and alien visitors. Newman had scored the original pilot (which had no Dr. Smith) using Bernard Herrmann's music for the previous Fox sci-fi films *The Day the Earth Stood Still* and *Journey to the Center of the Earth.*

Williams scored four of the first seven episodes, and many of the series' later hours were tracked with this music. Williams's main title, set to animation that hinted at the series' often youth-oriented outer space hijinks, featured an unusual electronic instrument invented by former Glenn Miller band trombonist and UCLA music professor Paul Tanner. Part theremin and part ondes martenot, Tanner's unnamed instrument could control the pitch of the electronic sound more precisely than a traditional theremin. (As a result, it was widely used, particularly on George Greeley's scores for the Bill Bixby-Ray Walston comedy "My Favorite Martian" [1963–66, CBS]; Tanner provided the weird sounds every time Uncle Martin's antennae went up or when he utilized his powers of levitation.)

John Williams. Photo by George Fields.

But Williams avoided electronics in his scores, preferring a more traditional orchestral approach to the drama. The "Lost in Space" ensemble, Williams recalled, "was mostly without strings. So we had a pretty healthy brass section, eight or ten [players], and some woodwinds and percussion—a little more generous than the Universal ensemble typically would be." Most prominent were his danger motif, in which brass and woodwinds signaled trouble for the Robinson clan; a lumbering tuba theme for the robot (reminiscent of Herrmann's music for the robot Gort in the *Day the Earth Stood Still* score); and a driving theme for the Chariot, a 1997 version of the all-terrain vehicle in which the family traveled while repairing their damaged Jupiter 2 spacecraft. Williams wrote additional themes for humorous moments, mostly arranged for upper woodwinds, usually involving Penny's extraterrestrial pet chimp or resourceful Will's quizzical reactions to Smith's antics; and otherworldly sounds for percussion, used to accompany a spacewalk sequence in the first episode.

Williams's diverse and interesting musical responses to the various environmental dangers that threatened the Robinsons turned out to be a kind of trial run for the disaster films that the composer would become famous for several years later: the heat of the planet's blazing sun (Allen's *The Towering Inferno,* 1974); the constant seismic activity (*Earthquake,* 1974); and the raging torrents of water as the Robinsons crossed the planet's inland sea (Allen's *The Poseidon Adventure,* 1972). More to the point, it was his first exposure to the science-fiction realm that, a dozen years later, would rocket him into the position of film's most famous composer.

"I guess the intention was probably to be pretty straight with it, but some of it, even at the time, was kind of campy," Williams recalled. "I remember doing some silly waltzes with four flutes and things. That just seemed right for this kind of carrying on that Irwin had there. It did get a little bit broad fairly quickly. I even sometimes think in my mind that it was a kind of precursor of *Star Wars* in a way, because [the series] had the robots, the various characters, and the broad musical treatment." Williams's grandly romantic, fully symphonic approach to George Lucas's 1977 space opera would win an Academy Award and almost singlehandedly rejuvenate the orchestral score in motion pictures.

Williams wrote a new theme for the third season of "Lost in Space," a far bolder, more adventurous musical signature that skipped the electronics entirely.

Herman Stein (b. 1915), who was no stranger to science fiction with past film scores such as *It Came from Outer Space* (1953) and *This Island Earth* (1954), contributed five other early scores to "Lost in Space" and, like Williams, avoided the use of electronic gimmicks. "Music has to appeal to you on a human level," Stein said. "I remember once Lionel [Newman] wanted me to use an electric violin for one of these things, and I hated the idea. It didn't fit and it was unnatural. I think that's the wrong approach with music. You've got all kinds of sound effects and [technicians] can do it much better than you can as a composer. But they cannot do what I can do: I can make you afraid, or I can make you sad. That's something else." Later composers on the series included Leith Stevens, Alexander Courage, Cyril Mockridge, and Robert Drasnin.

Allen engaged Williams for two more of his sixties sci-fi series: "The Time Tunnel" (1966–67, ABC) and "Land of the Giants" (1968–70, ABC). In each case, Williams—whose film career was beginning to take off—composed only the themes and pilot scores. For the time-travel series "The Time Tunnel," Williams complemented the colorful animated titles (which featured a man being buried in the sand inside an hourglass) with a rhythmic, brass-dominated theme that even incorporated a tick-tock sound. For the scenes of scientists Tony and Doug (James Darren, Robert Colbert) falling through time, he came up with swirling musical effects for flutes, vibes, chimes, and harps. Williams composed a different theme for each season of "Land of the Giants," both highly dramatic. (Williams's themes were actually the third and fourth for the series; Alexander Courage's original score for the pilot, as well as a second theme by Joseph Mullendore, was thrown out.) A measure of the trust that Allen placed in Williams is the fact that, although the producer was said to abhor dissonance, both Williams's "Time Tunnel" and "Land of the Giants" scores contain just such writing as appropriate to the bizarre, baffling happenings in each.

The roster of other "Time Tunnel" composers included non-Fox regulars such as Lyn Murray and George Duning, while the "Giants" episodes included scores by Leith Stevens, Mullendore, Harry Geller, and Richard LaSalle (who became Allen's regular TV movie composer when Williams went full-time into feature films in the 1970s).

While Irwin Allen was pleasing the kiddie audience on CBS and ABC, Gene Roddenberry was attempting to appeal to a more sophisticated demographic with "Star Trek" (1966–69, NBC). For this most famous of televised sci-fi programs, Roddenberry imagined a twenty-third-century federation of many civilizations and a giant, faster-than-light-speed starship with a human captain (William Shatner), a half-Vulcan science officer (Leonard Nimoy), a cynical Earth doctor (DeForest Kelley), and a multiracial crew that together confronted the unknown with a particularly humanistic philosophy.

Roddenberry relied on Desilu's unofficial music director Wilbur Hatch for advice on choosing a composer for his ambitious, special effects-laden hour. Hatch recommended Alexander Courage (b. 1919), an old friend from the days of CBS radio in the late 1940s. Courage spent much of the 1950s as an arranger-orchestrator at MGM; he scored the western classic *The Left-Handed Gun* (1958) and wrote music for dozens of series episodes including MGM's "National Velvet" (1960–62, NBC) and Fox's "Daniel Boone."

Courage was not a science fiction fan. "I never have been," he said. "But I

Alexander Courage. Courtesy BMI Archives.

thought, 'Well, what the heck. It's another show.' I visited the set down there in Culver City, at the old Selznick studios, and met Gene and so forth, and we got along fine." According to Courage, Roddenberry's dictum was: "I don't want it to sound like space music"—meaning, nothing "far out. He wanted something that had some balls and drive to it. In fact, he told me to always write that way through the show, all of it."

Searching for a theme, the composer recalled hearing, many years ago on the radio, the song "Beyond the Blue Horizon" in an unusual arrangement that suggested the heavens. Courage took his inspiration from that memory: "I figured that if I could get something that sounded like it was going off into space, and have a lot of motion underneath it, then that might work. That's what I came up with. I tried to have long intervals, which would make it kind of go 'out,' and then scales that went up and out. . . . And I wanted to have a strange kind of unearthly sound, so I had a very, very primitive early synthesizer, and Loulie Jean Norman, who was the great studio soprano, to do an 'ah' or an 'oh' on the tune. That really got to Roddenberry, because he was quite a sexpot and anything that had to do with a woman's voice was just right for him. So he mixed in more soprano and less of the instruments than I would have wanted. Aside from that, it's really right there."

In fact, the soprano voice was inaudible in the original mix of the series main title, replaced by an eerie, electronically altered violin sound manufactured by Jack Cookerly; Fred Steiner's more fully orchestral arrangement replaced it after a few episodes, and the wordless vocal was not heard until the start of the second season.

As a part of the pilot score, Courage also wrote an opening fanfare: eight notes for brass that would become among the most familiar musical signatures of the next three decades. "I had to fit that to the picture," Courage recalled. "So I just wrote a fanfare. Little did I know what was going to happen to it." Courage's fanfare for the USS *Enterprise,* even more than the series theme, became so inextricably linked with the "Star Trek" phenomenon that its inclusion in each of the *Star Trek* feature films was a foregone conclusion.

Courage also became involved with the sound effects of the pilot. "I told Gene that it might be kind of an interesting thing if we did some of the sound effects on the alien planet based on music. So we went into Glen Glenn [recording studio] one evening with about four or five [musicians], and we had them play certain things which we then fooled around with on the [mixing] board. We made the elevators opening and closing, the wind on the planet, and all kinds of stuff like that."

Courage's music for the first pilot, "The Cage," introduced the basic themes: the heraldic fanfare to announce the *Enterprise* (that would be used to underscore Shatner's opening narration in the series), the main theme (that soaring melody with its surprising beguine rhythm), and an alien motif (an ethereal sound, performed alternately by voice and flute). He also used an electronic organ on both "The Cage" and the second pilot, "Where No Man Has Gone Before," often in highly dramatic musical contexts, to stress the otherworldly nature of the drama.

In addition to the pilots (recorded in January and November 1965), Courage scored two early first-season shows ("The Man Trap" and "The Naked Time," in August 1966), and Roddenberry's unsold 1966 series pilot "Police Story." He then left "Star Trek" in order to take the prestige job of associate music director and chief arranger on *Doctor Dolittle* (1967), the major-screen musical that earned him an Academy Award nomination (for musical adaptation, with Lionel Newman) but nearly ruined Twentieth Century-Fox financially. After the debacle of *Doctor Dolittle,* Courage returned to score two more episodes in the series' third season. Unfortunately, however, Roddenberry's ill-advised attempt to write a lyric to Courage's "Star Trek" theme caused a rift with the composer.

Roddenberry's words ("Beyond the rim of the star-light/My love is wand'ring in star-flight. . . ."), which have rarely been performed, cost Courage 50 percent of his performance royalties from that point on. Courage protested, but because a clause in his Desilu contract permitted Roddenberry to add lyrics (and claim half the royalties), the composer had no legal recourse. Roddenberry never apologized, Courage said: "If he had told me about this, and we had come up with a really decent lyric—which it isn't—we both could have made more money out of it. He just knocked something out and that was it."

When "Star Trek" went to series, Roddenberry entrusted all decisions regarding music to his associate producer, Robert H. Justman. Justman, a television veteran who had recently worked on "The Outer Limits," knew the difference between Mozart and Mahler (and may have been the only producer in Hollywood with a harpsichord in his living room). Justman chose the composers, spotted the music (choosing where cues would begin and end, and deciding the nature of the score), and attended every scoring session.

Fred Steiner wrote more original scores for "Star Trek" than any other composer, including all or part of twelve episodes plus library music over the series' three seasons. "When they screened the pilot for me," he recalled, "I instantly knew what the approach should be: big adventure music. After I screened it, I went to Gene and he said the same thing. He wanted adventure music, for the *Captain Blood* of space. So the music reflects that—trying to get as big and noble a sound as possible." (As Roddenberry later wrote in the liner notes to Steiner's first *"Star Trek"* album, he told his composers, "Don't give us electronic beep-beep-beep music.") They undertook this despite a relative paucity of orchestral forces—as few as seventeen on Courage's pilots to a high of twenty-six on some of Steiner's scores.

Because of the thoughtful nature of the series, "Star Trek" tended to bring out the best in its composers. Steiner's music may have been his finest for the medium. Among his memorable 1966 contributions were what he called "harshly shocking, dissonant, glittery, clattering 'zap' chords," as well as his mysterious opening and closing music for "Charlie X"; the dark suspense-and-terror music of "The Corbomite Maneuver"; a militaristic theme for the alien Romulans in "Balance of Terror"; and lyrical passages for the title characters of "Mudd's Women."

The films of Sol Kaplan (1919–90) included *Halls of Montezuma* (1950), *Titanic* (1953), and *Lies My Father Told Me* (1975). He scored only two episodes of "Star Trek," but they were among the series' most dramatic, and their music was tracked throughout nonscored first- and second-season shows: the 1966 "The Enemy Within," with its complex rhythms and grim variations on the Courage fanfare; and the 1967 "The Doomsday Machine," which contained, in Steiner's words, "the brassy, cacophonous, persistently rhythmic motive so often sounding in moments of threatening danger or encounters with outer-space monsters."

Gerald Fried's five episodes included a lively, fun score, incorporating Irish influences, for the lighthearted 1966 "Shore Leave"; strange, rather primitive, music for Spock and the Vulcan ceremonies in the 1967 "Amok Time"; and exotic, American Indian-style woodwinds and percussion for 1968's "The Paradise Syndrome" that hinted at his later scores for such Indian-themed telefilms as "I Will Fight No More Forever" and "The Mystic Warrior."

Fried's approach to the music for Spock, who was forever in denial of his illogical human half, was particularly interesting: "I tried to write something which was emotionally expressive, espressivo, to show this part of him, but I played it with the bass guitar: this thumping, rhythmic drone which is anything but emotional. It doesn't have that ability to convey emotion."

Justman's admiration for George Duning's *Picnic* score led him to sign the composer for the more romantic episodes, including the 1967 alien love story "Metamorphosis," and a pair of sensitive 1968 episodes: the telepath tale "Is There in Truth No Beauty?" and "The Empath," in which Duning's haunting score speaks for the beautiful, mute title character of Gem (Kathryn Hays). Duning claimed to have been the first composer in Hollywood to employ the then-new Yamaha E-3 organ on the latter.

Jerry Fielding wrote just two scores, notable for very different reasons: the 1967 classic "The Trouble with Tribbles," a playful score including a theme for the ship's chief engineer Scotty; and the 1968 sci-fi western "Spectre of the Gun," which in tone, style, and orchestral color (including harmonica and accordion) presaged his Oscar-nominated music for *The Wild Bunch* (1969), on which he was just starting work.

When work began on "Star Trek: The Next Generation" (1987–94, syndicated), Roddenberry insisted on adopting Jerry Goldsmith's theme for *Star Trek: The Motion Picture* (1979) as the theme for the new series, while also approving Justman's idea to preface it with the Courage fanfare as a link to the classic original. The series starred Patrick Stewart as Jean-Luc Picard, captain of a new *Enterprise* in the twenty-fourth century. Three composers were primarily responsible for the music of "Next Generation": Dennis McCarthy, who worked on all seven seasons; Ron Jones (b. 1954), who worked on the first four; and Jay Chattaway (b. 1946), who succeeded Jones. McCarthy received five Emmy nominations for his music on "Next Generation," winning in the 1991–92 season for the two-part "Unification" story that guest-starred Leonard Nimoy as Spock. He also won an Emmy the following year for his main-title theme music for the second spinoff, "Star Trek: Deep Space Nine" (1993–, syndicated).

McCarthy (b. 1944), a former road musician and arranger-conductor for Glen Campbell and a veteran television composer on series including "V," "MacGyver," and "Parker Lewis Can't Lose," discovered early on that the producers of "Next Generation" wanted a markedly different approach from the music of its illustrious predecessor: orchestral, yes, but more subtle, establishing mood, and avoiding the bombast of the original. "I treated everything in the show as the second movement of a symphony," McCarthy said, "even the battle scenes." McCarthy and his colleagues were criticized by some "Trek" fans as failing to perform to the standards of the original, but McCarthy found the directive a creative challenge, "making it exciting, giving you the emotional impact, without making you say, 'Gee, the music's big.' Keeping the music almost subliminal."

Paramount didn't stint on the orchestral forces necessary. McCarthy and his colleagues averaged forty musicians, sometimes more than fifty, but never fewer than thirty-six. The same was true on "Deep Space Nine." McCarthy keyed on the isolation of the far-off outpost in coming up with the theme: "Solo horn in front, solo trumpet later on, big powerful subdued orchestra underneath it," he explained. "Nothing in your face. Restrained power, with the loneliness of the solo instrument."

McCarthy was freer to employ "strange harmonic and odd percussive effects" on "Deep Space Nine." "We had a fresh start and we could be a little more experimental," he said. McCarthy's impressive work on the two "Star Trek" series led to his massive orchestral and choral score for the seventh big-screen film, *Star Trek: Generations* (1994), whose initially ethereal main-title music segued to a spectacular arrangement of the original Courage fanfare—musically embodying the transition between the old and new "Star Trek" casts.

The latest spinoff, "Star Trek: Voyager" (1995–, UPN), with Kate Mulgrew captaining a starship lost in space, sports an original Jerry Goldsmith theme. Goldsmith's sweeping orchestral signature, set to stunning visuals of the ship cruising among the stars and planets, has an innate majesty and a grandeur that has few if any parallels in television music. Explaining his approach, Goldsmith spoke of space as "the last frontier," adding: "When any explorer goes into a new land, they're adventurers. There's always something of a nobility about that." The theme won Goldsmith his fifth Emmy.

In 1969, Rod Serling decided to return to television with a two-hour pilot for a proposed new anthology series to be called "Night Gallery." A huge success both critically and in the ratings, the TV movie spawned a series (1970–73, NBC) that combined fantasy, horror, and sometimes science fiction. Serling was the host (and, as on "Twilight Zone," often the writer), introducing each segment standing next to an original painting inspired by the piece.

Billy Goldenberg's assignment to score the two-hour "Night Gallery" was a direct result of his friendship with then-up-and-coming television director Steven Spielberg. He had already scored the occult telefilm "Fear No Evil" (1969), which included choral music based on devil-worship incantations. Spielberg's segment of the "Night Gallery" pilot starred Joan Crawford, who happened to be one of the composer's favorite actresses. Tipped off by Spielberg, he lobbied both Universal music director Stanley Wilson and producer William Sackheim and won the assignment.

Goldenberg's approach was different for each of the three segments. For the first, in which Roddy McDowall played a greedy young man responsible for his wealthy uncle's death, he scored McDowall's character with "a little synthesizer piece which was very hard-edged but almost sounded like bees buzzing or ants running"; for the second, about a blind woman's desperate ploy to see, he accompanied Crawford grandly with "giant orchestral chords" as she descended a staircase; for the third, he imagined fugitive German war criminal Richard Kiley's hopes of escape into a more peaceful life (as depicted in a gallery painting) with a thirties-era song, with an original German lyric, in the style of Kurt Weill.

Goldenberg's "dark, very Bernard Herrmann-like" theme for the film was not retained for the series because of a change in producers. For the new main title, producer Jack Laird turned to Gil Mellé (b. 1931), who was, at the time, in the midst of creating his groundbreaking all-electronic score for *The Andromeda Strain* (1971). Mellé's background was one of the most eclectic in Hollywood. Born in Jersey City, New Jersey, Mellé was: a self-taught musician; a jazz saxophonist signed to Blue Note Records when he was nineteen; a painter whose art appeared on albums by Miles Davis and Thelonious Monk; and a pioneer in the field of electronic music, building his own instruments and recording the first LP of electronic jazz (*Tome VI*) even before the term "synthesizer" was widely known. Mellé had already scored "Perilous Voyage" for Laird (a telefilm that sat on the shelf until 1976), utilizing a mix of orchestral and electronic music; "My Sweet Charlie" (1970), a landmark TV movie that would win Emmys for actress Patty Duke and writers Richard Levinson and William Link ("Columbo"); and "The Psychiatrist" (1971, NBC), a short-lived Roy Thinnes drama whose theme and episode scores again combined electronic with orchestral music.

His "Night Gallery" theme—television's first all-electronic main title—uti-

Gil Mellé. Courtesy BMI Archives.

lized the same unique inventions as his *Andromeda Strain* score. Its eerie sounds accompanied a series of images of weird paintings and ghoulish faces, setting the tone for the scary happenings to follow. Mellé also composed a small library of music for the series, but most of the scoring chores fell to other composers, including Universal regulars Benny Carter (who provided a nostalgic big-band sound for Serling's Emmy-nominated "They're Tearing Down Tim Riley's Bar"), Robert Prince (b. 1929), and Oliver Nelson. Noted concert composer Paul Glass (b. 1934) wrote superb scores for the Orson Welles-narrated "Silent Snow, Secret Snow" and "The Messiah on Mott Street," both in 1971. Laird's own background as an ex-musician led him to two more surprising choices for "Night Gallery": John Lewis (b. 1920), who had composed the music for *Odds Against Tomorrow* (1959) with his Modern Jazz Quartet, and Eddie Sauter (1914–81), who scored *Mickey One* (1965) with Stan Getz, contributed effective second-season scores. Sauter wrote a new theme for the third season, now as a half-hour series, and scored all of those episodes.

Mellé's association with the genre continued with "Kolchak: The Night Stalker" (1974–75, ABC). Darren McGavin first played irreverent, intrepid newspaper reporter Carl Kolchak in "Dark Shadows" creator Dan Curtis's TV movie "The Night Stalker" (1972), which was an immediate sensation. "The Night Stalker," about a vampire on the loose in modern-day Las Vegas, was scored by Robert Cobert using a unique approach that combined jazz with the musical melodrama of his earlier work for Curtis on the Gothic daytime soap "Dark Shadows" (which Cobert proudly characterized as "really great spook music"); the sequel, "The Night Strangler" (1973), employed the same theme.

McGavin, as executive producer of the weekly series, hired Mellé. Unfortunately, Mellé didn't have as much time to conceptualize the theme as he had hoped. "When do I start?" Mellé asked McGavin. "In twenty minutes," came the reply. "He was serious," recalled the composer. McGavin was about to shoot the main-title sequence, in which the reporter enters the newspaper office late at night and is whistling the theme on-camera.

Mellé protested, but with the clock ticking away, he came up with an idea. He had always liked a subsidiary theme that he had written for a sequence in another Universal pilot, Gene Roddenberry's "The Questor Tapes" (1974). They went into the music library, found the sequence, and whistled the theme into a tape recorder for McGavin—who promptly rode off on his golf cart to shoot the main title. Mellé scored the first four shows, but quit in a dispute with the producers who were at odds with McGavin on the direction of the music. ("Darren wanted me to play it straight," he recalled, despite the series' frequent lighter moments.) Jerry Fielding came in to score several subsequent episodes.

"The Sixth Sense" (1972, ABC), with Gary Collins as a parapsychologist, lasted less than a year but went through four different themes. David Shire wrote the first one and remembered thinking at the time: "At last, a series that uses the occult as a noble force, as a benevolent force. [The theme] was for Oriental cymbals and cello. It was a mantra, a very simple melody, very unlike what I usually do because I was trying to suggest in the theme the psychic ambiance of the guy's mind."

Shire's hypnotic, mystical music lasted just one week. "It was thrown out," Shire recalled, "and the feedback I got was that they wanted something that said 'exciting dramatic series' and 'solving crimes' and all of that." To replace it, Universal music editors went into the library and found an eerie melody that Billy Goldenberg had written for a 1970 episode of "The Name of the Game" (for a dream sequence in which Gene Barry was contemplating suicide); it became the new main title.

Eight months later, Lalo Schifrin recorded a theme that was never used. Again, the producers turned to Goldenberg for a new theme, although his music for the same season's "Ghost Story" (1972, NBC), with its electronically created wails and otherworldly orchestral sounds, was even spookier. Shire, meanwhile, went on to write the theme for the long-running Linda Lavin sitcom "Alice" (1976–85, CBS), and receive multiple Emmy nominations for prestige TV films such as "Raid on Entebbe" (1977, NBC) and the six-hour "The Kennedys of Massachusetts" (1989, ABC).

The success of *Star Wars* led to the inevitable television copycat shows. Writer-producer Glen A. Larson—who had successfully cashed in on several big-screen bonanzas with small-screen variations (*Butch Cassidy and the Sundance Kid* led to "Alias Smith and Jones," *The Sting* led to "Switch," etc.)—came up with two: "Battlestar Galactica" (1978–79, ABC) and "Buck Rogers in the 25th Century" (1979–81, NBC).

"Galactica" was the more watchable of the two, an ambitious saga of an ongoing space battle between the survivors of a devastated human civilization (now searching for their cousins on a far-off planet called Earth) and the race of mechanical beings out to destroy them. The ensemble cast included the fatherly commander (Lorne Greene), his good-guy son (Richard Hatch), his daughter (Maren Jensen), and a hotshot pilot (Dirk Benedict).

Larson had been a member of the Four Preps singing group of the early 1960s, both as songwriter and performer, and Stu Phillips (b. 1929) produced the Four Preps' last single in 1965. A pop record producer ("Blue Moon," "Johnny Angel") who had also achieved success as an arranger-conductor (the Hollyridge Strings) and film and TV composer (1966's *Dead Heat on a Merry-Go-Round,* "The Monkees" in 1966–68), Phillips began his long television association with Larson on "The Six Million Dollar Man" (arranging Dusty Springfield's vocal of Larson's title song for the series' original ninety-minute incarnation) and continued by cowriting the themes and scoring many episodes of "Switch" (1975–78, CBS), "Quincy, M.E." (1976–83, NBC), and "Knight Rider" (1982–86, NBC), among others.

On "Galactica," Larson came up with the brass fanfare that opened the theme, while Phillips did the rest. For the spectacular three-hour pilot (an

Emmy winner for its visual effects) and the subsequent one-hour episodes, Phillips achieved an appropriately *Star Wars*-style sound: swashbuckling, fully orchestral, and multithematic. The pilot score was even performed by the Los Angeles Philharmonic (from 85 to 105 players during the five days of recording) at Twentieth Century-Fox studios, which was ironic because Fox (which released *Star Wars*) was suing Universal at the time over alleged similarities between the film and "Galactica."

For the weekly scores, Phillips recorded with a studio orchestra ranging from 37 to 47 players (often achieving an even "bigger sound" despite the smaller ensemble, Phillips said). Although he wrote new themes for every episode, the formulaic nature of the show allowed him to recycle earlier material to ease the pressure caused by constant, last-minute recutting. "So the twenty-eight minutes [the average amount of music] basically became a jigsaw puzzle," Phillips said, combining new material with already familiar themes for the fighter-ship launches, battles, and love scenes. Phillips was rewarded with a 1978 Grammy nomination for the *"Galactica"* soundtrack album.

Phillips also launched "Buck Rogers," which cast Gil Gerard as the comic-strip hero and Erin Gray as his romantic interest Wilma Deering. Larson contributed a song, "Suspension," as the series theme. "Buck Rogers" later won a music Emmy, for Bruce Broughton's charming score for the 1981 episode "The Satyr."

From these pulp science fiction efforts, televised fantasy took a step back up with the introduction of two high-profile anthology series a few seasons later: "Amazing Stories" (1985–87, NBC) and a revived version of "The Twilight Zone" (1985–87, CBS). Steven Spielberg served as executive producer of the big-budgeted "Amazing Stories," and so naturally recruited his longtime feature film composer John Williams to supply the theme and score those episodes that Spielberg himself planned to direct. Williams's theme, a bravura orchestral fanfare, accompanied a cleverly designed main title that, in one minute, chronicled the history of American storytelling: from an Indian campfire to a family gathered around the TV. In between came computer-animated ancient scrolls, flying books, a ghost, a sword-wielding knight, and a spacecraft rocketing past the earth.

Williams also scored the premiere, the half-hour "Ghost Train" (about an old man's belief that he can atone for a disastrous childhood mistake by catching, seventy-five years later, a train that no longer exists), and the hour-long "The Mission" (a wartime drama, starring Kevin Costner, about a soldier trapped inside the gun turret of a crippled fighter plane). In addition to Williams, the generous musical budget of "Amazing Stories" brought many feature film composers back to the medium, including Jerry Goldsmith, Georges Delerue, James Horner, Michael Kamen, Bruce Broughton, and Johnny Mandel.

"The Twilight Zone" was something else altogether. Producer Philip DeGuere hired The Grateful Dead—the popular rock group with no experience in scoring film—to compose a theme and score early episodes. (Asked about his choice at a predebut press conference, DeGuere replied: "I wanted to go for the leading experts in the Twilight Zone.") Robert Drasnin, the veteran composer who was then CBS West Coast music director, recalled: "Just to get the first episode on the air was such a scene. They spent fifty-two hours in the studio to try to get the one-minute theme. The production costs were enormous. We were always trying to salvage something of theirs."

The new "Twilight Zone" main title was visually interesting but quite grim. The camera gradually receded from a bleak landscape through the window of an empty room, which dissolved into a revolving snow-globe containing images of a fetus, a spider, a doll, and a unicorn. A nuclear explosion gave way to a ghostly image of Rod Serling; the window frame mutated first into a skull and crossbones, then into the show title. The Dead's theme was a series of discordant, mostly percussive, sounds whose only recognizable element was a quotation from the original Marius Constant theme at the instant Serling's image appeared. The music disappeared into a heartbeat by the close of the main title.

In addition to the theme, the group attempted to score the first hour (which consisted of three stories) at their studios near San Francisco. "We ended up dropping music completely from one of them," Drasnin said. "It just wouldn't work and couldn't be fashioned into anything, so we just relied on sound effects. For the others, we kept some of the cues, as many as we could, but we were there [in dubbing] all night trying to salvage that thing."

After two or three disastrous episodes, Drasnin flew to San Francisco to work with them. Merl Saunders, a Bay Area keyboard player who had been friends with the members of the Dead for many years, improvised some scores with the group and handled the music for several others on his own. "By the fourth or fifth show," Drasnin said, CBS management convinced DeGuere that the Dead's attempts to score "The Twilight Zone" had been expensive failures and that film-experienced composers had to be hired. Drummer Mickey Hart, however, continued to do sound design for the series, including musical effects, and Saunders contributed occasional scores.

The roster of "Twilight Zone" composers wasn't the who's-who of "Amazing Stories," but several veterans did sign on. Apart from Drasnin and Fred Steiner, both of whom worked on the original "Twilight Zone," the composers included Morton Stevens, Dennis McCarthy, Basil Poledouris, Craig Safan, and Christopher Young. (Poledouris, incidentally, also arranged the Gounod melody for the updated version of "Alfred Hitchcock Presents" [1985–86, NBC]; he and Safan scored the two-hour pilot.)

The last of the decade's anthology series was "Tales from the Crypt" (1989–, HBO), expensive, high-gloss adaptations of the grisly, often dark-humored stories from the famous EC comics of the 1950s. Movie producers Joel Sill, Robert Zemeckis, and Richard Donner were among the executive producers of this half-hour series, which often featured top stars and directors (and, as on "Amazing Stories," scores by the composers who usually worked for those directors).

Upon hearing of the project, composer Danny Elfman (b. 1954) actually sought out Sill and asked to write the theme. "Nobody loves monsters more than me," Elfman explained, harking back to his childhood love of fantasy and horror and the morbid nature of some of the songs he wrote for his rock 'n' roll band, Oingo Boingo. His intent was simply to write "something dark, creepy, and fun."

Elfman's theme accompanied a virtuoso minute-and-a-half of camerawork and special effects, as the viewer entered an old house, proceeded down torch-lit stairways into a spooky dungeon where the ghoulish Cryptkeeper—part skeleton, part rotting flesh—resided, ready to introduce a new tale with bad, death-related puns. With the sepulchral notes of an organ and the quaint sounds of a harpsichord, it began menacingly and built in intensity, yet its play-ful theme and amusing finale suggested a musical "wink" reminding the viewer not to take all of this too seriously.

The "Tales from the Crypt" theme was actually recorded by the Sinfonia of London during the recording of Elfman's music for the big-screen *Batman* (1989), the result of a last-minute call from Silver. Elfman had "mocked up five or six little pieces on synthesizers" for Silver to choose. Hearing nothing, Elfman figured he had struck out. Two days before he was to leave for London and the *Batman* sessions, Silver called with his choice but said that he needed a finished theme in two weeks. Orchestrated in Los Angeles in Elfman's absence, the music was sent to London and arrived just in time for recording, mixing, and overnighting back to L.A.

"Beauty and the Beast" (1987–90, CBS) was a landmark in the genre. Cine-matically conceived, intelligently written, and classically scored, this modern-day version of the fairy tale won fans among many critics, and almost immedi-ately attracted a cult following. The premise centered on Vincent (Ron Perlman), a gentle, leonine figure who dwelled in a labyrinth beneath the streets of Manhattan, and Catherine (Linda Hamilton), an attorney whose life he had saved and with whom he fell in love.

Creator Ron Koslow gave Lee Holdridge (b. 1944) just five days to score the pilot. Holdridge, born in Haiti and raised in Costa Rica, moved to the United States in 1959 and became arranger/conductor for pop singer Neil Diamond in 1969 (which led to their collaboration on the film and album for *Jonathan Livingston Seagull* in 1973). His symphonic approach and melodic gifts had distinguished big-screen fantasies, including *The Beastmaster* (1982) and *Splash* (1984), and he consciously emulated the Erich Wolfgang Korngold style of swashbuckling music with a rousing score for the short-lived series "Wizards and Warriors" (1983, CBS).

Holdridge was impressed by Koslow's vision of the series as "a fairy tale set in modern-day New York" but was initially stumped for an approach. Watching

Lee Holdridge. Courtesy Academy of Television Arts and Sciences.

the scene in which Catherine is nursed back to health and about to leave Vincent's underground world, Holdridge was struck by the duality of the premise: "The world below is safe, the world above is dangerous. . . . Suddenly a concept hit me: if the music is very diatonic, very melodic, very pure when they're alone together, and then it's more discordant, more dissonant, more polytonal when they're out in the real world . . ."

Holdridge's conceptually simple, stunningly beautiful music set the tone for the wildly romantic series. He scored the first six episodes, and then turned the series over to composer Don Davis, who maintained the high orchestral standard on a weekly basis. Together, their music received five Emmy nominations, winning three (for Holdridge's 1987 pilot, for the song "The First Time I Loved Forever" that he later wrote with Melanie, and for Davis's 1990 "A Time to Heal"). An album, *Of Love and Hope,* featuring Perlman reading poetry to excerpts from their scores, became a best-seller in 1989.

For the bizarre "Twin Peaks" (1990–91, ABC), filmmaker David Lynch turned to his regular composer Angelo Badalamenti (b. 1937). Badalamenti, who composed the music for Lynch's film *Blue Velvet* (1986) and later won

Britain's Anthony Asquith Award for his score for *The Comfort of Strangers* (1991), created a moody, ominous ambiance for Lynch's endlessly quirky, often maddening series about deception and murder in a small town in the Pacific Northwest. The two-hour pilot introduced the characters: an FBI agent (Kyle MacLachlan) who arrived to investigate the brutal murder of teenage Laura Palmer, the local sheriff (Michael Ontkean), the diner owner (Peggy Lipton), the wealthy hotelier (Richard Beymer), his daughter Audrey (Sherilyn Fenn), the mysterious sawmill owner (Joan Chen), and her sworn enemy (Piper Laurie).

Badalamenti composed and performed the score for the pilot, and all of the episodes, at his studio in New York, with just seven musicians (including himself on synthesizers and piano): another synth player, electric guitars, clarinets, tenor saxophone, flutes, and percussion. His approach "came out of all the visuals, the characters and the mood of 'Twin Peaks' that feels very, very natural," the composer explained at the time. Lynch, in asking Badalamenti for a love theme, described in detail what he wanted in terms of musical moods, according to the composer: "He said, 'Well, we need some very slow, dark thematic theme that could tie scenes together and, from this minor feeling, go into a 'climb,' a very beautiful climb, then build to a climax. Let that climax just tear your heart out, just make it so beautiful and yet minimal. Let it peak, then fall down very, very slowly and make that fall go right back into that dark intro.' And I said, 'Oh, okay.'"

As realized, the love theme—which became the heart of the series score—was "kind of mysterious," Badalamenti explained. "It's dark. It covers a lot of

Angelo Badalamenti. Photo by L. Wong, courtesy ABC Television.

ground for 'Twin Peaks,' various types of mystery, certain kinds of darkness, shots of the fan in the hall, those kinds of things." Primarily played on keyboards, it became a frequently used device signaling unsavory activities in the town. First heard with the discovery of the girl's body, its extended version brightened considerably with ascending piano notes, transitioning from minor to major, and, in doing so, becoming a motif associated with Laura Palmer, particularly for flashbacks.

Badalamanti's main-title theme, underscoring bucolic images of life in Twin Peaks (Douglas firs, waterfalls, lumber mills), was a soft and dreamy tune primarily heard on synthesizers and electric guitar; with lyrics by David Lynch, it became a song called "Falling" (one of two hypnotic tunes performed in the pilot by Lynch-Badalamenti discovery Julee Cruise at the local hangout, the Roadhouse). Noted Badalamenti: "The main title theme has an intentional sixties sound; it's not really the sound of the sixties but some of the chord structure is. Julee Cruise in the club has a today kind of sixties sound. But it's not like any recording of sixties music that I've ever known."

Badalamenti wrote leitmotifs for several characters. Finger-snapping and brushes on snare drums were hallmarks of his sensuous theme for Audrey (who, in one of the series' more infamous moments, tied a cherry stem into a knot with her tongue), who would often be seen dancing by herself to some fifties-ish cool jazz tune in the diner. "She's in her own world," Badalamenti observed, "and the music seems to work very well when she's in her little naughty mood."

The pilot set the "retro" tone and launched so many of the themes that a number of cues were simply tracked into subsequent episodes, although Badalamenti continued to write new music, and new arrangements of old cues, throughout the series' run. He received three Emmy nominations (for series scoring, original song, and main title theme) and a Grammy (Best Pop Instrumental Performance) for his "Twin Peaks" music, then reprised many of the themes in his music for *Twin Peaks: Fire Walk with Me* (1992), the big-screen, postseries prequel.

"The X-Files" (1993– , Fox) demanded an altogether different approach: executed entirely with state-of-the-art synthesizers and sampling devices but without the clichés brought on by too many electronic scores in the wake of "Miami Vice" and its many clones of recent years. Executive producer Chris Carter, who created the series about FBI agents investigating unexplained phenomena, chose Mark Snow (b. 1946) as his composer. Snow was a Brooklyn-born, Juilliard-trained oboist and drummer who, with fellow Juilliard student Michael Kamen, was a founding member of the New York Rock 'n' Roll Ensemble during the late 1960s. Snow came to Los Angeles in the early seventies and found steady work in television, including writing the theme and weekly scores for the popular, lighthearted Robert Wagner-Stefanie Powers mystery "Hart to Hart" (1979–84, ABC). His reputation grew with his Emmy-nominated TV movie scores, including "Something About Amelia" and "Oldest Living Confederate Widow Tells All."

Carter gave Snow specific directives about the music for the "X-Files" pilot: "He said he hated melody, but he loved atmospheric and minimal," the composer recalled. Steve Reich and Philip Glass were among the modern composers cited as possible models for the score. Snow created the theme entirely apart from the visuals that came to accompany it: images of flying saucers, distorted faces, disconnected phrases like "government denies knowledge," the FBI identification tags of lead characters Fox Mulder (David Duchovny) and Dana Scully (Gillian Anderson), and finally a human eye that becomes a rapidly moving nighttime sky as the backdrop for the series' catch line "the truth is out there."

After several false starts, Snow came up with an echoing rhythmic figure—"dark, atmospheric, moody," in the words of the composer—and, later, "this light, eerie, whistling over it." Both elements were accidental discoveries: his synthesizer's delay-echo switch just happened to be turned on, and the whistling sound was a matter of turning a knob on one of his synthesizer units, completely altering the sound while playing the same musical notes.

In terms of the weekly dramatic scores, Snow explained, "Real melodic, obviously emotional music is out. But there can be dark, brooding chords with broad, Brahmsian or Bruckner-style melodies. Almost Wagnerian sometimes, or dark Liszt [in tone]."

Snow's music (an Emmy nominee in its first season) quickly became a crucial factor in setting the creepy, often unsettling mood of the series. Some weeks Snow, working in his own Santa Monica studio, writes and performs as much as forty minutes of music—including "a lot of quiet, sustaining, atmospheric stuff"—to underscore everything from low-key dialogue scenes to bizarre moments involving extraterrestrial visitors. "Through that first year, it was fine-tuned to what [the musical concept] is now," Snow said. "It's more adventurous than at the beginning, less self-conscious. I'm feeling completely uninhibited about doing and trying anything."

Man, Woman, Birth, Death, Infinity

Drama

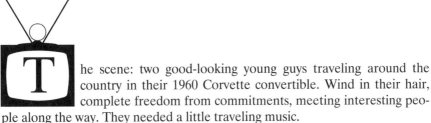

he scene: two good-looking young guys traveling around the country in their 1960 Corvette convertible. Wind in their hair, complete freedom from commitments, meeting interesting people along the way. They needed a little traveling music.

With Nelson Riddle at the wheel, they got it in "Route 66" (1960–64, CBS). Martin Milner and George Maharis were the actors, but they tooled along the highways of America to an infectious theme penned by one of the all-time great arrangers. Riddle (1921–85) had been a trombone player and arranger in the Tommy Dorsey Orchestra, and, after World War II, an arranger for NBC Radio in Hollywood. His hit arrangements of "Mona Lisa" and "Unforgettable" for Nat King Cole led to a long stay at Capitol Records and several significant album projects with Frank Sinatra, Judy Garland, and Ella Fitzgerald; and he was musical director on weekly TV variety shows headlined by Sinatra, Cole, and Rosemary Clooney in the late 1950s.

Riddle's "Route 66" theme—piano playing a jazzy little riff while a generous string section rises and falls, followed by building brass, all to a driving beat in the rhythm section—somehow said "open road" to millions of viewers (and, in 1962, record buyers who turned Riddle's theme into a hit, earning him two Grammy nominations for composing and arranging). Years later, Riddle observed: "I think [the music] gets the intriguing mysticism which often generates at the beginning of a trip. There's a big question mark, that notion that this is going to be a little different. There's the persistence of sound, of motion, the romance of seeing them drive down this highway." The composer's son, band-

Nelson Riddle. Photo by George Fields.

leader Christopher Riddle, later recalled his father saying that the "Route 66" theme should be played with "urgency, like the accelerator is down."

Producer Herbert B. Leonard, who filmed "Route 66" on location around the country, was an admirer who wanted Riddle to write the weekly scores for the series—but not, initially, the theme. "I chased Andre Previn for nine thousand years to sell me 'Like Young,'" Leonard recalled. "Like Young," written by Previn—then a popular jazz pianist as well as film composer (*The Subterraneans, Elmer Gantry,* both 1960)—and recorded with the lush strings of bandleader David Rose, had been a hit in 1959. Jazz piano, insistent beat, the famous Rose string section: some of the elements were there. "I couldn't get it," Leonard said. "So I said, 'Listen, Nelson, I love this piece. I don't want you to steal it, but I want you to capture the tempo and the style.' And he came up with the theme, and I fell in love with it."

Riddle not only wrote the theme, he scored the show on a week-to-week basis, with an orchestra that averaged twenty-six players. His orchestrator, Gil Grau, consistently received screen credit (a departure from television tradition). But, although the theme had a jazzy feel, much of Riddle's scoring consisted of straight dramatic writing: Buzz and Tod's encounters on the road brought them into all kinds of dramatic situations, enabling Riddle to write a wide variety of music.

The same was true of Leonard's other dramatic series, "Naked City" (1958–59, 1960–63, ABC). In its first-season half-hour format, with James Franciscus and John McIntire as New York City police detectives, the series had an original theme by George Duning (which, with Ned Washington lyrics, was turned into a "soundtrack" LP that had little connection to the series). The dramatic underscore consisted entirely of library tracks.

When "Naked City" returned in a one-hour format, Paul Burke and Horace McMahon became the stars, and Leonard commissioned Billy May (b. 1916) to write the theme and scores. Like Riddle, May was widely known for his arranging skills, having charted "Cherokee" for Charlie Barnet and a number of songs for Glenn Miller during the war years. His own successful big-band recordings of the 1950s led to a long stint writing for TV and films in the sixties and seventies. "Billy was perfect for New York," Leonard said, referring to the fact that "Naked City" was filmed on Manhattan locations. Leonard wanted a "sophisticated" sound, May recalled, one that May realized with a strong statement for orchestra, prominently featuring the brass section.

Another Leonard innovation, used in both "Route 66" and "Naked City," was the elimination of standard main-title sequences in favor of titles superimposed over the conclusion of the action in the teaser. To accommodate this format, a brief statement of the theme (often integrated into the score) was heard under the titles. Then, a more developed version of the theme was heard over the opening titles in the first act, and, in the case of "Naked City," a reprise over the famous concluding narration ("There are eight million stories in the naked city; this has been one of them").

May remembered the band as including six brass and four woodwind players, plus harp and percussion; only rarely was he able to use strings. "We had a theme for the detective's girlfriend [Libby, played by Nancy Malone], and when we introduced her, I talked them into letting me use six celli. Then every time there would be a show where she was prominent, they had to let me use the celli again. Over the budget, you know." As on "Route 66," the orchestrator (on "Naked City," often Bill Loose) received screen credit along with the composer.

Leonard, who disapproved of library tracks, insisted on original scores for most of his "Route 66" and "Naked City" episodes. All told, Riddle and May are believed to have written an estimated two hundred scores for these shows. Riddle created a new theme for the final season of "Naked City" in the fall of 1962.

Pete Rugolo created his own kind of traveling music for two successful series: "The Fugitive" (1963–67, ABC) and "Run for Your Life" (1965–68, NBC). Rugolo's earlier connection with David Janssen on "Richard Diamond, Private Detective," and the fact that they frequently socialized, may have been a factor in his getting the assignment to write "The Fugitive." Janssen played Dr. Richard Kimble, "an innocent victim of blind justice," as William Conrad's opening narration explained every week over Rugolo's propulsive theme:

Pete Rugolo. Photo by Alexander Courage.

"Falsely convicted for the murder of his wife, reprieved by fate when a train wreck freed him en route to the death house. . . ."

John Elizalde, then on loan from Daystar to producer Quinn Martin, worked with Rugolo to develop an entire library of cues for the series. The composer did not recall seeing a pilot. Elizalde "gave me an idea of what the character was about, and that in the main title he would be running and that [the music] should be a fast-moving piece," Rugolo said. Rugolo composed and orchestrated approximately ninety minutes of music. "I wrote a lot of variations," he said. "Every possible kind of suspense. I wrote a theme for Gerard [the police lieutenant, played by Barry Morse], a few love themes, some neutral cues, some sad cues. I wrote a lot of chases, because I knew he would be running a lot. Opening themes, act endings based on the theme. Dance pieces. All those things they used over and over."

Elizalde took the music to London, where it was recorded with a fifty-five-piece orchestra, "mostly members of the London Symphony Orchestra," Elizalde recalled; Harry Rabinowitz conducted. That library, recorded over a period of four days, formed the basis of the music for all four seasons of the series, because no single episode actually received an original score—an unusual situation for a prime-time hit in the sixties.

Supplementing the Rugolo library was music from the CBS library, which was licensed by Quinn Martin for tracking purposes. Because many of the cues heard in "The Fugitive" had originally been written for shows like "Gunsmoke" and "The Twilight Zone," "for all intents and purposes it was a Jerry Goldsmith-Benny Herrmann show," Elizalde said. (Elizalde, in fact, credits Goldsmith's agreement to write "Barnaby Jones" to the composer's substantial royalties from "The Fugitive"—a series he never actually wrote for. Elizalde ran into Goldsmith one day at lunch, right after the announcement that Kimble was soon to be exonerated in the two-part series finale. According to Elizalde, Goldsmith quipped, "John, what's this I hear, they're going to cancel our show?")

Roy Huggins, who created but did not produce "The Fugitive," had been a Stan Kenton fan and was aware that Rugolo's arrangements were a major factor in Kenton's sound. He hired Rugolo to score "Run for Your Life," a drama about a lawyer (Ben Gazzara) who learned that he had an incurable disease and had, at most, two years to live. Again, Rugolo wrote a bold and brassy signature, filled with movement, and remained with the show through its three seasons on the air. "I loved doing that show," Rugolo recalled. "I tried to write a fast theme, a moving theme, at the beginning. I would write jazz chases, and there were a lot of shows where Gazzara would go to different countries. He would go to Spain, and I would write a concerto with guitar. I had to write German music, Italian music, Japanese, Chinese. . . ."

He was rewarded with an Emmy nomination in the music-composition area for all three years of the series, and afterward became Huggins's virtual house composer, working on his subsequent series including "The Outsider" with Darren McGavin (1968–69, NBC), the lawyers segment of "The Bold Ones" with Burl Ives (1969–72, NBC), "Cool Million" with James Farentino (1972–73, NBC), and "Toma" with Tony Musante (1973–74, ABC). Both of his Emmys were earned for Huggins projects: the TV movie "The Challengers" (1970), about race-car drivers preparing for the Grand Prix, and for a 1971 episode of "The Bold Ones."

Meanwhile, at the hospital . . .

Two major medical dramas debuted within a span of five days in the fall of 1961: "Dr. Kildare" (1961–66, NBC) and "Ben Casey" (1961–66, ABC). "Kildare" starred Richard Chamberlain and Raymond Massey in the first television adaptation of the Max Brand characters that inspired a series of MGM films in the 1930s and 1940s; Chamberlain played the young intern James Kildare and Massey his crusty mentor Dr. Gillespie. "Casey," an original idea by James Moser (who created "Medic"), starred Vince Edwards as a neurosurgeon and Sam Jaffe as his wise old boss, Dr. Zorba.

Musically speaking, the approaches to a similar dramatic framework were markedly different. Producer Norman Felton, who had been impressed by Jerry Goldsmith's creativity on "Studio One in Hollywood," prevailed upon the up-and-coming composer to create a romantic musical signature for the hand-some Kildare. Goldsmith responded with a memorable fanfare, a series of stately brass chords that announced the setting: the modern and efficient Blair General Hospital. This formed the underpinning of the melody which, in a vocal version sung by Chamberlain himself, became a top-10 hit in early 1963. (The fanfare, incidentally, was originally written by the composer for one of the dramatic anthology series at CBS in the late fifties.) Goldsmith scored five of the first seven episodes. Carmen Dragon (1914–84), in what is believed to be his only work for television, composed two subsequent 1961 shows.

The vast majority—more than eighty episodes of "Dr. Kildare" over the five seasons—was scored by MGM workhorse Harry Sukman. Sukman won his own series the following year with "The Eleventh Hour" (1962–64, NBC), a literate psychiatry drama starring Wendell Corey; Sukman scored nearly forty of those hours as well. (An earlier "Kildare" pilot, produced in 1960 with a theme by "FBI" composer Bronislau Kaper, was never aired.)

For "Ben Casey," the producers sought out David Raksin (b. 1912), the venerable feature film composer whose score for *Laura* (1944) is one of the most memorable film scores ever written, and whose theme is also one of the most recorded tunes in history. The composer, who began his Hollywood career working with Charles Chaplin on *Modern Times* (1936), scored a wide variety of films including *Forever Amber* (1947), *Force of Evil* (1948), and *The Bad and the Beautiful* (1952).

Raksin, then in the midst of writing the jazz score for John Cassavetes's

David Raksin. Courtesy the composer.

film *Too Late Blues* (1962), was reluctant to take on a television pilot. A screening of the well-written hour, however, convinced the composer. There was no main-title sequence in the film; he was simply told that it would contain scenes of a desperately ill patient being wheeled through hospital corridors into an operating room where his/her life must be saved. Raksin's response was "oh, urgency and tension," and he immediately came up with the rhythmic concept for "Ben Casey."

Written in 5/4, then an unusual time signature for a TV theme, Raksin's brass and percussion propelled the viewer through the main-title visuals, which were shot entirely from the patient's point of view (on that rolling gurney, looking up at the lights and the doors being passed through) and concluding with Casey's arrival and the beginning of his examination. Preceding the main title is one of the sixties' most famous opening scenes: Zorba's solemn recitation of five words—"man, woman, birth, death, infinity"—while an anonymous hand draws the universal symbols for each of those five concepts on a blackboard.

Raksin composed the pilot score (although he did not conduct the recording, which took place in Belgium for financial reasons). A library of music based on Raksin's score was written by other composers, but the majority of first-season episodes were tracked with library music. George Bassman, Richard Markowitz, and Walter Scharf scored many subsequent episodes, and one 1965 episode (interestingly titled "Eulogy in Four Flats") was even scored by "Kildare" 's Jerry Goldsmith.

Raksin's theme for "Breaking Point" (1963–64, ABC), a psychiatry drama starring Paul Richards (and also produced by Bing Crosby Productions, which made "Ben Casey"), was equally sophisticated, with a melancholy opening played by four alto flutes.

Several years later, a similar dueling medical series competition began. "Marcus Welby, M.D." (1969–76, ABC) and "Medical Center" (1969–76, CBS) debuted on consecutive nights. "Marcus Welby" starred Robert Young as a kindly general practitioner and James Brolin as his young associate, while "Medical Center" featured Chad Everett as a surgeon and James Daly as his mentor.

Leonard Rosenman (b. 1924) scored all seven years of "Marcus Welby." The composer's roots were in the concert world, having studied with modern classical composers Roger Sessions and Arnold Schoenberg, and noted conductor Serge Koussevitsky. He happened to be James Dean's piano teacher when Dean was filming *East of Eden* (1955), which led Elia Kazan to commission Rosenman's first film score for the Steinbeck classic. He later scored Dean's *Rebel Without a Cause* (1955); for *The Cobweb* (1955), he composed the first twelve-tone score for a commercial Hollywood film.

From a dramatic orchestral opening, Rosenman's first-season "Welby" arrangement stressed the old-fashioned nature of Welby's practice by using a

Leonard Rosenman. Courtesy the composer.

harmonica to state his theme; subsequent seasons would feature a more conventional approach with strings, and later, solo trumpet, playing the melody.

During the first several seasons of "Welby," Rosenman wrote original music for an average of twelve of the twenty-four episodes. The remainder would be tracked with the earlier music, occasionally leading to unexpectedly comic—for the composer—transpositions of the material: "Sometimes during the operations I had a chance to do some odd music. I remember I wrote a sequence for a brain operation, and a few months later I happened to watch 'Marcus Welby' just to see what they were doing, and now the brain music was on during a mastectomy," he said. "Welby" occupied Rosenman's attention during the late summer and early fall (with an occasional single episode or two to be scored later in the season), enabling him to concentrate on concert-music commissions, teaching, and occasional big-screen film scores such as *A Man Called Horse* (1970), *Barry Lyndon* (1975), and *Bound for Glory* (1976), the latter two earning him Academy Awards.

The pilot for "Medical Center" was scored by Lalo Schifrin (b. 1932), an Argentinean composer who studied with noted modern composer Olivier Messiaen at the Paris Conservatory, later joined trumpeter Dizzy Gillespie's jazz band, and began scoring for films and television in the early 1960s. By the time he did "Medical Center," Schifrin had amassed two Oscar nominations (for *Cool Hand Luke,* 1967, and *The Fox,* 1968), four Grammys (for composing

"The Cat," 1964, and *Jazz Suite on the Mass Texts,* 1965, plus two for the *"Mission: Impossible"* soundtrack album, 1967), and four Emmy nominations (for "The Making of the President 1964" and three for "Mission: Impossible").

Schifrin's original "Medical Center" theme was a solemn affair, suggestive of the daily life-and-death struggles at the university medical facility; it was heard in the pilot and under the first-season end titles. (The original main-title sequence was without music, using only a heartbeat and a sound montage of the voices of anonymous hospital personnel.)

For its second season, "Medical Center" went hip with an upbeat new Schifrin theme that began with electric guitars and rhythm section and segued quickly into an ascending synthesizer tone to aerial shots of an ambulance en route to the facility. "I see an ambulance coming, and I thought, why not do the siren so that the same sound becomes [a musical] pitch? So I did it with a big Moog synthesizer. There was no other instrument that could do that [at the time]." He received two more Grammy nominations for the new "Medical Center" theme (composition and arrangement) in 1970. Schifrin wrote several "Medical Center" scores, and, although it was an MGM series, a number of Fox veterans came over to write individual scores including Alexander Courage, Arthur Morton, and (for the very first episode) "Ben Casey" composer David Raksin.

Schifrin's use of a Moog in the "Medical Center" main title was unusual for its era. Not so by the time of "St. Elsewhere" (1982–88, NBC), the theme of which was executed entirely electronically by composer Dave Grusin (b. 1934). A highly respected jazz artist as well as a multi-Oscar-nominated composer for films, Grusin's music had distinguished such pictures as *The Heart Is a Lonely Hunter* (1968), *Three Days of the Condor* (1975), *The Champ* (1979), and *On Golden Pond* (1981). He would later win an Oscar for his music for *The Milagro Beanfield War* (1988).

Ed Flanders, Norman Lloyd, and William Daniels headed the ensemble cast of this critically acclaimed drama about the professional and personal lives of the personnel at Boston's St. Eligius Hospital (derisively termed "St. Elsewhere" because of its hospital-of-last-resort reputation). The winner of thirteen Emmys over its six seasons, it was the finest hospital drama in the history of the medium.

Grusin's bright, catchy theme for "St. Elsewhere" played against images of the hospital and its characters, each of which began in black-and-white and became color. "The approach was just to try and find some alternative way to do what every TV show has to have anyway, but to try to do it electronically," Grusin explained. "If I had done it acoustically, maybe it wouldn't have been as unique in some way." Grusin created the sounds at his GRP record studios in New York City.

Discussing the television theme in general, Grusin said, "There needs to be something distinctive about the sound right off the top, because that's what will get people in from the other room or keep them from turning the dial. It's a constant challenge. It used to be a lot of energy, a lot of tempo, a lot of contemporary 'today' kind of feel and so forth. And that's not necessarily going to save you if everybody else is doing the same thing."

Grusin scored the pilot, but the remainder of the six years of "St. Elsewhere" was scored by J. A. C. Redford, who received two Emmy nominations for his consistently sensitive music for the series.

Courtroom dramas have been a staple of television entertainment almost from the beginning. "Perry Mason" (1957–66, CBS) became television's definitive lawyer show, adapting Erle Stanley Gardner's characters for the small screen in a way that captured the fancy of viewers for nine mostly high-rated seasons. Raymond Burr played the shrewd defense attorney; Barbara Hale was his secretary Della Street, William Hopper his investigator Paul Drake, William Talman was prosecutor Hamilton Burger, and Ray Collins was police lieutenant Tragg.

As the camera moves slowly through a courtroom, deserted except for Mason seated at the defense table studying some brief, the music begins with a decisive bit of orchestral drama. Pause: Mason looks up from his papers and smiles. The theme begins with swinging trombones and insistent piano notes, while muted brass and strings play the familiar melody as the credits appear. It sounds simple; it was anything but. Fred Steiner, who worked regularly at CBS

Fred Steiner, 1959. Courtesy the composer.

throughout this period, wrote the "Perry Mason" theme. Steiner and CBS music director Lud Gluskin "had this idea that the music for 'Perry Mason' should be a combination of his two sides: the suave, well-dressed man about town, so that you had a kind of sophisticated sound. And then you have him dealing with criminals and crime, and historically, you associate jazz with the lower, seamy sides of life.

"At that point, R & B [rhythm and blues] was the big thing, and the R & B rhythm, without associating it with crime, just seemed like what I was looking for. The idea became to write something that would have a contemporary beat for that side of him, and yet have this symphonic sound to represent him as the kind of guy who goes to the opera. So that was the idea, and the theme was very difficult to write. It sounds easy now, but I must have gone through four or five different versions," Steiner said.

Following standard practice in those days at CBS, the theme was recorded outside the United States (initially, in Mexico, Steiner recalled). The composer also wrote a library of theme variations and mood music for use in the series. Individual shows were tracked with this, and other music from the CBS library. Original scores were only rarely commissioned; Jerry Goldsmith wrote two in 1959 and Richard Shores composed several during the final season. Steiner wasn't given screen credit until late in the series' run.

"The Defenders" (1961–65, CBS) also dealt with the law, but it took a completely different approach. E. G. Marshall and Robert Reed played father-and-son defense attorneys in this hour drama filmed on location in New York City. Reginald Rose, who won an Emmy for writing "Twelve Angry Men" for "Studio One" in 1954, created "The Defenders"; neither he nor executive producer Herbert Brodkin ("Playhouse 90") shied away from potentially controversial subjects.

For "The Defenders," Leonard Rosenman created one of the great fanfares in television history. To scenes of the U.S. courthouse complex in Manhattan's Foley Square, a solo trumpet set the tone, followed by a sweeping orchestral theme, and, once again, that solo trumpet. Before he sat down to write the theme, Rosenman was asked to write music that would "express the law." Rosenman scoffed at the notion: "That's a literary idea, it's not a musical idea," the composer pointed out. "Music can't describe that. If music is associated with, let's say, a pictorial thing which describes a courthouse, then from then on when you hear it, you will think of the law." The association of music and image worked: Rosenman's theme, linked in viewers' minds with the courthouse and the faces of integrity-conscious Marshall and Reed on those steps, came to suggest the dignity of the American legal system.

Another filmed-in-New York series that tackled serious social issues was "East Side/West Side" (1963–64, CBS), which starred George C. Scott as a dedicated social worker, Elizabeth Wilson as his supervisor, and Cicely Tyson as the office secretary. Too controversial for network executives, too downbeat for many viewers, "East Side/West Side"—which attempted substantive stories

Kenyon Hopkins, 1963. Photo by Sheldon Secunda, courtesy R. A. Israel Collection.

about everything from drug addiction to child abuse—was canceled after a single season.

Executive producer David Susskind's music supervisor Bob Israel recommended Kenyon Hopkins (1932–83) to score the series. "What we wanted was a really gritty, angular sound," Israel recalled, the feeling that Hopkins had created in his score for the Paul Newman pool-hall drama *The Hustler* (1961). Hopkins had also scored *Baby Doll* (1956) and *The Fugitive Kind* (1959), and written a jazz album for producer Creed Taylor titled *The Sound of New York* (1959). That "sound" was what the series demanded. Hopkins's arresting main- and end-title music accompanied rapidly moving images of subway trains seen from several different perspectives: from the platforms, watching them pass by at high speeds; from the front, looking ahead into the tunnels; and from the final car, watching the lights recede into darkness.

Jazz was the predominant form in the series, and Hopkins received both an

Emmy nomination and a Grammy nomination for his work on "East Side/West Side." In a similar vein, although scored for smaller jazz combinations, was his work for "The Reporter" (1964, CBS), a short-lived series, created by playwright Jerome Weidman, with Harry Guardino as a New York City newspaper columnist.

Two decades later, social issues would be examined in a legal context on a regular basis in "L.A. Law" (1986–94, NBC), one of producer Steven Bochco's ensemble dramas. It originally featured actors Harry Hamlin, Susan Dey, Richard Dysart, and Corbin Bernsen in a weekly series of plots and subplots about a high-powered Los Angeles law firm, its personnel, and its always fascinating caseload. As he had on "Hill Street Blues," Bochco turned to composer Mike Post for music. But, with plenty of lead time before "L.A. Law" was to go on the air, Bochco made Post work overtime to come up with a theme. The one that finally ended up in the series was the composer's fifth attempt.

After four "respectful" rejections, Post said, he called Bochco and pilot director Gregory Hoblit (who had designed the main-title visuals, from the trunk closing to the Century City skyscrapers) into his Burbank studio and, piece by piece, with input from Bochco and Hoblit, assembled the now-familiar "L.A. Law" main title.

"Let's do this logically," Post recalled saying. "It's the law: it is grand, powerful, majestic, fair. French horns, right? Okay. Now, it's California, so it's got to have some sass to it, and I can't do the Beach Boys because it shouldn't be a shuffle. 'Born in the USA,' right? Here's the big snare drum thing: mm-mm-kish, mm-mm-kish, you guys like this tempo?" Post noodled various licks at the keyboard until Bochco and Hoblit agreed on a melody. "Now, I said, what else is this show about? It's about sex! Either the screwing that's being done or the screwing the lawyers are giving the clients. Alto saxophone. Nobody's done Junior Walker. . . . They sat on the couch, lick for lick, and when I was done, I said, that's your theme." It won a Grammy as Best Instrumental Composition.

Added Bochco: "Mike is very generous of spirit in the work process and he will work endlessly until you're happy. He's not happy until you're happy. And he's as creatively undefensive as anyone I've ever worked with. He makes it fun. He humors us, and helps us to understand his process." Both Post and Bochco speak wistfully of their favorite Post theme for a failed series: "Bay City Blues" (1983, NBC), about a minor-league baseball team. "It was like an anthem; it had a sad grandeur to it," Bochco recalled.

"Shannon's Deal" (1990–91, NBC) was a very different story. Filmmaker John Sayles (*Eight Men Out*) had written the pilot about a disillusioned Philadelphia lawyer (Jamey Sheridan) with a gambling problem. Producer Stan Rogow, remembering Duke Ellington's musical contribution to *Anatomy of a Murder* (1959), sought eight-time Grammy-winning trumpeter Wynton Marsalis to compose the score. "Wynton and jazz resonate into the past, but Wynton specifically has a very contemporary flavor," Rogow said. "That felt to be a perfect match to Jack Shannon and 'Shannon's Deal,' which is hopefully very contemporary, but the character and the style and the texture do go back even into the forties in terms of film."

Marsalis, then twenty-seven, had not previously scored a film. He explained that he spent "maybe a month" working out the themes, then two days in a New York recording studio with eight of his own sidemen, improvising to the picture. "The music is mainly there to give spice to the film," he said. "You don't really need a lot of instruments. What you need is music that will lend an air of drama or beauty. That can be one instrument or a hundred and one. Mainly," he added, "I'm just trying to use the language of the blues."

In addition to the two-hour pilot, Marsalis composed individual scores for several episodes of the critically acclaimed, short-lived drama series. Fellow jazz artists David Benoit, Tom Scott, and Lee Ritenour also contributed scores, making "Shannon's Deal" a rare and welcome excursion back into the jazz sound that made so many sixties series memorable.

Television went to war with "Combat!" (1962–67, ABC), which featured some of the most sophisticated music written for the medium to that point. Vic Morrow and Rick Jason starred in this black-and-white, war-is-hell chronicle of one infantry platoon's experiences in Europe during World War II.

Leonard Rosenman's lively march, punctuated by the sounds of bomb bursts and illustrated by a parade of rifles with fixed bayonets before portraits of Morrow and Jason, set the heroic tone during "Combat"'s main title. The dramatic underscores, however, were quite apart from the traditional "Caissons Go Rolling Along" style of so much war-movie music.

"I was living in Rome during that time," Rosenman said, "doing a great deal of conducting and also busy doing all the music for 'Combat,' which was a library. Some of it was very experimental. Since you were dealing with torture, pain, violence, war, human emotions on a large scale—the fact that it was not a period piece or a love story—I could utilize a lot of the techniques of the twentieth century. Also, since the film was not on the screen and I just did them as pieces, I could do them the way I wanted.

"These were basically sketches for compositions of my own. It was almost abstract, very dissonant," Rosenman said, comparing them in style to the music that would later bring avant-garde composer Gyorgy Ligeti to prominence (particularly after some of Ligeti's music appeared on the soundtrack of Stanley Kubrick's *2001: A Space Odyssey* in 1968). He even gave them titles like "Tortured Crawling" and "More Tortured Crawling."

Rosenman conducted a one-hundred-piece symphony orchestra for the "Combat" music, annually sending back new additions to the series library for tracking purposes. The pilot, and a handful of episodes, were actually scored "to picture," but the vast majority were cut together by music editors back in the states.

"After four years, I got so tired of writing music for Germans crawling through the bushes," Rosenman said, "I wrote a letter to the producer at the time, and typed it out like an army directive ('subject,' 'to'), requesting a transfer to the Pacific." In fact, the same producers were then preparing a pilot about the war in the South Pacific ("Attack" with Gary Conway and Warren Oates, 1966), which Rosenman scored; the show didn't sell. Rosenman did, however, score one more war series: "Garrison's Guerillas" (1967–68, ABC) with Ron Harper.

Equally interesting was Rosenman's music for one of the legendary unsold pilots of the sixties: "Alexander the Great" (1964, ABC) starring the pre-"Star Trek" William Shatner in the title role (and a surprising cast that included Joseph Cotten, John Cassavetes, and a pre-"Batman" Adam West). Rosenman consulted a Greek scholar on lyrics and, while in Rome, wrote a score for symphony orchestra (minus violins) and large men's chorus (singing, in Greek, about the conqueror of the ancient world). Highly dramatic, including colorful music suggestive of the era—using obscure instruments to evoke exotic sounds—the score for "Alexander the Great," like the show itself, was heard once and unfortunately forgotten.

Dominic Frontiere took a more traditional approach to his two war dramas, "12 O'Clock High" (1964–67, ABC) and "The Rat Patrol" (1966–68, ABC). "12 O'Clock High" was an adaptation of the 1949 Gregory Peck film, the story of air force bombardiers stationed in England during World War II, with Robert Lansing as their commander during the first season and Paul Burke as their leader during the second and third.

Frontiere, a pilot himself, wrote a patriotic-style anthem as its theme, and imbued the scores with an unmistakable wild-blue-yonder quality. He approached the series this way: "My theory was, everybody knew who won the war. What we were looking at were stories about how we won the war. And a lot of stories were going to be about people who died fighting that war. So I wrote this anthem, as opposed to a let's-go-to-war military march." He remained with the series throughout its duration, although he took time out in 1966 to write the theme and a library of music that was recorded in Munich for "The Rat Patrol."

Unlike "12 O'Clock High," which was an hour of Lansing scowling interrupted occasionally by some strong aerial footage, "Rat Patrol" was an action-packed half hour with Christopher George as the leader of a quartet that took on Rommel's Afrika Korps practically single-handed every week. The main title was particularly impressive, with images of American jeeps sailing over giant sand dunes in pursuit of German tanks set to Frontiere's upbeat martial music.

TV turned decidedly antiwar with "M*A*S*H" (1972–83, CBS), an adaptation of director Robert Altman's 1970 black comedy about a Mobile Army Surgical Hospital unit during the Korean War. The doctors and nurses initially stationed at the 4077th included Hawkeye Pierce (Alan Alda), Trapper John McIntire (Wayne Rogers), Henry Blake (McLean Stevenson), Hot Lips

Johnny Mandel. Courtesy the composer.

Houlihan (Loretta Swit), Frank Burns (Larry Linville), and Radar O'Reilly (Gary Burghoff). For music, writer Larry Gelbart and director Gene Reynolds turned to Johnny Mandel (b. 1935), who had scored the film for Altman, and who had suggested a key scene-linking device that the director used throughout the film: the loudspeaker announcements and playing of bad Japanese jazz from Radio Tokyo.

The composer created a new, instrumental, arrangement of his "Suicide Is Painless" film song, "but with the same flavor as the one over the main title of the movie, with the guitars," Mandel recalled. The music provided an unexpected and gentle counterpoint to manic main-title scenes of "people running with stretchers, and choppers coming in, the kind of thing you normally associated with very hyper music," he added.

Mandel, who arranged for Count Basie's orchestra and Sid Caesar's classic "Your Show of Shows" in the 1950s, worked only occasionally in television but had written some of the most significant film music of recent years: the innovative jazz score for *I Want to Live* (1958), and music for three films whose themes became popular standards: "Emily" from *The Americanization of Emily* (1964), the Oscar-winning "The Shadow of Your Smile" from *The Sandpiper* (1965), and "A Time for Love" from *An American Dream* (1966).

"China Beach" (1988–91, ABC) captured the Vietnam War experience in terms more dramatic and personal than any other series. Dana Delany, Marg

Helgenberger, Robert Picardo, Jeff Kober, and Michael Boatman were among the cast of this superbly written and acted chronicle of the experiences of personnel stationed at a medical facility near Da Nang.

John Rubinstein (b. 1946), the actor-composer who had scored *Jeremiah Johnson* (1972), written the theme for "Family" (1976–80, ABC), and scored the Emmy-winning Jane Fonda drama "The Dollmaker" (1984), composed a plaintive theme for harmonica, piano, and strings for "China Beach." He scored the two-hour pilot and the two-hour finale; Paul Chihara composed many of the weekly scores. However, the main-title theme, per network edict, wound up being "Reflections," the 1968 hit by Diana Ross and the Supremes, just one of dozens of period tunes used to evoke the era in the series. Rubinstein's theme was heard over the end titles.

Some of the most fertile ground for original music in television through the years has been in the realm of the dramatic anthology. What is generally thought of as TV's Golden Age, the live broadcasts of the 1950s, is based largely on the weekly dramatic anthologies that produced classic scripts such as Paddy Chayefsky's "Marty" (for "Philco Television Playhouse," 1953), Reginald Rose's "Twelve Angry Men" ("Studio One," 1954), Rod Serling's "Patterns" ("Kraft Television Theatre," 1955), Gore Vidal's "Visit to a Small Planet" ("Goodyear Playhouse," 1955), and JP Miller's "The Days of Wine and Roses" ("Playhouse 90," 1958). Sadly, most were "scored" with needle-drops and stock music acquired from libraries.

Most of the anthologies went to film or videotape by the late 1950s. As original scoring became commonplace in 1958 and later, many of these shows were scored with new music. The richest musical palette belonged—not surprisingly, considering Stanley Wilson's involvement—to a Revue series: "General Electric Theater" (1953–62, CBS). When Revue started scoring in the fall of 1958, the Ronald Reagan-hosted anthology was treated to an original score every week by Elmer Bernstein, his first regular work in television (and a coup for the series considering his demand in the motion-picture arena after the success of *The Man with the Golden Arm* and *The Ten Commandments*). Bernstein composed a new theme for the half-hour Sunday-night series and thirty scores in the 1958–59 season.

"I thought that television was the coming medium, and it was exciting," Bernstein recalled, finding the series "fun to do, because they were all different. Some were more exciting than others [but] it was a very nice atmosphere." With an orchestra of about twenty-five players, Bernstein gave every story a fresh musical treatment; only the title music remained the same from week to week. Highlights of the Bernstein scores, all for 1959 episodes, included a charming French melody for Fred Astaire in "Man on a Bicycle"; Hebraic influences for the biblical David story "The Stone"; a Scottish flavor for the Dan O'Herlihy tale "Robbie and His Mary"; and two shows in which the music spoke for mute characters: a heartbreaking motif for Joan Crawford in

"And One Was Loyal" and a tender treatment for Janice Rule in "Train to Tecumseh."

With Bernstein off to score "Riverboat" and "Staccato" during the following season, Stanley Wilson wrote a new series theme and assigned a number of different composers to handle individual episodes. The series' primary composer for the final three seasons was Conrad Salinger (1901–62), who was better known as a brilliant arranger and orchestrator, notably for such fifties MGM musicals as *Singin' in the Rain, Gigi,* and *Brigadoon.* Lyn Murray and Jerry Goldsmith contributed several scores; Morton Stevens's first credit was on a "GE Theater" that starred Sammy Davis Jr. ("The Patsy," 1960). Stevens was Davis's musical director, and it was Davis who brought him to Wilson. Wilson was sufficiently impressed to hire Stevens, who went to work on "Thriller" a few months later.

The music for "Alcoa Premiere" (1961–63, ABC) was entirely the work of Johnny Williams. With the jazz of "Checkmate" behind him, he graduated to a series that demanded a more orchestral approach. He began by writing an elegant theme—Fred Astaire, after all, was the series host—but continued to write diverse music for more than three dozen episodes over the next two years (including a lively score for a baseball story, directed by John Ford, that opened the second season). The television academy affirmed the quality of work: Williams was awarded an Emmy nomination in the original-music category for each season.

Williams looked back on that period as a training ground for his film career to come. "In the flurry and heat of battle, as a youngster with not a lot of experience, I was just very busy, extremely focused, and did my best to keep up with the work," he said. "Wilson was helpful by just being the kind of person he was. He was very avuncular, supportive, not controlling, always providing a safety net emotionally or technically or financially. I couldn't help but learn a tremendous amount. I certainly didn't know very much when I started, and whatever I may have gleaned out of the whole process, it certainly would have been the result of what was, in retrospect, a tremendous opportunity."

Williams went on to "Kraft Suspense Theatre" (1963–65, NBC), scoring most of its first season, including one of the scariest themes of the sixties. Set to animation of a single figure beset by silhouetted antagonists and searching for an escape, Williams's "Suspense Theatre" theme suggested terror in the Bernard Herrmann tradition. It was on the Kraft series that Williams met Robert Altman, the director who would later hire him to write the music for *Images* (1972), which garnered an Oscar nomination for the composer, and *The Long Goodbye* (1973).

Williams explained the process: "I would record all day on a Tuesday, let's say, in six hours. We'd have about twenty-five or thirty minutes of music to do. The next morning, Wednesday, we would spot the next episode to record the following Tuesday. At these spotting sessions, very often the producers or directors weren't even there. Wilson would spend two hours with me, then he'd spot a show with Benny Herrmann, or one with Elmer Bernstein, then go over on the stage and conduct something for someone else. And because of this volume, naturally the producers and directors couldn't babysit the projects all the way through editing and scoring and dubbing the way they do features. They would just shoot their film and go off and shoot their next episode.

"There were a few exceptions to this, however, and Altman was one of them. He didn't impose himself but he was tremendously interested. He was one of the few directors and/or producers who would turn up at these spotting sessions with Stanley Wilson. Some others did also, but very few, and it was very unusual if they did. Altman would also come to the [scoring] stage and offer suggestions and be very interested. But [on] most of the recording sessions that I did there, there was not a producer or director on the stage. If they came, they visited briefly and then went back to whatever it was they were shooting that week."

For the second season of "Suspense Theatre," Bernard Herrmann scored two episodes and Franz Waxman four, including a percussive score for the Robert Goulet war story "Operation Greif" (in the style of his *Objective Burma* score, 1945) and a Mexican-flavored one for "That He Should Weep for Her," which featured a rare dramatic performance by Milton Berle. About Waxman, Williams said, "I don't think he enjoyed doing television very much. I think he was annoyed that he had to write so quickly, and the orchestras weren't all that big, and the shows weren't all that good. He had come from the world of feature film where things were better. I think he was worried about working, and he felt that from the point of view of the development of performance revenue from music, a film composer was going to have to work in television.

"I think the same comments would apply to Herrmann. I think Herrmann, because of his character, dashed the things off more. I don't think he took it very seriously. It was just kind of a job, like doing a radio show, which he had done in his youth. So I don't think they were disdainful of the new medium; but I think they were certainly suspicious of it and disturbed by it."

Williams also wrote the classy theme for "Bob Hope Presents the Chrysler Theater" (1963–67, NBC) and scored a handful of its episodes including the acclaimed "One Day in the Life of Ivan Denisovich," based on the Alexander Solzhenitsyn book. The "Chrysler Theater" was, by this time, the most prestigious anthology series in television. Rod Serling, Edward Anhalt, Budd Schulberg, and William Inge were among the writers; Sydney Pollack won an Emmy for directing. Executive producer Dick Berg hired the composers, including Williams, with whom he had worked on "Alcoa": "I had come to trust in Johnny," he said. "He was dependable, and there simply wasn't a lot of time for philosophical discussions. People like Johnny were pretty much left to their own devices."

Berg was especially impressed with jazz artist Benny Carter, whom he hired to score the 1963 show "Something About Lee Wiley," a profile of the jazz vocalist starring Piper Laurie. "He wrote as melodic and moving a score as I have ever had. He was one of the few guys I've dealt with who had no problem expressing himself emotionally. Benny would let the stops out." Carter wrote more than a dozen additional scores over the series' four seasons.

Berg reluctantly hired Bernard Herrmann for one show, the 1963 "Seven Miles of Bad Road" with Jeffrey Hunter. He found the composer "very gruff and very opinionated," and the music—an especially dark score for brass and percussion—worried him because "it was extremely strong. The score became as prominent as what was going on visually, and I was unsure of it."

Unlike most composers on the series, Herrmann attended the dubbing session, and naturally objected when Berg chose to tone down a cue as "too loud or too intrusive. And he insisted that that was the point—that the point needed to be made, and that that kind of help was required.

"This debate went on for four or five hours," Berg said. "Every time I would say something he would snort. And there were occasions where the music was quite intrusive, as a matter of fact. Finally, for the only time in my life, I had to send somebody out of the room. I banned him from the dubbing session. It got very obscene between us and it was horrendous.

"But there's a postscript," the producer added. "When the film played, two weeks later, I realized that there was something almost camp about the film itself and that Herrmann had perceived that. And what he was doing was to help the film. A man and a score that I had resented during the process, I came to realize, had—to the extent to which it had been preserved—been our salvation." Herrmann wrote three more "Chrysler" hours, in 1965 and 1966.

Lalo Schifrin contributed two unique scores. The first, 1964's "Clash of Cymbals," concerned a talented pianist (Laura Devon) and her romantic involvement with a flamboyant conductor (Louis Jordan) who is also a judge in her upcoming competition. "I did a kind of classical score for that, because it took place in conservatories and concert halls," Schifrin recalled. Piano works by Mozart, Chopin, Schumann, Schubert, and Beethoven were included (performed by renowned pianist Pearl Kaufman), and Schifrin conducted excerpts from Mozart's Horn Concerto No. 4. "With that score, I was doing the groundwork for *The Competition*," Schifrin said, referring to his 1980 film about a piano competition with Richard Dreyfuss and Amy Irving. "It's a different movie, a different project, but a similar story, and I already knew how to prescore the classical pieces."

Even more unusual was "A Small Rebellion," a 1966 episode that won an Emmy for Simone Signoret, one of her only two dramatic-TV appearances. She played a major star whom a first-time playwright (George Maharis) hoped to convince to perform in his play. The entire hour, essentially a two-character dialogue, took place in an empty theater. Schifrin remembered the spotting session with Berg, Wilson, and director Stuart Rosenberg: "I said, 'I have an idea. Dizzy Gillespie a cappella.' They looked at me like I'm crazy." Schifrin proposed to sketch original music for the jazz great to improvise to. "With different mutes, I [felt that I] could do something very interesting. Not jazz; modern music performed by Dizzy Gillespie. They went for that. They flew in Dizzy, and he stayed at my house. And we did it: I was conducting Dizzy, all alone, no more musicians. It worked great." (Schifrin and Rosenberg later did several films together, including 1967's *Cool Hand Luke,* 1976's *Voyage of the Damned,* and 1979's *The Amityville Horror,* all of which resulted in Oscar nominations for the composer.)

Actor Richard Boone, meanwhile, created a repertory company to bring original plays to TV on a weekly basis. Clifford Odets was his story editor, and Buck Houghton ("Twilight Zone") was the producer of "The Richard Boone Show" (1963–64, NBC), a noble experiment. Henry Mancini wrote a lyrical theme for harpsichord, and Houghton hired several of his former "Twilight Zone" composers to contribute music, including Herrmann (four scores), Fred Steiner, Nathan Scott, Nathan Van Cleave, and Rene Garriguenc.

For "Profiles in Courage" (1964–65, NBC), based on John F. Kennedy's Pulitzer Prize-winning book about past American political leaders, Nelson Riddle created a stirring musical backdrop for Saul Bass's title visuals featuring an eagle and tolling bells.

By the late 1960s, the dramatic anthology was passé in television. But Universal kept the basic ingredients alive with creative packaging, beginning with "The Name of the Game" (1968–71, NBC), a ninety-minute series with three rotating stars: Gene Barry as a powerful magazine publisher; Tony Franciosa as an investigative reporter; and Robert Stack as a senior editor. Susan Saint James won an Emmy as their research assistant.

"Fame" was the name of the game, as expressed in the title of the 1966 TV movie that led to the series. Benny Carter scored the film, one of two pilots he worked on that became series—both of which went to Dave Grusin for new themes (the other was "A Thief Is a Thief Is a Thief," the pilot for "It Takes a Thief," 1968–70, ABC). Grusin's "Name of the Game" theme was one of the most dynamic of the era. Jazzy, exciting, kinetic, with an undeniable contemporary sound, it accompanied forty seconds of colorful graphics: the names of the three stars filled the screen, then merged into the images of each (the order rotating depending upon who starred in that week's story).

Later, Grusin wrote the theme for Universal's "The Bold Ones" (1969–73, NBC), which combined three different series under one umbrella title. Grusin commented on those themes: "At the time, I don't think I was very analytical about it. To try and make something—in thirty-five or forty-five seconds—complete or maybe a little memorable in terms of having something strong. It's like writing a short story as opposed to a novel, where you have a limited number of words and you have to make your point quickly. Beyond that, I don't think I took it apart too much. I just tried to write it so that I could like it."

Grusin wrote two early scores for "Name of the Game," but Universal new-

David Grusin (left) and Artie Kane (a top studio keyboard player of the sixties and early seventies). Photo by George Fields.

comers Billy Goldenberg and Robert Prince were mainstays of the series. Normally, they would work on separate installments, but in one case they divided a show, earning an Emmy nomination for their efforts: the remarkable 1971 Gene Barry episode "LA 2017," written by science fiction author Philip Wylie and directed by Steven Spielberg. Goldenberg and Prince created a partly orchestral, partly electronic smorgasbord of scoring, source music, and futuristic sounds for the environmentally ravaged, twenty-first-century totalitarian nightmare world that Barry's character imagined.

At Christmas 1971, CBS aired a TV movie titled "The Homecoming" with Patricia Neal and Richard Thomas. A touching memoir by writer Earl Hamner, Jr., of a special holiday he experienced as a boy in Virginia's Blue Ridge Mountains during the Depression, it won a Christopher Award, several Emmy nominations, and the hearts of millions of viewers.

Director Fielder Cook, who worked with Jerry Goldsmith on "Playhouse 90," called in the composer. Taking his cue from the nature of the film, Goldsmith wrote a simple, spare score for "The Homecoming," imbuing the music with regional flavor by using two guitars, banjo, accordion, harmonica, and recorder as his instrumentation. It was restrained but heartfelt; the composer repeated that accomplishment on half a dozen scores for the series that the network quickly commissioned, based on the film: "The Waltons"

(1972–81, CBS). Richard Thomas and several of his younger costars returned for the series; the parents were played by Michael Learned and Ralph Waite, with Ellen Corby and Will Geer as the grandparents. As he did in "The Homecoming," writer-producer Hamner narrated the opening and closing of each episode. "The Waltons" was an unexpected hit, a touch of homespun Americana that was reminiscent of simpler times and family warmth in the post-Woodstock, mid-Vietnam, and imminent-Watergate era.

Although Goldsmith returned for the series, the producers asked for a new theme. "They thought [the original] was too gentle," the composer recalled. "Today, I would have argued with them. I like the theme for 'The Homecoming' better. It was certainly more authentic." The "Waltons" theme had much the same flavor, with guitars, accordion, and harmonica, plus auto-harp—but added a solo trumpet as the primary voice for the melody. "I was thrilled with the themes from the very first time I heard them," creator Hamner later said, adding that "for a long time in the beginning, we didn't have that much [original] scoring available. We had to go on the air rather quickly, so we used a lot of Jerry's themes from 'The Homecoming,' which I think is one of the loveliest scores I ever heard."

Goldsmith's original "Waltons" scores were supplemented by music by

Arthur Morton. Courtesy BMI Archives.

Arthur Morton (who scored most of the second season) and, later, Alexander Courage (who took over the series with its third season and wrote 123 individual scores). Courage described his "Waltons" approach as "Appalachian mountain music with a lot of heart." As on Goldsmith's scores, Courage utilized a small ensemble, averaging seventeen pieces: strings and woodwinds but no brass, often with an accordion, harmonica, and acoustic guitar for a similar regional sound.

In a far different vein was the music for the prime-time soaps. The granddaddy of them all was "Peyton Place" (1964–69, ABC), which aired twice a week (and, during the height of its popularity, even three times). Based on the scandalous Grace Metalious novel and the popular 1957 film, it starred the now-famous Ryan O'Neal and Mia Farrow, as well as Dorothy Malone, Barbara Parkins, Ed Nelson, and Chris Connelly. The producers naturally chose Franz Waxman's memorable film theme for the main title, but Arthur Morton wrote the vast majority of music for the series.

Although better known as an orchestrator of the highest rank, Morton had contributed original scores of his own to "Shirley Temple's Storybook" (1958–61, NBC/ABC) and, for "Bus Stop" (1961–62, ABC) with Marilyn Maxwell and Rhodes Reason, a theme that colleague Hugo Friedhofer later called "most tasteful and haunting." Morton's lyrical scores for "Bus Stop" led to "Peyton Place," another Fox series. "I had a whole set of themes for the characters," Morton recalled. He estimated that he scored about four hundred of the half-hour shows—a recording session was held practically every week—over the course of the series' five-year life. Even those he didn't write (which were scored by Fox colleagues such as Cyril Mockridge) usually contained Morton's material. "At Fox, I had a wonderful orchestra," Morton said. "I had ten violins, four violas, four cellos with a bass. I had one of each woodwind and three horns. And occasionally I had a harp or a piano or, because we had a wonderful trombone player out there, Dick Nash, I'd write a piece for trombone."

After "Peyton Place," other series attempted to mine the same territory. Best-selling trash novelist Harold Robbins created "The Survivors" (1969–70, ABC), which starred Lana Turner, George Hamilton, and Ralph Bellamy in an expensive, high-gloss soap that was canceled after just fifteen episodes. Maurice Jarre scored the pilot, but by the time the much-troubled series hit the airwaves, newly arrived French composer Michel Colombier (b. 1939) had replaced him, scoring the first six hours with a sense of contemporary music and high drama.

One of the decade's most expensive flops was "Beacon Hill" (1975, CBS), an American "Upstairs, Downstairs" set in Prohibition-era Boston and taped in New York with a large cast of Broadway actors including Stephen Elliott, Nancy Marchand, David Dukes, Kathryn Walker, George Rose, and Beatrice Straight. Marvin Hamlisch (b. 1944), who was then the hottest composer in Hollywood, coming off his triple 1973 Oscar win (song and score for *The Way*

We Were and adaptation score for *The Sting*), took a chamber approach to his music for the series, composing a yearning theme for solo saxophone and strings, also adding harp, piano, and flute. "Beacon Hill" lasted all of eleven weeks, but it couldn't have mattered to Hamlisch: his *A Chorus Line* was, at literally the same time, becoming Broadway's biggest smash, eventually earning him a Tony and the Pulitzer Prize.

Then came "Dallas" (1978–91, CBS), the undisputed king of prime-time soaps. The tales of intrigue within and without the oil-rich Ewing family on Texas's sprawling Southfork ranch grew in popularity until the "Who Shot J.R.?" episode of November 21, 1980, became the most-watched TV program to that time. Larry Hagman was the conniving J.R. Ewing, Patrick Duffy his nice-guy brother who married the daughter (Victoria Principal) of his father's longtime rival; Linda Gray was J.R.'s alcoholic wife, while Barbara Bel Geddes and Jim Davis were the husband-and-wife ranchers who ran Southfork.

Jerrold Immel (b. 1936) was on the short list of both producer Leonard Katzman and creator David Jacobs (the latter of whom had just seen a TV movie of Immel's and admired the music) to provide the series' music. A former copyist at Four Star and supervising copyist/music librarian at CBS, he had worked with Katzman scoring "Gunsmoke" and had written the spectacular theme for "How the West Was Won." About "Dallas," Immel recalled: "I had read the script, and I had a conversation with Len in which he told me that he would like it to be big, like the movie *Giant*, but contemporary and urban. Contemporary and urban at that time meant disco. That was really all I had to go on." Set against images of the city skyline, the oil fields of Texas, and the cast, the "Dallas" theme successfully combined an urban glamour with a rural ambiance to become the familiar aural signature of the Ewing family.

Bruce Broughton, who came aboard with the third season, received four Emmy nominations, winning two, for his "Dallas" scores (both for 1983 episodes). Observed Broughton: "You could play 'Dallas' any way you wanted and you couldn't hurt the show. I would try to see how far I could go before it went over the side. You could play J.R. as dark and evil as you wanted, or you could play him with a lot of charisma and character, or say he was cute and charming. You could play sentiment, dripping violins over Miss Ellie, or Jock's nobility. These people could be doing despicable things with each other, but you could find almost any facet of human experience and play to that, and it would fit. The bigger the better.

"I started experimenting with the music itself," Broughton added, "making the music more strident or more dissonant, almost more elegant, and [the show] actually just sopped it all up. I always loved working on 'Dallas.'" While the orchestra numbers usually averaged twenty, Broughton enjoyed mixing up the ensemble: "one was all strings and a flute; another was for English horn, trombone, and strings; another was practically all woodwinds."

When "Dallas" creator David Jacobs spun off "Knots Landing" (1979–93,

CBS), he again turned to Immel. "I looked at it as four marriages on a cul-de-sac," the composer explained, "and went for a much gentler, more lyrical theme," including an alto sax solo that was performed, in early seasons, by the great Bud Shank. As with "Dallas," Immel would return to score an episode or two at the start of each new season. For five years toward the end of the "Knots" run, however, Immel—together with partner Craig Huxley—created and performed all of the "Knots" scores electronically.

With "Dynasty" (1981–89, ABC), composer Bill Conti (b. 1942) created what may be, next to his score for *Rocky* (1976), his most familiar theme. The Rhode Island native and Juilliard graduate spent seven years studying and composing in Italy before returning to the United States to score films, notably *Harry and Tonto* (1974) and *An Unmarried Woman* (1978), and scoring a number-one hit with *Rocky*. He would later win an Academy Award for writing the heroic score for *The Right Stuff* (1983).

Conti came to "Dynasty" at the suggestion of actor George Peppard, who played the role of Blake Carrington in the original series pilot and who liked Conti's score for his film *Five Days from Home* (1978). Peppard was replaced by John Forsythe, but Conti stayed with the project. According to the compos-

Bill Conti. Courtesy the composer.

er, creators Esther and Richard Shapiro asked for "an elegant, movielike, rather than televisionlike" main theme. The problem was the original title of the script, which was not "Dynasty" but "Oil"—a concept that Conti found hard to musicalize. Once the network changed the title to "Dynasty," however, the composer was immediately inspired and, in his words, "came up with the theme and wrote it before dinner. It was one of the only times in my life that it actually flowed through me. I'm not a mystic," Conti noted. "I know how to write music in a prepared way and feel quite craftsmanlike about it. But not with 'Dynasty.' I sat down and played it. It was so painless."

Conti's demand for a minimum orchestra of thirty-two on the pilot ("Nineteen guys is not going to sound like a movie," he explained to the producers) turned out to be less of a problem than expected. A musicians' strike forced the Aaron Spelling production to take the score to France, although Conti did not go abroad for the recording.

The "Dynasty" theme, particularly as heard throughout Conti's pilot score, said "elegant" from start to finish. The flourishes, the classically styled bridge, and the beautifully played trumpet solo set against strings provided a lush backdrop for the Shapiros' Denver-based, wealthy Carrington family melodrama (with Linda Evans as Blake's long-suffering wife Krystle, Pamela Sue Martin and later Emma Samms as daughter Fallon, and Joan Collins as Blake's scheming ex-wife Alexis).

For "Falcon Crest" (1981–90, CBS), Conti got a very different kind of direction. For this serialized drama of an ongoing battle for control of a northern California winery—starring Jane Wyman as its ruthless matriarch—creator Earl Hamner asked the composer for an "Italian baroque" sound. "I could tell you what that meant in terms of Italian baroque composers," Conti said, "but I don't know what he meant in terms of his own musical contacts. But I obviously understood something conveyed by that term, because when he heard it he liked it."

Conti's soaring theme, set to visuals of the lush Napa Valley vineyards, began with a regal brass fanfare—perhaps suggested by the winery's coat of arms in the title—and had an "Italianesque" style, in the composer's view. And, like "Dynasty," it had a timeless quality that only an orchestral theme can provide. "That was, I thought, the era to not do what everybody was doing in the genre, stylistically putting it in a place that time-dated it. Once you take away the rhythm section, you take away the time element."

Conti also wrote a batch of first-rate themes that unfortunately died along with their shows. Most notable among them were "Emerald Point N.A.S." (1983–84, CBS), a grand military march for a Shapiro-created serial set on a naval base; "The Colbys" (1985–87, ABC), a dignified fanfare for the "Dynasty" spinoff starring Charlton Heston and Barbara Stanwyck; "Mariah" (1987, ABC), a combination of classical elements and contemporary beat for a prison drama; "Ohara" (1987–88, ABC), which added mystical Oriental sounds to a catchy, synthesizer-performed tune for a Pat Morita cop show; and "HeartBeat" (1988–89, ABC), wordless female voices for an hour about a women's medical clinic with Kate Mulgrew and Gail Strickland.

One of the most musically interesting dramas of the late seventies was "Lou Grant" (1977–82, CBS), which ran at the height of the MTM dynasty of high-profile comedies and drama series. The music was entirely entrusted to one composer: Patrick Williams.

Williams (b. 1939) was the only composer active in Hollywood to have won a Pulitzer Prize nomination (for his *American Concerto,* a 1976 work for orchestra that combined jazz and classical elements). He studied music at Duke and Columbia universities and became active as an arranger-conductor in New York in the 1960s. He moved to California in 1968 to write for films and television. An Oscar nominee for scoring *Breaking Away* (1979), Williams was practically a house composer for MTM, having scored the popular "Mary Tyler Moore Show" and "The Bob Newhart Show" (and more short-lived efforts including Paul Sand's "Friends and Lovers" and "The Tony Randall Show"); his hour dramas included "The Streets of San Francisco" and Bill Bixby's "The Magician" (1973–74, NBC). He won a Grammy for his 1974 LP, *Threshold.*

"Lou Grant" was a dramatic spinoff from "The Mary Tyler Moore Show," sending Ed Asner's gruff newsroom character to Los Angeles to become the city editor of a major newspaper. Emmy-nominated as Outstanding Drama Series for each of its five seasons, it won twice. In the 1979–80 year alone, it received fifteen nominations (including seven for writing and direction) and won in six categories—including one for Williams for original music composition. He was nominated three other times for "Lou Grant" scores.

The "Lou Grant" main title was one of the cleverest in television drama: a sixty-second look at the life of a page of newsprint. Starting quietly with a chirping bird on a tree branch in the woods, it chronicled a logging operation, the manufacture of pulp, the delivery of paper to the newspaper operation (followed by a twenty-second interlude for scenes of the cast in the newsroom), newspapers rolling off the presses, delivery to a suburban home, someone reading the paper over morning coffee, and finally a section being shoved into the bottom of a bird cage—under, once again, a chirping bird.

As for music, Williams recalled: "The idea was something that had some energy and some hipness, because it wasn't supposed to be serious like 'The Defenders.' But we wanted it to cook." And cook it did, with Tom Scott performing the alto saxophone solo in the original main title and a rhythm section comprised of the best players in Los Angeles.

About the individual episodes, Williams said: "It wasn't formula time. Every show had a different theme, so there was a different musical approach for each. And [producers] Gene Reynolds and Allan Burns pretty much left me alone. . . . We had great success using smaller, interesting combinations of players you wouldn't normally put together, [for example] a show using a small string section and two or three classical guitars. Things that would be stimulating to write for."

After the barrage of electronic sounds throughout the seventies and eighties, a fresh voice emerged—and it was a throwback to yesterday: acoustic guitar. W. G. Snuffy Walden (b. 1950) introduced it on "thirtysomething" (1987–91, ABC), kept it fresh through "The Wonder Years" (1988–93, ABC), and augmented it with solo piano on "I'll Fly Away" (1991–93, NBC).

Born in Louisiana and raised in Texas, Walden got his training in Texas clubs and as a rock 'n' roll road musician, touring with his own bands and others (including Emerson, Lake and Palmer, Donna Summer, Laura Branigan, and Chaka Khan) before he began playing on film and television scores for other composers. Without prior experience in the field, Walden found a partner in Stewart Levin (b. 1954), who not only was a talented keyboard player but understood the technical aspects of scoring to film and had a studio. Detroit-born Levin grew up in Los Angeles, studied classical piano, became a studio musician, and acquired a facility with synthesizers.

Together, Walden and Levin performed the pilot score (along with a percussionist and an accordion player) for "thirtysomething." In fact, their main title theme was "a demo that we actually sped up to make it run sixty seconds," Walden laughed. "It didn't fit a minute, so we sped it up. It's now in E-flat instead of D." The other fresh sonority in the theme, playing the melody, was Levin's Kurzweil-sampled sound of air blowing across the mouth of a soda bottle. "It was a really neat sound, and not like anything else in the world," Levin said.

The guitar-and-piano approach resonated with viewers who identified with the realities of this original baby boomer series, about the daily lives of seven Philadelphia friends: two couples (Ken Olin and Mel Harris, Patricia Wettig and Timothy Busfield) and three singles (Melanie Mayron, Polly Draper, Peter Horton), with its life's-big-questions scripts, often so superbly written and played. Walden and Levin created and performed the scores for the first season; they dissolved the partnership but continued to score the remainder of the series on an alternating-episode basis.

Walden and Levin also began "The Wonder Years," a critically acclaimed comedy-drama set in 1968, with Fred Savage as twelve-year-old Kevin Arnold, trying to make sense of the world and relationships, particularly that with his sometime girlfriend Winnie (Danica McKellar), which was narrated by Daniel Stern as the adult Kevin. Because the score turned out to be largely acoustic guitar-based, Walden became the sole composer after several episodes.

For "I'll Fly Away," the critically praised civil rights-era drama with Sam Waterston and Regina Taylor, Walden said, "I wanted it to be gospel in nature without being over the top. So I bought a piano." Although the pilot featured a thirty-five-piece orchestra, Walden created many of the first-season scores on his own at the piano, and returned to score the two-hour series finale, the PBS-aired "Then and Now."

Walden and Levin were jointly Emmy-nominated for their "thirtysomething" theme; Walden, nominated for his "I'll Fly Away" main title; and Levin, nominated for his sensitive, piano-dominated theme for "Picket Fences" (1992–, CBS).

Just Sit Right Back and You'll Hear a Tale

The Sitcoms

One of the most familiar tunes in the history of television, the theme for "I Love Lucy" (1951–57, CBS), was dashed off in an afternoon, for a pilot that no one knew would sell.

Eliot Daniel (b. 1908), the composer of "I Love Lucy," had been an arranger and pianist for Rudy Vallee in the 1930s, composer-arranger for Frank Morgan's radio show in the late forties, and an Oscar-nominated song-writer (for "Lavender Blue" from 1949's *So Dear to My Heart* and "Never" from 1951's *Golden Girl*) at both Disney and Twentieth Century-Fox. Daniel had known "Lucy" producer Jess Oppenheimer from radio in the early 1940s; Oppenheimer had gone on to produce Lucille Ball's "My Favorite Husband" radio show and was part of the planning process for the "I Love Lucy" pilot. Oppenheimer asked Daniel to write the theme for the proposed sitcom about a Cuban bandleader (Desi Arnaz) and his madcap wife (Ball).

Daniel was reluctant at first because of his already heavy studio commitments, primarily at Fox. "But Jess really wanted me to do it, and all it was, was a pilot show," the composer recalled. "That's all we thought at the time. I thought it would be done one day and they'd forget about it."

Daniel knocked out the tune in an afternoon. "I wrote the first phrase of the song so that it matched 'I love Lucy and she loves me' . . . It came pretty easily after I got that first phrase." The complete lyrics, by Harold Adamson (who would pen the words for "The Life and Legend of Wyatt Earp"), were written much later, specifically for Arnaz to sing in a 1953 episode about

Eliot Daniel (in white jacket) and Desi Arnaz. Courtesy Eliot Daniel.

Lucy's birthday. Daniel's instrumental main-title arrangement, set to twenty seconds of simple visuals featuring the title and cast members' names on a satin heart, featured Latin percussion. But the theme itself, Daniel said, was not specifically conceived as a Latin number.

Daniel also composed the bridges and occasional underscore for the first few seasons. Arnaz's band, onstage for the filming of the innovative three-camera, live-audience show, would—earlier the same day—perform the score for the show shot the previous week. The composer also wrote occasional special material for the cast (including a mini-operetta for a 1952 episode and a baseball number for a Bob Hope episode in 1956).

Longtime Desilu musical director Wilbur Hatch—a composer in his own right, having scored "Our Miss Brooks" (1952–56, CBS) and later "The Lucy Show" (1962–68, CBS) and "Here's Lucy" (1968–74, CBS)—conducted the music. Also for Desilu, Daniel later wrote the themes for "December Bride" with Spring Byington (1954–59, CBS), "Willy" with June Havoc (1954–55, CBS), and "Those Whiting Girls" with Margaret Whiting (1955, 1957, CBS); and for Jess Oppenheimer, "Angel" with Marshall Thompson (1960–61, CBS).

Most situation comedies of the 1950s contained, like nearly all TV series, instrumental themes. For "The Honeymooners" (1955–56, CBS), star Jackie Gleason (1916–87) used his own song "You're My Greatest Love." In addition to his fame as a television star, Gleason recorded nearly three dozen popular-music albums in the fifties and sixties, choosing the tunes, overseeing the arrangements, and actually conducting them himself. (He had no musical training, and composed many songs, including his variety-show theme "Melancholy Serenade," by picking out the tunes at the piano and turning them over to an arranger for orchestration.)

A handful of shows featured songs with lyrics, but most themes—like the

Lionel Newman conducting at Twentieth Century-Fox. Photo by George Fields.

Lyn Murray-Richard Mack title song for "I Married Joan" (1952–55, NBC) and the Lionel Newman-Max Shulman theme for "The Many Loves of Dobie Gillis" (1959–63, CBS)—were almost generic in their approach: "I married Joan/What a girl, what a whirl, what a life . . ." and "Dobie wants a girl who's dreamy/Dobie wants a girl who's creamy . . ."

As the 1960s rolled around and television as a medium began to mature, a few especially creative producers began to take risks with their themes. For "Car 54, Where Are You?" (1961–63, NBC), producer Nat Hiken—who created and produced the hit "The Phil Silvers Show" (1955–59, CBS)—penned a clever lyric, set to music by "Phil Silvers" composer John Strauss (b. 1920), that clearly established the setting in less than half a minute of screen time:

> There's a holdup in the Bronx
> Brooklyn's broken out in fights
> There's a traffic jam in Harlem
> That's backed up to Jackson Heights
> There's a Scout troop short a child
> Khrushchev's due at Idlewild
> Car 54, where are you?

Set against comic visuals of Officers Toody and Muldoon (Joe E. Ross, Fred Gwynne) playing checkers while on patrol in New York City's 53rd Precinct, this tune (sung by a male chorus) didn't introduce the characters so much as it suggested the kind of wacky cop antics to which viewers would be treated. It also marked the first time that a living political figure was mentioned by name in, of all things, a sitcom theme.

The real breakthrough occurred the following season with "The Ballad of Jed Clampett," written for "The Beverly Hillbillies" (1962–71, CBS). The long-running comedy starred Buddy Ebsen as head of a clan of Ozark country bumpkins who became millionaires when oil was struck on their land and they decided to move into a southern California mansion. Ebsen played Jed, Irene Ryan his mother-in-law Granny, Donna Douglas his naive daughter Elly May, and Max Baer Jr. big, dumb Cousin Jethro; helping to "civilize" them were their Beverly Hills banker (Raymond Bailey) and his assistant (Nancy Kulp).

Paul Henning, the creator-producer of the show, auditioned a songwriting team for the theme but didn't care for their approach. Having been a singer on the radio as a youth, he knew a little about music. "So, of necessity," Henning said, "I did something I had not done before. I just composed a song, words and music, and performed it for a musician who played piano and who simply wrote out the music." From the time he conceived it, the "Beverly Hillbillies" theme was designed to outline the show's basic premise. "I thought it would save a lot of time and exposition on the screen," he explained.

Those now-famous lyrics chronicled, in fifty-five seconds, the entire story of the Clampett family:

> Come 'n listen to my story 'bout a man named Jed
> A poor mountaineer, barely kept his fam'ly fed
> An' then one day, he was shootin' at some food
> An' up through the ground come a bubblin' crude.
> Oil, that is! Black gold! Texas tea! . . .

Henning again broke with TV tradition by writing different lyrics for the end-title version of the theme:

> Well now it's time to say goodbye
> To Jed and all his kin
> An' they would like t' thank you folks
> fer kindly droppin' in
> You're all invited back next week to this locality
> T' have a heapin' helpin' of their hospitality . . .

(It can be argued that a hint of the premise, and the concept of a theme explaining the show's background, actually originated a few years earlier with "The Real McCoys" [1957–63, ABC/CBS], with Walter Brennan as patriarch of a West Virginia family that moved to central California. Veteran tunesmith Harry Ruby [1895–1974], whose career dated back to Broadway in the 1920s and whose film career included songs for the Marx Brothers movies *Duck Soup* and *Horse Feathers,* wrote a country-flavored title song that included the lyric ". . . from West Virginny they came to stay in sunny Californiay . . . " But the tune otherwise spoke only generally about the family, in particular Grandpappy Amos, and was not a ballad describing their life's journey.)

Henning's composer for the pilot and the first season, Perry Botkin Jr. (who would go on to later fame as co-composer of the "Young and the Restless" theme, even better known as "Nadia's Theme" for Olympic gymnast Nadia Comaneci), went to Nashville, Tennessee, at Henning's suggestion and signed popular country artists Lester Flatt and Earl Scruggs to perform the music. Botkin brought in Jerry Scoggins (a Texas singer who came to California in 1946 to perform on Gene Autry's "Melody Ranch" radio show) to sing the vocal. Flatt and Scruggs's bluegrass style, Henning reasoned, was "the music most descriptive of what I was trying to say," both for the theme and the show's underscore.

Composer Curt Massey (1910–91) retained that sound when he inherited "Hillbillies" the next season. Massey was "one of the most talented, versatile musicians I've ever known," Henning said, noting that Massey both wrote and performed (via overdubs) nearly all of the music for "Hillbillies" and its spin-off, "Petticoat Junction" (1963–70, CBS), by himself in his Los Angeles recording studio.

Henning went on to write other songs for the show, notably "Pearl Pearl Pearl" for Flatt and Scruggs when they made their first of several appearances playing themselves. In the 1963 episode "Jed Throws a Wingding," they played competing former suitors for Jethro's mother, Pearl Bodine (recurring guest star Bea Benaderet). Flatt and Scruggs recorded both "Pearl Pearl Pearl" and "The Ballad of Jed Clampett." The latter shot to Number 1 on the *Billboard* country chart (Number 44 on the pop chart) within the series' first year, becoming the first sitcom theme to score big with the record-buying public—just as the series became a giant hit in its first season and remained in the Nielsen top 20 throughout its nine years on the air.

Massey composed the music, Henning the lyrics, for "Petticoat Junction": "Come ride a little train that is rollin' down the tracks to the Junction . . ." The tune was sung to shots of the Hooterville Cannonball steam locomotive that passed by the Shady Rest hotel run by Kate Bradley (Bea Benaderet) and Uncle Joe Carson (Edgar Buchanan), with Kate's three attractive daughters (originally Jeannine Riley, Pat Woodell, and Linda Kaye Henning) apparently bathing in the town water tower. Flatt and Scruggs's recording of "Petticoat Junction" went to Number 14 on the country charts.

With most series, the music comes long after principal photography has been completed and the producers' attention has shifted to postproduction. But in a rare exception, the theme came first, and became one of the most famous tunes in TV history: "The Ballad of Gilligan's Isle."

Sherwood Schwartz, a former writer on "I Married Joan" and later Emmy-winning head writer on "The Red Skelton Show," created "Gilligan's Island" (1964–67, CBS). The idea was a comic variation on the classic Daniel Defoe novel *Robinson Crusoe:* a tropical storm throws off course a Honolulu cruise boat carrying several sightseers, stranding them on an uncharted South Pacific island where they manage to survive while awaiting rescue.

Schwartz sought funding from CBS for the pilot. But he fought a running battle with then-CBS president James Aubrey. Recalled Schwartz: "Aubrey contended that it was impossible to do the show because of the background that would have to be explained to the audience each week as to why these people were on this island. He said it would be deadly exposition." Schwartz's answer: incorporate the back-story into the lyrics of the show's theme, "an amusing, rollicking kind of song that will tell the audience, in sixty seconds, why they're there, how they got there and so forth." Aubrey apparently wasn't convinced. So, at the urging of his agent, Schwartz stayed up late the night before his presentation to CBS executives creating a song designed to assuage Aubrey's concerns.

"I'm not a songwriter," admitted Schwartz. "I used to play the violin, I have a good ear, and I can pick out a tune on the piano." But believing that CBS would not commission a pilot unless Aubrey's perceived problem was resolved, Schwartz went to work. "At that time, 1963, calypso was very popu-lar. So I tapped out a calypso tune on the piano, and wrote those lyrics. I must

Sherwood Schwartz in the 1960s. Courtesy Sherwood Schwartz.

say, it took me from seven in the evening to about midnight to get the lyrics and music together."

According to Schwartz, Aubrey insisted that he sing the song to a roomful of CBS brass. "Opportunity sometimes just knocks once," mused Schwartz. "So even though I couldn't sing and I might kill the pilot, I knew that if I didn't get up, there would be no pilot. So I had little choice. I got up and I sang. When I was through, there was silence in the room until big Jim had to make a decision.

"All he said was, 'I think you could work a little on the middle lyric.' Which meant, 'Okay, now I understand. With that song, there will be no exposition problem.' That's the test that I had to pass." Schwartz was given the go-ahead to produce the pilot for "Gilligan's Island."

Later, after the pilot was produced, Schwartz decided to ask a professional to help him revamp his theme song, so he called a composer friend, George Wyle (b. 1916). Wyle, then the music director on "The Andy Williams Show" and later music director for "The Flip Wilson Show," was also a successful songwriter (he penned the Christmas standard "It's the Most Wonderful Time of the Year"). As Wyle pointed out: "The boat goes down in the Pacific and [Schwartz] had written a Caribbean melody, a calypso."

Wyle suggested setting the lyrics to a sea chantey. "I wasn't really sure what a sea chantey was," he laughed, "but it sounded good." At the time, he was writing relatively simple arrangements for the Christy Minstrels on Williams's

George Wyle. Courtesy the composer.

variety series, and he felt the same approach would also work for the "Gilligan's Island" theme. Within hours, Schwartz and Wyle retooled the lyric to fit a traditional-sounding sailor tune.

Schwartz's main-title lyrics are familiar to anyone who has watched television in the past thirty years: "Just sit right back and you'll hear a tale, a tale of a fateful trip/That started from this tropic port aboard this tiny ship. . . ." Against scenes from the never-aired pilot episode and shots of the crew and passengers, the song detailed the "three-hour tour" that ended with the S.S. *Minnow*'s shipwreck on an "uncharted desert isle." Five of the seven castaways were shown during the first-season opening; the Professor and Mary Ann were added for the second and third years on the air. And, as Henning had done previously with "The Beverly Hillbillies," Schwartz wrote different end-title lyrics that urged the viewer to "Join us here each week, my friends, you're sure to get a smile/From seven stranded castaways here on Gilligan's Isle."

Wyle also found The Wellingtons, the vocal trio, who literally recorded the song in the living room of Schwartz's old friend, film director Mel Shavelson (*Beau James, Cast a Giant Shadow*), because there were only days left to complete postproduction. (The Wellingtons later appeared in a second-season episode as three of the four members of The Mosquitoes, a rock group seeking rest and solitude for a month.)

"It was the song that sold the show," said Schwartz. "Gilligan's Island" ran just three seasons but became a huge success in syndication and continues to rerun endlessly on stations to this day.

Schwartz later came to believe that Aubrey's original concerns were justified. "I believe that a puzzled audience cannot laugh. If they're trying to figure something out, the joke has passed them before they can analyze it. A song can bring people out of the kitchen, or wherever they are: 'Oh, I know that show.' It's highly identifiable when you can tell the story of a show in a lyrically and musically interesting way. It nails down the focus of the audience."

As for the underscore, Schwartz was fortunate to land a budding feature film composer early on: Johnny Williams was completing his five-year stay at Universal and was signed to score the "Gilligan's Island" pilot. Even though his previous chores (notably on "Checkmate") were largely jazz-influenced, Williams had scored many comedies, notably "Bachelor Father." In addition to interpolating the title tune in his underscore, Williams composed a lively theme for Gilligan that opened and closed nearly every episode. Later in the first season, Gerald Fried joined the "Gilligan" crew, providing a further sense of fun in his inventive use of exotic percussion instruments.

Schwartz created and produced several other shows in the 1960s and 1970s, each with a distinctive theme song that featured lyrics he had written. "It's About Time" (1966–67, CBS), a sitcom about time-traveling astronauts who had become stranded in the caveman era, lasted only one season. Yet the opening phrases of its theme—"It's about time, it's about space, about two men in the strangest place"—were instantly memorable. "Strangely enough, that's true," observed Schwartz. "I know people who never heard of the show but can sing the song."

Schwartz's other big hit of the 1960s—and, in its many incarnations, the seventies, eighties, and nineties—was "The Brady Bunch" (1969–74, ABC). The premise had a widow (Florence Henderson) with three daughters marrying a widower (Robert Reed) with three sons. The result was TV's first blended-family comedy, after two decades of nuclear-family and single-parent sitcoms. Again, Schwartz chose to explain the concept via an opening title song: "I explained what this marriage consisted of: two prior marriages, one with three girls and one with three boys and so forth. You now start fresh: you don't have to worry about how it happened."

For music this time, Schwartz turned to Frank DeVol (b. 1911). DeVol was a veteran bandleader and five-time Oscar nominee, for the original scores of *Pillow Talk* (1959) and *Hush . . . Hush, Sweet Charlotte* (1964), the adaptation scores for *Cat Ballou* (1965) and *Guess Who's Coming to Dinner* (1967), and the song "Hush . . . Hush, Sweet Charlotte." He scored more than a dozen films for producer-director Robert Aldrich, including *Whatever Happened to Baby Jane?* (1962), *The Dirty Dozen* (1967), and *The Longest Yard* (1974).

Frank DeVol. Courtesy Society for the Preservation of Film Music.

The appropriately dark musical tone DeVol brought to Aldrich's suspenseful and action-filled films contrasted sharply with the composer's television reputation, which was based on his success writing upbeat, happy music for lightweight comedy series. It began with "My Three Sons" (1960–72, ABC/CBS), about a consulting engineer (Fred MacMurray), a widower raising three boys with the help of his father-in-law (William Frawley, previously best known as Fred Mertz on "I Love Lucy").

DeVol's clever conception for the "My Three Sons" theme began with knowing that MacMurray had been, back in vaudeville, a saxophone player with a band called the California Collegians. This immediately suggested a saxophone as the lead instrument. For grumpy old Uncle Bub (Frawley), he added a bassoon ("a low comedy thing," DeVol said). "And for the children, I thought, well, I'll lay this very simple melody over 'Chopsticks.'" The casual viewer, caught up in the animated title sequence of toe-tapping and hand-clapping, might not have noticed the piano playing a variation of the traditional child's tune (although it was hard to miss the intentionally off-key harmonica that interrupted the melody, another musical reference to the kids).

DeVol's second hit was "Family Affair" (1966–71, CBS), which, like "My Three Sons," was from producer Don Fedderson. This one starred Brian Keith as a Manhattan bachelor (with Sebastian Cabot as his English valet) whose well-ordered life is disrupted by the arrival of three young orphans, the children of a brother and sister-in-law who died in an accident. This time, DeVol composed a jaunty tune featuring the harpsichord.

Along the way were "Our Man Higgins" with Stanley Holloway (1962–63, ABC), "Grindl" with Imogene Coca (1963–64, NBC), and others. But DeVol would attain lasting success, and a surprising on-screen familiarity, via two different cult series: scoring "The Brady Bunch" and appearing on the talk-show sendup "Fernwood 2–Night" (1977–78, syndicated).

"The Brady Bunch" became one of those shows whose popularity twenty years after its network run far outshone its Nielsen ratings success on the network. Reed, Henderson, Ann B. Davis (as nutty maid Alice), and the kids resurfaced time and again—in "The Brady Bunch Hour" (1977, ABC), "The Brady Brides" (1981, NBC), "The Bradys" (1990, CBS) and ultimately a 1994 feature—always accompanied by the Schwartz-De Vol theme song (sung, in the first season, by the Peppermint Trolley Company) that began, "Here's the story of a lovely lady/Who was bringing up three very lovely girls . . ." and continued with "It's the story of a man named Brady/Who was busy with three boys of his own . . ." Schwartz "came to me with the lyrics," DeVol recalled, "and I wrote the music to his words." The composer scored nearly three dozen episodes of the series over its five-year run, and even appeared in a 1972 episode.

On "Fernwood 2–Night," DeVol's role as Happy Kyne, leader of the house band The Mirth Makers, was perfectly suited to the composer's ham-actor side. He had previously performed in comedy sketches during his live-TV stints in the 1950s; was one of the original panelists on "Pantomime Quiz" (1950–63, CBS); and even played a recurring role as building contractor Myron Bannister in the John Astin-Marty Ingels sitcom "I'm Dickens, He's Fenster" (1962–63, ABC).

Words like "zany" and "wacky" now seem irredeemably associated with television comedy. Perhaps no composer in television history wrote more music that could be characterized in those terms than Vic Mizzy (b. 1922). Mizzy composed the themes and weekly scores for two of the 1960s' most beloved comedies: "The Addams Family" (1964–66, ABC) and "Green Acres" (1965–71, CBS). And, in a highly unusual collaboration with the producers, he even conceptualized both main-title sequences and directed the one for "The Addams Family" himself.

Mizzy came to TV from the songwriting world. Born in Brooklyn, he appeared on radio's famous "Major Bowes Amateur Hour"; arranged for bandleader Ray Bloch; composed special material for singers like Perry Como and Frank Sinatra; and wrote the popular songs "There's a Faraway Look in Your Eyes," "My Dreams Are Getting Better All the Time," and "Pretty Kitty Blue Eyes," several of which wound up on radio's famous "Hit Parade."

David Levy, who was then a programming vice president at NBC, gave Mizzy his first television assignment on a live, summer-replacement dramatic

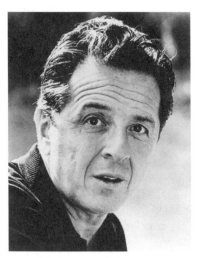

Vic Mizzy. Courtesy the composer.

anthology called "Moment of Fear" (1960). "Shirley Temple's Storybook," which had just moved to NBC from ABC, and the James Coburn action-adventure series "Klondike" (1960–61, NBC) quickly followed. Mizzy moved to Los Angeles, where he scored episodes of "The Richard Boone Show" and the Dennis Weaver comedy-drama "Kentucky Jones" (1964–65, NBC).

Levy, who by this time had gone into the production side of the business, was shepherding a risky, offbeat concept in 1964: turning Charles Addams's macabre magazine cartoons into a series called "The Addams Family." According to Mizzy, Filmways had made a ten-minute presentation reel to screen for ABC executives. To save money, they planned to track in preexisting music rather than commission an original score. Mizzy loved the outrageousness of the concept—a dark-humored comedy about an endearingly ghoulish family with bizarre tastes and hobbies—and volunteered to write a theme gratis.

Mizzy recalled demonstrating the theme for Filmways executive Al Simon at an appropriately cobweb-covered rehearsal piano in the rear of a dimly lit soundstage. For the recording sessions, however, Mizzy chose a harpsichord because "it denoted something quaint, something outside the realm; a small, intimate sound." In fact, the composer played the harpsichord not only for the main title but in all the cues (including the many occasions when butler Lurch was seen playing for the family in the Addams living room). That was also Mizzy's voice singing his lyrics (overdubbed three times) because budget-conscious Filmways, again, "didn't want to pay for singers"; and actor Ted Cassidy, who played Lurch, uttering "neat, sweet, petite" in those familiar sepulchral tones. The entire series was scored with the same four-piece ensemble: harpsichord, woodwind player (usually clarinet or flute), bass violin, and drums (doubling on other percussion instruments).

Mizzy composed themes for most of the main characters, including a graceful flute motif for Morticia (Carolyn Jones), a merengue for Gomez (John Astin), and even signature themes for the Addams mansion (which opened every episode), and Thing, the hand that mysteriously appeared from ornate tabletop boxes scattered throughout the house.

The composer's musical conception was so specific that he became deeply involved with the filming of the main-title sequence, which involved all seven actors snapping their fingers in carefully timed rhythm to Mizzy's music. The composer remained on the set to guide the actors in specific movements designed to coincide with his individual character themes. He recalled advising Astin to "walk pseudo-Groucho Marx" and Jones to "take little short steps" so that she would appear to glide along the floor, both in time to Mizzy's music. "It's strictly a songwriter's crazy imagination," he said.

Perhaps no composer in TV was more suited to "The Addams Family" than Mizzy. The theme reappeared in the 1991 feature film of the same name, but without those famous lyrics: "They're creepy and they're kooky, mysterious and spooky, they're altogether ooky: the Addams Family . . ."

"Green Acres" followed the next season. The show, a spinoff of "Petticoat Junction" with a similarly rural theme, cast Eddie Albert and Eva Gabor as New Yorkers who escaped the hubbub of city life for the more bucolic existence of farming. Again, Mizzy conceived the title song as intertwined with the visuals of the main title, beginning with an aerial shot of the barn emblazoned with the words "Green Acres," and telling the story of Oliver and Lisa Douglas (Albert, Gabor) moving from city to country. The final scene, as Mizzy envisioned it, would be an amusing variant of Grant Wood's classic midwestern-farmer painting "American Gothic," with Albert stamping a pitchfork in time to the final notes of the song.

Mizzy described the "Green Acres" theme as "bright country," with downhome instrumentation including fuzz guitar and harmonica. The lyrics were instantly memorable: Oliver begins with "Green Acres is the place to be/Farm livin' is the life for me . . ." while Lisa responds with "New York is where I'd rather stay/I get allergic smelling hay . . ."

Unlike "The Addams Family," the stars of "Green Acres" also sang the title song. Albert had a background as a musical-comedy star, so Mizzy knew that he could perform; Gabor was "a sweetie pie," Mizzy recalled, but after several tries, she was unable to sing the lyrics properly. Finally, he asked her to "talk it. Blasé. Park Avenue. Do it in that bored, rich tone that you can do so well"—which she managed. The only line she had to sing was the final one ("Green Acres, we are there") in harmony with Albert. "That was the biggest luck-out in the history of singing," Mizzy said, "but she hit the right notes."

Mizzy did other comedies with Levy, including "The Double Life of Henry Phyfe" with Red Buttons (1966, ABC), "The Pruitts of Southampton" with

Phyllis Diller (1966–67, ABC), and "Captain Nice" (1967, NBC). At the movies, he scored the William Castle spine-tingler *The Night Walker* (1964), the Tony Curtis satire *Don't Make Waves* (1967), and five Don Knotts films including *The Ghost and Mr. Chicken* (1966) and *The Reluctant Astronaut* (1967).

Competing with "The Addams Family" during the same two seasons was another monster-family comedy, "The Munsters" (1964–66, CBS) with Fred Gwynne and Yvonne DeCarlo as Herman and Lily Munster, and Al Lewis as Lily's father Grandpa. Herman may or may not have been the original Frankenstein monster, and Grandpa may or may not have been Dracula. Little Eddie Munster (Butch Patrick) sported a definite werewolf look, and niece Marilyn (Beverly Owen, later Pat Priest) was the "normal"-looking one of the family.

Unlike "The Addams Family," the humor of "The Munsters" wasn't dark but rather sunny: a broadly played, traditional family sitcom that happened to star a bevy of happy monsters living in a literally haunted house at 1313 Mockingbird Lane. Guitarist-composer Jack Marshall ("The Deputy") wrote the theme and scored the episodes in a cartoony Halloween fashion, with organ, brass, and twangy electric guitar, for a kind of Bernard Herrmann-meets-Duane Eddy sound.

Vic Mizzy wasn't the only television composer to write wild music for wild concepts. Veteran songwriters Jay Livingston and Ray Evans, who wrote the title tune for "Bonanza," came up with the perennially popular theme for "Mister Ed" (1961–65, CBS).

"Mister Ed" was essentially a variation on the *Francis the Talking Mule* pictures (1949–56). Arthur Lubin, who directed the first six of the seven *Francis* movies, created "Mister Ed," about a palomino whose new owner (Alan Young, as architect Wilbur Post) is startled to discover that the horse can speak. He only talks to Wilbur, naturally, and most of the episodes centered on Ed getting Wilbur into one jam after another.

Livingston and Evans's memorable lyrics ("a horse is a horse, of course, of course . . .") were actually performed by Livingston on the soundtrack. Recalled Livingston: "Raoul Kraushaar, who scored all of Filmways's pictures, went to Rome to record it. They got an Italian opera singer to sing 'Mr. Ed.' I'd like to have heard that," he laughed. According to Livingston, producer Al Simon called just a week before the show was to go on the air, panicked because the operatic version was—to no one's surprise—unusable. Simon had liked the way Livingston had performed the song at an early demonstration, and asked if he would pinch-hit until a professional singer could be engaged to perform the song for the show's soundtrack.

"I said, okay. I thought it was a temporary track. And I had a lot of trouble with it because there's no place [for a singer] to breathe. My wife [popular singer] Jo Stafford coached me; otherwise I would never had gotten through it." Livingston's voice was never replaced. That was even Livingston saying, in his deepest bass tones at the end of the song, "I am Mister Ed." Even though longtime B-western star Allan "Rocky" Lane did the voice of the horse—and was, according to some reports, originally considered to perform the entire song—he apparently wasn't approached.

Livingston and Evans's Oscar-winning "Que Sera, Sera (Whatever Will Be, Will Be)," originally written for Alfred Hitchcock's 1956 thriller *The Man Who Knew Too Much* and thereafter star Doris Day's signature tune, later became the theme for "The Doris Day Show" (1968–73, CBS). They also wrote the title song for the John Forsythe comedy "To Rome with Love" (CBS, 1969–71), for which Frank DeVol supplied the underscore.

Earle Hagen's first job in television lasted more than a decade: "The Danny Thomas Show" (1953–64, ABC/CBS). He and partner Herbert W. Spencer spent the late forties and early fifties as arranger-orchestrators at Twentieth Century-Fox (including work on two films that won Oscars for musical direction, 1947's *Mother Wore Tights* and 1953's *Call Me Madam*). "In 1953, when the studios cut back [on music departments], Herbie and I formed a partnership and we went into television," Hagen recalled. "We did three pilots that year, and two of them sold: 'The Danny Thomas Show' and 'The Ray Bolger Show.' Ray stayed on two years and Danny stayed on eleven." Both were filmed situation comedies.

The Thomas show secured Hagen's future in the business, not just because of its longevity but because of the professional relationships Hagen forged. Six weeks after the launch of the Thomas series, Sheldon Leonard came aboard as director and executive producer. The former B-movie character actor would go on to become one of TV's most successful producers, and Hagen scored nearly all of his shows.

"Sheldon was unique," Hagen said. "The first time I met him, he said, 'Do you know your business?' and I said, 'Yeah, I do.' He said, 'Good, you'll never hear from me.' In seventeen years, he never ran a picture with me, he never went to a dubbing or a recording, and he never second-guessed me. It was like Camelot. The implication was that he hired the best people he could get and then stayed out of their way. He had plenty to do himself." Leonard broke with then-standard television practice of tracking shows. "Every episode of every show that Sheldon Leonard ever did was scored," Hagen said, recalling a memorable Leonard quip that the practice of tracking music originally intended for another show would be like "wearing somebody else's underwear."

"The Danny Thomas Show," originally titled "Make Room for Daddy," was a family comedy that cast Thomas as a nightclub entertainer. Jean Hagen played his first wife, Marjorie Lord his second, and Rusty Hamer, Sherry Jackson, and Angela Cartwright played his children. It was filmed before a studio audience. Hagen recalled the showmanship that was involved with staging an episode: "I would come in at six o'clock and record the two previous weeks' scoring to stopwatch. Then we would rehearse; if there were any [live] num-

bers, we would rehearse them. And then we would go on the stage and introduce people [the cast] with fanfares. During [camera] setups, we would play
dance music. And we would go home at nine o'clock." The same routine was
followed on "The Dick Van Dyke Show" (1961–66, CBS).

Hagen arranged "Londonderry Air" ("Danny Boy") as the theme for "The
Danny Thomas Show." He composed most of the incidental music for the
show and conducted; Spencer composed some of the cues and wrote most of
the arrangements. Their partnership, publicly known as the Spencer-Hagen
Orchestra, lasted until 1960. Spencer later became orchestrator for John
Williams, working on the *Star Wars* and *Indiana Jones* trilogies.

Thomas and Leonard, now production partners, sold "The Andy Griffith
Show" (1960–68) to CBS in the spring of 1960. Griffith was to play widower
Andy Taylor, sheriff of tiny Mayberry, North Carolina, raising a young son
named Opie (Ronny Howard) with the help of his maiden Aunt Bee (Frances
Bavier); his high-strung deputy, Barney Fife (Don Knotts), was among the
many townspeople whose stories would make up the series.

"We had a whole summer to come up with the theme," recalled Hagen.
"Herbie and I fiddled around with it—we were still partners at that time, and it
was after the show sold that we went our separate ways—and we couldn't get
anything that we really liked. One day I got up and I just thought, here's a guy
who's a simple character. And I started whistling a theme. I called a bass guitar-
and-drum session in a little studio on Fairfax Avenue, and I whistled the theme.
My son, who was eleven years old at the time, did all the finger-snapping. I
played the demo for Sheldon and he said, 'That's perfect. I'm going to shoot
the main title next week and I'll just have Andy and Opie walking along the
lake with a couple of fishing rods.' That was it. And I've never whistled since."

For "The Dick Van Dyke Show," another Leonard series, Hagen opted for
a big-band sound, although Hagen noted, "our bands weren't that big. I think I
had five brass, four saxes, probably four rhythm: fifteen or sixteen pieces
total." Van Dyke's penchant for physical comedy was apparent from the
beginning, so Hagen recalled adding "that little fillip" in the main title, "and
they shot a scene with him tripping over a couch."

"Gomer Pyle, U.S.M.C." (1964–69, CBS), a spinoff from "The Andy
Griffith Show," had the naive gas-station attendant enlisting in the Marine
Corps. Hagen composed a lively military march for the main title, in which the
hapless Pyle was being screamed at by his tough sergeant (Frank Sutton). Still
another Thomas-Leonard show, "That Girl" (1966–71, ABC), starred Danny's
daughter Marlo Thomas in the first of a trend of young-career-woman comedies. Hagen's theme for "That Girl" was light and airy (pizzicato strings) with
a brassy jazz kick.

Amazingly, every episode of these sitcoms boasted an original score
(although sometimes only a few minutes of music, in addition to the main- and
end-title themes, was required). For most of the 1960s, Hagen was juggling
three shows at once: at one time, the Thomas, Griffith, and Van Dyke shows;

later, the Griffith, Van Dyke, and Nabors series; still later, Nabors plus "I Spy" and "That Girl." Observed Hagen: "We had it better than anybody before or since. Thomas and Leonard had [their own] postproduction company. We were so organized that we would book our studios a season in advance. There was a discipline involved. We had one producer/story writer per show. In the case of 'Dick Van Dyke,' it was Carl Reiner; for 'Andy Griffith,' it was Aaron Ruben. There was a minimum amount of duplication. And the head honcho, the executive producer of all the shows, was Sheldon Leonard.

"Today you look at a credit and you see two executive producers and nine other producers, so that in order to get a decision you have to have a committee meeting. Anybody down the line can hang up the turning-over of a film. The way we had it organized, they had a certain amount of time to prepare the film, and if they were supposed to turn it over on a Thursday, it was turned over Thursday, not a week from Thursday. So that we [composers] had two weeks on an hour show, a week on a half-hour comedy show. Today you get a day. And nobody wasted anybody's time. It was totally professional."

"The Patty Duke Show" (1963–66, ABC) featured another favorite TV theme. This comedy was about look-alike cousins, both played by young Oscar winner Duke (*The Miracle Worker*). She played Patty Lane, a fun-loving teenager from Brooklyn Heights, New York, and Cathy Lane, her elegant and refined Scottish cousin who lived with Patty's family (the parents were played by William Schallert and Jean Byron). This typically silly sixties sitcom—identities switched, mischief ensues—joined the trend of shows whose themes outlined the series' premise. With lively music by Sid Ramin (b. 1924) and clever lyrics by Robert Welles, the song introduced each twin and described them in a memorably sixties fashion: ". . . where Cathy adores a minuet, the Ballet Russe and crepes suzette/our Patty loves her rock 'n' roll, a hot dog makes her lose control—what a wild duet!"

Ramin began his television career as an arranger on Milton Berle's "Texaco Star Theater" (NBC, 1948–56) and became a well-known Broadway orchestrator, winning an Oscar and a Grammy for his work on the 1961 film version of *West Side Story*. He landed "The Patty Duke Show" when writer Robert Alan Arthur—with whom he had been working on the stage show *Kwamina* in Toronto—introduced him to series creator-producer Sidney Sheldon. Welles had written the lyrics for Mel Tormé's internationally popular "Christmas Song" ("Chestnuts roasting on an open fire . . ."). Ramin recalled that their approach was upbeat: "I composed the front of [the song]. Then I presented that to Bob and he put lyrics to it. Then we both sat down and extended it; that we kind of worked out together from his lyric. We practically wrote the song side by side, sitting on his piano bench."

Ramin achieved the honor of composer credit during the main-title sequence, a then-unprecedented move that he attributed to his friendship with creator Sheldon. Few other composers (aside from Dave Brubeck on "Mr.

Broadway" in 1964, and Mike Post on several Stephen J. Cannell shows more than two decades later) ever received such front-end credit.

While scoring "The Patty Duke Show" in New York, Ramin gained considerable fame on Madison Avenue for writing commercial jingles, notably the "Come Alive" campaign for Pepsi-Cola (1964). He then was signed to score Peter Falk's first series, "The Trials of O'Brien" (1965–66, CBS), about a disorganized but brilliant lawyer. Ramin composed a jaunty theme for "O'Brien" (and got the great Johnny Mercer to write a lyric, which the producers never used) as well as subsidiary themes for several of the series' running characters. The series died but the main theme lived on, in a way: it was quite similar to Ramin's 1966 Diet Pepsi jingle, "Music to Watch Girls By," which became a worldwide hit and was recorded nearly two hundred times.

It is hard to imagine a greater contrast between a composer's film and television careers than that of Jerry Fielding. In films, he was well known for his music for the grim, often bloody pictures of directors Sam Peckinpah and Michael Winner (*The Wild Bunch, The Mechanic*), yet in TV, he was often called to score light music for half-hour comedies.

Fielding lent an appropriately military tone to the music for the Ernest Borgnine wartime comedy "McHale's Navy" (1962–66, ABC), although its jaunty theme was actually composed by former Frank Sinatra bandleader Axel Stordahl (1913–63). Fielding wound up scoring both big-screen films based on the show (about the misadventures of the crew of a navy PT boat in the South Pacific), as well as "Broadside" (1964–65, ABC), a female variation on the formula that starred Kathy Nolan as one of a quartet of women mechanics stationed on a South Pacific island.

"McHale's Navy" was just a warmup for Fielding's most popular series, another World War II sitcom called "Hogan's Heroes" (1965–71, CBS). Bob Crane starred as an American officer in charge of Allied soldiers in a German prisoner-of-war camp run by an incompetent colonel (Werner Klemperer). The show's content offended some survivors as making light of Nazi atrocities and remains controversial in reruns decades later. Fielding's main theme was a bouncy march that made an impression because of its surprising orchestration and dynamics: starting boldly with heavy, military-style percussion (establishing the POW camp locale) then segueing to a jovial mood with woodwinds and brass, as the individual cast members were introduced and the lighthearted premise became clear.

Fielding, who also composed the incidental music for the series, would work on about two dozen other comedies in his career but never have a bigger hit. Many lasted just a season or two: "Run, Buddy, Run" (1966–67, CBS), with Jack Sheldon as a man on the run from inept mobsters; "The Good Guys" (1968–70, CBS), a Bob Denver-Herb Edelman show about a diner; "The Governor and J.J." (1969–70, CBS), with Dan Dailey and Julie Sommars as a midwestern state's chief executive and his daughter; "The Little People"

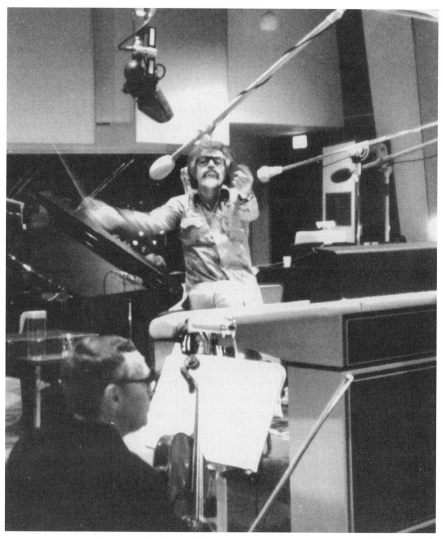

Jerry Fielding. Courtesy Screen Archives Entertainment.

(1972–74, NBC) with Brian Keith and Shelley Fabares as father-and-daughter pediatricians in Hawaii; and "Diana" (1973–74, NBC), Diana Rigg's American debut as a solo comedy star.

Three of Fielding's series became minor classics. The critical favorite "He and She" (1967–68, CBS) cast real-life spouses Richard Benjamin and Paula Prentiss as a cartoonist and his wife, along with Jack Cassidy as the egomania-cal star of a TV series based on Benjamin's comic strip. The short-lived "Chicago Teddy Bears" (1971, CBS), set in a 1920s Chicago speakeasy, was renowned for its classic cars and Fielding's delightful score, which incorporated both ragtime and Dixieland elements. "Bridget Loves Bernie" (1972–73, CBS) was much debated, and finally canceled (despite its top-10 ranking in the Nielsen ratings), because of its interfaith marriage theme: Catholic girl (Meredith Baxter) wed to a Jewish man (David Birney).

"Bewitched" (1964–72, ABC) was the longest-running of the Screen Gems comedies and an early beneficiary of the coming trend of pop songwriters involved with television music. Songwriter-publisher Don Kirshner had, in 1963, sold his company Aldon Music to Columbia Pictures-Screen Gems and was named president of the company's music division. The deal included the contracts of several top songwriters for the pop market, including Neil Sedaka and the hit-producing songwriting teams of Barry Mann and Cynthia Weil, Carole King and Gerry Goffin, and Howard Greenfield and Jack Keller. Composer Keller (b. 1936) and lyricist Greenfield wrote the hits "Breakin' in a Brand New Broken Heart," "Ev'rybody's Somebody's Fool," and "My Heart Has a Mind of Its Own" for Connie Francis, and "When Somebody Loves You" for Frank Sinatra. With Neil Sedaka, Greenfield had also written "Breaking Up Is Hard to Do," "Calendar Girl," and "Where the Boys Are."

Greenfield and Keller, still writing in New York's Tin Pan Alley, were assigned to view the pilot for the Elizabeth Montgomery sitcom about a witch named Samantha who was married to an advertising executive (Dick York, later Dick Sargent). "The pilot had used [Frank] Sinatra's 'Witchcraft,' but they didn't want to pay for 'Witchcraft,' so they asked us to write something," Keller recalled. "We only had a week to write the song, do the demo, and get it out to California. And they accepted it and they put it on. The show was a smash. We had thirteen recordings the first year [including] Peggy Lee and Steve Lawrence."

The series, however, adopted an instrumental version. The animated main title—of a gorgeous witch riding sidesaddle on a broom across the night sky, writing the word "Bewitched" over the city—was underscored with a light orchestral arrangement by series composer Warren Barker. (There was talk of a vocal during the second year, Keller said, but "they didn't want to spend $2,500 to pay for that portion of the session that Jerry Vale agreed to do.")

Barker (b. 1923) was called to do "Bewitched" on the basis of an album that he had recorded using the exotic instruments that actor William Holden had collected on his around-the-world travels. "The producer thought it was exactly the type of music that they were looking for. It was full of bells and tinkling sounds, and they thought that it fit the mood of 'Bewitched,'" Barker said. The xylophone signature for Samantha's trademark nose-twitch was Barker's idea, and he incorporated it into the main title. "We caught a lot of the action musically," Barker said, "and because things happened so fast on the show, most of the music cues were very short. If we had a cue that lasted ten to fifteen seconds, that was a long piece of music."

Greenfield and Keller went on to write the theme for "Gidget" with Sally Field (1965–66, ABC)—"Wait'll you see my Gidget/you'll want her for your Valentine . . ."—as well as lesser Screen Gems efforts, "Camp Runamuck" (1965–66, NBC) and "The Wackiest Ship in the Army" (1965–66, NBC). They also penned a new theme for the hugely popular "Hazel" with Shirley Booth (1961–66, NBC/CBS), although its original Sammy Cahn-Jimmy Van Heusen theme song also continued to be used (one as the main title, the other for the end credits).

Keller had an even bigger hit with "Seattle," the theme for the David Soul-Bobby Sherman western sitcom "Here Come the Brides" (1968–70, ABC), which he cowrote with Ernie Sheldon. Hugo Montenegro, who arranged the main title (in its original instrumental version, replaced after a few weeks by a vocal version by The New Establishment), also received songwriting credit. Perry Como's version of the song went to Number 2 on the adult contemporary charts and was a top-40 hit on the pop charts.

Songwriters Mann and Weil, meanwhile, wrote the theme for "The Farmer's Daughter" (1963–66, ABC), and producer Kirshner went on to oversee the music for the first season of "The Monkees" (1966–68, NBC), including hiring pop writers Tommy Boyce and Bobby Hart to compose the title song ("Hey, hey, we're the Monkees . . ."). Mike Nesmith, Davy Jones, Mickey Dolenz, and Peter Tork were the fictionalized, fun-loving rock 'n' roll group based loosely on the Beatles (and their antics on the freewheeling format of the Fab Four's 1964 film *A Hard Day's Night*). Stu Phillips composed the scores, but the songs—including the hits "Last Train to Clarksville," "I'm a Believer," "Pleasant Valley Sunday," and "Daydream Believer"—were written by established rockers such as Boyce and Hart, Neil Diamond, King and Goffin, and John Stewart, respectively.

Two sitcoms took to the airwaves with outrageous songs in the fall of 1965. "F Troop" (1965–67, ABC) sent up the western with Forrest Tucker and Larry Storch as scheming, Bilko-style con artists at a cavalry post in the post-Civil War West. The song, a snappy march by William Lava ("Cheyenne") with a lyric by Irving Taylor, explained how their bumbling captain (Ken Berry) took command of Fort Courage. Its funniest line would later become politically incorrect: ". . . where Indian fights are colorful sights and nobody takes a lickin'/Where paleface and redskin both turn chicken . . ."

"My Mother the Car" (1965–66, NBC) was one of a kind as a sitcom. Not only did it open with a song that set up the bizarre premise, the lyrics were actually printed, follow-the-bouncing-ball-style, on the screen during the entire main-title sequence. Written and sung by Paul Hampton (b. 1940) to a bouncy Dixie accompaniment (plus ooga horns) and images of Jerry Van Dyke tooling around town in his 1928 Porter, it explained: ". . . Well you all may think my story is more fiction than it's fact/But believe it or not my mother dear decided she'd come back—as a car. . . ."

The potential for controversy surrounding another strange sitcom actually trickled down to the composer. "I was doing a pilot," Dominic Frontiere recalled, "and I got a call from Leonard Goldenson." Goldenson was the president of ABC; Frontiere was floored. "Are you sure he wants to talk to me?" he asked the secretary. According to the composer, Goldenson expressed enormous concern about the show he was scoring. "I hope you realize what a serious situation you're in. Sixty million dollars worth of product is hanging on your shoulders, and you're going to be totally responsible if you do this wrong," Frontiere remembered Goldenson saying.

The series was "The Flying Nun" (1967–70, ABC), about Sister Bertrille (Sally Field), a novice at a Puerto Rican convent who discovered that, owing to her stature and her cornette, she could easily become airborne with the winds. "They were so worried about Catholicism, and how the music would play," Frontiere said. He described his approach to Goldenson: "As far as I'm concerned, it's a Broadway musical. I'm going to write a show opener, and the title of the song is, 'Who needs wings to fly? Certainly not I.'

"I had already come to the conclusion that I wasn't going to write any organ music. And in those days, we had a brand-new music that didn't have any gender attached to it, called the bossa nova. So I put a lot of bossa novas into the show, because it could represent almost anything."

Three sixties and seventies comedies took the then-unusual tack of hiring pop singer-songwriters to supply distinctive themes: "The Courtship of Eddie's Father" (1969–72, ABC), whose title tune was penned by Harry Nilsson; "Chico and the Man" (1974–78, NBC), by José Feliciano; and "Welcome Back, Kotter" (1975–79, ABC), by John Sebastian. All three had one individual in common: producer James Komack.

Komack's surprising composer choices extended back even farther, to his role as producer on "Mr. Roberts" (1965–66, NBC), a sitcom adaptation of the Broadway and movie hit starring Roger Smith in the title role. Komack had been the president of the first Stan Kenton fan club back in the forties, so for his World War II comedy he decided to hire the bandleader to score his show (although his original, quickly discarded, notion was to have Kenton play the captain). Kenton (1911–79) actually scored the first two episodes. "It was a terrific score, a lot of great Kenton music," Komack recalled. "But it wouldn't fit [the picture]." Both scores were thrown out as unusable, with Warner composer Frank Perkins writing a new theme and scoring the first episode, and Johnny Mandel replacing the second score. The Kenton music went into the library, but during the entire thirty-episode run only one piece of original Kenton material—a cue called "Elysium Anchorage," lasting all of twenty-three seconds—was ever used in the series.

For "Eddie's Father," about the relationship between a widower (Bill Bixby) and his constantly matchmaking son (Brandon Cruz), Komack went searching for a fresh sound: "something that hadn't been done before," he said. "Otherwise, with a standard music track, 'The Courtship of Eddie's Father' would sound like every other show on television: 'Father Knows Best' or 'My Mother the Car.' I didn't want that. I wanted to do something that was very up, and hip, and accessible."

He discovered Nilsson, whom he had not heard of, by listening to a stack of contemporary pop records he had been loaned. At the time, by coincidence, Nilsson was actually on the MGM lot (where Komack was making "Eddie's Father") acting in director Otto Preminger's all-star bomb *Skidoo* (1968), which he later scored. Nilsson (1941–94) came up with a song that began, "People, let me tell you 'bout my best friend . . ." and included, at the end, a number of offbeat vocal effects, which sounded a bit old-fashioned to Komack. "It sounds like Rudy Vallee with a megaphone," the producer recalled telling Nilsson. Still, Komack liked it and went a step further, asking the singer-songwriter to interpolate musical commentary within the episodes themselves.

Nilsson's happy tune played over main- and end-title visuals of Bixby and Cruz strolling, running, and frolicking along the seashore. The performer's end-title credit was certainly unique in television history: "music and lyrics written and sunged by Nilsson." Nilsson's friend George Aliceson Tipton arranged and conducted the scores (Tipton would later go on to write the music for the seventies and eighties sitcoms "Soap" and "Benson"). To Komack's chagrin, however, Nilsson never recorded the theme for commercial release. He later wrote and sang the delightful song score for the animated TV movie "The Point" (1971, ABC).

When he created "Chico and the Man," a sitcom set in East Los Angeles, Komack again sought a musical sound that would seem right for the story: the often comic relationship between a white garage owner (Jack Albertson) and his Mexican-American employee (Freddie Prinze). Prinze played a Chicano, although he was of partly Puerto Rican descent; José Feliciano (b. 1945) was also Puerto Rican and, a few years earlier, had a top-10 hit with his cover of the Doors' "Light My Fire."

Komack traveled to Las Vegas, where Feliciano was performing, to ask him to provide a theme. Later, the producer played the pilot for the blind musician. "He listened to the entire dialogue," Komack said, "and I told him what it was about." Feliciano and his wife, Janna Merlyn Feliciano, wound up writing not one but two songs: the Latin-flavored title tune ("Chico, don't be discouraged/the man, he ain't so hard to understand . . ."), featuring Feliciano's trademark acoustic guitar sound, which won an Emmy nomination; and a second song ("Hard Times in El Barrio") that Komack chose to play under the end titles. Feliciano also appeared in a 1976 episode.

On "Welcome Back, Kotter," Komack never even met his composer, former Lovin' Spoonful singer-songwriter John Sebastian (b. 1944); they only spoke on the phone. It was Alan Sacks, cocreator (with Gabriel Kaplan, the

John Sebastian. Courtesy Reprise Records.

star) of the series, who initially suggested a John Sebastian-style, easy-rocking theme for the show about a teacher (Kaplan, a popular standup comedian) who returns to his old Brooklyn high school to instruct a group of hopeless misfits known as the "sweathogs" (including later film star John Travolta).

Sacks spoke with agent Dave Bendett, an old friend and fellow Brook-lynite; as it happened, Bendett had just taken over management of John Sebastian, and a meeting was set. Sebastian had not previously written a TV theme, although the Lovin' Spoonful had contributed songs and music to the 1966 films *What's Up, Tiger Lily?* and *You're a Big Boy Now.*

Sebastian did not see the pilot; he read a ten-page synopsis and two scripts before calling Sacks back to say: "Look, Alan, I know you want this [series] to be called 'Kotter,' but don't make me write something called 'Kotter' because nothing rhymes with it except 'otter.' Let me go for the gist of the story and put it together that way." The songwriter recalled spending about twenty minutes on one tune before deciding that "it was only close" and discarding it. "I started again, and I really wasn't halfway through writing 'Welcome Back' before I thought that this thing could not only go on the television [show], it could go on the radio."

Sebastian's "Welcome back/your dreams were your ticket out . . ." hooked Sacks, Komack and company—so much so that they actually changed the title of the series from "Kotter" to "Welcome Back, Kotter" to capitalize on Sebastian's catchy tune. On the television theme, Sebastian both sang and played acoustic guitar; in the single version, he played harmonica as well. Commenting on the sound, Sebastian said, "We knew what guys from Brooklyn would sound like. So part of the spirit in the studio was being the 'sweathogs' for the afternoon. Just being very New York in everything that we played." The song went to Number 1 on the *Billboard* pop charts in 1976, the second TV tune to do so that year (the "S.W.A.T." theme preceded it by several weeks).

No one had more hit sitcom themes than Charles Fox. One of the busiest film and TV composers of the 1970s and 1980s, Fox counted among his successes "Love, American Style" (1969–74, ABC), "Happy Days" (1974–84, ABC), "Laverne & Shirley" (1976–83, ABC), "The Love Boat" (1976–86, ABC), "Angie" (1979–80, ABC), and "The Hogan Family" (1986–91, NBC). Fox (b. 1940) arrived in Hollywood just in time to update the sound of the television underscore. He was in the vanguard of composers who brought a more contemporary sensibility to TV music after a decade of classically oriented composition.

Fox graduated from New York's High School of Music and Art, and continued his musical studies with Nadia Boulanger in Paris. Robert Russell Bennett introduced him to bandleader Skitch Henderson, who hired Fox to write original material for "The Tonight Show" band in 1962. After scoring documentaries, writing sports themes (including ABC's "Wide World of Sports" in 1965 and the original "Monday Night Football" in 1970), and scoring a rare dramatic special (Mia Farrow's "Johnny Belinda," 1967, ABC), he entered the film-scoring arena with songs and underscore for the Jane Fonda sci-fi picture *Barbarella* (1968).

While working on *Goodbye, Columbus* (1969) at Paramount, he was offered the pilot of "Love, American Style." "It was a great experience for me, because music was very much a part of that show," Fox recalled. "They wanted to go with a more contemporary-sounding score, as opposed to a more traditional one.

Charles Fox, c. mid-seventies. Courtesy the composer.

"'Love, American Style' may have been one of the first television series that really used a pop rhythm section," Fox said. "It was like a record-oriented score. I had completely free range to develop my musical ideas, which combined pop sounds and styles with classical music influences." Fox worked with writer-producer Arnold Margolin on songs for the pilot (which was "almost a musical," Fox recalled) and remained with the series for its entire run. Of four consecutive Emmy nominations, Fox won twice for his "Love, American Style" music: the first season for his title song with Margolin; and the fourth season (1972–73) for his scores.

Because "Love, American Style" was essentially a comedic anthology (three or four different segments per hour, usually light, amusing romantic tales with new casts), Fox was expected to create original scores for each. Yet some of his most creative work was reserved for the blackouts, brief (sometimes just twenty seconds) bits between playlets. "I either scored them with the theme, crisper, faster-moving versions, or in the style of a classical composer—like a Chopin waltz or a Beethoven sonata," Fox said. "So if you had a silly romantic scene and played it with a Brahmsian kind of piano flourish, the juxtaposition of the two things made it fun."

The pilot for "Happy Days" was originally a sketch on "Love, American Style." The show, according to Fox, didn't initially sell; only when the movie *American Graffiti* (1973) became a hit did ABC buy the series, which was set in the 1950s and, like *Graffiti,* starred Ron Howard as a high school kid, this time in Milwaukee. Fox and lyricist Norman Gimbel (who together had written the Grammy-winning 1973 hit "Killing Me Softly") were asked to write a song similar to the Bill Haley tune "Rock Around the Clock," which was such an important component of the *American Graffiti* score. Gimbel's response to "one, two, three o'clock, four o'clock rock" became "Sunday, Monday, Happy Days/Tuesday, Wednesday, Happy Days . . ."

"I wasn't into the pop music of the fifties," Fox admitted. "I really had very little familiarity with those records at that time. I started listening to pop music in the sixties. So for this project, I immersed myself in the records of the fifties in order to write a new song that would sound like a hit from the fifties, and yet one that could become a hit in the seventies." ABC decided against using the Fox-Gimbel song and, for the first season, bought "Rock Around the Clock" for use over the series' main title (again, to reinforce the actually nonexistent *American Graffiti* connection). An instrumental version of the "Happy Days" theme ran over the end titles.

Only later, as part of the many changes made during the series' run (shooting with three cameras before a live audience, playing up Henry Winkler as The Fonz), did "Happy Days" make its main-title debut as a song. The show, and the song, were almost immediate hits. "Happy Days" shot to the top of the Nielsen ratings for the 1976–77 season, and the single, sung by Pratt & McClain, reached Number 5 on the *Billboard* charts in 1976.

For its first spinoff, "Laverne & Shirley," Fox and Gimbel were again enlisted for a title song, although the presentation reel was hastily assembled before the characters were fully developed. According to Fox, the producers' original descriptions of the girls (played by Penny Marshall and Cindy Williams) were "two blue-collar brewery workers who had dreams of getting out and achieving things in life."

So Fox and Gimbel wrote a song about "these girls wishing and hoping that their dreams would come true." The producers' reaction to that initial effort, however, was that the girls "were not going to sit around and just wish and hope—they're going to make it happen, come out and take the world by storm." That, said Fox, is how the "Laverne & Shirley" theme went from "wishing our dreams will come true" to "Making Our Dreams Come True." Cyndi Grecco's vocal, produced by Fox and Gimbel, climbed the charts at about the same time that "Happy Days" was also a hit record.

Between feature assignments like *The Other Side of the Mountain* (1975) and *Foul Play* (1978)—both Oscar-nominated for Best Song—Fox found time to write still another now-classic theme. "The Love Boat" was written for the 1976 TV movie pilot. Producer Doug Cramer, according to the composer, had told him that he and Aaron Spelling were effectively shooting "'Love, American Style' on the ocean," and that the theme should be "filled with romance and adventure and the kind of excitement that you'd get from taking off on a cruise."

Fox reprised the theme in the 1977 sequel; for a third movie, also in 1977, he asked Paul Williams (with whom he had collaborated on the movie *One on One,* writing songs for Seals & Crofts) to pen a lyric ("Love, exciting and new . . ."). Jack Jones sang it, and the song accompanied the series when it premiered that fall. Jones's vocal was heard every season except the last; Dionne Warwick performed a new version in 1985.

For "Angie," a sitcom about a poor waitress (Donna Pescow) who fell for a rich doctor (Robert Hays), Fox and Gimbel wrote "Different Worlds," sung by Maureen McGovern (the vocalist who had made a hit of "The Morning After," from *The Poseidon Adventure,* and went on to become one of the foremost interpreters of the songs of Gershwin and Porter). The series lasted only a year and a half, but McGovern's record went to Number 18 on the charts. Other memorable Fox themes included "The First Years" for "The Paper Chase" (1978–79, CBS), with a Gimbel lyric sung by Seals & Crofts, and "Together Through the Years" for "The Hogan Family" (with lyrics by Stephen Geyer), performed on the soundtrack by Roberta Flack. Fox also wrote several acclaimed scores for television films, including "Victory at Entebbe" (1976, ABC), "Baby M" (1988, ABC), and "Crash Landing: The Rescue of Flight 232" (1992, ABC).

"Who can turn the world on with her smile? Who can take a nothing day and suddenly make it all seem worthwhile? . . ." A tune that is as instantly identifiable as the image of Mary Tyler Moore tossing her hat in the air on the streets of Minneapolis: "Love Is All Around," singer-songwriter Sonny Curtis's theme for "The Mary Tyler Moore Show" (1970–77, CBS). The premise had the ex-"Dick Van Dyke Show" actress playing a single young career woman, associate producer at a second-rate TV news operation with a gruff boss (Ed Asner), a moronic anchorman (Ted Knight), and a cutup newswriter (Gavin MacLeod); and, at home, a wisecracking neighbor (Valerie Harper) and a vain landlady (Cloris Leachman). "The Mary Tyler Moore Show" went on to become one of the most beloved of all television comedy series.

Texas-born Curtis (b. 1937) had played guitar behind Buddy Holly in the late 1950s and written hits for other artists (including "I Fought the Law" for Bobby Fuller in 1966 and, later, "More Than I Can Say" for Leo Sayer in 1980). As it happened, an old friend was working in the office of Arthur Price, manager for Mary Tyler Moore (and later president of the MTM production company), and tipped off Curtis that they might need a theme song. "He came by my house that very day at lunch and dropped off a four-page format—just a treatment of what the show was going to be about," Curtis recalled. "So I wrote [the song] in about two hours. And I called him back and said, 'Where do you want me to go sing this thing?'" Curtis, who lived in Studio City at the time, was sent over to the nearby offices of cocreators James L. Brooks and Allan Burns.

They had barely settled into their new digs, Burns remembered: "Sonny Curtis, a bearded guy, walked in. He was very shy, kind of mumbled in his beard. He took out a scrap of paper, put it on his guitar case and just started singing this song. And Jim and I just looked at each other [and said] 'It's perfect. How can this be so easy?' We never wanted anything else other than that song."

At the time, Curtis had the title "Love Is All Around" and a verse that asked, "How will you make it on your own?", reflecting Mary Richards's new arrival alone in Minneapolis. "Fortunately, Doug [Gilmore, his pal at the Price agency] didn't give me very much information," the songwriter explained. "I think too much information can really bog things down. You don't want to write too much. What Doug gave me was a story about this girl from a small town in the Midwest who had been jilted and gotten a job at a TV station in Minneapolis, and couldn't afford her apartment, that sort of stuff. That's all I had to go on, so I just took it from there. Of course, it wasn't like rocket science or anything, just a one-verse little song," he laughed.

"Jim called a whole bunch of people in, had me sing it five or six times, and finally ordered a cassette recorder and put it down. He wanted to take it to Minneapolis with him," Curtis said. "They were going to shoot the [main title] that weekend." Curtis originally concluded the song with the line "You might just make it after all . . ." but, at the request of the producers, altered it for the second season to a more assured "you're gonna make it after all." It was also in the second season that Curtis added that memorable opening line: "Who can turn the world on with her smile?" (Curtis later wrote the theme for the

Patrick Williams. Photo by John Rose, courtesy the composer.

short-lived 1977 Ned Beatty sitcom "Szysznyk" and one of the themes for Burt Reynolds's "Evening Shade," in 1991.)

That "Love Is All Around" seemed so right for Moore was a testament to the sound that arranger-conductor Pat Williams was able to achieve, with a little orchestral massaging. Williams's assignment was also something of a fluke. In 1970, the former New York big-band arranger had only been in Hollywood for two years. His wife and Burns's wife had been friends; Burns knew of Williams's jazz records. Recalled Williams, "It wasn't a particularly big deal. I don't think the network even cared about it that much. It was just a three-camera show."

Curtis had already composed the song, so there was never any intent for Williams to compete. "My job was to do whatever the underscore situation was, mostly bridges," he says. And, when it came time to record the theme, "we put some strings on it, tried to warm it up a little bit so that it fit [Moore's] character. Make the arrangement somewhat appropriate. Years later, one of the things that [Twentieth Century-Fox musical director] Lionel Newman told me was that he really liked what I had done with 'The Mary Tyler Moore Show' and some of the other [MTM] shows.

"It's very difficult to write all those little bridges and make them sound reasonably interesting. It may be a three- or four-bar cue but there are so many starts on a [recording] date. You have to do maybe ten or twelve cues a particular show, so there are thirty to thirty-five starts to record. And you have to keep the orchestra's attention level up. It's not as easy as it sounds."

Williams struck gold with "The Mary Tyler Moore Show." The series became a hit, and MTM Enterprises became one of television's leading independent production companies. Williams—while also pursuing other scoring opportunities, like Quinn Martin's "The Streets of San Francisco"—became a fixture at MTM, scoring all seven seasons of "Mary Tyler Moore" as well as "The Bob Newhart Show" (1972–78, CBS), Paul Sand's "Friends and Lovers" (1974–75, CBS), "The Tony Randall Show" (1976–78, ABC/CBS), "Lou Grant" (1977–82, CBS), "FM" (1989–90, NBC), and many others.

The original "Bob Newhart Show," like the Moore series, posed an arranging as well as a composing challenge. The comedian played a Chicago psychologist, harassed at work by clients and fellow office denizens (Peter Bonerz as an orthodontist and Marcia Wallace as their receptionist) and at home by an airline navigator (Bill Daily), with only his understanding wife (Suzanne Pleshette) to provide some stability in a life filled with crazies. Producer Lorenzo Music and his wife Henrietta had composed a theme that Williams was asked to adapt for the series' main-title sequence.

Williams's brassy sound, designed to establish the Chicago setting, bookended the more relaxed love theme (composed by the Musics). As for the underscore, "the approach was not wildly different," Williams recalls, "but the bands were completely different. 'Newhart' had a couple of saxophones and some brass. It was more like a little hot jazz band, with no strings at all. On Mary's show, we always used a string section, which was more feminine. 'Newhart' was a little edgier."

Producer Jay Tarses, whom Williams met on the "Newhart" show, continued to commission music from the composer into the eighties and nineties. Williams's theme for "The Days and Nights of Molly Dodd" (1987–91, NBC/Lifetime), the thoughtful and nuanced Blair Brown comedy-drama about a single woman in New York, featured jazz violin as the solo instrument. "We talked about an uptown kind of jazzy feel," Tarses said, "and he came up with that Stephane Grappelli kind of 'le jazz hot' violin" as the musical voice for Molly. Her boyfriend was a jazz saxophonist, so music became an integral part of many scores; Williams was twice Emmy-nominated for "Molly Dodd."

The groundbreaking comedy series of producer Norman Lear, from "All in the Family" to "Maude" and "Sanford and Son," made him the single most successful TV producer of the 1970s. Unlike Sheldon Leonard, however, Lear rarely stuck with the same composer.

For "All in the Family" (1971–79, CBS)—Lear's controversial sitcom about Queens, New York, bigot Archie Bunker, his good-hearted wife Edith, daughter Gloria, and liberal son-in-law Mike—the producer defied TV conventions not only in program concept but in theme music as well. Having worked with

Broadway songwriters Charles Strouse and Lee Adams on his 1968 feature film *The Night They Raided Minsky's,* Lear asked them, rather than the usual Hollywood-based composers, to write a theme. Strouse (b. 1928) and Adams (b. 1924), who had a major hit with *Bye Bye Birdie* and who would later write *Annie,* came up with "Those Were the Days," a nostalgic paean to simpler times in America, with a hint of ragtime influence: "Boy, the way Glenn Miller played/Songs that made the hit parade/Guys like us, we had it made . . ."

Strouse recalled: "He paid us a few hundred dollars; it was all he could afford. And he said that he would like it scored for chorus and orchestra. I told him at the time that you couldn't even get a studio for that amount of money. I suggested that, when I was a kid, my mother used to sit at the piano and we all stood around to sing. [The Bunkers] are a lower-middle-class family; why doesn't somebody sit at the piano and everyone just gather around and sing?"

In fact, Strouse added, "There was no choice because there was no money to do anything else. So I sat down and played it, off-camera," while Carroll O'Connor and Jean Stapleton (as Archie and Edith) sang on-camera. (Strouse's original piano performance, heard in the initial episodes, was eventually replaced with that of a studio pianist.) Surprisingly—considering Stapleton's in-character screeching of lines like "and you knew who you were then"—the song, as released commercially, went to Number 30 on the *Billboard* easy-listening chart. The Strouse-Adams tune was used only over the show's main title. Jazz composer Roger Kellaway (b. 1939) contributed a player piano-style tune (subsequently titled "Remembering You" with an O'Connor lyric, one he sang on an album but that was never heard in the show) for the end titles.

The immediate success of "All in the Family" led to the inevitable spinoffs. First was "Maude" (1972–78, CBS), Edith Bunker's loud, outspoken cousin, winningly played by Beatrice Arthur. Again, Lear called for a vocal to accompany the main title, but this time he turned to composer Dave Grusin (another previous collaborator, having scored Lear's 1967 feature *Divorce American Style*) and now-famous Hollywood lyricists Marilyn and Alan Bergman (Oscar winners for "The Windmills of Your Mind" and, the year after "Maude," for *The Way We Were*).

Alan Bergman recalled that Lear initially asked for "something like *Mame.* And we said, 'That's already been written.'" Added Marilyn Bergman: "That was really obvious. We knew that we wanted something to set up the entrance for Bea." Grusin, they said, came up with a novel concept: a gospel-flavored song. Donny Hathaway, with piano, organ, and small choir, performed the tune. The Bergman lyrics introduced the character by recalling, with a cheeky wit, courageous women throughout history: "Lady Godiva was a freedom rider/She didn't care if the whole world looked/Joan of Arc, with the Lord to guide her/She was a sister who really cooked . . ."

"Good Times" (1974–79, CBS) was spun off from "Maude," although this

Marilyn and Alan Bergman. Photo by Spike Nannarello, courtesy the Bergmans.

time the gospel approach of the title music seemed a little more obvious. Esther Rolle, as Maude's ex-maid Florida Evans, was the focal point of this sitcom, about a lower-class black family in Chicago. Grusin and the Bergmans penned a theme similar in style but with a lyric that characterized the series' underlying premise of a positive outlook despite trying economic times: "Temporary layoffs, easy-credit ripoffs/scratching and surviving . . . Ain't we lucky we've got 'em/Good times . . ."

Lear (with partner Bud Yorkin) Americanized another British series (as they had with "All in the Family") and turned it into another top-10 hit: "Sanford and Son" (1972–77, NBC), with Redd Foxx and Demond Wilson as a crotchety old junk dealer and his restless son, living together in Los Angeles.

Yorkin chose Quincy Jones, at that time Hollywood's leading black composer, to compose an instrumental theme.

Recalled Jones: "I said, Redd Foxx on nationwide TV? I had worked with him thirty years ago at the Apollo in Billy Eckstein's band, and I couldn't believe it," based on Foxx's reputation for blue material. Yorkin asked Jones to look at the pilot, but the composer replied, "It's Redd Foxx. I don't need to see the first episode." Jones remembered having to compose a play-on for Foxx in a hurry at the Apollo, and the "Sanford" theme (subtitled "The Streetbeater") came just as fast: "In about twenty minutes, and we recorded it in about twenty minutes, too, because I had known Foxx so well for so long. It just fell out."

The sound was decidedly funky, featuring a harmonica and an organ. "It was like an Earl Bostic kind of feel," Jones said. "We used a washboard and it felt just right. Dave Grusin [on keyboards] and [bassist] Chuck Rainey were on that date, and Ernie Watts [on electric sax], and it just happened so fast."

Jones's most creative work in the comedy genre actually came three years earlier, on "The Bill Cosby Show" (1969–71, NBC). Cosby, then a major TV star coming off his triple-Emmy win for "I Spy," had asked his old friend to contribute the music for his new sitcom, about a Los Angeles physical education teacher and coach named Chet Kincaid. Jones had written a lighthearted jazz theme featuring a tenor saxophone. What happened at an early scoring session, which Jones described as "an accident," led to his first Emmy nomination (1969–70) for music composition in a series.

"Bill loves jazz so much," Jones pointed out. "That's his real frustration. He'd rather be a jazz musician, and he knows a lot about it; he hears it and he understands it. He used to come over from the shooting stage all the time [to the scoring stage]. So one day, I'm watching the screen with the streamers and everything else, and I hear all this noise coming out of the earphones. I said, 'What the hell is that?' I look back and there's Cosby with a sweatsuit on and he's playing Coltrane on a bassoon!

"You know, Cosby can't play a bassoon. But he knows what Coltrane's attitude is about. He's such a maniac. I said, 'No, Bunions'—I've been calling him Bunions for years—'Bunions, you got to get up out of that chair. Here's a cowbell.' And he took the cowbell and he had a cigar in his mouth and I'll never forget it—we went into the theme and he said, 'Woooo Lord! Hikky-burr!'" And he continued with the half-spoken, half-sung but undeniably funny gibberish that Jones then incorporated into both the main- and end-title themes. The tune, which Jones later recorded as "Hikky-Burr," was cocredited to Jones and Cosby.

Even more interesting was Jones's handling of the individual scores, which were largely improvised using an all-star jazz group whose membership changed from week to week.

"We had a very unusual style," Jones explained. "Only Bill [who was executive producer] would let you get away with that. I had a whole sheet of themes for the orchestra. I never wrote the scores; it was like free-form, right to syn-chronization and everything. I would point to the guys and we would go through it once with the thematic material and it was just like creating on the spot. Bill loved that, because every week we'd have Oscar Peterson or Roland Kirk or Cannonball Adderley or Jimmy Smith or Milt Jackson. Every week they'd check in, they'd play the theme and all of the spots, and we'd have those little bridges, and so forth. Just the most incredible lineup of musicians you ever saw.

"I wrote a lot of thematic material. I'd have bass lines and three or four dif-ferent themes, and we had a kind of master sheet. It was like skydiving. You have to have somebody that understands and lets you do that, like Cosby. He really knew where I was coming from; I said, 'Let's try it, it'll be fun.' And it was."

"Making your way in the world today takes everything you got / Taking a break from all your worries sure would help a lot . . .": the opening of the "Cheers" theme, perhaps the most famous song about a bar ever written. It was certainly the most memorable sitcom tune in recent years, owing partly to the series' longevity and partly to its clever lyric and infectious melody. "Cheers" (1982–93, NBC) centered on a Boston bar, its management and patrons. Ted Danson (as Sam Malone, a former Red Sox pitcher and the tavern's propri-etor) remained a constant presence over the show's many seasons, although other key players changed; Shelley Long began the run as Sam's literate wait-ress, replaced later by Kirstie Alley as his boss and, still later, bar manager.

The story of the "Cheers" theme, also known as "Where Everybody Knows Your Name," illustrated the often-haphazard way that crucial elements were arrived at in contemporary network TV. In the spring of 1982, New York songwriters Gary Portnoy and Judy Hart Angelo were working on a new musi-cal called *Preppies*. Angelo had sent a cassette containing several of the num-bers to a California friend whose brother happened to be Emmy-winning director James Burrows ("Taxi"). With writers Glen and Les Charles, Burrows was developing "Cheers" at the time; he heard the tape and thought that one of their songs, "People Like Us," would make a fine theme for their new show.

Angelo recalled: "You have to understand that we now were caught between a rock and a hard place. Since 'People Like Us' was essential to our theater proj-ect, we knew that we couldn't remove it; what we did do was look at each other and quickly blurt out over the phone that we would be happy to write another theme song for their new television show. And they said, 'Great, go to it.'

"Now, it would be nice to be able to say that we went to the piano and promptly tossed off the theme to 'Cheers' as it is known today. In actuality, since they already wanted our other song, we did what any songwriter would do: we sat down and attempted to clone it. The new song was promptly rejected. But, along with the rejections came their encouragement to not box ourselves into our original concept and to do whatever we felt was right for the show.

"Thus freed," Angelo said, "we wrote two more potential themes. One of

Gary Portnoy (at piano), Judy Hart Angelo, and Jay Leno singing the "Cheers" theme during the post-"Cheers" finale festivities, May 1993. Courtesy NBC.

them pleased us enough to write a full-length version in which we speculated on all sorts of life situations that might compel a person to take refuge at a place like Cheers. That song was 'Where Everybody Knows Your Name.' We immediately went into a tiny eight-track studio and made a piano-voice demo."

The original opening lines ("Singing the blues when the home teams lose—it's a crisis in your life/On the run 'cause all your girlfriends wanna be your wife . . .") were changed when the producers asked for a "more general approach [that] might wear better over the course of what everyone hoped would be a long run for the show," noted Angelo. "And thus, 'making your way in the world today . . . ' They were happy. We were happy."

Portnoy, who sang the original demo, was asked to perform the theme for the show itself. Enhancing the song were the creative graphics behind the titles, a series of drawings and still photographs of people in taverns over the past century (which won an Emmy at the end of the show's first season; the song was nominated as well). Portnoy and Angelo subsequently supplied the themes for the comedies "Punky Brewster" (1984–88, NBC), "Mr. Belvedere" (1985–90,

ABC), with a vocal by cult favorite Leon Redbone, and "Marblehead Manor" (1987, syndicated).

When standup comedian Roseanne Barr got her own sitcom, "Roseanne" (1988–, ABC), creator Matt Williams ("The Cosby Show") was very specific about the music he wanted, according to composers Dan Foliart and Howard Pearl, who cowrote the theme and scored the series' first five seasons. Oklahoma native Foliart (b. 1951) and Connecticut-born Pearl (b. 1948) become songwriting partners in the mid-1970s and scored several of Paramount's popular sitcoms including "Angie" and "Bosom Buddies." They met Williams and, according to Pearl, "Matt had definite ideas about what he wanted the tone of the show to be. He told us that he wanted some kind of raw, rural feel."

Foliart recalled coming up with an early version of the theme that Williams rejected as "not earthy enough," yet close enough that the producers gave the team a go-ahead to modify their musical ideas and make a studio demo. "We had the germ of the theme, but it had to be a lot bluesier," Foliart said. They recruited six key musicians and went to Sound City, "the funkiest studio in L.A.," where Bob Dylan had often recorded in the past.

"We started jamming," Foliart said. "It was the same melody that Howard and I had written, but there was something about the mood of the studio, having these great players, and also having Matt sitting there where he could immediately say 'yes' or 'no.'" The sound of "Roseanne"—tenor sax, harmonica, acoustic guitar, bass, drums, and piano—was "accomplished in no small part by the musicians," Pearl said. "I would say that a good part of that theme song was ad-libbed around the melody. And it's their performances that really made it come to life." On-screen, the theme accompanied a camera panning around the Conner family dinner table, with Barr's laughter added to the end of the sequence.

Foliart was called again when Williams created "Home Improvement" for comedian Tim Allen. According to the composer, Williams asked for "something primitive and visceral" to fit Allen's standup persona of a grunting, tool-obsessed macho guy with little understanding of women. Foliart saw Allen's standup act and decided to interpolate not only tool sounds but also Allen's apelike noises into the theme.

As a result, the "Home Improvement" theme was assembled with as many as fifty tracks of various sound effects (jackhammers, drills, breaking glass, wheel sounds, even trains crashing) combined with a small band including electric guitar, organ, and bass harmonica: as Foliart described it, "a hip-hop groove underneath a tapestry of all these different tool sounds," plus Allen's trademark grunt. A flute track was added to represent Tim's wife Jill (Patricia Richardson); Foliart added even more percussion the second season and "a raunchier guitar, with more bite" the third.

Another standup who achieved major television success commissioned a wildly different musical approach. For "Seinfeld" (1990–, NBC), comedian Jerry Seinfeld came to composer Jonathan Wolff (b. 1958) with "more of a sound design problem than a musical one," in the words of the composer.

The main title sequence (at the time a pilot called "The Seinfeld Chronicles") featured Seinfeld, in a nightclub setting, performing material that related to the episode's storyline. Recalled Wolff: "He wanted a catchy, recognizable signature theme that would play along with his comedy monologue but not interfere with the audio of his standup material. So I watched a lot of his comedy material and noticed that his delivery had a unique, quirky rhythm to it. The pacing of his words, phrases, and inflections has a musical quality. So I based the rhythm of the 'Seinfeld' theme on the rhythms of his speech patterns. Jerry's human voice became the 'melody' of the theme, and I built the rest of the music around him. Instead of using drums and percussion, I used digital samples of my finger snaps, and tongue, mouth, and lip noises, to accompany him. The prominent bass line of the 'Seinfeld' theme is in an audio range that does not compete with his voice."

According to Wolff, Seinfeld—who had previously rejected another composer's music for the pilot—"wanted it to be weird and unique, as all [producers] claim they want their themes to be. When it comes right down to it, a lot of people are scared. They hear something unique and they say, 'That's too weird,' and you have to bring it back to conventional standards. Jerry was not afraid of theme music from Mars." Because the routine was different every week, Wolff had to modify the music to match the monologue. "The 'Seinfeld' music theme remains basically the same from week to week," Wolff explained, "but since he says different things every episode, each week his 'melody' is like a variation on the 'Seinfeld' theme."

The producers of "Frasier" (1993–, NBC) wanted a song that alluded only obliquely to the content of the "Cheers" spinoff starring Kelsey Grammer as a Seattle psychiatrist and radio personality. Bruce Miller (b. 1944), veteran composer for "Designing Women" (1986–93, CBS) and "Wings" (1990–, NBC), submitted a tune that was not only accepted but also sung by the show's star and Emmy-nominated in its first year.

According to Miller, the producers told him: "Don't mention shrinks, don't mention radio, don't mention crazy people—which is what the show's all about—but do something that's appropriate." Miller came up with "a real light, quirky, jazzy, upscale" tune and called an old friend, lyricist Darryl Phinnessee, to write a few lines that might meet the parameters. Phinnessee's line "tossed salads and scrambled eggs" actually refers to "things that are mixed up," like so many of Frasier Crane's callers, Miller explained. They wrote the tune with someone like Mel Tormé in mind, but the producers offered it to Grammer instead.

Grammer, a trained singer with off-Broadway credits, initially performed a straightforward version of the tune at the recording session. "Then the producers said, 'Stretch out with it, have more fun,'" Miller recalled. "Kelsey came up with all the shtick, all the laughs, and the funny stuff. At the end, he did a little line over the guitar lick: 'Goodnight, Seattle!' and everybody started getting into that—'give us more of those.'" Then came "Frasier Crane has left the building" and others, five or six in all. "It was just a kick," Miller said. "So Kelsey essentially took this silly little ditty and made it his own. I'm a great fan of the recognized jazz singers, but Kelsey brought a real personality to this song that may not have happened with somebody else. He made it the 'Frasier' theme."

The most unexpected hit of all may have been the theme for "Friends" (1994–, NBC), an ensemble comedy about the lives of six friends (three men and three women) in Manhattan. "I'll Be There for You," the infectious, lighter-than-air song by composer Michael Skloff (b. 1959) and lyricist Allee Willis (b. 1947), spent seven weeks at Number 1 on the *Billboard* adult contemporary charts, and eight weeks at Number 1 on its radio airplay chart, during the summer of 1995.

Skloff had written the theme for HBO's "Dream On," which, like "Friends," was created and produced by his wife Marta Kauffman and her longtime partner David Crane; Willis was a 1985 Grammy winner for her contribution to the *Beverly Hills Cop* soundtrack, the Pointer Sisters smash "Neutron Dance." The song was performed by The Rembrandts, a pop duo who only reluctantly added an extended version of the TV theme to their 1995 album *LP* when it became clear that the series was shaping up into a giant hit and the demand for a recording of the theme was growing.

Skloff was initially inspired by the Beatles' "Paperback Writer": "It just felt so right for the show, that sort of happy, guitar-riff feeling." Skloff came up with the song hook, the title, and the melody; Willis, brought in by another of the series' producers because of her pop-tune track record, wrote the now-famous words: "So no one told you life was gonna be this way/Your job's a joke, you're broke, your love life's D.O.A. . . . ."

"The bulk of my hits have been very black, funky, pop stuff, and this was as white as could be," Willis laughed. "However, for some bizarre reason, I actually had a very good time writing it." The lyrics "went back and forth on rewrites" (with Crane and Kauffman, who had written musical theater works with Skloff, including a musical based on the movie *Arthur*) until just two weeks prior to the series' premiere. For the extended version, Crane, Kauffman, and Rembrandts Danny Wilde and Phil Solem received additional writing credit.

Said Skloff: "It's a perfectly likable song that's reminiscent of the Beatles and the Monkees, which is from a time in our history that was idealistic and fun, that whole 'our generation' kind of thing, and just brings back good feelings. And it's connected with a wildly popular show. . . . People like the song on its own, but they also say, 'Oh, God, I love that show.'" The commercial success of the "Friends" theme caused network executives to rethink earlier policies about cutting back main-title themes to just a few seconds.

Your Mission, Should You Decide to Accept It

Action-Adventure

elevision, particularly in its infancy, frequently looked to the movies for inspiration. The advent of the James Bond films in 1962, and their increasing popularity, sent producers scurrying for material with which to emulate the successful Bond formula.

As it happened, producer Norman Felton (who had a top-10 hit in NBC's "Dr. Kildare") had long wanted to do an escapist hour of pure entertainment. Even before the arrival of the 007 movie extravaganzas—but during the heyday of Ian Fleming's popular Bond novels, which were said to be a favorite of President John F. Kennedy—Felton had met with Fleming in hopes of enticing him to create an American TV series, perhaps based loosely on his nonfiction travelogue *Thrilling Cities.*

Fleming came up with very little: a vague concept about a mysterious man, named Napoleon Solo, who was a globetrotting troubleshooter frequently seen near centers of power in Washington and Moscow. Felton turned to producer Sam Rolfe (who had created the western "Have Gun—Will Travel" and was then working on Felton's psychiatry series "The Eleventh Hour"), who created a fictitious worldwide peacekeeping organization, some subsidiary characters, and a format for weekly adventures—to be filmed on the "international" locales of the MGM backlot in Culver City, California.

The result of their labors was "The Man from U.N.C.L.E.," TV's first successful spy show and the vanguard of an entire subgenre of action-adventure series that would dominate the medium throughout the mid-1960s.

Jerry Goldsmith in the 1960s.

"U.N.C.L.E." (1964–68, NBC) starred Robert Vaughn and David McCallum as the American-born Solo and his Russian partner Illya Kuryakin, doing constant battle with larger-than-life, world-threatening villains, often in the service of the evil organization Thrush. Leo G. Carroll played their boss, Alexander Waverly.

Felton's sole choice for composer of the pilot was Jerry Goldsmith. The two had collaborated on several previous projects, and Goldsmith's "Kildare" theme had become a pop hit. In fact, by the time he scored the "U.N.C.L.E." pilot (then called simply "Solo"), Goldsmith was a fast-rising feature film composer with an Oscar nomination (for 1962's *Freud*) and more than a dozen other movies (including the critically acclaimed *Lonely Are the Brave*, 1962, and *Lilies of the Field*, 1963) to his credit. The involvement of Goldsmith was of such significance that he merited a photo and biography that was the same size as those for Felton and Rolfe in the lavish advertisers' brochure—a rare tribute to a composer in television.

As with all of his television scores, Goldsmith derived most of his musical material for "The Man from U.N.C.L.E." from his distinctive, and quite unusual, 5/4 theme. "If you noticed," he recalled, "every one of the themes I wrote for television, including 'U.N.C.L.E.,' had two elements. There are a main theme and a secondary theme, a countermelody. [In the scores] I milked the hell out of them. That's how I could do those shows so fast. That, I believed, was the way to do it. In those days, we took pride in what we did for television."

The striking look and sound of "U.N.C.L.E." was established in the opening sequence of its first episode, "The Vulcan Affair," as viewers were introduced to the high-tech, concrete-and-steel structure of the organization's headquarters behind an innocent-looking tailor shop facade. A Thrush operative, bent on assassinating Waverly, manages to enter the building but is confronted by Solo. The killer fires four shots in rapid succession, only to find that Solo is behind a wall of bulletproof glass—a moment of high drama that cuts directly to the series' main title (and, in fact, was used as a teaser for most of the first season).

Goldsmith's orchestra was without strings, and its small size (twenty-seven musicians for the pilot; usually just fifteen players during the first season) forced the composer to become particularly creative in his use of brass, woodwinds, and percussion. His three original "U.N.C.L.E." scores (a dozen other episodes were tracked with the same music) accompanied early, dark episodes that were less characteristic of the series than its later, more widely popular tongue-in-cheek shows.

The unconventional main-title theme contained both jazz and martial elements—some rather wild trumpet flourishes over militaristic snare drums—that musically conveyed both the high-style heroics and serious drama elements of the series. Deceptively simple upon first hearing, it was also the source for Goldsmith's secondary action theme (which was extensively developed in chase and suspense sequences). Stylistically, his music for "U.N.C.L.E." resembled his score for MGM's all-star thriller *The Prize* (1963) and presaged the action music in the war picture *Morituri* (1965) and the far more flamboyant spy spoof *Our Man Flint* (1965).

Goldsmith's theme was nominated for an Emmy, surprisingly during the series' second season, which didn't even use his powerful original arrangement; Lalo Schifrin created a "cooler" version in 4/4 for flute and the then-popular bongo drums. Schifrin was one of several composers who followed Goldsmith on the series; they, together with fellow first-season composers Morton Stevens and Walter Scharf, were nominated for a Grammy for their music as it appeared on the first of two soundtrack albums. Gerald Fried and Robert Drasnin wrote most of the music for the series' second and third seasons; Richard Shores worked on the fourth. Its spinoff, "The Girl from U.N.C.L.E." with Stefanie Powers (1966–67, NBC), also used Goldsmith's theme but in a harpsichord-dominated arrangement by jazz composer Dave Grusin.

Because the series started as a serious spy drama and gradually became lighter and broader in approach, the underscore naturally reflected these changes. It was during its second season that the debonair Vaughn and the turtleneck-wearing McCallum became teen idols and the show jumped into the Nielsen top 10. That's when Fried signed on, eventually composing some two dozen scores for "U.N.C.L.E.," more than any other single composer on the series. "It was just plain fun," he recalled. "Nobody took it seriously. The more gimmicks and the more smartass things we could do, and the stuntmen and prop men could do, the better [the producers] would like it. It wasn't challenging musically; it was a craft job. You'd use the same material basically, just with an Arabian version, a Japanese version, a Greek version, being imaginative in those prescribed areas. This was a game, and a very enjoyable game." Fried's scores sported a lively, jazzy feel, befitting the series' less serious tone as the seasons wore on.

By the fall of 1965, TV's spy craze was in full swing. The most successful, creatively speaking, of the season's new espionage-themed entries was "I Spy," from producer Sheldon Leonard (whose previous hits had all been in the comedy field, from "Make Room for Daddy" to "The Dick Van Dyke Show"). Whereas "U.N.C.L.E."'s derring-do was rooted in a utopian fantasy about a global peacekeeping organization, "I Spy" (1965–68, NBC) took Cold War politics somewhat more seriously.

What distinguished "I Spy" from the many other cloak-and-dagger series of the period was the casting of comedian Bill Cosby as one of the two leads, and producer Leonard's insistence on shooting the series on location around the world. Robert Culp played American agent Kelly Robinson, whose cover was that of a top tennis player on the international circuit; Cosby was his partner, Alexander Scott, a Rhodes scholar and linguist who was supposed to be Robinson's trainer. Cosby, the first black actor to star in a dramatic series, won three consecutive Emmy Awards for his performances.

As he had before, Leonard turned to composer Earle Hagen to provide the musical score. As a valued and longtime member of Leonard's production team, Hagen often traveled with the company. In fact, he recalled: "Before we started the show, Sheldon and his wife and my wife and I went around the world, scouting locations for the show. We went west from here [California] to Japan, Hong Kong, Bangkok, India, Israel, the Greek islands, Rome, Paris, New York, and home. Fifty-two days. It was a great trip. And wherever I went I sampled [indigenous music] and bought records. I probably had, at one time, about as good an ethnic [music] library as you could get."

The result was arguably the richest musical palette ever composed for any American television series. Although the scores were recorded in Los Angeles, Hagen regularly visited the company's far-flung locations to record, on-site, the unique local sounds that would provide authentic musical flavor for each episode. "For example, in the marketplace in Marrakech," Hagen recalled, "they had Berber tribes' bands with just clapper cymbals and drums. You'd have had to hire one hundred men to duplicate that [in the states], and then you'd never get it right. So we just shot them, recorded them, and synched the tracks."

On a Mexican location, Hagen said, "they shot in the Floating Gardens in Chapultepec and there were seven different mariachi combinations playing at the same time. We had to build that, do that from scratch, because they would cut to Culp sitting in the middle of a marimba band, playing just odd notes, and an accordion would go by in another boat. There were seven orchestra tracks going at the same time."

The globe-trotting even became a little dangerous on one occasion. Flying into Athens after the coup in Greece in April 1967, "We were the first plane to land after the military takeover," Hagen said. "We were taken into custody and we had to get off the mainland the next day. Sheldon had chartered a boat that slept sixty, which he used in a couple of the shows. And that was our hotel; we stayed on the boat. Two weeks later I came back into Athens alone and set up a recording with a bouzouki player."

The majority of on-location source recordings—many made using just a battery-pack tape recorder—were mixed into the background. For his dramatic

Earle Hagen accepting his Emmy for "I Spy." Courtesy Academy of Television Arts and Sciences.

scoring, Hagen generally used an orchestra of eighteen to twenty players. And, as with his experiences in comedy, every one of the eighty-two episodes boasted an original score (two-thirds by Hagen, the rest by Hugo Friedhofer, a longtime friend and colleague).

Hagen's main-title theme was an exciting, up-tempo melody for saxophone, and then strings, over a bass guitar ostinato, all liberally flavored with brass. According to the composer, the "I Spy" main title was the first to combine live action, animation, and graphic art: it was cut specifically to a tempo that Hagen had requested, so that the transformation of the animated tennis player into an armed spy, running into the "I" of the title, was perfectly timed. Sometimes the editors working on individual episodes would even consult Hagen when cutting chases, so that the tempo of his score would match the rhythm of the editing.

"The approach was semi-jazz," Hagen said, although the range and depth of "I Spy" scores actually defied easy labeling. Hagen and Friedhofer lent orchestral color to the varied locales, paced the drama, enlivened the humor, and underscored the emotion of the moment. Hagen's personal favorite, the 1967 "Mainly on the Plains" (with Boris Karloff as a college professor in Spain who thinks of himself as a reincarnated Don Quixote), featured flamenco guitar; his Emmy winner, music for the 1967 "Laya," was set in Greece with a bittersweet denouement underscored by a vocal version of Hagen's romantic theme.

Then, in the fall of 1966, came the most famous spy music ever, for what certainly qualifies as one of television's most dynamic series: "Mission: Impossible" (CBS, 1966–73). A veteran intelligence agent (Steven Hill in the first season, Peter Graves in succeeding years) would assemble a team of experts—in the first few seasons, usually including a master of disguise (Martin Landau), a model-actress (Barbara Bain), an electronics whiz (Greg Morris), and a strongman (Peter Lupus)—to undertake an espionage mission, often abroad, that was deemed too dangerous or difficult for most agents. And, many years before the phrase "plausible deniability" entered the public discourse, the voice on all of the assignment recordings invariably cautioned, "Should you or any member of your IM Force be caught or killed, the Secretary will disavow any knowledge of your actions."

Lalo Schifrin wasn't sure why producer Bruce Geller called him to score the pilot for "Mission." "He asked specifically for me to do this show," the composer later recalled. "I don't know who else he had in mind, but he called my agent—and this was quite unusual—to say that he wanted me to go to see the sets while they were shooting the pilot." For "Mission," Geller asked Schifrin to compose themes for each of the characters. Schifrin declined. "When I saw the pilot, I said I think that would be wrong. There are so many characters, it would be confusing," he told Geller. "There would be no cohesion. They have one common goal; it's almost a paramilitary operation." His solution was a march, "but a march with suspense." Called "The Plot" on the best-selling LP recording,

Lalo Schifrin. Photo by George Fields.

Schifrin's familiar "Mission" march worked—in dozens of variations over the series' seven-year life—to link visually disparate scenes.

(As often happened in television scoring, a theme that becomes famous for one show may, in reality, have had its germination in another. "The Plot" was a variation on a theme Schifrin had already composed for "U.N.C.L.E." producer Norman Felton's World War II spy drama "Jericho," whose pilot Schifrin scored at MGM in December 1965. Schifrin had been ideally suited for this episode, about underground efforts to spirit a famous conductor out of Germany. Schifrin used a forty-eight-piece orchestra to record classical music for several concert-hall scenes. The march, with a few variations identical to "The Plot," bound together the military operation scenes. Felton later asked his old friend Jerry Goldsmith to score another episode and used Goldsmith's own, quite different, march as the "Jericho" theme.)

But "The Plot" was not the "Mission" theme. According to Schifrin, "We needed a theme for the main title that had to be a little more tongue-in-cheek. I wanted a little humor, lightness, a theme that wouldn't take itself too seriously." He chose—like Jerry Goldsmith two years before, with "The Man from

U.N.C.L.E."—5/4 for his time signature. "There is something unpredictable about five/four," he said.

At the time, there were no main-title visuals per se. In fact, according to Robert H. Justman, who was associate producer on the pilot, what became the "Mission: Impossible" theme "was a cue that Lalo had written for an escape sequence on the road, after they get away from the dictator." Added Jack Hunsaker, music editor on the pilot: "A piece of music came up that was really exciting, that had nothing to do with the rest of the show. Bruce [Geller] got very excited about it" and decided to use it as the main-title theme. Said Geller, in his liner notes for the *"Mission: Impossible"* LP: "So integral to the show did Lalo's themes become, that when the main title of 'Mission: Impossible' was made, it was built around the music, not scored afterwards. Many times since then whole sequences of film have been handled the same way: the music dictating the editing."

The "Mission" theme was built around a series of three-note phrases for flute, punctuated by sharp brass notes over a driving, heavily percussive beat (featuring those great sixties bongos). The now-famous fifty-second main-title sequence opened with a hand lighting a match that ignited an animated fuse which, in turn, crossed the screen six times over a rapid-fire sequence of exciting scenes from that night's episode. The word "Mission" appeared in typescript, timed precisely to Schifrin's music, before the camera zoomed in on a series of cast portraits. The word "Impossible" appeared, "stamped" diagonally across the screen as Schifrin's music reached its climax.

No music accompanied scenes of Hill (or later, Graves) receiving his assignment; it routinely began after the voice announced that "this tape will self-destruct in five seconds" and smoke began rising from the tape or record. Schifrin cleverly intertwined the "Mission" and "Plot" themes as Hill/Graves evaluated the various Impossible Missions Force member dossiers for the week's assignment.

Music was more important in "Mission" than in any other action drama of its time. In most of the early episodes, the missions were complex and often accomplished by team members working silently behind the scenes; Schifrin's music, mostly variations on the "Plot" theme—the backbone of most "Mission" scores—served as the connective tissue for many sequences and made a major contribution to the suspense.

In all, Schifrin scored a total of twelve episodes, including three in the first season and one or two for most succeeding years. Many of "Mission's" other composers were spy-show veterans: Walter Scharf, Gerald Fried, Robert Drasnin, and Richard Markowitz; jazz-oriented composers like Jerry Fielding and Benny Golson also scored a number of episodes. All were obligated to use Schifrin's "Plot" theme extensively throughout.

Schifrin was nominated twice for Emmy Awards for his "Mission" scores (in the 1966–67 and 1968–69 seasons). Although denied the statue from his peers in the television industry, other and perhaps more satisfying rewards followed: the soundtrack album was nominated for four 1967 Grammy Awards, and Schifrin won two (for Best Instrumental Theme and Best Original Score for a Motion Picture or TV Show). It spent thirty-one weeks on *Billboard*'s Hot 100 chart and, to this day, remains Schifrin's best-known work (despite six Oscar nominations, scores for film classics such as *Cool Hand Luke* and *Dirty Harry,* and a busy career as a classical music conductor). The Grammy win as Best Original Score remains, more than a quarter-century later, the only time that a TV soundtrack has ever won in that category.

The irony of a *"Mission"* LP was that, despite the crucial role of music in the series, Schifrin had only two major themes (along with dozens of fragments, phrases, and musical devices that worked well in the context of the show but weren't substantial enough to make album cuts). So, belatedly following Geller's original instructions, Schifrin composed all-new leitmotifs for the characters to fill out the album. These surfaced in later seasons of the series, but only occasionally and usually as source music.

That Schifrin failed to compose a single score in the series' second season is not surprising considering his next major assignment: Geller's new series "Mannix" (1967–75, CBS), with Mike Connors as a contemporary private eye whose agency was heavily computerized. The "Mannix" theme broke with detective-show tradition by being in 3/4 time. According to the composer, Geller had heard a jazz tune he liked on the radio and tried to hum it. Schifrin interpreted Geller's suggestion as "a syncopated jazz waltz" and proceeded to create the "Mannix" theme.

Again, Geller created the main-title visuals as a showcase for Schifrin's surprising music. After the first season (a more conventional opening in which a computer punchcard emerged with the show title), the main title was redesigned. A brassy opening with timpani introduced the character, who appeared in various scenes (making breakfast, shaving in the car, shooting a gun, practicing judo, and others) that multiplied into split screen as the letters *M A N N I X* appeared. The lively tune, beginning with saxophones playing the melody and trombones the countermelody, swept the viewer away—and its upbeat tone belied the frequent mayhem during the hour to come.

"Mannix" thrived on two-fisted action. In the second season, Joe Mannix left his high-tech agency, hired a smart secretary (Gail Fisher), and opened his own one-man firm. Although the series ran longer than "Mission: Impossible" (eight seasons), Schifrin scored just eight episodes. And, as he had with his two *"Mission"* albums, the composer created mostly original material for the *"Mannix"* LP, which became one of his finest efforts in the realm of orchestral jazz of the sixties: alternately charming and beautiful, dark and exciting.

Schifrin created the musical formats for several other action-adventure shows of the sixties and seventies, but none would match the longevity and popularity of his "Mission" and "Mannix." A cult favorite was "T.H.E. Cat" (1966–67, NBC), a half-hour drama in the "Peter Gunn" mold with Robert Loggia as a former circus aerialist and cat burglar turned professional bodyguard. Schifrin's theme for flute and brass had an appropriately stealthy feel, and he filled many moments in Cat's hangout (a nightspot called the Casa del Gato, for House of the Cat) with Latin jazz.

Later came "Starsky and Hutch" (1975–79, ABC), a buddy-cop show with David Soul and Paul Michael Glaser as unconventional, odd-couple plain-clothes detectives in Los Angeles. Schifrin's theme, drawn directly from his pilot score for the Aaron Spelling-Leonard Goldberg-produced action hour, seemed inspired by the Scorpio motif from his *Dirty Harry* score and elements of its sequel *Magnum Force* in its grim tone, electronic textures, and heavy beat. Schifrin's theme was subsequently replaced by new ones by two different composers (Tom Scott and Mark Snow).

The success of the spy shows, starting with "U.N.C.L.E.," combined with the still-growing popularity of the James Bond movies starring Sean Connery (notably *Goldfinger* in 1964 and *Thunderball* in 1965), caused network pro-grammers to buy practically every international intrigue show in sight. First to arrive were a wave of British series, nearly all from England's ATV company. The reasons were obvious: they were inexpensive, already produced, and ready to air; and, originating in the land of 007's birth, they could be perceived as classier and more authentic than their American counterparts.

"The Saint" wasn't strictly a spy show, but the debonair Simon Templar was something of a jet-setting troubleshooter in this incarnation of the Leslie Charteris-created character (who had been played in the movies by the likes of George Sanders and Louis Hayward). Roger Moore, in his best role ever—and the one that ultimately persuaded the Bond producers to cast him, a decade later, as 007—played the charming rogue. "The Saint" was shown on independent stations starting in late 1963, becoming one of the biggest syndi-cation hits of the sixties; NBC picked up the series as a summer replacement for three years beginning in 1967.

The "Saint" theme, by Edwin "Ted" Astley (b. 1922), was one of the most recognizable of the era, although its specific origins are somewhat shrouded in mystery. Templar's calling card, which figured prominently in the graphics of the main title, was a stick figure topped by a halo. The teaser of every episode ended with an animated halo appearing over Moore's head, accompanied by the opening of the "Saint" theme: a female voice with muted brass in a seven-note intro, answered first by guitar and drums, then by flute. Writer Charteris was actually credited with the opening bars of the theme in later "Saint" episodes—and, indeed, the "Saint" radio show of the 1940s featured a whis-tled version of it—although the earliest episodes and the RCA soundtrack credited only Astley with the music. Nonetheless, Astley's scores were the first hint that British television had become hip to the jazzier sounds of the sixties (which had already made an impact on American TV).

Astley's greatest achievement in sixties scoring was ironically overshadowed by the American pop-hit mentality that would soon overtake the movies as well, displacing veteran screen composers in favor of songs by writers thought to be more in touch with the youth market. "Secret Agent" (1965–66, CBS) became the first British spy show to be purchased by an American network. Another ATV production, its title in Great Britain was "Danger Man." "Danger Man" was first produced in 1960 as a half-hour series with Patrick McGoohan as North Atlantic Treaty Organization (NATO) operative John Drake; CBS aired the show as a summer series in 1961. An hour-long version of "Danger Man," in which Drake was now an agent of the British Secret Service, was picked up by CBS just as the spy craze began.

The one-hour "Danger Man" was distinguished by a memorable main title theme that Astley called "High Wire." Its sound was unique: jazz harpsichord as the primary voice, backed up with brass and mounted at a fast pace to introduce the ultraserious adventures of Drake, the secret agent who rarely carried a gun or kissed a woman. Astley's episodic scores were equally colorful, often taking the then-exotic Latin American rhythms of the tango and samba and deploying them in creative new ways previously unheard in American TV.

For its American broadcast, the McGoohan series was retitled "Secret Agent" with a new theme commissioned by CBS. The precise circumstances of the commission are not clear; in any case, the "Secret Agent" song broke new ground as the earliest successful television theme with a rock 'n' roll beat. CBS went to Lou Adler, who managed then-hot rocker Johnny Rivers, for the new theme. Adler asked two of his staff writers, Phil Sloan and Steve Barri (who would, later in 1965, have a Number 1 hit with "Eve of Destruction," sung by Barry McGuire), to compose a song. According to Barri, they never even saw the program: "We were just trying to write something that fit what we were told the show was like. They said it was like a TV version of James Bond—it's British and not as much action, but it's pretty intelligent, a real spy kind of thing."

John Barry's *Goldfinger* theme, sung by Shirley Bassey, was riding high on the charts at the time and may have been a factor in CBS's decision to replace Astley's instrumental with a title song. "Basically, we were thinking that we were writing a James Bond theme," Barri recalled. A further influence was the guitar sound of the original "James Bond Theme," because, said Barri, "we wanted to come up with a guitar hook for the beginning, since the Bond theme had a guitar hook."

Sloan, the guitarist of the pair, wrote the now-famous opening guitar riff. "And then we both sat down and basically came up with the melody together, and we both worked on the lyrics," said Barri. "I remember we were laughing through most of it, because the lines just seemed so silly to us. At that particular time we were trying to get away from writing surf songs and hot-rod things—and it was about the time that [Bob] Dylan was starting to become a really important artist, and the Beatles [were popular]—so we were trying to write songs that had some kind of political commentary, or that were a bit more serious. And here we are writing about a guy laying in a Bombay alley. It was kind of dumb, but obviously it worked."

Barri's reference to the "Bombay alley" ("sunnin' on the Riviera one day, then layin' in a Bombay alley next day") was to a later verse heard on the record but not in the TV version. In fact, correspondence between Adler and then-CBS music head Lud Gluskin indicated, Sloan and Barri wrote the song in March 1965 as "Danger Man," but a last-minute title change resulted in the alteration of the song to "Secret Agent Man."

The demo featured Sloan singing "look out, Danger Man" and "think fast, Danger Man" (along with a female backup group echoing "Danger Man") in the spots where we became accustomed to hearing "Secret Agent Man." "We wrote and submitted it as 'Danger Man' and then, for some reason and I have no idea why, they decided they wanted to change the show to 'Secret Agent.' So all we did was change the line. It worked okay, although it never really worked as well as 'Danger Man' as far as I was concerned," Barri said.

CBS replaced the brief, thirteen-second "Danger Man" main title (which contained the opening of Astley's "High Wire" theme) with a forty-second opening, part animation and part live-action clips of McGoohan, scored with Johnny Rivers's vocal version of the Sloan-Barri tune. Within months, thousands of kids taking guitar lessons would spend hours learning to play the memorable opening electric guitar riff; and the lyrics—"There's a man who leads a life of danger/To everyone he meets he stays a stranger/With every move he makes, another chance he takes/Odds are he won't live to see tomorrow. . . ."—were indelibly marked in the minds of spy-show fans nationwide. In less than a year, "Secret Agent Man" went to Number 3 on the *Billboard* pop charts. (Astley's original theme was relegated to the opening first-act credit sequence of each episode.)

Other Astley series that aired in America included "The Baron" (1966, ABC), based on the John Creasey character of a London-based American antiques dealer (Steve Forrest) who routinely became involved in criminal cases; and "Department S" (1970, syndicated), about a specialized unit of Interpol that included a crime-fiction writer (Peter Wyngarde), a computer specialist (Rosemary Nicols), and an American (Joel Fabiani).

Perhaps the biggest critical favorite of the mid-1960s British imports was "The Avengers" (1966–69, ABC), a stylish hour of derring-do that, like "The Man from U.N.C.L.E." at its best, both emulated and parodied the big-screen adventures of James Bond (and, by this time, Derek Flint, Matt Helm, and others). Bumbershoot-toting, bowler-topped John Steed (Patrick Macnee) and the jumpsuited Emma Peel (Diana Rigg) took on a succession of outlandish villains bent on taking over England or the world. The plots were often so broad that the fun of "The Avengers" had far less to do with the story's resolution than in listening to the witty banter and savoring the sophisticated chemistry of Steed and Mrs. Peel.

American audiences were treated to the third incarnation of "The

Avengers." The series began in Britain in 1961 with Macnee playing second fiddle to Ian Hendry. It was improved in 1962 after Hendry's departure led to Macnee's teaming with Honor Blackman (whose leather suits and black boots became a sensation in England). Composer Johnny Dankworth's low-key, minimally scored "Avengers" music accompanied those early episodes (not seen in the United States until 1990). When a new production team took over "The Avengers" in 1965, Laurie Johnson was signed to compose a new theme and write the episodic scores; that's what American audiences heard when ABC picked up "The Avengers" in early 1966.

Johnson (b. 1927), educated at the Royal College of Music, was already an old hand at film and TV music. He had written scores for Stanley Kubrick's *Dr. Strangelove or: How I Learned to Stop Worrying and Love the Bomb* and the science fiction film *First Men in the Moon* (both 1964), in addition to composing for the London theater and the concert hall. Johnson's approach was diametrically opposed to the dark ambiance of Dankworth's music, but perfectly in keeping with the fresh new tongue-in-cheek attitude of the series. His "Avengers" theme employed a wave of elegant strings over a rapidly moving, jaunty repeated figure for electric keyboard, all of which built into a big-band sound. This synthesis of orchestral and jazz textures, very much in tune with the sixties, and the more generous orchestra (including strings) than was common in American television scoring, made "The Avengers" a surprising listening experience as well as fun to watch.

Johnson scored many episodes during the two Rigg seasons, as well as the single final season in which Linda Thorson (as the younger, less experienced Tara King) replaced Rigg as Steed's partner. When the series was resurrected as "The New Avengers" in 1976–77 (screened on CBS in a late-night timeslot in 1978), with Macnee joined by Joanna Lumley and Gareth Hunt, Johnson—now a full production partner with producers Brian Clemens and Albert Fennell—reprised only the opening bars of his original "Avengers" theme. He segued into military-style snare drums with a new brass fanfare, and (emphasizing the new younger partners) busy bass and electric guitar riffs.

Australian-born Ron Grainer (1922–81) contributed two memorable themes for late-1960s spy shows. After the end of "Secret Agent," star Patrick McGoohan produced a seventeen-episode series that contained elements of the fiction of Orwell and Kafka, called "The Prisoner" (1967), which CBS ran during the summer of 1968; it became an almost instant cult classic. McGoohan played an unnamed British agent (probably John Drake, although that was never formally stated) who resigned under mysterious circumstances, was abducted, and found himself in a seaside town with a carnivallike atmosphere where the residents were identified only as numbers; everyone was under constant surveillance and the ruthless captors would use any means to discover the reasons behind the agent's angry departure from the Secret Service.

Grainer's theme for "The Prisoner" was a rousing piece for brass, electric guitar, bass, and percussion that was apparently intended to underscore the boundless determination of No. 6 (McGoohan) to escape. The end title, an even livelier arrangement, provided a strong musical finale even though nearly every episode ended with No. 6's efforts being foiled again.

Grainer's distinctive sound and style also distinguished "Man in a Suitcase" (1968, ABC), a rather grim affair starring the scowling Richard Bradford as McGill, an unjustly disgraced American agent on an odyssey that took him all over Europe trying to clear his name. Any other composer might have taken a dark approach, but Grainer chose an entirely unorthodox musical route: bouncy, almost boogie-woogie piano with peppy brass and an offbeat percussion section including xylophone and timpani. For both "The Prisoner" and "Man in a Suitcase," Albert Elms provided the bulk of the episodic underscore.

The last of the great British adventure series on American TV was "The Persuaders!" (1971–72, ABC), Tony Curtis's first and Roger Moore's last series for television (the latter, just before he became the movies' James Bond). Curtis played a self-made millionaire from the Bronx and Moore was a titled aristocrat with a penchant for daredevil adventure; both were playboys with lots of money and an eye for the ladies. Laurence Naismith, as a retired judge who sought to right wrongs outside of the legal systems of Europe, brought the two together and effectively blackmailed them into helping him achieve his goal. The show was light and often amusing, thanks to Curtis's frequent ad-libbing, which won him legions of fans in Britain.

"Saint" producer Robert S. Baker, with the backing of ITC's Sir Lew Grade, poured money into expensive location filming throughout Europe, especially the Côte d'Azur; and hired "Avengers" writers Brian Clemens and Terry Nation, and veteran feature directors Basil Dearden, Val Guest, and Roy Ward Baker, among others, as behind-the-camera talent. Flamboyant music producer Don Kirshner, who had just taken over ATV Music in England (and thus supervised the scoring of their TV shows), sought an equally high-profile talent for the music: John Barry (b. 1933), composer for the James Bond films and by then the recipient of three Oscars (two for *Born Free,* one for *The Lion in Winter*) and a Grammy (for *Midnight Cowboy*). At the time, he was arguably the world's most in-demand film composer. Roger Moore, whose own company was also involved in the production, "courted me with lunches and such," Barry remembered.

Barry's "Persuaders" theme remains (despite the failure of the series after just a single season) one of the most stylish ever written for the medium. "The whole point about television," Barry observed, "is that you've got so little time. People are looking at television, this wall-to-wall visual thing they've got, day in and day out. How do you break through that? I always used to think, if a person's in the kitchen and they hear this in the living room, is it going to grab them? Are they going to say, 'What the hell is that?' I always went for a really intensely individual shot right off the top. You know, a sound that would grab you, very distinctive and very memorable. And you have to capture that audience within, hopefully, the first four bars."

Barry wanted "a strange sound" and went to a London musician with a penchant for offbeat instruments. John Leach, who had played the cymbalum on Barry's score for the spy thriller *The Ipcress File* (1965), had discovered an unusual Middle Eastern stringed instrument called the qanun. "It had a strange scale," Barry said. "It was not a chromatic instrument. I loved the sound of it, so I figured out a melody that worked on this very odd scale. I think there was one interval that was a semitone and there was another with three notes missing." With the qanun and a pop rhythm section including synthesizers—at that time, still an unusual choice for television—Barry recorded the theme at former Beatles producer George Martin's new studio with "a lot of reverb and studio effects around the sound," the composer recalled.

The theme accompanied a very classy series of main-title visuals that depicted the diverse backgrounds of the Moore and Curtis characters, then shifted to shots of their Aston-Martin and Ferrari tooling around the French Riviera, plus the usual champagne/roulette wheel/bikinied beauty shots that told the viewer they lived the good life. Barry's upbeat and undeniably catchy tune became a hit in England (reaching Number 13 on the charts in early 1972) but, because ABC relegated the series to a dismal Saturday night time-slot in the United States, never caught on with American record-buyers. Barry later composed musical signatures for Gene Barry's "The Adventurer" (1972) and the anthology "Orson Welles' Great Mysteries" (1973), both produced for first-run syndication, and both themes written for mandolin and synthesizers.

The superhero subgenre that began with the syndicated "Adventures of Superman" in the fifties hit the network big time with "Batman" (1966–68, ABC). A sensation upon its first appearance, in the middle of the 1965–66 season, "Batman" became synonymous with the newly coined term "camp": an outrageous takeoff on a serious subject.

Like "Superman," "Batman" brought a DC Comics hero to life. Unlike "Superman," however, executive producer William Dozier saw the exploits of the Caped Crusader as more effective when played for laughs. So Adam West and Burt Ward, as Gotham City crimefighters Batman and Robin, played their roles absolutely straight. But writer Lorenzo Semple Jr.'s looney dialogue, and the cockeyed pilot direction of Robert Butler, made quite clear that none of this was to be taken seriously. The villains—Joker (Cesar Romero), Penguin (Burgess Meredith), Riddler (Frank Gorshin), Catwoman (Julie Newmar), and others—were all far larger than life, their schemes diabolical, and their gadgets wild. Even the colors in "Batman" were garish, the violence so cartoonish that animated titles containing words like "pow" and "bam" were superimposed during fight scenes.

Dozier asked Neal Hefti (b. 1922) to score the presentation film for "Batman." Hefti, a veteran jazz arranger and bandleader who had composed such standards as "Girl Talk," had only recently moved into the film-scoring arena, doing such comedies as *Sex and the Single Girl* and *How to Murder Your*

Wife (both 1965). Hefti was stumped. What should the musical approach be when the heroes are deadly serious, the villains are smirking madmen, the situations are ludicrous, and the audience is expected to howl with laughter? "I tore up a lot of paper," Hefti recalled. "It did not come easy to me. It sounds easy, after it's all over; it sounds so natural. But I just sweated over that thing, more so than any other single piece of music I ever wrote. I was never satisfied with it.

"This was not a comedy. This was about unreal people. Batman and Robin were both very, very serious. The bad guys would be chasing them, and they would come to a stop at a red light, you know. They wouldn't break the law even to save their own lives. So there was a grimness and a self-righteousness about all this," the composer said. It took him "the better part of a month" to come up with the theme. "I was almost going to call them and say, I can't do it. But I never walk out on projects, so I sort of forced myself to finish."

Hefti's "Batman" tune wound up winning a 1966 Grammy as Best Instrumental Theme (beating out entries by Henry Mancini and Alex North, among others). His musical solution to a combined dramatic and comedic problem was perfect: bass guitar, low brass, and percussion to create a driving rhythm, while an eight-voice chorus sings "Batman!" in harmony with the trumpets. It was part serious, part silly: just like the series.

Hefti's theme played against animated images drawn, for the main-title

Neal Hefti. Courtesy the composer.

visuals, in the style of the DC Comics characters. For the presentation reel, he also wrote a chase-sequence variation on the main theme. Hefti recalled the makeup of the band: two trumpets, four trombones, two keyboards, four guitars, a bass, and two drums. The eight singers (four sopranos, four tenors) "sang in perfect unison, not octaves apart," Hefti said. "The tenors were up there screeching, so they sounded like boy sopranos." He offered to create separate tracks, so that Dozier could eliminate the voices if he desired, "but he liked the idea," Hefti says, so the chorus stayed.

"Batman" was originally planned as a fall 1966 entry, but ABC's fall 1965 schedule was falling apart in a hurry. So Dozier was forced to speed up production to make a January 1966 airdate. Hefti, otherwise committed (with 1966 films including *Duel at Diablo* and *Barefoot in the Park*), was unable even to complete the pilot.

Enter Nelson Riddle. With "Route 66" and "The Untouchables" behind him, he had no trouble following Hefti's lead in scoring "Batman." Riddle frequently fell back on Hefti's ostinato from the theme for the speeding Batmobile, but he wrote new themes for the villains: shrill, laughing brass for the Riddler; waddling woodwinds for the Penguin; a darker, cackling musical laughter for the Joker; and so forth.

Riddle had previously worked for Fox TV head William Self as musical director on Frank Sinatra's ABC variety show in 1957; Self suggested Riddle to producer Dozier. According to Riddle's son, bandleader Christopher Riddle, his father saw scoring "Batman" as "an opportunity to enhance his BMI [royalties] by writing a lot of stuffing music, music to be punched by— they even spelled it out on the screen, pow-biff-bash—despite the fact that he hadn't been commissioned to write the theme."

Riddle scored most of "Batman," although for the third and final season (1967–68) another big-band veteran, Billy May, came aboard. He composed a theme for the new character of Batgirl (Yvonne Craig) that received unusual end-title credit by itself. (Hefti, meanwhile, turned his quick stint on the series into two successful LPs, *Batman Theme* and *Hefti in Gotham City,* both composed of almost entirely original material.)

The immediate success of "Batman" (whose Wednesday and Thursday half hours finished among the Nielsen top 10 for the season) led ABC to commission from Dozier another series about a masked crimefighter. "The Green Hornet" (1966–67) was adapted not from a comic book but from the long-running radio series about Britt Reid, crusading newspaper editor whose secret identity was that of the Green Hornet, wanted by the police but in reality a dedicated foe of organized crime. Van Williams ("Surfside 6") played Reid, and Bruce Lee played his faithful manservant Kato (who demonstrated, for the first time to American viewers, the kung fu skills that would make him a movie star in the 1970s and an enduring cult figure after his death).

Hefti was asked to pen this theme as well. But he turned down the assignment when Dozier asked him to base the music on Rimsky-Korsakov's famous

"Flight of the Bumblebee," which had been the theme of the radio show. Billy May agreed to the parameters, and came up with a clever reworking of the musical concept that, while taking its initial cue from the Russian composer, became an original theme on its own as played by trumpet virtuoso Al Hirt. May also scored the entire season (moving to "Batman" after "The Green Hornet" was canceled).

May said that his longtime friendship with Fox music director Lionel Newman led him to do "The Green Hornet," and that the idea of the theme was "to make it sound close enough that people would think it's 'Flight of the Bumblebee,' but different enough so that we could get the copyright." He had recently done some albums with trumpeter Hirt, so the connection with the

Billy May. Photo by George Fields.

New Orleans jazzman was both obvious and natural. May's scores, while similar in tone to Riddle's "Batman" music, were largely jazz-based and marked by plenty of blaring brass during action sequences. Says May: "You didn't have to work as hard with 'Batman' as you did with 'Green Hornet.' 'Batman' was easier because he had all those 'pows' and everything, you know. With both, you had your tongue in your cheek, a little bit."

It was 1974 before another network decided to take a chance on a superhero. ABC tried "Wonder Woman," a ninety-minute pilot with former tennis star Cathy Lee Crosby as the Amazon princess of DC Comics fame, now an intelligence agency secretary in contemporary times. Its failure led to a second pilot in 1975 by a new production team: "The New, Original Wonder Woman," with former Miss USA Lynda Carter in the title role. This time, the show was set in the 1940s, with Wonder Woman and good guy/romantic interest Steve Trevor (Lyle Waggoner) fighting the Nazis.

The campy attitude was reflected in the score, composed by sitcom veteran Charles Fox ("Love, American Style," "Happy Days"). He set the tone with a title song that featured lyrics by his longtime partner Norman Gimbel: "All the world is waiting for you and the power you possess/In your satin tights, fighting for your rights, and the old red, white and blue . . ." The lyric was funny, the music was bouncy, and the pilot sold. Recalled Fox: "We were dealing with a cartoon character, a superhero. The series was set in the forties, with the Nazis and all that. So everything was larger than life. We just went for a song that had a lot of energy, a dynamic quality."

Fox scored the early episodes of the series, called simply "Wonder Woman" (1976–79, ABC), in lively, campy style, maintained by composer Artie Kane when an arm injury sidelined Fox. Kane, one of Hollywood's most celebrated keyboard players, turned to a composing career in the early 1970s, and Fox became one of his early benefactors.

Television shifted its comic-book attention from DC to Marvel in 1977 with the addition of "The Incredible Hulk" (1978–82) to the CBS schedule. Universal's adaptation of the legend of scientist David Bruce Banner (Bill Bixby)—whose exposure to deadly gamma rays turned him, at moments of extreme stress or high emotion, into the green, superstrong, and primitive Hulk (Lou Ferrigno)—was entrusted to composer Joe Harnell (b. 1924), who came from the same studio's "Bionic Woman" series after several years as music director of daytime's "Mike Douglas Show." Harnell had, earlier, studied with Nadia Boulanger, William Walton, and Aaron Copland, and won a 1962 Grammy for his *Fly Me to the Moon* LP. He eschewed the camp approach in favor of straightforward orchestral scoring. Explained the composer: "I really try to work up a feeling of empathy for a show, regardless of how silly it may seem. I've got to believe in it.

"To me, the Hulk represented the human condition. Sometimes we don't behave very well, and in my life, there's been a lot of that. When I get angry, I don't turn green but I get ugly. So I really searched for an identification with that character, and with David's hysterical need to get rid of this thing." Much of his music emerged from two key themes: his "lonely man" motif (for Banner, who remained aloof from most human contact, often scored for solo piano) and a "snarling" element for the Hulk.

Harnell was permitted a surprising degree of freedom in composing weekly scores for "The Incredible Hulk." One week, a solo harmonica for Banner's friendship with a retarded boy; another, an energetic march for the Hulk's capture by a military organization; another, a forties-style big-band score for a film noir episode; even a choir for Banner's tragically short marriage (in 1978, to a character played by Mariette Hartley, who won an Emmy for her performance). Harnell was nominated (in the 1981–82 season) for an "Incredible Hulk" score, and went on to greater success with his Emmy-nominated score

Joe Harnell. Courtesy the composer.

for the science fiction miniseries "V" (1983, NBC) and his theme for the series "Alien Nation" (1989–90, Fox), both from "Hulk" producer Kenneth Johnson.

Short-lived attempts to adapt fellow Marvel characters "The Amazing Spider-Man" (1978, CBS) and "Captain America" (1979, CBS) followed. Two "Captain America" movies, with scores by Mike Post and Pete Carpenter, and a brief "Spider-Man" series, with music by Stu Phillips and Johnnie Spence, met with disinterest on the part of viewers.

It took the success of the big-screen *Batman* (1989) to revive interest in comic-book heroes. "The Flash" (1990–91, CBS) was the first to reach fruition, and, because it also was a DC Comics property (owned, like DC's Batman, by Time-Warner and therefore produced at Warner Bros.), the route was obvious: clone the many elements that turned *Batman* into a runaway box-office hit, including the music. The producers immediately sought composer Danny Elfman, whose massive, pseudo-operatic score for Batman—featuring large-scale orchestral histrionics, achieved with the Sinfonia of London—complemented director Tim Burton's grim vision of the Dark Knight.

"The Flash" was a hero of superhuman speed. Central City police scientist Barry Allen (John Wesley Shipp), victim of a crime-lab accident involving lightning and chemicals, donned a red suit and fought crime with the help of a smart researcher (Amanda Pays). Like the TV "Batman," there were several supervillains (Mark Hamill as the Trickster, David Cassidy as the Mirror Master) and a healthy dose of tongue-in-cheek humor. The special effects were superb, but the show's scheduling was so erratic that the expensive, beautifully designed "Flash" never caught on.

Stylistically, Elfman's theme for "The Flash" was virtually identical to his *Batman* motif: constantly moving, building to a big climax, fully orchestral, and—because, like "Batman," the show was about a reluctant hero out to avenge the murder of a family member—essentially dark in character. As Elfman recalled, the producers essentially said, "Can you give us something with a *Batman* vibe for 'The Flash'? And, as these things tend to be, it was real quick, I jotted something down, spent two hours, there it is."

Elfman submitted a sketch for the theme, but the orchestration, the entire score for the two-hour pilot, and virtually every note of the episodic scores were the work of composer Shirley Walker (b. 1945). Walker had co-orchestrated and conducted all of Elfman's music for *Batman* (as well as other Elfman projects) and was the obvious choice for "The Flash" series. Walker was one of Hollywood's best-kept secrets for years. Long known as one of the finest orchestrators and conductors working in films, she became one of the first women to score a major-studio release with *Memoirs of an Invisible Man* (1992). Similarly, her work on "The Flash" made her the first female composer ever entrusted with the music of an entire series.

Warner Bros. wanted a big sound for "The Flash," so Walker requested a big orchestra (for episodic TV) of forty-seven players. Unfortunately, "China Beach" was considered the studio's "prestige" show and had been given forty-

Shirley Walker, 1993. Photo by Dana Ross, courtesy the composer.

five players, so for political reasons Walker wound up with forty-two. In Walker's words, the series "started in Danny's area, but I took it into regions away from there and in my own direction." "The Flash" became one of TV's richest-sounding series, with Walker composing original scores, quirky themes for the villains, and warmly romantic melodies for Barry's love interests. Unlike the big-screen *Batman,* which was so overscored that Elfman's music became musical wallpaper, the more astute spotting and varied textures that Walker brought to "The Flash" created a far more listenable score. Surprisingly, it was Walker's work on "The Flash" and not her prior experience with Elfman that won her the job of supervising composer on the subsequent "Batman" animated series (1992–95, Fox).

The music of only a handful of animal-adventure series stood out. The long-running "Lassie" (1954–74, CBS/syndicated), a television adaptation of the 1943 film about a resourceful collie, began with library music supplied by former Republic composer Raoul Kraushaar. In the late 1950s, the show switched to music by veteran composer-arranger Les Baxter (1922–96) that included a whistled main theme. After Nathan Scott took over composing chores on

"Lassie" in 1963, he was asked to create an arrangement of the traditional English folk tune "Greensleeves" that remained with the series to its end.

"Flipper" (1964–67, NBC), spun off from the 1963 movie about a smart dolphin, utilized the same composer, Henry Vars (1902–77), and his familiar title song ("Flipper, Flipper, faster than lightning . . ."). Vars went on to launch the African adventure series "Daktari" (1966–69, CBS), including a drum-dominated but otherwise conventional theme that was replaced at the start of the series' second season.

"Daktari" was also a spinoff, from the 1965 film *Clarence the Cross-Eyed Lion,* starring Marshall Thompson as an American conservationist at an African animal-behavior research center. Clarence and chimpanzee Judy were favorites of the youngsters who made up the bulk of the series' audience. Producer Leonard Kaufman, while shooting location footage in Mozambique,

Shelly Manne. Photo by George Fields.

was listening to native drums and happened across a magazine that featured a profile of the great West Coast drummer Shelly Manne (1920–84). He vowed to contact Manne about a new score upon his return home.

Manne, who was not a skilled composer, was reluctant (although he had dabbled in low-budget films a few years before) but elicited a promise from Kaufman that he could have freedom to experiment and choose the instruments and players he felt appropriate. A student of African music, Manne used only three percussionists, two woodwind players, and an amplified bass guitar for all of his "Daktari" music over the next three seasons.

Among his unusual choices were "hollowed-out Thailand bamboo, suspended in a rattan framework, and an African marimba, which was more or less in quarter tones and which was employed for the main title. Once," he recalled in 1970, "we did a whole cue with flute players just using the keys— not actually playing notes, but getting a wild percussive sound by striking the holes." In his notes for the *"Daktari"* album, Kaufman also pointed out that Manne and company, all top jazz sidemen, often improvised to the on-screen action during the recording sessions.

"Tarzan" (1966–68, NBC), with Ron Ely as Edgar Rice Burroughs's immortal ape man, sported two themes with strong martial elements, one by Sydney Lee for its first season and another by Nelson Riddle for its second. Both interpolated Johnny Weissmuller's memorable original jungle call from the classic MGM films.

"Scarecrow and Mrs. King" (1983–87, CBS) cast Kate Jackson and Bruce Boxleitner in a tongue-in-cheek spy adventure as a suburban housewife and an American intelligence agent with whom she becomes involved. The creator-producers repeated a popular refrain to composer Arthur B. Rubinstein (b. 1938): "We don't want TV music." According to Rubinstein, their suggestion was the music of Hitchcock's *North by Northwest,* in which composer Bernard Herrmann elevated the stakes of an essentially larger-than-life intrigue scenario with a rich and exciting orchestral score. "I knew the slant they were taking on this," Rubinstein said. "It was this frothy kind of thing, but they wanted to surround it with the doom and drama and humor of a feature. So it became like a sandbox for me."

The composer offered an example: "Kate Jackson is on this parapet; she's been drugged, and she's trying to keep her footing. I thought, this is a lot like a Prokofiev ballet. And I wrote this cue, which encompasses the spirit of a Prokofiev ballet score. Where else on television could I do that?" In another instance, he recast the "Scarecrow" theme in the style of a Bach *Brandenburg Concerto* for a scene in which Jackson was waiting for Boxleitner on a Munich bridge.

Rubinstein won an Emmy for a third-season "Scarecrow" episode. Born in Brooklyn, he studied at Yale, wrote music for plays in New York and

Williamstown, and began his television career with the 1971 Hallmark Hall of Fame production of "The Price" with George C. Scott. His feature scores included the thrillers *Blue Thunder* and *WarGames* (both 1983); he later scored several of the "Janek" television crime dramas with Richard Crenna (starting in 1985, CBS).

He preceded his clever work on "Scarecrow" with similarly lively scores for an earlier Boxleitner series, "Bring 'Em Back Alive" (1982–83, CBS), loosely based on the adventures of 1930s explorer Frank Buck, but styled more like a TV version of *Raiders of the Lost Ark.*

When producer George Lucas decided to make "The Young Indiana Jones Chronicles" (1992–93, ABC), the story of the globe-trotting archaeologist's adventures as a boy, he faced extremely high expectations: Lucas's Indiana Jones pictures, starting with *Raiders of the Lost Ark* (1981), drew moviegoers with action-filled, high-adventure tales set in exotic locales.

The series was more of a coming-of-age tale involving the ten-year-old Indy (Corey Carrier) and the sixteen-year-old Indy (Sean Patrick Flanery) encountering new ideas and new places along with the usual bad guys. Set during the early years of the twentieth century and filmed around the world, the series was introduced by the ninety-three-year-old Indy (George Hall) and—because of its consistent placement of historical figures in fictional contexts—was designed to educate as well as entertain. ABC aired twenty-eight hours over two seasons before giving up because of low ratings.

Lucas had used John Williams for his features, including the *Star Wars* and Indiana Jones trilogies, but could not expect the Oscar-winning composer to return to episodic television. "I tend toward a more classical kind of composition in film scores," Lucas explained. "In this case, I was looking for [a composer with] background in various ethnic areas of music. I talked to Johnny Williams about it early on, and asked for his recommendations.

"One of the things that I'm trying to do," he said at the time, "is a geography lesson: to introduce people to different parts of the world and give it a kind of authentic ethnic quality. So music is obviously very important in that."

Williams recommended Laurence Rosenthal (b. 1926) for the job. Born in Detroit, he studied with Howard Hanson and Nadia Boulanger, and wrote extensively for the Broadway theater beginning in the late 1950s. An Oscar nominee for *Becket* (1964) and his adaptation of *Man of La Mancha* (1972), Rosenthal's other film scores included *The Miracle Worker* (1962), *The Comedians* (1967), and *The Return of A Man Called Horse* (1976). For television, he had written the themes for "Coronet Blue" (1967, CBS) and "Fantasy Island" (1978–84, ABC), and won three consecutive Emmys (in 1986, 1987, and 1988) for his music for miniseries, including "Peter the Great."

"When these assignments started coming in, of Egypt and Mexico and Kenya and China and India and Istanbul and Prague and Vienna and Ireland

Laurence Rosenthal with Henry Mancini. Courtesy Academy of Television Arts and Sciences.

and northern Italy and Florence, it was overwhelming," Rosenthal recalled. "There appeared a new range of possibility for me to pursue my lifelong interest in all kinds of ethnic and national music. This study has always fascinated me, even in early childhood. And here it was, handed to me on a platter. George was all for exploring it in depth. 'I don't want Hollywood Turkish,' he said. 'I want real Turkish.'"

Rosenthal began by writing a rousing new theme for young Indy, quite different from Williams's familiar *Raiders* music. "The feeling of youthfulness, lightheartedness, and humor, as well as great energy and excitement [was the intent] as contrasted with the more 'grown-up,' almost militant heroism of John's wonderful march. In 1916, Indy may have been a potential hero," the composer explained, "but mostly he was a nice kid having a hell of a good time." Lucas set Rosenthal's theme to main-title visuals of Jones's diary, black-and-white photos of the young Indy, and his fedora and whip trademarks. The episodes themselves were like mini-movies, each with its own themes and frequently indigenous musical sounds.

Rosenthal's two-hour pilot score, because of network-ordered time restrictions, was recorded by members of the San Francisco Symphony at Lucas's Skywalker Ranch. "I think in the first two shows we used up half the [music] budget for the whole season," the composer said. Most later shows were orchestrated in London and recorded in Munich. The music of "The Young Indiana Jones Chronicles" received six nominations over four successive Emmy periods, winning three: for Rosenthal's "Ireland 1916" score, his "Young Indiana Jones and the Hollywood Follies," and fellow composer Joel McNeely's Gershwin-flavored "Young Indiana Jones and the Scandal of 1920."

For "Peking 1910," Rosenthal employed bamboo flute and a Gu-zheng, a multistringed Chinese zither; for "British East Africa 1909," he delved into African folk music; for "Vienna 1908," he evoked the music of Mahler and Hugo Wolf; for "Northern Italy 1918," he turned to Italian lyricism and hints of Rossini. "The Young Indiana Jones Chronicles" may have had the richest, most lavish orchestral scoring on a weekly basis in the history of television.

8

You Are There

Documentaries and News Programming

Henry Salomon's outlandish notion to have Richard Rodgers write the score for "Victory at Sea" met with skepticism, even derision, at the time. Yet the music for this landmark documentary on the maritime battles of World War II set the standard for all television documentary programming to follow. "Victory at Sea" (1952–53, NBC) was ex-naval officer Salomon's twenty-six-part history of recent naval warfare, drawn from millions of feet of footage from the archives of ten different countries. It was his inspiration to ask the composer of such popular Broadway successes as *Oklahoma!*, *Carousel,* and *South Pacific* to supply a musical score.

Even Rodgers wasn't sure. According to Richard Hanser, cowriter of the script, "Salomon screened some rough, uncut combat footage for him of a kind he had never seen before, and Rodgers came away with a dawning enthusiasm for the project. He sketched out some preliminary themes, but was still not sure enough to proceed until he had played them for Russell Bennett." Rodgers (1902–79) had come to rely on the good taste and immense skills of Robert Russell Bennett (1894–1981), who had orchestrated several of his shows, as well as many other classics of the American stage (Jerome Kern's *Show Boat,* Cole Porter's *Anything Goes,* George Gershwin's *Of Thee I Sing,* Irving Berlin's *Annie Get Your Gun*). He had also written several symphonies, three operas, and a number of chamber works.

Rodgers first came up with the series theme, which he called "The Song of the High Seas," and a fuguelike motif for German U-boats. Bennett's approval

227

and willingness to collaborate on an essentially new musical form—original symphonic underscore for a television documentary series—signaled the beginning of what Hanser called "the most fruitful musical collaboration in the history of television." Rodgers later confessed that he had "neither the time, patience nor aptitude to sit in a cutting room hour after hour going over thousands of feet of film with a stopwatch in my hand in order to compose themes that fit an inflexible time limit. . . . As a result, what I composed were actually musical themes. For the difficult technical task of timing, cutting, and orchestrating, I turned to my old friend Russell Bennett, who has no equal in this kind of work. He fully deserves the credit, which I give him without undue modesty, for making my music sound better than it was."

But what themes: the majesty of the oceans, realized orchestrally in "Song of the High Seas"; the Pearl Harbor bombing, as remembered in the urgency of the music in "The Pacific Boils Over"; the patriotic fervor of American resolve in the jaunty "Guadalcanal March"; the hopeful tone of "D-Day"; an unexpectedly lilting "Theme of the Fast Carriers"; an insouciant tango for the South Atlantic in "Beneath the Southern Cross" (which Rodgers borrowed for a song, "No Other Love," in his 1953 musical *Me and Juliet*); the fugue for the undersea wolf packs of "Danger Down Deep"; melancholy solo violin for memories of home in "Mediterranean Mosaic"; icily austere and howling, wind-blown sounds for the Arctic in "The Magnetic North"; colorful, exotic music for the South Pacific in "Peleliu"; and an aptly titled "Hymn of Victory" to conclude.

Still, as scriptwriter Hanser pointed out, the exigencies of film required a great deal of technical expertise: "The music had to be so arranged—conceived, designed, paced—to coincide with the film as it raced through the projector at ninety feet a minute, twenty-four frames a second. Artistry and creativity had to conform to rigid and unbending mechanical requirements. It was Russell Bennett who mastered this complex procedure, besides contributing the soaring orchestrations that gave symphonic sweep and majesty to the Rodgers themes. He did more. The themes, superlative as they were, supplied only a part of the musical ideas and background which the thirteen-hour score of 'Victory' required. . . . Much of the music of 'Victory at Sea' was originated, note for note, by Robert Russell Bennett."

Bennett described it this way: "Richard and I set to work on Henry Salomon's magnificent film story, he composing his inimitable melodies based on broad situations, scenes, and events; and I putting in the colors of the orchestra and filling out the musical forms to cover every foot of 62,100 feet of film." For the score, Bennett conducted the NBC Symphony Orchestra. Throughout the series, sound effects and narration were often bypassed in favor of music, which in conjunction with the visuals frequently communicated all that was necessary for the viewer to understand the scene.

Critics were wowed. Partly because of the prominence of the score, partly because it was written by a famous composer (who, with Bennett, was given main-title credit in the series), they actually noticed the music. *Time* said

Robert Russell Bennett. Photo by Sheldon Secunda, courtesy R. A. Israel Collection.

"[the] music is often the only description the action needs." *Newsweek* called it "monumental." *Variety* opined: "No small measure of credit for the series' impact and success goes to composer Richard Rodgers." *The New Yorker* termed it "an extraordinary achievement: a seemingly endless creation, now martial, now tender, now tuneful, now dissonant, but always reflecting the action taking place in the films."

"Victory at Sea" called attention to the potential of original music in television in a way that no previous score had done. The reaction was so great, to both the series and the music, that Bennett arranged a suite from the score that RCA Victor released in 1953 (followed in 1958 by a second suite and in 1959 by a third). All three became best-selling albums.

After the success of "Victory at Sea," the same unit of filmmakers and craftspeople embarked on a new series of films under the umbrella title "Project XX" (1954–70, NBC), a reference to the century with an eye toward historical documentaries along the lines of "Victory at Sea" (although the scope later was broadened to include cultural and social issues as well). Bennett scored more than thirty of these programs, receiving three Emmy nominations, winning one of those for the 1962 "He Is Risen," the second of three shows dealing with biblical subjects.

The trilogy—begun by "The Coming of Christ" (1960) and concluded by "The Law and the Prophets" (1967)—utilized the unit's innovative stills-in-motion technique, which photographed works of art with a subtly moving camera to create the illusion of movement. In "The Coming of Christ," the entire half hour consisted of approximately three hundred paintings, mostly from the Renaissance (including works by Rubens, Raphael, and Rembrandt), that depicted the life of Jesus through the Sermon on the Mount. The distinguished actor Alexander Scourby read the narration, drawn largely from the New Testament, and Bennett created an evocative score whose main theme was based on the Gregorian chant *O Dulcissime Jesu.* It met with unanimous critical acclaim, which led to the Easter-week sequel, "He Is Risen," using the masterworks of the fifteenth to eighteenth centuries (including paintings by El Greco, Velázquez, and Titian) to depict Christ's later ministry, crucifixion, and resurrection. "The Law and the Prophets" used a similar technique to illustrate key moments of the books of Genesis and Exodus.

As Bennett explained in a 1957 seminar, "Our music is emotionally deeper than Broadway music. It's a much more responsible task than just bringing out the tunes of Broadway. . . . For one thing, we use a symphony orchestra. There are many more notes to be written. The scope of the music is much wider—requires not prettier music, but in many cases better music." He added: "An entirely original score fits the picture better, but arranging other men's themes is easier and often more fun for all concerned."

In fact, several of Bennett's scores incorporated popular tunes of the period being chronicled, or were adaptations of classical works. His "Life in the Thirties" (1959) perfectly captured the sound of that era, from wailing clarinet solos to lively dance-band arrangements of such tunes as "Anything Goes" and "Happy Days Are Here Again." "Not So Long Ago" (1960), a Bob Hope-narrated look at American life between the end of World War II and the start of the Korean War, interpolated some two dozen tunes from "Beer Barrel Polka" to "Sentimental Journey." For "Call to Freedom" (1957), a recent history of Austria that included footage of a Vienna production of *Fidelio,* Bennett built his entire ninety-minute score on themes from the Beethoven opera and elements from other Beethoven works.

NBC president Sylvester "Pat" Weaver was credited with several innovative television concepts including the creation of the "Today" and "Tonight" shows. Another was "Wide Wide World" (1955–58, NBC), a live, ninety-minute Sunday afternoon cultural and informational series that aired twice a month with Dave Garroway as host.

"Wide Wide World" was designed to take advantage of the latest technology, using live remote cameras to take viewers around the country, and occasionally across the Atlantic, ambitiously exploring a single theme from many places and points of view. Despite the attention given to the complex visual elements, NBC also budgeted for original music for each program.

David Broekman (1899–1958) was the composer-conductor whose music immeasurably enhanced "Wide Wide World" for its first two seasons. A native of Holland, he was a violinist with the New York Philharmonic under famed conductor Arturo Toscanini, had scored early sound films, including *All Quiet on the Western Front* (1930), and worked as musical director on variety shows including Ken Murray's CBS series (1950–52).

Broekman compared scoring the live "Wide Wide World" to "a helmsman steering 34 rowers in a frail craft down uncharted rapids at terrifying speed for 90 minutes, with scarcely a moment in which to draw a breath." Given a week's notice about the segments planned for the following Sunday, Broekman wrote the necessary music in five days and rehearsed it with the orchestra during a two-hour run-through a few hours before air. Because the shows were live, though, anything could happen, from cameras failing to segments running shorter or longer than planned.

"The conductor must be alert for these changes, which come more frequently than is suspected," Broekman wrote in 1957. "He must be able to communicate them to his 34 musicians and they must be able to make the transition required in so smooth a manner that the right bar of music is always heard for the picture and action on the screen. To achieve this 'instantaneous synchronization,' I must work with two different headphones, one supplying the outgoing sound of the program and the other hooked up to Central Control and feeding me the conversation and instructions of the New York director and all of the location directors. At the same time I must keep one eye on the script and the other on the monitors showing me not only the picture being telecast, but the shots coming up next. I must instinctively be directing my score and bring forth a performance from the orchestra."

Broekman's ability to write descriptive music served him well on "Wide Wide World." From cable-car music in San Francisco to side-wheeler music for a Mississippi riverboat, and from a majestic overture for the first televised shots of the Grand Canyon to a warm and touching theme for a visit with painter Grandma Moses, Broekman met a variety of musical challenges. "The gamut has included 100 Salt Lake City kids dancing to a ballet written and played in New York, a battalion of tanks thundering along to a march composed to fit the tempo and timbre of the clanking monsters, and a jam session on the Brooklyn Bridge," he wrote.

For a segment set in New Mexico's Carlsbad Caverns, Broekman asked pioneering electronic music composers Otto Luening and Vladimir Ussachevsky to create strange electronic sounds, around which the composer then wrote orchestral music. But Broekman's finest hour may have come with the April 29, 1956, telecast, in which instrumentalists stationed all around New York City played his "City Symphony" together with the ensemble back in the studio. He received a 1955 Emmy nomination for his efforts on the series.

The success of "Victory at Sea," both as a program and in terms of its music, was not lost on competing networks. CBS, with the cooperation of the United States Air Force, launched "Air Power" (1956–57) with similar fanfare.

Writer-producer Perry Wolff (who had made the educational series "Adventure" for the network) sought an even broader audience by exploring the entire history of aviation and not simply aerial combat during World War II.

The footage was sometimes even more spectacular than that of "Victory at Sea," and the score was certainly equally impressive. Most of the music in "Air Power" was the work of Norman Dello Joio (b. 1913), the composer and educator who had studied with Paul Hindemith and had won several awards for his concert music. His *Meditations on Ecclesiastes* for string orchestra, composed during roughly the same period as his "Air Power" score, won him the Pulitzer Prize in 1957; his opera *The Trial at Rouen* was staged on NBC in April 1956 (later revised as *The Triumph of St. Joan* for the New York City Opera in 1959). The composer, interviewed at the time, explained his work process: "First, I

Norman Dello Joio. Photo by Sheldon Secunda, courtesy R. A. Israel Collection.

met with the producers and musical director to determine just how many minutes of music was required for the half-hour film. Then, I simply showed the movie over and over again to myself until it eventually gave me an emotionally binding unit, and I got an idea of the kind of music required."

"Air Power" differed markedly in style from "Victory at Sea," every minute of which was scored. As CBS musical director Alfredo Antonini explained at the time, "Where the action is strong by itself, it would detract from the story to have a 50–piece orchestra playing in the background. In fact, silence can be used sometimes with enormous dramatic effect. It's all a question of sensing, of feeling spontaneously where music has to come into the picture."

In addition, unlike the endless stream of unconnected melodies with which Rodgers filled "Victory at Sea," Dello Joio's concept was more one of theme and variations plus occasional stand-alone pieces. "I want to make all the episodes I'm responsible for sound like a symphonic entity," he said. "Musically, that is, they should be one profile from beginning to end." (This became most apparent when he arranged much of the basic musical material into a symphonic suite for recording by Eugene Ormandy and the Philadelphia Orchestra after the series ended.)

For his main theme, Dello Joio stressed the romance of flying with a lyrical motif for the opening sequence of planes aloft and drifting through cloud-dotted skies. For an early episode about the barnstorming daredevils of the 1920s, he created a buoyant, happy mood; for scenes of aerial warfare, orchestral bombast with especially difficult passages for brass and percussion. Individual highlights included an off-kilter march for the German military, a sprightly dance for Russian soldiers, and Oriental color for later episodes depicting the war with Japan.

Also, unlike "Victory at Sea," Antonini assigned other composers to specific "Air Power" episodes, including two fellow concert-hall composers: George Antheil, who wrote what Antonini termed "very modern, mechanical, destructive-sounding music" for the story of the bombing of German oil refineries in Rumania; and Paul Creston, whose Italian heritage and lyrical bent were considered appropriate for the episode about the liberation of Rome. Both aired in early 1957.

Antonini returned to Antheil, Creston, and other notable composers outside of the usual film and television ranks when, the following season, CBS News inaugurated "The Twentieth Century" (1957–66). Walter Cronkite was the on-camera host and narrator for this distinguished Sunday-night series of documentary half-hours that examined mostly historical subjects from the first half of the century. Burton Benjamin, who with Isaac Kleinerman produced most of the series, told an interviewer in 1959 that he believed that composers from the "serious" music field would supply more sophisticated music appropriate to a series devoted to the twentieth century.

Antheil (1900–59), who was no stranger to film scoring (with twenty-five films to his credit, including *The Pride and the Passion,* 1957), composed the

"Twentieth Century" theme and wrote a dozen scores for its first two seasons, including music for profiles of Churchill and Gandhi and several programs relating to World War II. Creston (1906–85) produced nearly as many over the first five seasons. Alan Hovhaness (b. 1911), who had scored NBC documentaries on India and Southeast Asia in 1955 and 1957, contributed to "Twentieth Century," as did Gail Kubik (1914–84), Ulysses Kay (1917–95), and, most intriguingly, Darius Milhaud (1892–1974).

Milhaud, who had been a member of France's rebellious school of radical composers known as Les Six, was also familiar with film (having written more than two dozen scores including *Madame Bovary,* 1934). His two "Twentieth Century" scores are believed to have been his only work for American television. Both were for subjects with exotic backdrops: the Argentina political story "Peron and Evita" (1958) and the World War II film "Burma Road and the Hump" (1959). Another member of Les Six, Georges Auric (1899–1983), scored the series' wartime story "Stalingrad" (1959), while Franz Waxman scored a two-part 1960 examination of the world's oceans that featured undersea expert Jacques Cousteau.

Richard Rodgers was lured back to the documentary form for "Winston Churchill—The Valiant Years" (1960–61, ABC), a twenty-six-part adaptation of the British leader's World War II memoirs in which Richard Burton spoke the words of Churchill.

Daniel Melnick, later a producer who would make the films *Straw Dogs* and *All That Jazz* (and the man who introduced composer Jerry Fielding to director Sam Peckinpah, on television's "Noon Wine" in 1966), was vice president in charge of programming at ABC at the time. Fellow network executives were reluctant to commit to a documentary series that was likely to garner only low ratings; Melnick convinced them that a Richard Rodgers score for "The Valiant Years" might turn into another bonanza as "Victory at Sea" had been for NBC.

Rodgers happened to be Melnick's father-in-law. "It was after Oscar Hammerstein had died," Melnick recalled, "and Dick became very depressed. I knew that if I could give Dick a project that allowed him to write but didn't demand a lyricist, that could go a long way toward ending his depression." Rodgers agreed to write "The Valiant Years," and to do so in the same manner in which he had scored "Victory at Sea." "He wrote for every section," Melnick said, "but he wrote in chunks, the way he composed on Broadway. He would write the melody and the harmony, but then turn it over to an orchestrator. They were more than themes; they were really full-blown pieces." With Robert Russell Bennett busy on "Project XX," "The Valiant Years" was orchestrated by Robert Emmett Dolan, Hershy Kay, and Eddie Sauter.

Rodgers's main theme for Churchill was a triumphal statement for orchestra that had decidedly Waltonesque overtones. There were variations and secondary themes that represented Churchill's various moods: determined, depressed, jubilant, and peaceful. He also wrote a hopeful motif for the survivors of Dunkirk; one of his most lyrical pieces, "Deep Sea," for the Mediterranean Theater; a lightly pastoral theme for Churchill's country home Chartwell; a hymn to suggest the spirituality of many of the Allied leaders, later associated with the death of President Roosevelt; and several marches, including a jubilant one for the English resolve and a triumphant one for the Allied victory. Rodgers won the Emmy for original music for his score.

Producer David L. Wolper significantly altered the way documentary programming was produced and aired on commercial television. With "The Race for Space" (produced in 1958–59, aired on an ad hoc network of stations in 1960), which utilized then-unseen film of the Soviet space program, he demonstrated that a public affairs program that had not been produced by one of the networks could not only be informative and compelling but also find an audience.

Wolper was a filmmaker. A key element in his conception of documentary programming for a mass audience was music. "Music is a language of film-making," he explained. "Words are one language, the photography is one, and music is another. It creates movement, tension, mood, beauty, fright . . . With music, sometimes you don't even need words. CBS said for a long time, 'We don't want any music in our documentaries.' I always laughed when they said that. I said, 'Well, let's not have words or cameramen either.' Music is part of the language of making films. If you don't have that language, you don't have a film. So why not use it?"

In choosing composers for his early documentary films, Wolper started at the top. He hired Elmer Bernstein for "The Race for Space," and returned to him again and again throughout the 1960s. Bernstein's "Hollywood: The Golden Years" (1961, NBC) opened with an elegant theme and, because the subject was the silent-film era, featured a score that ranged from the raucous (for two-reeler comedies) to the grand (for D. W. Griffith epics) and melodramatic (for cliffhangers). He reprised the theme in two sequels, "Hollywood: The Fabulous Era" and "Hollywood: The Great Stars" (1963, ABC), and for the subsequent series "Hollywood and the Stars" (1963–64, NBC) hosted by Joseph Cotten.

For "D-Day" (1962, NBC), Wolper's definitive study of the Normandy invasion, Bernstein composed a score as dramatic as those for any of his war movies. He won an Emmy for his stirring music for "The Making of the President 1960" (1963, ABC), based on Theodore H. White's Pulitzer Prize-winning chronicle of the Kennedy-Nixon campaign.

Still, none of this was easy, the composer said: "They were very, very difficult to do because you're not dealing with specifically dramatic situations. You're trying to keep something alive which is basically information. It's very hard to write music for information. Being an emotional art, you [normally] write music for emotional situations."

Lalo Schifrin received his first Emmy nomination for a Wolper documentary: "The Making of the President 1964" (1965, CBS), Theodore White's examination of the Johnson-Goldwater campaign. Schifrin wrote themes for both candidates, but the highlight was his two-minute fugue for strings that underscored a montage of Election Day scenes throughout the country.

Even more impressive was Schifrin's grim and complex score for the now-classic "The Rise and Fall of the Third Reich" (1968, ABC), Wolper's three-hour, three-night adaptation of William L. Shirer's history of Nazi Germany. "Third Reich" was particularly significant as the first television score to inspire a dramatic cantata, which received public performance even before its screen debut.

This was no "Victory at Sea"—no happy melodies here. As described in a 1967 *Life* review, the cantata ranged in idiom "from traditional German classicism to contemporary tone clusters that occasionally flirt with atonality. There are few jazz elements, beyond a section in which a banal fox-trot conjures up, in the style of Kurt Weill, the decadence of post-World War I Germany." All of those elements could be found in the television score. *TV Guide,* only rarely given to mentioning the composer, singled out "Lalo Schifrin's powerful score" in its program preview. *Newsweek* found influences of Wagner, Bartók, and Stravinsky in the score. Alternately dissonant, martial, bombastic, and mournful, Schifrin's television score achieved much wider notice because of its development into the cantata (performed in August 1967 at the Hollywood Bowl, with Laurence Harvey narrating the Alfred Perry text). Reflecting on the writing process, Schifrin later said, "I went into a kind of madness, an intricate kind of writing, and I used that in the creation of [music for] Hitler."

Stravinsky also inspired Lyn Murray, who was Emmy-nominated for his sophisticated, yet primitive-sounding, music for Wolper's "Primal Man" series (1973–74, ABC), an elaborate depiction of the lives of man's ancestors as far back as five million years.

The last of the outstanding weekly network documentary series was "World War I" (1964–65, CBS), produced by the veteran "Twentieth Century" team of Burton Benjamin, Isaac Kleinerman, and John Sharnik. Narrated by Robert Ryan, it told the entire story of the Great War from its historical and social context to the aftermath of the 1914–18 conflict across Europe.

Because all of the footage was silent, music was even more important to "World War I" than to most of its documentary predecessors. CBS News followed its choice of Norman Dello Joio to score "Air Power" with another leading figure in American symphonic music to score "World War I": Morton Gould (b. 1913). Gould's *Spirituals for Orchestra, Latin-American Symphonette,* and *Fall River Legend* embodied a distinctly American flavor and were as accessible to popular-music audiences as to concert-hall regulars. A former radio conductor, he wrote for Broadway (including *Billion Dollar Baby,* 1945) and movies (including *Windjammer,* 1958) as well as symphony orchestras. His two earlier assignments on "Twentieth Century"—a 1960 episode about turn-of-the-century Europe and a 1963 episode about the bloody 1916 battle at Verdun—led to his commission to write the music for "World War I."

Like the earlier series, "World War I" consisted of twenty-six half-hour episodes, and like "Victory at Sea," it was scored from beginning to end. With the exception of a 1965 episode, "Tipperary and All That Jazz," that drew on songs of the era, Gould's music avoided literal quotations from period tunes in favor of evoking the atmosphere; as the liner notes of the soundtrack put it, "the bittersweet nostalgia, the doomed romanticism, the optimism, the tragic human drama."

Gould's main-title theme was played against footage of a doughboy rising out of the trenches to aim his rifle over barbed wire-fenced terrain. While it contained martial elements appropriate to a study of war, there was also a melancholy element suggestive of the monumental loss of life and the permanently changed world that resulted from the conflict. And, although there was considerable lighter music when called for, that somber, even world-weary tone pervaded much of Gould's score. Other recurring themes included his lyrical waltz for Sarajevo; music of elegance for the royal courts of Europe; staccato bursts of percussion and brass for battle scenes, sometimes incorporating variations on the main theme; Americana, including parade music, for scenes of soldiers preparing to depart for Europe; and more ethnically flavored motifs for scenes of Russians, Frenchmen, and other nationalities.

Gould recalled the circumstances: "They would screen a rough cut of [the episode]. I would look at this and jot down the general atmosphere. As an example, there was one segment that had to do with Jutland, the famous sea battle. Well, obviously that's ocean music, you know, dreadnoughts and destroyers and all that business. Then the specifics would be done; I worked off a log and footage sheets. The log would have certain descriptive things, and I made my own pencil notations. Then I would do a very full sketch, or sometimes go right to the score." CBS musical director Alfredo Antonini conducted the recording sessions in Bayside, Queens; the band, Gould said, averaged about twenty-four players.

One of the decade's most remarkable documentary scores was composed by Alex North (1910–91) for "Africa" (1967, ABC), an unprecedented four-hour, single-night exploration of the land, the peoples, and the problems facing the continent at that time. North was one of the most highly respected composers in films. The composer of *A Streetcar Named Desire* and *Death of a Salesman* (both 1951), *Spartacus* (1960), *Cleopatra* (1963), *The Agony and the Ecstasy* (1965), and *Who's Afraid of Virginia Woolf?* (1966), he had studied with modern composers Aaron Copland and Ernst Toch, composed ballet scores for Martha Graham and Agnes DeMille, and continued to write for the concert hall. In 1986 he would be presented with the first Academy Award ever given to a composer for lifetime achievement.

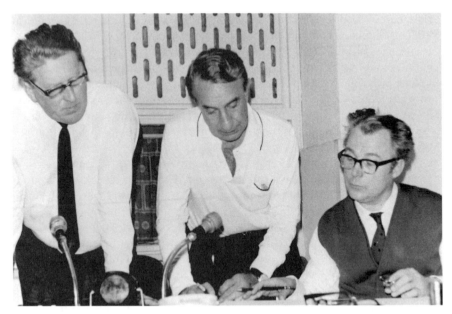

Alex North (center) reviewing the "Africa" score with his engineer (Hans Endrulat, left) and conductor (Kurt Graunke, right) during the 1967 "Africa" sessions in Munich. Courtesy Anne Marie North.

North had spent little time, however, writing for television. His best-known work was the theme for "Playhouse 90" (1956), although he had scored the little-seen documentary series "F.D.R." (1965, ABC), which was made by the producing team from "Winston Churchill—The Valiant Years," and featured Charlton Heston reading the words of Franklin D. Roosevelt.

About "Africa," North later recalled: "This was a rare assignment from ABC. They were doing a four-hour special on Africa, and I went to New York and looked at thousands of feet of the material as they assembled it. My unique commission was to write a four-movement symphony and then the producers would lay in the music after the show had been properly put together. In other words, I was able to sit down and write a four-movement work without the crutch of scenes and footage to catch and support. I did intensive research at the New York Public Library and collected some thirty or so records of authentic African music.

"Finally, after all the study and assimilating of the rhythms and instrumental sounds, I decided to write music that would reflect the birth of a new continent with all its turmoil, joys, and dramatic upheaval. I just couldn't include many of the hundreds of native instruments in existence, but I did have ABC ship over to Munich (where Henry Brandt and I recorded the score) $17,000 worth of more-or-less orthodox percussion instruments." In addition to his thirty-minute symphony, he wrote a main theme and additional music designed to meet a variety of dramatic needs. All of this was recorded with a 108–piece orchestra in Munich, Germany, in March 1967, with both North and orchestrator Brandt conducting different parts of the score.

As producer Jerry Bredouw related in his notes for the album of the score: "During the actual tapings, the superb 11–member percussion section wove subtle and intricate cross-rhythms over unusual tonal combinations. A total of 38 pairs of mallets were employed. The battery of tympanists moved like ballet dancers from boo-bam to log drum to lou-jons; from steel drums to a bank of odd-looking, instantly tunable tom toms."

Bredouw went on to describe the composer's "fragmentary themes in poly-tonal combinations" and to explain the approach: "North first uses aboriginal instruments for the jagged cross-rhythms and weird, wailing melodies which express emotions not readily comprehensible to Western ears. Then the primi-tive sounds are translated into the language of the Western world's instru-ments and musical devices. What seemed like discordant shrieks are fashioned into majestic, compelling themes."

"Africa" aired September 10, 1967. Gregory Peck's narration, together with North's thoughtful, complex score, and the spectacular cinematography, helped the program win an Emmy as the year's outstanding news documentary.

Throughout the 1960s, the documentary genre continued to attract a variety of composers, often from outside the usual television ranks. Eddy L. Manson (b. 1922), the harmonica virtuoso who had scored films such as *The Little Fugitive* (1953) and received an Emmy nomination for his music for "Harvey" with Art Carney on "DuPont Show of the Month" (1958), received another nomination for his unusually exotic music for "The River Nile" (1962, NBC).

English composer John Barry wrote two memorably lyrical scores for famous actresses touring their favorite cities: the Emmy-nominated "Elizabeth Taylor in London" (1963, CBS) and "Sophia Loren in Rome" (1964, ABC), which included an original ballet and a song performed by Loren. Elsewhere on the Continent, popular-music conductor Percy Faith created a lush, evoca-tive backdrop for Princess Grace in "A Look at Monaco" (1963, CBS).

Two of producer Lucy Jarvis's Emmy-winning cultural documentaries prominently featured outstanding scores by major composers. Georges Auric wrote music of a decidedly Russian character for the extensive historical sequences of "The Kremlin" (1963, NBC), while Norman Dello Joio was inspired by the world's great art masterpieces for "The Louvre" (1964, NBC). He won an Emmy for his stunning score, which augmented the traditional sym-phony ensemble with a cathedral organ, and interpolated Renaissance music for scenes of the changing face of the Paris landmark through the centuries.

Three other composers drew inspiration from great painters for notable documentaries of the period. For "I, Leonardo da Vinci" (1965, ABC), part of the critically acclaimed "Saga of Western Man" series, Italian-born composer Ulpio Minucci (b. 1917) created Renaissance fanfares and, for the *Last Supper,* a fugue for orchestra. For "Gauguin in Tahiti: The Search for Paradise" (1967, CBS), Gerald Fried invoked South Seas rhythms and musically imagined the native innocence sought by the French postimpressionist artist. Both programs won Emmys; both composers were nominated for their scores.

Laurence Rosenthal won his first Emmy for "Michelangelo: The Last Giant" (1965–66, NBC), a two-part chronicle of the artist's life, with Peter Ustinov reading the words of Michelangelo. Rosenthal, who scored the special in Rome ("echoing some of the feeling of late medieval and early Renaissance music," the composer said), was given the rare opportunity to spend an hour alone in the Sistine Chapel prior to writing that sequence.

Two documentary series carried the tradition of orchestral scoring from the sixties into the seventies and beyond: the *"National Geographic* Specials" (1965–, CBS/ABC/PBS/NBC) and "The Undersea World of Jacques Cousteau" (1968–76, ABC).

David L. Wolper produced the earliest *"National Geographic*s," and it was his longtime relationship with Elmer Bernstein that led the composer to write the series theme, the familiar brass-and-percussion motif that the series retained throughout the next three decades. In creating the theme, Bernstein said, he sought to write music "with a sense of importance . . . I was thinking of fanfares that Aaron Copland had written during World War II, and I suppose I thought of [the *'National Geographic'* theme] as a fanfare for the world, which is really what *National Geographic* is all about." Bernstein scored one of the earliest hours, "The Voyage of the Brigantine *Yankee*" (1966), a chronicle of the around-the-world trip of a Massachusetts sailing vessel for which Bernstein wrote a rousing hornpipe and similarly old-fashioned seafaring music.

For "The Hidden World of Insects" (1966), Lalo Schifrin contributed off-beat sounds that, he later observed, laid the groundwork for his brilliantly eclectic score for Wolper's Oscar-winning insect documentary *The Hellstrom Chronicle* (1970). His improvisational approach, essentially the creation of aleatory music, was highly unusual for television at the time.

For the seventh *"National Geographic,"* Wolper initiated a relationship that would last for the next several years and result in some of the finest scores written for documentary television: he hired Walter Scharf (b. 1910) to score "Alaska!" (1967). Scharf's career had embraced show music of all kinds. He orchestrated *Girl Crazy* for George Gershwin on Broadway, was accompanist for singer Helen Morgan, and wrote arrangements for Alice Faye musicals in the thirties. A multiple Oscar nominee, he was musical director for pictures such as Danny Kaye's *Hans Christian Anderson* (1952) and the then-in-production *Funny Girl* with Barbra Streisand (1968). He scored several Jerry Lewis movies including *The Bellboy* (1960), would later have a hit single with *Ben* (1972), and had scored dozens of television dramas including "Ben Casey," "The Man from U.N.C.L.E.," and "Slattery's People."

The playground of the *"National Geographic"* series was the entire natural

Walter Scharf, 1988. Courtesy the composer.

world. Always informative, spectacularly photographed, and often enthralling, the programs quickly became the cream of commercial television's documentary crop. It was through the *Geographic* series that the American public became familiar with Jane Goodall and her chimpanzees, Dian Fossey and her mountain gorillas, and numerous other pioneering researchers.

This varied turf provided an endless series of fresh challenges to the composer, and the freedom permitted by the filmmakers often resulted in small-scale tone poems within many programs. Scharf scored sixteen "*National Geographic*s" including such diverse topics as "Siberia: The Endless Horizon" (1969), "Ethiopia: The Hidden Empire" (1970), "Journey to the High Arctic" (1971), the Philippines-set "Last Tribes of Mindanao" (1972), the nocturnal species show "Strange Creatures of the Night" (1973), and the volcano study "This Violent Earth" (1973).

"We went to terrific expense," Scharf recalled. "We never had an orchestra of less than thirty-five [musicians], all the way up to fifty and sixty. We recorded at the major studios, at major prices. Mixing of these films took three, four, five days; ordinarily [in television], they take six to eight hours and slap it together." Scharf avoided a simplistic approach. "I felt that we shouldn't portray a bird with a piccolo or a whale with a tuba. I thought that was a little childish," he said. "I felt that the music should be humane, dramatic, and relate to people, giving heart to the creatures . . . I never regarded them as animals, or treated them in cartoon fashion. I tried to give them understanding."

Among Scharf's successors on the *"Geographic"* series were Billy Goldenberg, who successfully combined electronic and acoustic elements for a unique look inside the human body in "The Incredible Human Machine" (1975); Lee Holdridge, whose soaring theme musically captured the majesty of special creatures in "The Great Whales" (1977); Paddy Moloney, whose flavorful Irish music, performed by his group The Chieftains, lent authenticity to the equine study "Ballad of the Irish Horse" (1985); and Jay Chattaway, who combined a twenty-six-member gamelan orchestra with conventional Western music for "Bali, Masterpiece of the Gods" (1990).

Shortly after assuming musical direction of the *"Geographic"* series, Scharf was called to score the Cousteau series. Celebrated French oceanographer Jacques-Yves Cousteau (who had been profiled on a *"National Geographic"* hour) and the crew of his research ship *Calypso* circled the globe studying undersea life in these acclaimed, highly rated specials.

Scharf started with the initial offering, "Sharks" (1968), and as quickly as the second, "The Savage World of the Coral Jungle" (1968), his music was being noticed in the press; *TV Guide* pointed out that "Walter Scharf's score accents the graceful movements of ocean life." According to Scharf, Rod Serling—who narrated the series for its first seven years—often attended the scoring sessions, making notes about the dynamics of the music that he would take into account when later recording his narration. "We did maybe ten or twelve like that," Scharf recalled. "It gave me the latitude to do what I wanted."

Scharf scored twenty-eight hours in the Cousteau series, including studies of whales, manatees, walruses, penguins, and other species of marine life. For "A Sound of Dolphins" (1972), he reflected the intelligent mammals being portrayed with playful, exuberant music, including a miniature ballet. He received two Emmys for original music on the series, for "The Tragedy of the Red Salmon" (1970) and "Beneath the Frozen World" (1974), third in Cousteau's four-part series on the Antarctic. He also composed an original symphonic work, "The Legend of the Living Sea," for a Cousteau Society museum exhibit in the early 1970s.

Succeeding Scharf on the retitled "Cousteau Odyssey" series and its successors (1977–, PBS/TBS) with especially colorful scores were an international collection of composers including Elmer Bernstein, who penned a new series theme as well as a ghostly serenade for Cousteau's exploration of a sunken

World War I ship in "*Calypso*'s Search for the *Brittanic*" (1977); Greek writer Manos Hadjidakis (*Never on Sunday*), whose bouzoukis and panpipes lent authentic flavor to "*Calypso*'s Search for Atlantis" in the Greek islands (1978); and French composer Georges Delerue, whose threnody for a long-lost civilization haunted "The Blind Prophets of Easter Island" (1978) and whose music underscored the awesome power of the great African river in "The Nile" (1979).

British composer John Scott (b. 1930) became the most consistent musical voice of the later Cousteau series. A former jazz musician and sixties session player for colleagues including John Barry and Edwin Astley, his diverse scores for films, including *Antony and Cleopatra* (1973), *The Final Countdown* (1980), and *Greystoke: The Legend of Tarzan, Lord of the Apes* (1984), demonstrated an equal facility with the symphony orchestra.

Scott appreciated the broad scope and musical freedom afforded him by the producers. "Generally in feature films," he said, "one doesn't have the encouragement that I received from Jacques Cousteau and from [his son] Jean-Michel Cousteau." Their unusual interest in the music of their films led them to contract with London's prestigious Royal Philharmonic Orchestra on a number of occasions.

Scott composed a number of memorable, richly melodic scores for the series. His sometimes extensive musical research paid dividends in scoring exotic locales, notably the six-part "Cousteau/Amazon" series (1984), for which Scott utilized indigenous South American sounds including Brazilian rhythms, Peruvian flutes, a guitar made from an armadillo shell, and various percussion ensembles. His three-part "Papua New Guinea" series (1991) took a daring approach involving jazz soloists performing on wind and percussion instruments. "The last thing that it [would have] called for was a big orchestral tapestry," Scott explained. "The native instruments are all kinds of drums. Therefore I found every reason for using drums and jazz musicians. There is a definite relationship between jazz and primitive music; it's music from the soul of the people."

For "Cape Horn: Waters of the Wind" (1986), he created a forbidding musical landscape depicting the icy conditions at the bottom of the world, eliminating violins and utilizing a wordless soprano as a lament for the hundreds of wrecked ships and lost sailors over the centuries, evoking "a ghostly feeling of the presence of these souls," Scott said. The score won an Emmy.

News themes over the years have been contributed by an array of composers, usually anonymous. Often, they were little more than a variation on the old click-clack teletype sound that was heard in the background of so many newsrooms of the 1960s (and, before that, on radio).

"The Huntley-Brinkley Report" (1956–70, NBC) concluded with an excerpt from the second movement of Beethoven's ninth symphony. The rechristened "NBC Nightly News" (1970) sported a new theme by composer Ray

Ellis (b. 1923), whose arrangements for Johnny Mathis, Barbra Streisand, and Lena Horne had made him successful in the popular-music field of the 1960s; Ellis later composed a new theme for NBC's "Today" show, which previously had used the standards "Sentimental Journey" and "Misty" as signature tunes.

Henry Mancini created a new "NBC Nightly News" theme that ran for two seasons beginning in the fall of 1977. The use of rototoms (a drum with various pitches) made the sound highly percussive, but, Mancini reflected later: "I think it was a little too hip for its time. It was too involved. The news themes on now are [mostly] four- and five-note phrases, which is probably the only part of the theme that gets played a lot. So [mine] did not have that kind of identification."

Far more successful was a theme that Mancini wrote the previous year. His "Decision '76" theme, an exhilarating march that NBC commissioned for its election-night coverage, became the network's standard election theme for years thereafter. Mancini recalled: "'Seventy-six, you know, they wanted Americana. The original was written for band: six trumpets, six trombones, lots of French horns, baritone horns, clarinets, a bunch of piccolos, and percussion. It really sounded like a brass band coming down the street."

NBC radically altered the sound of all of its news programs in September 1985, when it debuted a new series of news themes by composer John Williams, who by that time was not only the world's most famous film composer but also musical director of the Boston Pops Orchestra. An NBC executive said at the time that the division's intent was to replace the all-too-familiar "synthesizer 'news noise'" that had become commonplace around the dial with a "world-class composition."

The main theme, called "The Mission," became widely known as the new signature music for "NBC Nightly News"; brisk, dignified, featuring a fanfare, and signifying a "nobility of purpose," as Williams said at the time, it appeared in a number of versions throughout the day. Williams wrote three other themes, however, all classically styled, which were seldom heard in their entirety: "Fugue for the Changing Times," sometimes used on special reports; the bright "Scherzo for 'Today,'" written for, but only occasionally heard on, the morning news program; and "The Pulse of Events," the urgent opening and closing of which became the theme for the Sunday news show "Meet the Press." Williams conducted these, plus four shorter versions of "The Mission" theme, and eleven five-second "bumpers," with an eighty-piece orchestra. He later arranged a three-and-a-half-minute concert version of "The Mission."

CBS News, on the rare occasions when it demanded a musical signature, often turned to the classics. Aaron Copland's "Appalachian Spring" was the source of the main theme for "CBS Reports" (1959) for many years, while the "Albason" of eighteenth-century German musician Gottfried Reiche—who played all of Bach's first trumpet parts for the last ten years of his life—

became the opening fanfare for the weekend news and cultural affairs magazine "Sunday Morning" (1979–).

ABC's "Good Morning America" (1975), initially produced by the network's entertainment division, commissioned an upbeat theme by Marvin Hamlisch. The network's news division, however, turned to Bob Israel (b. 1928) and Bill Conti for most of its news music. In 1977, Israel created the ABC News "umbrella theme" whose first four notes became familiar as the opening of the themes for "World News Tonight," "Nightline," "This Week with David Brinkley," and various special reports. "In terms of news," Israel said, "there has to be a very quotable entity in the theme. It has to say what it says quickly and to the point, so that if people are out of the room but hear that piece, they'll know that it's time to go and watch and listen.

"It also has to have a kind of urgency, without resorting to the cliché of the ticker-tape thing which goes way back to radio," he added. "I think the reason [the ABC News theme has] been so successful is that anybody can hum it. We've developed that into endless variations for all kinds of subjects, from the inaugural of a president—with a big orchestra—to the beginning of '20/20,' or any of those [news] shows."

Conti was frequently signed to write new main-title themes for ABC's newsmagazines and specials, including the three-hour historical retrospective "45/85" (1985), "Our World" (1986–87), "Business World" (1986–), and "PrimeTime Live" (1989–). His connection with the staff of Roone Arledge, who oversaw both news and sports at ABC, led to his most unique television commission: live music for the New York City Marathon in November 1989, performed by the Juilliard Orchestra at Lincoln Center while the race was being run, and televised live around the world.

As described by host Jim McKay at the start of the telecast, their goal was "music that will reflect the emotions that a person feels while running twenty-six miles through the streets of New York. This will be television the way it began—live, with an unknown ending, cameras, commentators, and musicians working without a script, reacting to the events of the morning as they unfold."

Conti had written a triumphant theme, a baroque-style fugue for early moments of the race, music for various city montages, and a finale for the first runners who would cross the finish line more than two hours later. Organized much like the many Academy Awards telecasts he conducted, the scheme had Conti responding to the action and the directions of the telecast's producers, communicating which pieces and tempos were appropriate to the fifty-two young musicians, and hoping for the best when it came time to count down the seconds to the finish. This ambitious and largely successful venture won two Emmys for Conti (one for the concept, another for the music itself), and was probably the most original idea for musical scoring in the history of televised sports.

Flintstones!
Meet the Flintstones!

Cartoons in Prime Time

A Schlitz commercial changed Hoyt Curtin's life.

The composer, who had been scoring industrial films and commercials since 1948, scored an animated spot for the popular beer in 1957. The animation directors happened to be former "Tom and Jerry" cartoon creators William Hanna and Joseph Barbera. So when the duo created their first Saturday-morning cartoon series for television—"Ruff and Reddy" (1957–64, NBC)—they called Curtin to supply the music. In fact, the process that began with that show remained nearly identical for the next thirty years of work with Hanna-Barbera Productions: "I got a call, and it was Bill and Joe on the same line, asking me if I could write a tune to this lyric which they gave me over the phone. I said 'Sure.' I wrote down the lyric, I wrote the tune, and I called them back. It was about five minutes. Something like that."

Hoyt S. Curtin (b. 1922), the king of television cartoon music, went on to create the music for nearly 150 series, including all of Hanna-Barbera's prime-time entries: "The Flintstones," "Top Cat," "The Jetsons," and "Jonny Quest." Along with the prime-time series, Curtin was responsible for the music on all of Hanna-Barbera's many syndicated and network cartoons airing during the afternoons and on Saturday mornings. The early hits included "Huckleberry Hound," "Quick Draw McGraw," "Yogi Bear," and "Magilla Gorilla"; the later ones included "Scooby-Doo," "Josie and the Pussycats," and "The Smurfs." At the height of the studio's success, in 1970, Curtin wrote and supervised music for nine new series in one season.

His most famous tune, the now world-famous theme for "The Flintstones"

William Hanna (left) with Hoyt Curtin at the piano. Courtesy Hoyt Curtin.

(1960–66, ABC), didn't even hit the airwaves until the series' third season. Hanna and Barbera had borrowed an idea or two from Jackie Gleason's fifties series "The Honeymooners" but cleverly modified the setting to the Stone Age. The sitcom antics of suburban Bedrock neighbors—blustery Fred Flintstone, his dimwitted but good-hearted neighbor Barney Rubble, their wives Wilma and Betty, pet dinosaur Dino, and (later) their children Pebbles and Bamm-Bamm—kept audiences laughing for six seasons.

Curtin's original main-title theme for the series was an instrumental he called "Rise and Shine," a brassy, bouncy tune with lots of xylophone (for Fred's foot-powered car). The more familiar "Flintstones" theme actually originated as a part of the first-season underscore (in a Dixieland arrangement for the pilot). "And the second year," Curtin recalled, "we all decided to change it to a more 'caveman' sound. I had all the timpanists in town. It was like Swiss bell ringers, you play this note and you play that. And it was the present theme. That stayed on a year, and then Bill wrote a lyric to that tune. I got a jazz band and some singers and recorded that [for the third season], and they haven't changed it since." "Flintstones! Meet the Flintstones! They're the modern Stone Age family/From the town of Bedrock, they're a page right out of history. . . ." went the lyric, incorporating Fred's familiar "yabba-dabba-doo!" that voice-over artist Alan Reed came up with at a recording session.

The jazz approach to the scoring of many Hanna-Barbera shows was directly attributable to Curtin's love of big-band music, although the composer points to Hanna and Barbera as his original inspiration: "Their idea was to write a piece of music that's happy. These cartoons are not World War Three. They are happy, and if you write a piece of music that's happy, it's pretty much got to go with it. 'Happy' to me is jazz." Curtin found comedic sounds throughout the orchestra, but especially in the contrabassoon, the tuba, and percussion. He even created a musical guffaw: an eight-note, descending figure for clarinets and tuba that became an aural punch line on many Hanna-Barbera series for years.

"The Flintstones" often indulged in musical shenanigans, as when Leonard Bernstone conducted Rockmaninoff, or when songwriter Hoagy Carmichael performed in a 1966 episode, asking would-be tunesmith Fred: "You want this allegro, pianissimo, or andante?" and Fred replied, "Look, I don't want to talk about Italian food. Play."

For "Top Cat" (1961–62, ABC)—". . . the most effectual Top Cat/whose intellectual close friends get to call him T.C. . . ."—Curtin found the jazz approach especially appropriate for the story of a smart, urban, and very hip alley cat and his gang.

A year later, Hanna and Barbera decided to follow up their Stone Age hit with a sitcom set in the future. "The Jetsons" (1962–63, ABC) would alternate its focus between the workplace (hapless George beset by his blowhard boss Mr. Spacely) and the home (his wife and two children, dog Astro, and domestic robot Rosie). Curtin recalled: "The first time I did [the 'Jetsons' theme] was with a little band because nobody had any faith in the picture. It was from left field." Positive network feedback, however, resulted in a new directive: "Rescore with a really big band. Instead of writing a whole new score," Curtain explained, "I just had the musicians listen to, on headsets, the first try-out with a small band. I wrote an arrangement to include the large group, all the strings and everything."

In fact, the "Jetsons" main title is one of Curtin's most orchestral. More of an instrumental intro than a song, the words simply introduced the cast ("Meet George Jetson, his boy Elroy, daughter Judy, Jane his wife"), leaving it to Curtin score the action. Camera moves through the stars and galaxies to Earth, where George is piloting his family in an airborne craft to their various daily destinations: Elroy, off to the Little Dipper School; Judy (to the tune of a sexy-sounding trumpet), to Orbit High School; and Jane, who grabs George's wallet, to the local shopping center in the sky. In the final seconds, George arrives at Spacely Space Sprockets, where his entire craft folds up into a brief-case and he rides the conveyor belt into his office.

In contrast to all this zany music was Curtin's work on "Jonny Quest" (1964–65, ABC), television's first prime-time animated action-adventure series. Jonny was the precocious twelve-year-old son of world-renowned scientist Dr. Benton Quest; they—together with their bodyguard Race Bannon, his young Indian pal Hadji, and pet bulldog Bandit—roamed the world, encountering villains and facing danger on a weekly basis.

Curtin was always hearing trombone players complain about "falling asleep playing goose eggs," a reference to whole notes, on other sessions. So he wrote the "Jonny Quest" theme to feature six trombones. "I wrote it in a killer key," Curtin said, "because I know how to play trombone and I know the hardest place to play is all of the unknown, odd positions. There wasn't anything open. Just murder, E-flat minor . . . And they killed themselves because nobody wanted to make a mistake. Nobody wanted to get outcarved."

In addition to the trombones, the "Quest" band included five trumpets, four woodwinds, three French horns, and a large rhythm section, all heard to spectacular advantage in the series main title: a series of action sequences designed to establish the fantasy, adventure, and science fiction elements that would appeal to the target younger audience. A flying pterodactyl, soldiers battling a spiderlike robot, a walking mummy, Bannon swinging to the rescue, and Quest preparing to fire some futuristic weapon, segue to scenes of Quest's jet, piloted by Bannon, and introductory shots of the characters.

Curtin's music, jazz-based but undeniably dramatic, enhanced the sense of excitement and adventure that the sequence promised. With the underscores, the composer demonstrated that he was as capable of scoring action and danger as well as lighter moments (although there was also room for comedy in the frequent antics of rambunctious Bandit).

Curtin often attracted star players ranging from trumpeter Pete Candoli and flute player Buddy Collette to drummer Frank Capp and guitarist Barney Kessel. His cartoon bands averaged around twenty players. According to Curtin, plans for the new season would be made around April, with recording to begin in early June, whether or not film was available. Arranger Jack Stern was Curtin's right-hand man in the early days; later he would have several orchestrators working to create the scores based on his sketches. At the height of the work, "I had eight guys working around the clock," the composer recalled. "We scored four times a week, four three-hour sessions, and we'd just blast through it." Only a handful of shows would be individually scored "to picture"; in most cases, Curtin would time out storyboards, record enough music to meet union regulations, and track future episodes with music already recorded.

Animation in prime time was not the sole province of Hanna-Barbera. "The Bugs Bunny Show" (1960–62, ABC) drew on the vast backlog of theatrical cartoons produced by Warner Bros., but added new animation (directed by such Warner greats as Chuck Jones and Friz Freleng) to open, close, and bridge the various shorts aired during this weekly half hour. As had become the custom—given the success of such theme songs as "77 Sunset Strip" and "Hawaiian Eye"—the studio assigned songwriters Jerry Livingston and Mack

David to create a musical signature for the show. What they came up with would ultimately rank as their most familiar Warners tune. "77 Sunset Strip" was famous for years, but their theme for Bugs and company, "This Is It!," lasted for decades, when "The Bugs Bunny Show" (later, "The Bugs Bunny/Road Runner Hour") became a fixture among Saturday-morning cartoon shows.

Bugs first appeared from behind the studio shield ("This, folks, is a Warner Bros. television production"). Four spotlights lit up with the words "The Bugs Bunny Show," and a theater curtain rose to Livingston and David's Broadway-style melody as Bugs and Daffy Duck—attired as song-and-dance men, in straw hats and carrying canes—entered from stage right. A spotlight followed them across the stage as they sang: "Overture! Curtain! Lights! This is it! The night of nights . . ." Nine of their fellow Warners cartoon stars (including Elmer Fudd, Pepe LePew, Porky Pig, Foghorn Leghorn, Sylvester, and Tweety) paraded across the stage behind them in time to the music, as the number ended and the announcer introduced "the Oscar-winning rabbit" as host.

The Warner cartoons were smart, often sassy, and superbly animated. The animation produced by Jay Ward's studio, on the other hand, was often crude, but the writing was so satirical and so clever that it was soon obvious that "The Bullwinkle Show" (1961–62, NBC) wasn't aimed at children at all. "Bullwinkle" was a prime-time version of the earlier "Rocky and His Friends" (1959–61, ABC), which ran on weekday afternoons. Producer Jay Ward had made the cult favorite "Crusader Rabbit" (1957, syndicated), and partnered with writer-director Bill Scott for "Rocky and Bullwinkle"; Scott did the voices of such characters as Bullwinkle, Dudley Do-Right, and Mr. Peabody.

In the adventures of Frostbite Falls, Minnesota, residents Rocky the Flying Squirrel and his dimwitted pal Bullwinkle J. Moose, the writers regularly lampooned Cold War politics, starting with the presence of sinister spies Boris Badenov and Natasha Fatale. The nogoodniks reported back to the monocled Fearless Leader in the vaguely Eastern European dictatorship of Pottsylvania. No institution was safe. In one series of adventures, Rocky and Bullwinkle discovered that the world's economy was actually based on the value of cereal boxtops; in a visit to alma mater Wossamotta U., they learned that American college fortunes rested entirely on the success of their football teams; mixed up with the government in a story involving space travel and moon men, they declared that "military intelligence" was "a contradiction in terms."

The puns alone were worth the tune-in. Boris's name was a funny turn on a Mussorgsky opera (*Boris Godunov*). The boys once climbed Whynchataka Peak; found a gem-encrusted toy boat known as the Ruby Yacht of Omar Khayyam; came into possession of a hat known as the Kurwood Derby (a take-off on sixties TV personality Durwood Kirby); and became embroiled in the politics of Moosylvania, located on the Isle of Lucy near the shores of Veronica Lake.

The irreverence extended to the series' various subordinate features: "Fractured Fairy Tales," twisted versions of classics drolly narrated by actor Edward Everett Horton; "Peabody's Improbable History," in which a canine scientist and his pet boy visited famous figures throughout time; "Dudley Do-Right," a silent-movie sendup with Hans Conreid as the voice of villainous Snidely Whiplash; and "Bullwinkle's Corner," outrageous variations on famous poems.

For the prime-time "Bullwinkle," Ward commissioned Fred Steiner to do a Broadway show tune version of his carousel-style "Rocky and His Friends" theme for a new main title that had the moose, in top hat and tails, kicking up his hoofs. For the opening music of the adventures of Rocky and Bullwinkle, the mini-fanfare and rollicking original music of Frank Comstock was heard on some cartoons, while Steiner's new light and airy theme for Rocky could be heard in others.

Steiner also wrote the silent-movie-style music of Dudley Do-Right, the idiot Canadian mountie who usually managed to foil Snidely Whiplash in spite of himself. From Steiner's galloping orchestral theme to his old-fashioned, delightfully melodramatic four-hand piano cues (which sported titles like "Chase the Heavy," "Ardent Swain," and "Our Hero"), played on a tinny-sounding piano and speeded up to impossible tempos, the music of "Dudley Do-Right" was as funny as the on-screen antics of Dudley, beautiful Nell Fenwick, and the evil Whiplash. Steiner's father George Steiner also contributed music to "Dudley Do-Right."

Comstock (b. 1922) wrote the charming lullaby for "Fractured Fairy Tales," a demented march for "Peabody's Improbable History," and a comic tuba-and-bassoon motif for "Bullwinkle's Corner." The composer became far better known for his music for the Jack Webb crime dramas "The D.A.'s Man" with John Compton (1959, NBC), "Adam-12" with Martin Milner and Kent McCord (1968–75, NBC), and "The D.A." with Robert Conrad (1971–72, NBC).

When producer Lee Mendelson and animator Bill Melendez made the first of their "Charlie Brown" specials, "We didn't want cartoon music," Mendelson recalled. "We wanted something that had a different sound." This "different sound" turned out to be jazz piano, as composed and performed by Vince Guaraldi (1928–76). Guaraldi's music would come to be as integral an element of the specials as the writing and art of "Peanuts" creator Charles M. Schulz, and be universally recognized as the aural signature of Charlie Brown, Linus, Lucy, Snoopy, and the rest of the "Peanuts" gang.

Guaraldi's involvement with the comic strip and films based on Schulz's famed creations actually predated the first animated special, "A Charlie Brown Christmas" (1965, CBS). Mendelson had made a documentary, "A Man Called Mays," about baseball player Willie Mays, which aired on NBC in late 1963. Having profiled "the world's greatest baseball player," he decided,

John Scott Trotter (left), music director on many of the "Peanuts" specials, with composer Vince Guaraldi (right). Courtesy Lee Mendelson Productions.

"now I'll do the world's worst": good ol' Charlie Brown. So he made "A Boy Named Charlie Brown," which featured Schulz and examined the "Peanuts" phenomenon; he needed a composer.

"I had always been a jazz fan," Mendelson said. "My dad used to play Art Tatum records. Everybody came through San Francisco: Shearing, Peterson, Garner," added the northern California-based filmmaker. He called veteran jazz critic Ralph J. Gleason at the *San Francisco Chronicle* for advice. With the comic strip's Beethoven-loving pianist Schroeder in mind, Mendelson told Gleason: "I'm looking for a piano player who plays jazz, who reads and knows 'Peanuts,' and who has his own children."

Gleason recommended Guaraldi, who had won a 1962 Grammy for his jazz tune "Cast Your Fate to the Wind" and recorded for Berkeley-based Fantasy Records. "I called Vince. It was that simple," Mendelson recalled. "He lived and worked there, and I lived and worked there. It was just very fortunate.

"About two weeks later, after we hired him, I remember he called me and said, 'I've got to play something for you.' That's the first time I heard 'Linus and Lucy,'" Mendelson said. "I just went crazy, because it was so right, just perfect. It set the standard not only for the first show, but for all of the other shows." In fact, "Linus and Lucy" was just one of several themes that Guaraldi wrote for the documentary that later became popular in the animated "Peanuts" specials. Mendelson couldn't sell his documentary (it aired years later in a revised version) but Guaraldi recorded nine themes for a 1964 Fantasy LP, *Jazz Impressions of "A Boy Named Charlie Brown"*. Gleason wrote in his notes for that album: "He took his inspiration from the creations of Charles Schulz and made music that reflects that inspiration, is empathetic with the image and is still solidly and unmistakably Vince Guaraldi. . . . All the characters in 'Peanuts' are artists confronted with the illogical, blind and mechanistic world. It was natural that Vince Guaraldi's music should fit so well."

Guaraldi was the obvious choice when Mendelson and Melendez made "A Charlie Brown Christmas." Although he revived his "Linus and Lucy" and "Charlie Brown" themes from the documentary, the main theme of the initial half hour was a new one, "Christmas Time Is Here," a contemporary carol (with Mendelson lyrics) performed by a children's choir and, later, Guaraldi's jazz trio.

Guaraldi wrote at least one new theme for every new "Peanuts" special that came along, scoring a total of fifteen until his untimely death. Most memorable—in addition to the energetic and undeniably catchy "Linus and Lucy"—were his elegant waltz for the Halloween special "It's the Great Pumpkin, Charlie Brown" (1966), the "Pebble Beach" samba heard in "Charlie Brown's All-Stars" (1966), his fun theme for irrepressible Snoopy in "He's Your Dog, Charlie Brown" (1968), and a wistful waltz for "You're in Love, Charlie Brown" (1967).

Snoopy's sunglasses-wearing, ultrahip persona Joe Cool made his first appearance in "You're Not Elected, Charlie Brown" (1972) to a funky new theme written and sung on the soundtrack by Guaraldi ("Joe Cool, back in school/Hangin' round the water fountain, playin' the fool . . ."). Later, for "A Charlie Brown Thanksgiving" (1973), he added another vocal, "Little Birdie," as a theme for Snoopy's hapless pal Woodstock. And he took second billing, behind Ludwig van Beethoven, as author of the score for "Play It Again, Charlie Brown" (1971), which focused on Schroeder's classical music interests and featured a number of Beethoven sonatas. Guaraldi began with an all-acoustic sound but, as time went on, became more and more amplified, including not only electric piano and electric guitar but eventually synthesizers as well. It was a way of keeping up with the times, but the later music never seemed quite as simple and honest as in those early scores.

"Linus and Lucy," although initially written for the Van Pelt siblings in the documentary, was never specifically associated with them in the specials. Even in "A Charlie Brown Christmas," it's simply a lively piece to which the kids dance while preparing for the holiday pageant. It quickly emerged as the overall theme for all of the "Peanuts" specials, and was retained by later composers even after Guaraldi's death.

"There's no doubt in my mind," Mendelson said, "that one of the reasons for the longevity of [the series] is the music. It appealed to adults, and kids liked it. And it wasn't 'cartoon music.' Jazz and the comic strip are very American, and that's probably why they work so well together."

Sticking with the Guaraldi tradition, Mendelson later hired a star-studded group of jazz composers to score various segments of his ambitious eight-part historical miniseries, "This Is America, Charlie Brown" (1988–89, CBS), including George Winston ("The Birth of the Constitution"), Wynton Marsalis ("The Wright Brothers at Kitty Hawk"), Dave Brubeck ("The NASA Space Station"), and Dave Grusin ("The Smithsonian and the Presidency").

When Arthur Rankin Jr. and Jules Bass made their stop-motion animation classic "Rudolph, the Red-Nosed Reindeer" (1964), they signed "Rudolph" composer Johnny Marks to compose eight new songs for the score. A key musical element that made "Rudolph" work, as well as dozens of other Rankin-Bass productions over the years, was the musical direction of Maury Laws (b. 1923).

Laws, a guitarist and singer who became an arranger-conductor in New York, had an extensive background as a commercial composer. He served as musical director on the Rankin-Bass "Return to Oz" special (1964), but his success with the wildly popular "Rudolph" ensured him the post of musical director on all future Rankin-Bass productions, both fully animated and stop-motion. In most cases, he not only arranged the standards involved, he also composed the underscore and wrote many original songs with lyricist Bass.

His holiday perennials, in addition to the beloved "Rudolph," included "The Little Drummer Boy" (1968) with the Vienna Boys Choir, "Frosty the Snowman" (1969) with Jimmy Durante, "Santa Claus Is Comin' to Town" (1970) with Fred Astaire, and " 'Twas the Night Before Christmas" (1974) with Joel Grey. He also scored two sequels to the original "Rudolph," both with new songs by Johnny Marks: "Rudolph's Shiny New Year" (1976) and "Rudolph and Frosty" (1979).

Laws's most impressive solo scores for television animation projects included two lavish, all-star films based on books by J. R. R. Tolkien, "The Hobbit" (1977), with songs performed by Glenn Yarborough, and "The Return of the King" (1980); an adaptation of a literary classic, "The Wind in the Willows" (1987), with songs performed by Judy Collins, Roddy McDowall, José Ferrer, and Eddie Bracken; and an original, "The Flight of Dragons" (1986), with a title song performed by Don McLean.

"The Simpsons" (1990–, Fox) was not only an early hit for the fledgling network, it was also the first significant prime-time animated offering in years. Spun off from brief segments in Fox's "Tracey Ullman Show," it dealt with a

Danny Elfman.

dysfunctional middle-class, Middle America family including a not-very-bright nuclear power plant technician named Homer, his wife Marge, and three children (smart Lisa, wiseacre Bart, and infant Maggie).

When cartoonist Matt Groening created the series, he decided that Danny Elfman would be "a natural" to compose the theme. "I've been a fan of Elfman's since the days of the Mystic Knights of the Oingo Boingo," Groening said, referring to Elfman's eclectic Los Angeles rock band. But he didn't know the composer, who by then had gone on to movie fame with his quirky carnival music for *Pee-wee's Big Adventure* (1985) and his dark orchestral score for

Batman (1989). "Not only did I not know him," Groening pointed out, "I used to be a rock critic, and during the days of Oingo Boingo, I gave them a review that annoyed Elfman so much that he wrote a letter to the editor of the *Los Angeles Reader.*

"I didn't know if he would remember that I was the one who had panned him in this review, and when we had our first meeting, he said, 'So you're the one.' But he forgave me," Groening laughed, "because I also went on to make fun of rock critics a lot in my cartoon scripts."

Groening's direction to Elfman: "I want something that's frantic and frenetic, like the scores of the great shows of the 1960s. I always thought that the shows of the seventies and eighties were so wimpy and very tentative, saying, 'Oh, here's our little show, we're trying not to be too offensive, please give us a chance.' Whereas in the sixties, show themes were big fanfares and swoops and swooshes—they said, this is a show!" Recalled Elfman: "I was inspired by a lot of different stuff including 'The Flintstones' and 'The Jetsons,' and just the style of those times. When they sent me a pencil sketch of their opening it really had, to me, the feel of a sixties-flavored fun opening, and I should play it that way."

Elfman's "Simpsons" theme began with, surprisingly, a choir singing the title as it emerged from the clouds. An aerial shot of Springfield, the animated family's hometown, led to a look inside a school window where Bart was writing the same sentence over and over on the chalkboard (a line that changed every week). Scenes of Homer at work, Marge at the grocery store, and Lisa playing a saxophone solo (also different each week) during practice with her awful school band, followed; Homer driving home, Bart skateboarding, Maggie pretending to drive in Marge's car, segued into a final scene of the family gathering in front of the TV (the "couch gag," the third element to change from week to week).

Richard Gibbs, former keyboard player for Elfman's Oingo Boingo band, scored the first season of "The Simpsons." Alf Clausen came in during the second season and remained with the show. Although he had not previously worked in animation, his versatility, speed, and familiarity with a wide range of musical styles made him perfect casting for the show (and resulted in at least one Emmy nomination every year for his music).

"Early on, I was told that this is not a cartoon," Clausen said. "This is a show where the characters are drawn. There's a difference, according to [the producers]. They are saying that they want me to score the real emotion of the characters; they don't want me to 'Mickey Mouse' anything." Clausen found that his extensive variety-show background came in handy "because I have to do everything under the sun on this show. I've honed the orchestra down to the smallest group of players [thirty-five] that can perform all of these styles without having to pay any extra people.

"The basic premise of this whole series is the joke," the composer

Alf Clausen. Photo by Ted Soki, courtesy the composer.

explained, "and the jokes come rapid-fire. An old bandleader friend once told me, 'You can't vaudeville vaudeville.' Meaning, the joke is much funnier if you play the music real with the situation as opposed to playing the music funny. You pull the audience into the reality of the situation, so that the payoff becomes much more hilarious. . . . If you try to 'Mickey Mouse' it, or play the comedy of the situation, you're already tipping your hand."

Clausen's touch was also apparent with the sometimes subtle, often intentionally obvious quotations from classic film and television scores, and in some cases outright parodies of them. Among the many examples were his use of Elmer Bernstein's theme from *The Great Escape* for Maggie's day-care adventures, John Williams's *Raiders of the Lost Ark* opening for Homer chasing a mischievous Bart through the house, and even David Raksin's "Ben Casey" theme as an intro for Homer's hospitalization.

For the "Itchy and Scratchy" cartoons that Bart and Lisa often watched, Clausen got to write real cartoon music; for the "McBain" action-movie clips, he adopted a "Michael Kamen-esque *Die Hard* style"; his annual "Treehouse of Horror" Halloween show music ranged from Bernard Herrmann-style suspense music to Jerry Goldsmith-style alien cues.

My Name Is Kunta Kinte

Made-for-TV Movies and Miniseries

THE BEGINNINGS

s television matured and became, however slightly, more respected by filmmakers and artists in the theater, increasingly ambitious productions were mounted both in New York and Hollywood. The "dramatic special" of the late 1950s and early 1960s gradually evolved into what commonly became known as the made-for-TV movie.

The dramatic anthology series of the late 1950s, notably CBS's hour-and-a-half "Playhouse 90," led inevitably to larger-scale, one-shot film productions. Although billed as "dramatic specials," these were essentially made-for-TV movies before the term had been coined. Producers sought name talent both before and behind the cameras for these prestige projects. Pulitzer Prize-winning composer Norman Dello Joio wrote a symphonic score for a two-night adaptation of Thackeray's "Vanity Fair" (1961, CBS), while Laurence Rosenthal composed the darkly passionate music for Graham Greene's "The Power and the Glory" (1961, CBS) with Laurence Olivier and George C. Scott.

Some historians mark 1964 as the starting point of the telefilm, with the launch of Revue's "Project 120" series of two-hour films made especially for the medium. The first of this series was "The Killers," a remake of the 1946 film with Lee Marvin, Angie Dickinson, and Ronald Reagan that featured a fast-moving, jazz-driven score by Johnny Williams. Sadistically violent, "The Killers" was rejected by NBC and released theatrically by Universal instead.

The earliest "Project 120" films to make it on the air, both in late 1964, were two other crime melodramas: the Lalo Schifrin-scored "See How They Run" and "The Hanged Man," with music by Benny Carter. (Carter, with lyricist Sammy Cahn, wrote a Brazilian-flavored song, "Only Trust Your Heart," that was performed in the film by vocalist Astrud Gilberto and saxophonist Stan Getz, whose "Girl from Ipanema" was then riding high on the pop charts.)

CBS's most high-profile projects continued to be billed as dramatic specials. Just as Alex North had composed a grand and beautiful orchestral theme for its "Playhouse 90" showcase, the network sought a major composer to create a new theme for "CBS Playhouse" (1967–70), a prestigious series of New York-originated plays from Golden Age drama producer Fred Coe. The network commissioned one of North's teachers: the great Aaron Copland (1900–80). His highly unusual forty-second fanfare for brass and percussion received an Emmy nomination as the year's outstanding music for television.

The television film attracted a number of high-profile composers, several in the waning days of their careers: Franz Waxman's last score was for a television film, "The Longest Hundred Miles" (1967, NBC). So was Hans J. Salter's, with "Return of the Gunfighter" (1967, ABC), and Malcolm Arnold's, for "David Copperfield" (1970, NBC). Producer Norman Lloyd, who had frequently used Bernard Herrmann on "The Alfred Hitchcock Hour," hired the temperamental composer for "Companions in Nightmare" (1968, NBC), a psychological thriller with Gig Young, Anne Baxter, and Melvyn Douglas. (Herrmann's score—his only one for a TV movie—was a particularly strong element, alternately melancholy and suspenseful, and in several respects hinted at his later score for Brian De Palma's 1973 suspense film *Sisters* in the use of chimes and bells for scenes of murder and its aftermath.)

Waxman, Salter, and Herrmann were old pros who were finding big-screen assignments harder to come by. John Williams, on the other hand, was an up-and-comer who had toiled for years in episodic television, and, with a few feature films (mostly silly comedies) to his credit, was beginning to establish himself as a composer of talent. "Heidi" (1968, NBC) unveiled a Williams that television had not previously heard. This adaptation of the Johanna Spyri classic, written by Earl Hamner Jr. and directed by Delbert Mann ("Marty"), starred Michael Redgrave and, in the title role, Blake Edwards's daughter Jennifer; Maximilian Schell and Jean Simmons completed the cast.

Fox musical director Lionel Newman recommended Williams to producer Frederick Brogger. "The first thing he needed was a song for the little girl to sing," Williams recalled. "The company was already in Switzerland shooting. So I wrote this little melody and had my daughter Jennifer, then about age six, tape the melody; I sent it to Delbert Mann, who loved it."

Postproduction, including scoring, was slated for Hamburg. "So I flew over to Germany, and it was during the holiday season," Williams said. "I loved the place, and I thought the film was exciting. . . . The members of the orchestra came from the Hamburg Opera. I met some of them before we recorded; I had gone to a few of the productions of the opera and heard them play, and I was inspired by that. . . . I did my best to write a score that would allow the orchestra to show some of their beautiful sound, to the degree that the film allowed the space to do that. We recorded it in the Deutsche Grammophon studio in Hamburg which was technically very advanced, so the original recordings were, I would say, superior to what I'd been used to getting in Hollywood. The whole experience was a happy one."

Williams's song (with Rod McKuen lyrics) became the film's main theme, although the score also contains a romantic secondary motif, and much of the music complements the spectacular Alpine scenery. Williams won his first Emmy for the score, but "Heidi" would become a footnote in television history for a very different reason: to start the much-promoted "Heidi" on time, NBC cut away from a hotly contested football game between the New York Jets and Oakland Raiders, drawing the ire of thousands of gridiron fans and jamming the network's Manhattan switchboard.

Williams's second Emmy was for another Brogger production: "Jane Eyre" (1971, NBC), based on the Charlotte Brontë novel and directed in England by Delbert Mann, with George C. Scott and Susannah York as the stars. The composer happened to be in Great Britain at the time, having finished the prerecordings for the film version of the musical *Fiddler on the Roof.* While preparing the score, Williams and Mann actually visited the fabled Yorkshire moors together. "We drove around that most beautiful county in England," the composer remembered. "Del showed me some of the old castles and locations that he photographed in the film, and I found it all very touching. We also went to the Brontë house and parsonage, which are open to the public. I was interested in that because I'd heard Bernard Herrmann talk about that for years when he was writing [his opera] *Wuthering Heights,* and being so obsessed with the Brontës and all things relating to their short lives." (Herrmann, in fact, scored the 1944 film of *Jane Eyre* with Orson Welles as Rochester.)

So while he was awaiting the *Fiddler* company's return from filming in Yugoslavia, Williams—inspired by the real-life settings of the Brontë fiction—wrote the "Jane Eyre" score: "What I tried to do," he explained, "was create 'new' folk material, if you like, which film composers have done so often all through the years. I wrote, I felt, in the modalities that gave the ambiance of nineteenth-century Yorkshire—somewhat in the same way that Vaughan Williams had taken his Welsh and Celtic airs and put them into his works. I don't mean to compare my humble scribblings with his great music, but the process of creating in the atmosphere and the modality of these folk tunes, new melodies which could then be manipulated and metamorphosed throughout the whole score."

Williams's music for "Jane Eyre" remains one of the composer's most haunting works. The sixty-piece orchestra eliminated all brass but included two harps, two pianos, an organ, and two harpsichords. The score included an evocative love theme for Jane, an ominous motif for Thornfield Manor, an exciting scherzando for the Yorkshire carriage ride, a quasi-liturgical theme for St. John Rivers, and even a string quartet for a celebration at Thornfield.

During this period—the early 1970s—top feature film composers were still intrigued by the television medium and its possibilities, and knowledgeable filmmakers not only sought out the best collaborators but made sure the music budgets accommodated them. One of the earliest, and most celebrated, was Michel Legrand's score for "Brian's Song" (1971, ABC). The poignant story of

Michel Legrand. Courtesy of F Sharp Productions.

the friendship between white football player Brian Piccolo (James Caan) and his black Chicago Bears teammate Gale Sayers (Billy Dee Williams), which grew even closer when Piccolo was diagnosed with terminal cancer, drew huge ratings and won five Emmy Awards (including Outstanding Single Program for the 1971–72 season).

Producer Paul Junger Witt flew to Paris to convince Legrand—the French composer whose music for *The Umbrellas of Cherbourg* (1964) and *Pieces of Dreams* (1970) had been Oscar-nominated, and who had won a Best Song Oscar for "The Windmills of Your Mind" from *The Thomas Crown Affair* (1968)—to score the TV movie.

"I had never done a film for television before," Legrand said. "They had a working copy of the picture, black-and-white, ragged. I looked at it and I cried. I said, 'This is extraordinary, beautiful: what a story, what a man.'" Legrand agreed to write the score but had to do so in just two weeks. "When I started to write the theme I knew it had to contain three elements: joy, death, and childhood—childhood because they really were just boys at the start," the composer explained after the sessions. As for the football sequences, he trusted drummer Shelly Manne and his fellow percussionists on the session: "I wanted

John Barry. Photo by E. J. Camp, courtesy Epic Records.

improvisation and instinct, because that is what guides a football runner," he added. Legrand's music provided the tender touch that helped propel "Brian's Song" into the hearts of fifty million viewers in a single night. Nominated for an Emmy, it won a Grammy and was the first theme for a television film to become a popular standard.

John Barry's first score for an American television film wasn't actually the first to be televised. The English composer was on holiday in Majorca when he got a call about "Love Among the Ruins" (1975, ABC), directed by famed filmmaker George Cukor (*The Philadelphia Story*). James Costigan's charming, witty script cast Laurence Olivier as a brilliant barrister and Katharine Hepburn as his client, a wealthy widow whose recent affair with a much younger man has scandalized upper-class London. The twist: he has been in love with her ever since their brief affair forty years ago—one she claims to have forgotten.

Hepburn had been a fan since Barry had written the dramatic, medieval music for *The Lion in Winter* (1968), which had won Academy Awards for both of them. The idea to hire Barry for "Love Among the Ruins" was apparently hers. "So I got on the plane, flew back to London, and met with Cukor. We talked about it, he showed me some footage, and that was it," the composer recalled. Upon his return to Majorca, he wrote a theme that was needed before the end of shooting: a song that Olivier sings briefly to Hepburn in a restaurant. (Veteran Barry collaborator Don Black wrote the lyric.)

The score was built around that theme. It had, said Barry, "a days-gone-by, Old World charm." *Variety* described it as music evoking "a mood of romantic nostalgia." The main-title sequence, in fact, consisted of color-tinted photographs of turn-of-the-century London; Barry's simple waltz theme, flavored with the antique sound of a harpsichord, suggested an elegance and sophistication befitting the legendary actors and the romantic comedy to come.

First on the air, however, was Barry's unique contribution to "The Glass Menagerie" (1973, ABC), the Tennessee Williams play starring Hepburn (plus Sam Waterston, Michael Moriarty, and Joanna Miles) and directed by Barry's *Lion in Winter* colleague Anthony Harvey. The entire score was performed by the composer at the piano. It hadn't been planned that way. "I did a piano demo for Anthony, and he liked it very much. He laid it against the movie and it worked wonderfully well," Barry remembered. Harvey thought it so effective that he asked Barry to write and play the entire score as a solo piano piece.

The delicate, fragile nature of the theme was perfect for Williams's wistful reminiscence of the 1930s, but it had actually been written somewhat earlier. "I was planning a concert work," Barry said, "basically [about] my childhood in World War II, what it was like going through, and then the emotional reflection on that childhood when one became sixteen, seventeen, eighteen years old and you really started to realize what it had all been about. That [theme] was the opening scene for the piece, very childlike, but it also had a strange kind of quality to it. . . . It was not written for 'The Glass Menagerie' but it just had a fragility about it that worked for the story." Williams later told Harvey that he thought it was the best score his play had ever had.

Barry would go on to score the final Hepburn-Cukor collaboration for television, "The Corn Is Green" (1979, CBS). "All the years she's been in the business, she'd never been to a recording session," Barry recalled. "So she came down [to the sessions] and brought chicken sandwiches with grapes for lunch for everybody, and wine, and had a few cute comments. She was great, she loved it. And the orchestra, of course, were over the moon having her around."

The composer's other major work in the television field was for "Eleanor and Franklin" (1976, ABC), a four-hour miniseries based on Joseph P. Lash's Pulitzer Prize-winning biography of Eleanor and Franklin Roosevelt. "I thought it was a wonderful piece," Barry recalled. "It was a personal story; it wasn't a grand political statement." Barry's main theme—voiced first by solo horn and strings, then harpsichord and flute—possessed a dignity and strength, touched by a hint of sadness, and much of the score was built around that motif.

Highly acclaimed, with bravura performances by Jane Alexander and Edward Herrmann in the title roles, "Eleanor and Franklin" won the Emmy as Outstanding Special. Barry returned to score the three-hour sequel, "Eleanor and Franklin: The White House Years" (1977, ABC) and received an Emmy nomination.

The miniseries—multiple-night airings, usually consecutive, of a single production, often mammoth in scope—began with "The Blue Knight" (1973, NBC), a four-hour, four-night adaptation of the Joseph Wambaugh novel about a soon-to-retire Los Angeles beat cop. William Holden won an Emmy for his performance as Bumper Morgan, and the dramatic score by Nelson Riddle was his last great work for television.

"QB VII" (1974, ABC), however, convinced the networks of the creative viability of long-form television. An adaptation of the Leon Uris best-seller, "QB VII" ran six-and-a-quarter hours over two nights in April, and at $2.5 million was the most expensive television film made to that time. The story, loosely based on Uris's own experience after writing *Exodus,* concerned an American writer (Ben Gazzara) who was sued for libel by a Polish physician (Anthony Hopkins) over accusations that the latter had committed war crimes while a surgeon in a Nazi concentration camp.

Part one followed the parallel courses of their lives over a thirty-year period: the trash-novel author who discovers his Jewish heritage and writes a book about the Holocaust, and the doctor who devotes his life to public service in the Near East and the London slums and is knighted for his efforts. Part two chronicled the lawsuit and trial in London's Queen's Bench courtroom No. 7. Leslie Caron, Lee Remick, Juliet Mills, and Anthony Quayle were among the supporting cast.

Jerry Goldsmith. Courtesy the composer.

Jerry Goldsmith agreed to write the score, the longest and most complex in his television career. He interwove more than half a dozen themes throughout the more than two hours of music. As he explained in his liner notes for the album: "One central musical statement or theme was impossible for a drama of this scope and dimension. It was necessary to treat each part with its own identifying musical statement, a formidable task considering the number of elements involved and the need to unify them overall." Goldsmith wrote a fanfare for the exterior scenes of the royal court, which he used to open and close the main title of each night; a theme for each of the two protagonists; variations on them for different love relationships; and subsidiary themes that depicted the Kuwaiti desert, postwar Poland, and modern-day Israel.

His most significant musical problem, however, involved the concentration camps and the memories of human suffering, the composer explained. "Musically, there had to be pain but yet culmination in a feeling of hope," he wrote. "I used the text of the Kaddish, the Jewish mourners' prayer, as the words to this theme. The words, in Hebrew, were sung abstractly, spoken abstractly and sung purely [at various points in the score]." The dramatic impact of the voices in the Jadwiga concentration camp sequences was stunning. The music suggested that the ghosts of the Jewish victims were all around; the wailings of a women's choir were grim, echoing reminders of the hideous experiments that had gone on in these and other places. The complete choral performance of this theme, which Goldsmith subtitled "A Kaddish for the Six Million," was heard as the finale of the miniseries.

The score was recorded in Rome with a sixty-piece orchestra and—ironically, considering the Hebrew texts—the Sistine Chapel choir. Orchestrator Alexander Courage conducted the choral elements when Goldsmith took ill during the sessions. The composer won his second Emmy for the score and received a Grammy nomination as well.

"QB VII" broke new ground for television drama. Nazi horrors had never been discussed with such candor or conveyed with such shattering impact in an entertainment program. The nine-and-a-half-hour "Holocaust" (1978, NBC) addressed the issues even more directly, and as a result became one of the most controversial miniseries in television history.

Gerald Green's "Holocaust" script told the story of two German families and their changing fortunes between 1935 and 1945: a prosperous Jewish physician, his cultured wife, and their three children; and a struggling lawyer whose ambitious wife pushes him into service with the Nazi SS. Fritz Weaver, Michael Moriarty, James Woods, and Meryl Streep were among the stars. Critically praised but hotly debated among Holocaust survivors for its depiction of concentration camp life and Hitler's "Final Solution," the miniseries won eight Emmys including Outstanding Limited Series. And regardless of its merit as drama, it called attention to the unspeakable crimes of Auschwitz, Buchenwald, Treblinka, and the other nightmarish sites of the attempted genocide like no previous mass communication effort.

To score this obviously important project, the makers of "Holocaust," including former "Playhouse 90" producer Herbert Brodkin, chose a composer with few credits in film: Morton Gould, who had done a stellar job with the sixties documentary series "World War I" but who had not written for television drama apart from an earlier Brodkin film, "F. Scott Fitzgerald in Hollywood" (1976, ABC). Gould looked at a rough cut and turned it down. "I felt that the picture did not need music. I thought, 'How can you do music for this?' I thought that much of it. It was such a powerful, wrenching show," he said. His music publishers, and another conversation with the producers, changed his mind. He composed a score that touched on all of the themes, the characters, the locales, and the entire scope of the project.

Yet there was very little music in "Holocaust" apart from source cues (Wagner played by Nazi leaders, Mozart performed by musicians in the camps). In fact, of seventeen themes represented on Gould's Grammy-nomi-

Morton Gould. Courtesy ASCAP.

nated *"Holocaust"* soundtrack album, only seven were actually heard in the program, and those mostly in severely truncated form (usually as "curtain music" at the end of an act). Although Gould had agreed with the producers on specifically where music should be included—all of which was recorded—the vast majority was removed before the film went on the air. "A tremendous amount of music was taken out," Gould recalled. "I understand that there was some conflict within the production staff about doing it. Some felt that it should go out, some felt that it shouldn't."

What remained were Gould's profoundly mournful main theme, a trio of motifs for various members of the tormented Weiss family, music for the rail transport to the death camps, a portion of Gould's exuberant finale, and, perhaps most dramatically, the dirgelike music that underscored scenes of the slaughter of tens of thousands at Russia's Babi Yar. The composer said that he hoped to "convey the tenderness and the tragedy in as unostentatious a way as possible. In the opening theme, I did something that I hoped would make an important statement. I did not want a trivial theme. . . . I meant it to have a never-ending sadness." Despite the massive cuts in his sophisticated original score, Gould received an Emmy nomination from his peers in the Television Academy.

It remained for "War and Remembrance" (1988–89, ABC) to deal with the Holocaust again, and in even more graphic visual terms. "War and Remembrance" was the twenty-nine-hour, $100 million sequel to "The Winds of War" (1983, ABC), an eighteen-hour adaptation of Herman Wouk's best-seller. For both scores, producer-director Dan Curtis turned to his frequent collaborator Bob Cobert (b. 1924), whose music had helped popularize the daytime soap "Dark Shadows," and who went on to write the scores for virtu-ally all of the director's television and film projects. Just as the two films, con-sidered together, are a massive historical-fiction look at World War II, the

Bob Cobert (in white tux) with director Dan Curtis on the set of "War and Remem-brance." Courtesy the composer.

music for "The Winds of War" and "War and Remembrance" is essentially one long single score: the longest, in fact, in the history of television.

Educated at Juilliard and Columbia, Cobert first met Curtis on "Dark Shadows," when he was in New York City writing music for game shows ("To Tell the Truth," "Password") and soaps ("The Doctors"). The success of "Dark Shadows," including a pop hit with his Grammy-nominated "Quentin's Theme" and a top-20 soundtrack album in 1969, cemented the partnership between producer and composer. His memorable music for Curtis pictures included "The Night Stalker" (1972), the Jack Palance "Dracula" (1974), the period detective drama "Melvin Purvis: G-Man" (1974), and his Western Heritage Award-winning score for "The Last Ride of the Dalton Gang" (1979).

Because Curtis had a long professional relationship with Cobert, he gave the composer more freedom than usual at the start of the "Winds of War" project. Cobert spent six weeks writing a total of forty-five original themes, which were demoed at the piano for Curtis, who then pared them down to twenty for recording by a full sixty-piece orchestra. Having heard those, Curtis selected his five favorites for Cobert to utilize as his main motifs in the underscore.

The main theme for "The Winds of War" and "War and Remembrance," a simple but haunting melody that was published as the "Love Theme from 'The Winds of War,'" was not conceived as such. It was one of several proposed main-title themes that were auditioned for Curtis. "I wrote it not as a love theme but as an expression of the sadness and valor of World War Two," the composer recalled. But, because Curtis was not initially enthusiastic about the piece, "I only had sixteen bars," Cobert added. "I didn't bother to develop it because I thought, well, he's not going to like it." However, when a piano demo of that theme was played against the scene of Byron and Natalie (Jan-Michael Vincent, Ali MacGraw) meeting in Siena, Curtis became excited, Cobert said. "We started running it against other Byron-and-Natalie scenes. That's how it became their theme," and ultimately, the main theme for both series.

In addition to that, Cobert's score included a heroic fanfare and march for Pug Henry (Robert Mitchum); themes for Pamela (Victoria Tennant), Pug's wife Rhoda, and her lover Kirby (Polly Bergen, Peter Graves); and a theme for the Henry family. In addition, there were grim martial sounds for the Nazi leaders, a patriotic march for President Franklin Roosevelt (Ralph Bellamy), and considerable ethnic-flavored music suggestive of Poland, Russia, and the plight of the Jews in Europe.

Cobert recorded seven hours of music for "The Winds of War." Besides writing the dramatic underscore, Cobert served as musical director on the miniseries, which involved responsibility for all of the source music—which ranged from Hitler favorites (Franz Lehár) to dance music (Glenn Miller and other period tunes). In all, there were more than one hundred such pieces, all of which Cobert arranged; there were another hundred for "War and Remembrance" (including one big bash where Cobert can be spotted conducting the orchestra on-screen). Veteran Jack Hayes orchestrated Cobert's under-score on both miniseries.

"The Winds of War" built up to the Pearl Harbor bombing and America's entry into World War II. "War and Remembrance" followed the same charac-ters through the war itself, including horrific scenes set in the Nazi concentra-tion camps. Cobert devised a dirgelike death march that first appeared in the Babi Yar sequences and reappeared in the Auschwitz gas chamber scenes where, in some of the most affecting moments in the series, Aaron Jastrow (John Gielgud) met his fate. "I wanted to do something that had dignity, that had heart, that was sad, that had power—and dramatic value," Cobert said. "I think I achieved it."

"War and Remembrance" contained approximately twelve hours of dra-matic underscore alone, and interwove fifteen different themes throughout the narrative, including all of the original ones from "Winds" and several new ones. As with "Winds," Cobert conducted a sixty-five-piece studio orchestra. His "War and Remembrance" score complemented Curtis's harrowing scenes of World War II, enhancing the high drama with music of emotion and inten-sity. He received an Emmy nomination for his efforts; "War" itself won as Outstanding Miniseries for the 1988–89 season.

AMERICANA

American history and Americana subjects provided the inspiration for several composers in the movie and miniseries realm. Perhaps the first great Americana score was Jerry Goldsmith's music for "The Red Pony" (1973, NBC), an adaptation of the John Steinbeck novella with Henry Fonda, Maureen O'Hara, Ben Johnson, and Clint Howard as the boy Jody.

The composer recalled the film as "one of the most joyous" experiences of his career. "I'd get up and I could hardly wait to get to work," he said. The Aaron Copland score for the 1949 film version, in its concert suite form, has become a part of the American musical repertoire and so, Goldsmith acknowl-edged, "comparisons were inevitable. Note for note, no, there's no resem-blance. But stylistically, yes. It's me, with a heavy influence of Copland."

Sweet and gentle, fully orchestral but flavored with traditional western sounds including acoustic guitar and accordion, Goldsmith's "Red Pony" music beautifully complemented Steinbeck's coming-of-age tale of a boy, his gruff father, and his ill-fated pony. The composer won his first Emmy Award for the score (the third of four Frederick Brogger-produced classics to win for its music); the film itself won a Peabody Award.

For "The Autobiography of Miss Jane Pittman" (1974, CBS), Fred Karlin (b. 1936) drew on his extensive knowledge of American music and folk idioms. Cicely Tyson won an Emmy for her extraordinary portrayal of the title character, a 110–year-old woman whose life had begun in slavery but ended as a part of the civil rights movement. Eight other Emmys went to this sensitively written and directed character study, including one for Karlin's heartfelt score.

Karlin, whose film career had begun in New York with scores including *Up the Down Staircase* (1967) and *The Sterile Cuckoo* (1969), had won a Best Song Oscar for his "For All We Know" from *Lovers and Other Strangers* (1970). A talented trumpet and flugelhorn player, Karlin had begun his career in jazz but grew to embrace all kinds of American music, particularly in the sixties, when he and his wife Megan founded the Historical Institute of American Music. With only ten days to score "Miss Jane Pittman"—and a subject that covered an entire century of the black American experience—Karlin was the right composer for the film, with no time to spare for musical research.

Karlin was moved from his first screening of the picture. "'Pittman' had the kind of depth of characterization and evolution that you don't usually get within a two-hour film. Usually it takes a miniseries or a longer feature. That's one of the things that made it so extraordinarily successful, and such a landmark television project. I found the musical language that I thought was appropriate for the texture of the film and the characters."

His work included period military music for the Confederate soldiers at the start of the story; southern folk and blues colors, including harmonica, banjo, guitar, and fiddle, for Jane's cross-country odyssey and plantation work; and ragtime for scenes set at the turn of the century. During the final five minutes, scenes of the 110–year-old Miss Jane walking slowly up to a "whites only" drinking fountain in 1962 are accompanied only by Karlin's quietly powerful, gospel-flavored piano, flute, and strings, with touches of harmonica, banjo, and guitar.

Karlin's later Americana scores for television included "Minstrel Man" (1977, CBS), a turn-of-the-century tale that included several original songs, as well as the seven-hour miniseries "The Awakening Land" (1978, NBC) with Elizabeth Montgomery and Hal Holbrook, and the seven-hour "Dream West" (1986, CBS) with Richard Chamberlain as explorer John Charles Frémont.

"Roots" (1977, ABC) is remembered today as one of the most important television programs of all time. But, during its production, it was considered a tremendous gamble. Hoping to maximize the credibility of a twelve-hour miniseries about the first black Americans, producers David L. Wolper and Stan Margulies enlisted the one composer they felt was perfect for the job: Quincy Jones.

"Roots" was a dramatization of journalist Alex Haley's best-selling book that traced his ancestry back to eighteenth-century Africa and a Gambian named Kunta Kinte. Wolper and Margulies had enlisted a notable cast including Cicely Tyson, Maya Angelou, Moses Gunn, and newcomer LeVar Burton for the opening two-hour chapter set in Africa. The behind-the-camera talent was equally impressive; filmmakers and actors alike knew that "Roots" was special, although no one could have guessed that it would become the most-watched miniseries in television history.

Quincy Jones quit writing film and TV scores in 1972, returning to the record world for the most part in a producing capacity. But *Roots,* written by his friend Alex Haley and undertaken for television on a large scale, seemed too important a project to pass up. Jones was signed to score the entire miniseries.

In 1971 Jones had written *Black Requiem,* a fifty-minute work performed by the Houston Symphony Orchestra with Ray Charles, a gospel choir, a concerto grosso group, and jazz and soul musicians including Billy Preston, Grady Tate, Joe Newman, and Toots Thielemans; it traced the black experience from 1510 through the assassinations of Malcolm X and Martin Luther King Jr. Through the 1970s, Jones continued to research the evolution of black music with an eye toward a concert work, a film, or both. "So," Jones decided, "this was right up my alley. I had gone through a lot of credible research on African music back to 479 A.D." But, he added, "emotionally, I fell in. We had a very limited budget to do the whole project, and I was concerned about that, and just a lot of things that happened. I was so focused on the importance of it—it was just very meaningful to me, and that transcended the pragmatic aspect of it in terms of time and deadline."

Jones's attempt to achieve an authentic African sound in the opening episode took longer than anyone expected. He hired vocalist Letta Mbulu and African-music expert Caiphus Semenya to contribute their unique talents. "If the culture was going to get lost, stolen, or traded in the next episode," Jones pointed out, "we really had to do something of significance in the first one, just from a musical standpoint. Dramatically [the producers] could have done without it, and I don't think it was as important to them as it was to me." Jones recorded most of the music for the opening installment, including three crucial and highly evocative pieces cocredited to Jones and Semenya, all of which involved traditional African chants and phrases: "Mama Aifambeni," the rhythmic main title featuring Mbulu; the dramatic "Behold, the Only Thing Greater than Yourself" sequence, as the baby Kunta Kinte is held aloft to the stars; and "Oluwa," the primary African motif. The words *"ishe oluwa, koleba jeo,"* from the Nigerian Yoruba tongue, mean "what God has created, no man can destroy."

Jones became consumed with the effort. "I was really almost unprofessional in terms of time," he admitted, "because I was trying to solve the mystery of making it authentic and still do it within the constraints of the budget." In addition, he said, "I was trying to get a theme that would last all the way through the twelve [hours] but still would have a strong African basis to it, and I hadn't solved that problem yet musically."

Producer Stan Margulies became concerned. "It was an interesting phenomenon because it happened with a number of actors," he pointed out, "and it happened with Quincy. They wanted to do the best work they had ever done, the best work they could ever imagine, because of the project. And that thought crippled them. Quincy kept saying, 'It's not good enough, I've got to work some more on it. Let's not do the session today.' Or tomorrow, or whenever. And eventually I had to say, 'Quincy, we'll never get this show on the air.' We had a rush airdate.

"There came a point where I couldn't wait for Quincy anymore, and Quincy understood that," Margulies said. "It broke his heart, but he totally understood it." The producer called Gerald Fried, who had created authentic-sounding American Indian music for the Wolper-Margulies TV film "I Will Fight No More Forever" (1975). "Part of what drew me to Gerry was the way in which he had immersed himself in Native American sounds and instruments, and I felt he would bring that sensibility to a combination of African

Gerald Fried accepting his Emmy for "Roots." Courtesy Screen Archives.

themes for blacks in America and various country music [sounds] for the whites in Virginia."

Fried remembered it this way: "I got a call from Wolper saying, 'Gerry, we're going to give you one thousand dollars to keep your pencils sharp and your mouth shut. But get a lot of sleep.' I finished the first episode, wrote the main theme, and did everything from then on. The first three or four shows, we did in something like twenty days. It was madness. It was the most brutal schedule I ever had. But they warned me. I was ready and I did research." Fried immersed himself for several days in ethnomusicological studies at UCLA and consulted with studio percussionist Emil Richards, whose fabled collection of unusual instruments from around the world also came in handy on the scoring stage (and was utilized in Jones's score for the first episode).

Reflecting on his memorable main theme for "Roots," Fried explained, "I wanted to write the strongest, most powerful [music] in a kind of early Americana way. There wasn't time to be nervous or worried about it." The bass marimba figure that opened the "Roots" theme, and Fried's attempt to keep the notes within scales that would apply to West African music, immediately suggested Africa; the harmonica in the bridge reminded viewers of the South, where most of the series took place. As the series progressed, the "Roots" theme became a key musical subtext, a reminder of Kunta Kinte's homeland and heritage—still echoing with African percussion and woodwinds—and finally emerging orchestrally triumphant when Chicken George (Ben Vereen) became the family's first free man.

Despite the haste in which it was written, "Roots" may have been Fried's most inspired score. The rousing hornpipe with which he opened night two (as Edward Asner's sailing ship brought the slaves to America); the down-home banjo-and-harmonica theme for Lorne Greene's Virginia plantation; lively new themes for Chicken George and for Kizzy (Leslie Uggams), daughter of the adult Kunte Kinte (John Amos); and dramatic passages for Civil War and Ku Klux Klan night-rider sequences rounded out Fried's music. (A few minutes of Jones's previously recorded arrangements of several source pieces were also heard in subsequent episodes.)

The "Roots" sweep at the 1976–77 Emmy Awards resulted in nine wins, including one for Outstanding Limited Series and one shared by Jones and Fried for the music of part one. Controversy arose, however, when Jones quickly released an album titled "music from and inspired by" the series. Fried felt that the LP unfairly implied that it was the soundtrack of the series, when much of it was not, in fact, heard in the score, and only Fried's main theme was included. Fried's music could barely be heard in the "official" soundtrack, a three-record set containing narration and dialogue drawn from the twelve hours.

Fried reprised his "Roots" theme but also created considerable new material for the fourteen-hour sequel, "Roots: The Next Generations" (1979, ABC), which continued Haley's saga to the present day (with James Earl Jones as

Haley and, in one riveting sequence, Marlon Brando in his TV debut as American Nazi leader George Lincoln Rockwell).

Fried's penchant for musical research and ability to combine authentic sounds with the dramatic necessities of television made him the obvious choice for Wolper and Margulies's next major miniseries on an American theme: "The Mystic Warrior" (1984, ABC), based on Ruth Beebe Hill's novel *Hanta Yo,* about a band of Lakota Sioux in the late eighteenth and early nineteenth centuries.

Utilizing authentic Indian poems, chants, and writings, the composer created a wide range of music including choral anthems, ritualistic chants, ethereal voices, and a variety of exotic percussion and woodwind instruments designed to simulate authentic Indian sounds. His efforts did not go unnoticed: *Newsweek,* for example, referred to "Gerald Fried's dazzling musical score, with its suggestions of Indian, Oriental and Gregorian chants." The composer received another Emmy nomination, and the Roger Wagner Chorale performed a suite from the score while on tour for several months prior to its television airing.

One miniseries dared to attempt an overview of the entire American experience: "Centennial" (1978–79, NBC), a sprawling, twelve-part, twenty-six-hour adaptation of James A. Michener's epic saga of American history as seen through the people of fictional Centennial, Colorado. And, as with "Eleanor and Franklin," this quintessential American story was scored by an English composer.

Producer John Wilder, with whom composer John Addison had worked on "The Bastard" (1978, syndicated), called upon the Englishman again for "Centennial." Addison wrote the theme and scored the three-hour opening installment, which introduced the key early characters of French-Canadian fur trapper Pasquinel (Robert Conrad) and the Scotsman Alexander McKeag (Richard Chamberlain). "I had read Michener's book," Addison said, "and it was particularly interesting to me as a foreigner having come to live here on the West Coast. I was more or less an immigrant myself. As I got more involved in the show, there came a time when I really didn't want to hand it over to anybody else."

Addison didn't initially intend to score all twenty-six hours. But Wilder talked him into doing the second installment of two hours, and, according to Addison, pointed out that "there are all these themes and many of them will go right through the whole thing." So Addison stayed with the entire series, a six-month commitment of time that resulted in approximately six hours of dramatic music, all recorded at Universal with a forty-five-piece orchestra.

For his "Centennial" main-title theme, Addison composed a series of fanfares to suggest the heroism and courage of the pioneers who settled the West, along with a hint of Indian drums to remind listeners of the true native

John Addison. Courtesy the composer.

Americans who were there long before the white people came. Within the body of each show, Addison said, "there were a great many themes. New characters would come in, but then there would be a reference to previous characters. Whatever situation the character was in, the music would be adapted to suit that. So there were endless variations on some of those themes." (Among them: a theme for the majesty of the Indians; another for man in harmony with nature; a love motif; another for man in conflict with fellow man; even a theme for the small wandering river near Centennial.) Addison researched and consulted experts in ethnic instruments of the various periods chronicled. "Any research I did might have influenced the style," the composer explained, "but the music I wrote was original to me and was inspired by the characters, situations, and mood of the film."

Addison effectively wrote a dozen full-length film scores, reprising old themes and creating new ones as Michener's tale developed through the nineteenth and twentieth centuries, involving a German merchant (Raymond Burr), an army officer (Chad Everett) sympathetic to the Indians' plight, a fanatic Indian hater (Richard Crenna), a German farmer (Alex Karras), a peacekeeper (Brian Keith), a trail boss (Dennis Weaver), a cowboy (William Atherton) who falls for a cultured Englishwoman (Lynn Redgrave), and a Mennonite trader (Gregory Harrison) who becomes the community's founding father. David Janssen narrated the entire series and appeared in the final episode as a contemporary descendent of the founders of Centennial.

Addison returned to early American history with another miniseries, the seven-hour "Ellis Island" (1984, CBS), for which he composed nine Irving Berlin-style songs (with lyricist Douglas Brayfield) that were performed by Peter Riegert (as the songwriter), Ann Jillian (as an ambitious music-hall singer), and Melba Moore (as a Harlem nightclub performer).

"East of Eden" (1981, ABC) was a milestone in the career of Lee Holdridge. An eight-hour adaptation of the John Steinbeck classic, it explored the entire novel instead of just the final third (as had the 1955 film with James Dean). Holdridge had loved the book and, having been signed to write the music, knew that "this wanted a big dramatic score." What's more, the project was treated like a feature: Holdridge was given ten weeks to write and orchestrate, and was, he recalled, "basically left alone."

"What's fun about a miniseries," Holdridge observed, "is that you have a very big canvas to work with. It's not unlike writing an opera in the sense that you spread yourself out over a long period of time. You can take a theme and develop it and come back and revise it later, do something different with it. It's a very intriguing format for a composer."

Holdridge wrote "at least five or six" primary themes for "East of Eden," including the main theme, motifs for the patriarch (Warren Oates) and his sons (Timothy Bottoms, Bruce Boxleitner), and the evil Cathy (Jane Seymour) who comes between them. Cathy's theme was particularly interesting: "Early in the film, she's very beautiful," Holdridge said. "I remember scoring mostly classical piano and strings for her. As she becomes twisted and turned, all the themes become polytonal and atonal." By late in the film, the disfigured Cathy was reflected in what Holdridge called "the ultimate evolution of this once-beautiful theme, pulled apart into all sorts of discordant sounds." The composer wrote about two hours of music for the score, which was recorded in Rome with a fifty-five-piece orchestra. He later extracted key themes for an eighteen-minute concert suite.

"The Blue and the Gray" (1982, CBS) required a different kind of Americana score. An all-star cast populated this much-anticipated, eight-hour miniseries about the Civil War, based in part on a story by Civil War historian Bruce Catton. Gregory Peck made his dramatic television debut as Abraham Lincoln, as did Sterling Hayden as abolitionist John Brown. Stacy Keach and John Hammond were the leads, as a government agent and a newspaper artist, respectively; Rip Torn played General Ulysses S. Grant.

For "The Blue and the Gray," Bruce Broughton composed as authentic-sounding a score as any American historical miniseries ever had. His main-title theme opened with a barrage of military flourishes and fanfares, then segued into a memorable Americana theme (actually of Irish folk origin), all played against sepia-toned drawings of the people and places of the Civil War era.

The main title offered an appropriately grand sound (an orchestra of about forty), but Broughton was warned early on by one of the producers that they

Bruce Broughton. Courtesy Society of Composers and Lyricists.

were looking for a smaller, simpler approach, "in the sense that you'd have a harmonica playing around the campfire. He wanted to play the people and the time," the composer explained. As a result, much of the two-and-a-half hours of music was for reduced ensembles, often incorporating highly atmospheric sounds that were period-specific: fiddle, Jew's harp, banjo, acoustic guitar, or dulcimer.

Broughton was rewarded with an Emmy nomination for the score—which subsequently was used as the temporary music track and partial model for the big-screen western *Silverado* (1985), itself an Oscar nominee for Broughton's music. He later composed an Emmy-winning score for "O Pioneers!" (1992, CBS), based on the Willa Cather novel—"music that spoke of the prairies," Broughton said—with Jessica Lange portraying a turn-of-the-century Nebraska farm woman.

When producer David L. Wolper hired Bill Conti to write the music for his lavish adaptation of John Jakes's pre-Civil War epic "North and South" (1985, ABC), he didn't want a small score. "I really want *Gone with the Wind*," he whispered, according to Conti. The composer was on the spot, not only in the sense of creating a theme to rival Max Steiner's famous music for the 1939 classic—but also due to the fact that the miniseries consumed twelve hours of television time, and he had only three weeks to write and record the entire score.

The "North and South" theme, according to Conti, came quickly and easily. Grand and majestic, it was nothing like *Gone with the Wind,* but Conti had correctly interpreted Wolper's request. Performed by a sixty-piece orchestra, Conti's sweeping main-title music played against beautifully drawn pen-and-ink portraits of the principals and scenes of antebellum America, setting the stage for Jakes's saga of two West Point soldiers—Pennsylvanian George Hazard (James Read) and South Carolinian Orry Main (Patrick Swayze)—and their families and feuds. Key facets of the storyline involved Orry's true love, the Creole Madeline Fabray (Lesley Anne-Down), and Orry's scheming vixen of a sister (Terri Garber).

"I began writing from the minute that I could and [one week later] began recording every night, from seven until midnight, for two weeks," Conti said, "because you could not stay ahead of them [the sound mixers]." He wrote about three hours of dramatic underscore, relying on the main theme for the large-scale set pieces, "Dixie"-style music for the southern settings, and secondary themes for several characters throughout the drama.

In terms of general approach, however, Conti chose an unlikely model. "I did it in a style that I was so familiar with: Italian opera," he said. "It had nothing to do with the program itself, musically, but when you have to do stream-of-consciousness writing, you had better go to your strong suit. Because you're not going to use your eraser." It was a perfect choice. So much of "North and South" was melodramatic hokum that the grandiose musical gestures were entirely appropriate—for example, Conti's four-minute buildup to the love-making scene of Orry and Madeline in a deserted chapel, as passion-filled and overwhelming as any of its predecessors in the realm of romantic Hollywood.

Conti received an Emmy nomination for his opening-night score. He reprised all the themes in his score for the twelve-hour sequel, "North and South, Book II" (1986, ABC), which reunited the cast and crew for Jakes's chronicle of the Civil War years in the lives of the Main and Hazard families.

Basil Poledouris (b. 1945), unlike many of his contemporaries, didn't start out in television. A film major at USC, he counted among his classmates and friends future filmmakers John Milius, George Lucas, Caleb Deschanel, Randall Kleiser, Hal Barwood, and Matthew Robbins. An aspiring concert pianist (who also sang in a folk group during the sixties), his film studies made him unique among contemporary composers. He created the romantic score for Kleiser's *The Blue Lagoon* (1980), the powerful orchestral and choral music for Milius's *Conan the Barbarian* (1982), and scored several subsequent Milius films including the Soviet-takeover thriller *Red Dawn* (1984). Ironically, the militaristic *Red Dawn* did nothing to prepare the composer for his longest and most complex work: "Amerika" (1987).

"Amerika" was the most controversial and misunderstood miniseries in television history. For months prior to its airing, it was the subject of wild speculation, attacks by both liberals and conservatives, and ill-informed commentary about its content. In fact, writer-director Donald Wrye's political fantasy about the aftermath of a bloodless coup and Soviet occupation of the United States was thoughtful, provocative, and often moving. At nearly fifteen hours, it was far too long, but Wrye's point—that freedoms taken for granted could easily be lost by a generation of complacent Americans—was forgotten in all the brouhaha. In a sense, "Amerika" was television's *Heaven's Gate:* a well-intentioned, beautifully filmed epic that spun out of control, was in postproduction up to the very last minute, and cost an unnecessary fortune (an estimated $40 million).

Kris Kristofferson played a recently released political prisoner who led the Resistance; Robert Urich, the well-meaning politician who wound up collaborating with the new government despite the misgivings of his wife (Cindy Pickett); Sam Neill, the KGB colonel who oversaw the governing of Middle America while sleeping with an American actress (Mariel Hemingway); and Christine Lahti was the Resistance leader's sister, who had been raped by the Soviet invaders.

"Amerika" started out with a $300,000 music budget. By the time the show went on the air, it had ballooned to an estimated $1.25 million, and become the most expensive score in the history of television to that time.

Poledouris wrote five-and-a-half hours of music in total. His first scoring date was in late November 1986, but he started working on the project during the summer months in order to write the music that is actually performed in the program, notably the "Heartland" anthem when Urich's character is inaugurated (as well as "outlaw theater" pieces performed by Hemingway). At the same time, the composer began developing themes for Wrye and was looking at dailies as the film was shot—a highly unusual perk for a composer, but one that turned out to be invaluable. "It probably would have been impossible to just start out cold in October and [to have] finished it without some kind of understanding of where it was going," he said.

Wrye "wanted to have a real Americana flavor," Poledouris recalled. "We both agreed that it shouldn't be jingoistic from either side. In fact, what we tried to do musically was represent both the Russians and Americans as being the same, with the same kinds of concerns. I didn't use balalaikas; I tried to give the KGB colonel a kind of jazzy, New York type of motif because he was so understanding of the American system."

However, Poledouris added, "as opposed to individuals, the themes really represented the larger [issues] of the piece. . . . The theme for Alethea [Lahti] represented America and the rape of the land. There was a theme for the squatters, the homeless people who were herded into camps; then there was a theme for the Resistance. A lot of the underscore was oppressive at times, until the end, where the Resistance takes over and then, of course, it becomes more hopeful and bright."

Basil Poledouris with his Emmy for "Lonesome Dove." Photo by Craig T. Mathew, courtesy the composer.

Poledouris's powerful main-title music represented the resolve and defi-
ance of the American people as it would ultimately emerge, with a hopeful
subtheme and triumphant coda that became the voice of the Resistance. This,
plus Alethea's alternately soaring and heartbreaking theme, and the grim, sad
motif for the political exiles (the "squatters")—who became a grass-roots
movement for new freedom—were among the strongest musical statements
that television had ever inspired.

Poledouris used a sixty-five-piece orchestra for much of the score and
recorded off and on in an estimated thirty sessions between November 1986
and February 1987, with the final scoring session held literally the day before
the final episode was televised. "The very last night was mixed down, dubbed,
and finished one hour before it hit the air," the composer said. "I didn't receive
the cut for the last two hours until twelve hours before I had to score it. And it

went on the air twenty-four hours after that." Poledouris managed to write twenty-four minutes of original music for the final two-hour episode. "There may have been as much as forty minutes [of score] so the music editors had to jump in and put that together from the other five hours that we had," he said.

Like so many talented professionals on "Amerika," the composer's work was ignored by the television academy as a direct result of the controversy surrounding the program. *Variety,* at least, noted that "Poledouris's immensely profound score forcibly moves in lockstep with the action."

By contrast, "Lonesome Dove" (1989, CBS) was an undisputed masterpiece in every sense. Probably the finest western in the history of the medium, it won seven Emmys and restored faith—if only temporarily—in commercial television's ability to do great things. Robert Duvall and Tommy Lee Jones starred in this eight-hour adaptation of Larry McMurtry's Pulitzer Prize-winning novel about a nineteenth-century cattle drive from Texas to Montana, with an outstanding supporting cast that included Diane Lane, Danny Glover, Robert Urich, Ricky Schroder, and Anjelica Huston.

Poledouris had not previously scored a western. It didn't matter; his familiarity with folk music had already laid the necessary groundwork, and the film itself was inspiration enough. And, Poledouris believed, the folk idiom "is a wellspring for very powerful, simple, eloquently stated musical renderings of the human spirit. This is really what 'Lonesome Dove' is about."

At the start, "I knew that I needed one very strong, central melodic notion for the piece," the composer said. "In terms of scoring Gus [Duvall] and Call [Jones] specifically, it didn't seem like that was necessary because they are so much one entity that I didn't really feel the need to separate the two of them. They were Lonesome Dove." In composing this main theme, Poledouris sought "a little bit of yearning, of longing . . . a kind of romance, a sense of lost youth, perhaps, and a sense of striving toward regaining some of that spirit." (Later, each character would be associated, only briefly, with his own motif: philosopher Gus with a bawdy "whorehouse piano" tune, and stoic Call with solo trumpet playing the traditional song of the Texas Rangers.)

Poledouris's second major theme involved the cattle drive itself: "So I made up this cowboy song about driving cows along. . . . And I knew that I wanted somewhat of an up-tempo, galloping motif that would represent the excitement of going to Mexico and stealing horses—a kind of high-adventure, high-romance theme." Within three days of landing the assignment, he had created three of the key themes in the score; later, at the request of director Simon Wincer, he wrote love themes that represented Gus's feelings for Clara (Huston) and Lorrianna (Lane).

Although most of the three-hour, forty-five-minute score was orchestral (fifty-eight players at its height), about forty minutes—notably those involving the Arkansas sheriff and his wayward, wandering wife—featured a small band playing authentic-sounding western music on instruments appropriate to the time and place: dulcimer, harmonium, banjo, guitar, mandolin, and fiddle. "We had talked about contacting the Nitty Gritty Dirt Band, who were a favorite of mine, and other artists, but in the end, when you are confronted with the realities of picture-scoring budgets, those sorts of ideas go out the door," the composer explained.

All of Poledouris's themes embodied folk-flavored Americana without resorting to Coplandesque cliché. His "Lonesome Dove" theme, at once elegant and bittersweet, captured the essence of the story in such a memorable and enduring way—"reflecting both the intimacy and the grandeur of the work," noted *Variety*—that, four years after the composer's Emmy win for Outstanding Achievement in Music Composition for a Miniseries or Special, an enterprising label finally released excerpts from his score and made a success of the album.

HISTORICAL, RELIGIOUS, AND LITERARY SUBJECTS

"Moses: The Lawgiver" (1975, CBS) not only was among the first of the network miniseries, it was the first to focus at length on a biblical subject, and a rare early instance of an international coproduction (by Britain's ATV and Italy's RAI) to be acquired by an American broadcast network. Burt Lancaster played the title role in this six-hour miniseries (telecast on consecutive Saturday nights during the summer months) that was filmed on location in Israel. Anthony Quayle played his brother Aaron, Ingrid Thulin his sister Miriam, and Irene Papas his wife Zipporah; Lancaster's son William played the young Moses in the first part. British novelist Anthony Burgess (*A Clockwork Orange*) was one of the screenwriters who adapted the Old Testament chronicle, in an unusually intelligent fashion (Moses's debate with Pharaoh in the second hour being a particularly riveting example). Equally intelligent was the choice of the eclectic and innovative Ennio Morricone as composer.

Morricone had written for television before, although not for a project of this size or one that required such an unusual musical backdrop. Only a fraction of his approximately two hours of original music was heard in the American version of "Moses," although all of the key themes made at least abbreviated appearances.

Morricone's theme for Moses was the backbone of the score. Rendered variously for mixed chorus (over the main titles), for wordless alto with chorus, and for solo viola with strings, it was infused with a quiet spirituality that was quite removed from the large-scale orchestral scores that Miklós Rózsa and Elmer Bernstein had written for big-screen biblical epics.

A second recurring theme was his song of joy for the Jews beginning their Exodus out of Egypt, featuring women's and men's choirs singing the single

Ennio Morricone.

word "Israel," over and over, to the accompaniment of organ and percussion.
For scenes where Moses heard God's voice, the composer created an atmosphere of strange percussive sounds. Only briefly heard was his mournful
"Lamentation" (in scenes of a stoning in part five and Aaron's death in part
six), for female soloist and a cappella mixed chorus.

Much of Morricone's "Moses" music, particularly the source music for the
Egyptian palaces and Jewish camps, was designed to imitate sounds that might
have been heard in the Middle East circa 1500 B.C.: music for voice, simple
flutes, and harps. "I did keep in mind ancient Jewish music," Morricone
explained, "but in a very liberal sense. Otherwise we would have had to have
the pieces played on original instruments; I did not have at my disposal the
performers or the instruments to do that. I [scored] with modern instruments,
so I could not be rigorously Jewish in style or form." Morricone's frequent collaborator, Bruno Nicolai, conducted the score in Rome. Music consultant Dov
Seltzer created many of the songs and dances for the series, including an
"Israel" chant (sung by Aaron as high priest in part six) that Morricone incorporated as a part of his "Moses" theme.

Morricone returned to the ancient world for "Marco Polo" (1982, NBC), a
ten-hour miniseries that marked the first cooperative filmmaking venture
between Western producers and the People's Republic of China. "Marco
Polo," which by virtue of its mammoth spectacle won the Outstanding Limited

Series Emmy, gave American audiences their first views of the Great Wall of China, Peking's Forbidden City, and the steppes of Inner Mongolia in an entertainment program.

Ken Marshall played young Marco Polo, the thirteenth-century adventurer who accompanied his father and uncle on a twenty-year, ten-thousand-mile journey from Venice to Cathay. The usual all-star parade of cameos (Burt Lancaster as Pope Gregory X, John Gielgud as the Doge of Venice, and Anne Bancroft as Marco's mother) was overshadowed by Chinese film star Ying Ruocheng in a completely convincing performance as the legendary Mongol emperor Kublai Khan.

For "Marco Polo," Morricone was reunited with two previous collaborators: "Moses" producer Vincenzo Labella and director Giuliano Montaldo (*Sacco and Vanzetti*). On the project for eleven months, the composer responded with one of his most memorable and complex scores: more than six hours of music incorporating three major themes, twelve secondary themes, and an untold number of source-music pieces appropriate to the many cultures visited by Marco Polo en route to the Far East.

"That 'Marco Polo' is an epic film is obvious," Morricone told an interviewer in Rome during the recording. "But it also has a nostalgic side to it: Marco's desire to return to Venice." With that notion as his initial inspiration, the composer created a main theme for viola, orchestra, and chorus that embodied a sense of longing for home but also, perhaps, a touch of sadness for the profound level of human suffering Polo encountered in his travels. The viola solos (played by Dino Asciolla, who also performed the solos in "Moses") often expressed the inner voice of Marco Polo.

A second motif, effectively a love theme, was associated with the three women in Marco's life: his mother; his first love as a youth in Venice; and a European woman named Monica whom he discovered in south China. Written for recorders, strings, harp, and women's chorus, it may have been the most beautiful melody that Morricone ever wrote for television: at once haunting and heartbreaking. The third primary theme, "On the Way to the Orient," was Marco's traveling music: constantly in motion, arranged in its most prominent incarnation for strings, harp, woodwinds, and percussion.

The secondary themes encompassed a wide range of styles and sounds: subdued brass fanfares and grim male chorus for the horrors of the Crusades; frenzied woodwinds for the first sighting of the Mongol hordes; a primitive march for Kublai Khan going to war; plaintive strings and male chorus for the story of the thousands who died building the Great Wall of China; and a graceful Oriental-flavored melody for Mai-Li (Monica's doomed stepsister).

Morricone said at the time that he based his incidental music on forms of Eastern music and known instruments of the period, although (as with "Moses") his challenge was to create a score that would resonate with twentieth-century viewers without negating thirteenth-century musical principles.

The composer came to Los Angeles to assist with the final music mix. The experience forever soured him on scoring for American television. "It was scandalous how they were treating the music," he later recalled. "They should have been ashamed of themselves. I left before it was over. In America, they don't care about the music in TV. All they care about is the dialogue. They sacrificed my music in a terrible way. . . . They reduced 'Marco Polo' to a soap opera, cutting [the music] to a very low level [resulting in] a pure discussion, a verbal account."

"Jesus of Nazareth" (1977, NBC) bears a dual distinction. Not only was it director Franco Zeffirelli's only work for American television, it is widely considered the finest life of Christ ever committed to film. Originally aired as a six-hour film over two nights, it was later expanded to eight hours over three or four nights for subsequent showings. Anthony Burgess, once again, created the original script outline. The great advantage "Jesus of Nazareth" held over other reverent big-screen retellings of the story was his, and Zeffirelli's, setting of the biblical accounts within a clearly defined historical and social context. Robert Powell's outstanding performance as Jesus, and a number of memorable guest-star turns (including Olivia Hussey as Mary, Peter Ustinov as Herod, Michael York as John the Baptist, James Farentino as Judas, and Laurence Olivier as Nicodemus), added to the credibility of the film.

Zeffirelli's insistence upon period realism (as on such previous films as 1968's *Romeo and Juliet* and 1973's *Brother Sun, Sister Moon*) gave "Jesus of Nazareth," filmed in Tunisia and Morocco, an authentic look. That approach extended to the musical score, entrusted to composer Maurice Jarre (b. 1924). Jarre had, by that time, written three scores for celebrated English director David Lean, and won Academy Awards for two of them: *Lawrence of Arabia* (1962) and *Doctor Zhivago* (1965). He scored a diverse range of other films including Alfred Hitchcock's *Topaz* (1969), Luchino Visconti's *The Damned* (1969), John Huston's *The Man Who Would Be King* (1975), and Elia Kazan's *The Last Tycoon* (1976). Apart from his "Cimarron Strip" theme and his romantic music for the Michael York-Sarah Miles version of "Great Expectations" (1974), Jarre had written no major scores for American television. (In fact, like the Dickens film, "Jesus" was an international coproduction, made by "Moses" and "Marco Polo" producer Vincenzo Labella for Britain's ITC and Italy's RAI.)

According to Jarre, Zeffirelli's first choice as composer was Leonard Bernstein. Bernstein had written only one film score (*On the Waterfront*, 1954) and was, interestingly enough, writing his *Mass* at the time. Bernstein recommended Jarre (having known the French composer since his days as musical director of the French National Theatre). "I worked very closely with Franco," Jarre said. "He asked me to go on location, to a monastery in Tunisia. We talked, and he told me of his view: really to try to [tell the story] in a very

Maurice Jarre conducting the "Shogun" score. Courtesy NBC.

human way instead of going to too much of the 'miracle' business with a lot of special effects. He wanted it to be more realistic, more human. And from there, I started to have my own view of Jesus. And I tried to use interesting instruments."

Jarre's tasteful, often understated, three-hour score for "Jesus of Nazareth" reflected Zeffirelli's vision. Although powerful and fully orchestral when called for throughout the miniseries, the music was more often subtle and reverent, as contrasted with Jarre's music for *Mohammad, Messenger of God* (1977), the birth-of-Islam epic whose Oscar-nominated score is quite grand in nature.

Jarre's theme for Jesus suggested the gentle nature of the Galilean and the hopeful nature of his message—yet was also transformed into music of overwhelming sadness during the crucifixion scenes. The composer also wrote individual themes for Mary and John the Baptist (and included all three themes during his overture to part one). Adding unusual colors throughout the score were an ondes martenot, the electronic keyboard heard during the annunciation scenes; the santur, a dulcimerlike instrument played in ancient times in Assyria, for scenes of the three kings arriving to worship the baby Jesus; the kithara, a lyrelike instrument popular in Greco-Roman times; the uggav, a shepherd's pipe; and the chalil, "a flute that one of the musicians in London found in Nazareth," the composer recalled.

Zeffirelli, in his memoir of the making of "Jesus," praised the composer's research into the "musical texts of the ancient Jewish tradition. He studied the poetic structure of the psalms for hints of possible musical cadences. He uncovered archaic instruments; others, he recreated, such as aulos, a flute that the apostle Thaddeus plays." The director was especially impressed with Jarre's handling of the Way of the Cross sequence: "[These scenes were] commented upon, animated and embellished by a heavy, provocative passage full of surprising blendings of sound, supported by a wealth of rhythm and a fury of percussion—harsh and disturbing sonorities over which, from time to time, an exalted but mournful theme emerges—a funereal but at the same time triumphant march."

Jarre's facility with unusual ethnic instruments within scores designed for Western audiences made him an obvious choice for "Shogun" (1980, NBC). Another expensive ($20 million) and ambitious effort, this twelve-hour miniseries was based on the James Clavell best-seller about the English captain of a Dutch vessel shipwrecked off seventeenth-century Japan. Richard Chamberlain starred along with Japanese actors Toshiro Mifune (as the powerful warlord) and Yoko Shimada (as Chamberlain's interpreter and eventual love interest). Filmed entirely in the Far East, Clavell's adventure introduced viewers to sights and, in fact, a culture not previously seen: samurai swordsmen, political intrigues in feudal Japan, even the language itself, since much of the original telecast was in Japanese without subtitles and with only occasional narration by Orson Welles to explain what was happening.

"It's like a ballet," Jarre said at the time. "There is such grace and style to the film, I didn't need to understand the scenes in Japanese to know what was going on." Having studied Japanese music while a student at the Paris Conservatoire, the composer based much of his score on traditional Japanese scales. "For me, it was very interesting to [write for] some interesting ethnic instruments, not only Japanese but period [instruments], and I found a lot of great Japanese players," he later recalled.

The shakuhachi (a bamboo flute), koto (a Japanese zither), biwa (a four- or five-stringed lute), and shamisen (three-stringed lute) were featured prominently in Jarre's score. During one early recording session in Los Angeles, Jarre said, "the entire television department, from accountant to driver, probably, peeked into the studio just to see how the musicians were going to play all of these strange instruments." "Shogun" won the Emmy as Outstanding Limited Series, as did Phill Norman's titles—twisting samurai swords that introduced images of the stars and scenes of Japan, all immeasurably enhanced by Jarre's orchestral overture, flavored with the sounds of those colorful Japanese instruments.

The composer intertwined themes for Blackthorne (Chamberlain), Mariko (Shimada), and Toranaga (Mifune), as well as non-character-specific music for the romance and adventure of the story. More than three-and-a-half hours of music were recorded over thirteen sessions between late May and late July 1980, several with a sixty-piece orchestra. Unfortunately, at the time, a musicians' strike was brewing and the sessions had to be speeded up to the point that, Jarre confessed, "I was not very happy about the recording. We had a lot of problems." The result was that not all of the miniseries was scored specifically "to picture," and some tracking of earlier music was required in the later segments.

Still, the American public tuned in to the five nights of "Shogun" in droves, reestablishing Richard Chamberlain as a major television star, and setting a new high standard for miniseries production. Jarre later returned to Clavell territory with his score for the big-screen *Tai-Pan* (1986), set in nineteenth-century Hong Kong.

Jerry Goldsmith's final large-scale work for television, and one that brought him a fourth Emmy for original music, was "Masada" (1981, ABC). Set in the first century A.D., it recounted the heroic struggle of 960 Jewish men, women, and children who successfully held off a 5,000–man Roman legion for nearly six months in a mountaintop fortress in the Judean desert. Rather than face capture, the entire Hebrew contingent ultimately committed suicide. Part tragic history, part fictionalized duel of wits between military leaders, "Masada" benefited from Joel Oliansky's fascinating script, the Israeli locations, and the Emmy-nominated performances of Peter Strauss (as Eleazar ben Yair, leader of the Jewish Zealots) and Peter O'Toole (in his dramatic TV debut as Flavius Silva, the world-weary Roman general). Key supporting roles were played by Barbara Carrera, Anthony Quayle, and David Warner.

"I had wanted to do that story for so many years," Goldsmith later recalled. "I had read it in the writings of Josephus, who first chronicled it, and I had read the Ernest Gann book [*The Antagonists*]. I had just been fascinated with the whole story of Masada and thought it would be a great movie. Sydney

Pollack was going to do it [at one time], and like so many pictures it never got made. And it became a television show."

Goldsmith traveled to Israel to do musical research and write and record the martial source music. He found little guidance at a university in Jerusalem, however: "The only clue [a scholar] gave me was that the Romans beat their swords against their shields for rhythm to march to. That wasn't very helpful, but it was interesting. You take dramatic license and write music to what you feel," he explained.

Because the "Masada" schedule fell hopelessly behind, Goldsmith was able to score only the first four hours of the eight-hour miniseries. Committed to a big-budget feature (the even more troubled *Inchon*), he turned over the task to old friend Morton Stevens, who scored the final four hours using Goldsmith's themes (and won an Emmy nomination for the moving finale).

"Masada" was among Goldsmith's most inspired scores. Much of the music derived from three primary themes: a motif for the freedom fighters atop Masada, of clearly Hebraic origin and employing a dancelike rhythm at its most joyous; a fanfare and march for the Romans; and a mournful theme for the oppressed Jewish people, many of whom became slaves. All three themes were heard to greatest advantage in the second part of the four-night miniseries. Goldsmith skillfully blended the Roman and Masada themes in the main title, as the Roman legions marched toward the mountain and the Jews of Masada prepared for war. The music for the Jewish slaves made its most dramatic appearance as the Romans cruelly used the slave labor to build their ramp up to the fortress. Richly orchestrated throughout and performed by a sixty-five-member ensemble of Los Angeles musicians, Goldsmith's music became a key element in the success of "Masada."

The first century in Rome and Palestine was also the setting for "A.D." (1985, NBC), scored by Lalo Schifrin in his largest-scale American television project. Producer Vincenzo Labella sought to create a semi-sequel to his "Jesus of Nazareth" with this $30 million, twelve-hour chronicle of the early Christian Church, the Jewish zealots, and the Roman Empire between the years A.D. 30 and 69; Labella once again recruited Anthony Burgess as scriptwriter.

"A.D." meshed historical fact with dramatic fiction in its tale of a Roman soldier in love with a Jewish slave, a Jewish Zealot falling for a Roman senator's daughter, and the experiences of the apostles Peter and Paul—coupled with the rise and fall of emperors Tiberius, Caligula, Claudius, and Nero (James Mason, John McEnery, Richard Kiley, Anthony Andrews). Critics found fault with much of "A.D.," dismissing it despite its lavish look and multiple guest stars (including Susan Sarandon, Ava Gardner, and Mason in his final role).

Schifrin conducted the Paris Philharmonic and the chorus of the Paris Opéra in the score. His main theme, associated with Jesus and the Christians, was gentle and uplifting; his "Golgotha" music, for the film's postcrucifixion scenes, was eerie and chilling. He wrote love themes for Valerius and Sarah (the soldier and slave) and Caleb and Corinna (the Zealot and senator's daughter); strident marches for the Romans; a choral "Alleluia" for Pentecost; and, perhaps most striking, a theme for King Herod that coupled the expected martial rhythms with a bright choral accompaniment (this last theme was so memorable that NBC used it in all its "A.D." promos).

After the phenomenal success of "Brian's Song," Michel Legrand returned occasionally to television, creating two memorable works for now-forgotten films, both with period settings: "The Adventures of Don Quixote" (1973, CBS) and "Casanova" (1987, ABC).

"Don Quixote" was an American-British coproduction based on the Cervantes classic, with Rex Harrison in the title role and Frank Finlay as his sidekick Sancho Panza. This quintessentially romantic tale of an avid reader who imagines himself as a knight-errant in sixteenth-century Spain inspired Legrand to write a score specifically for one instrumentalist: violinist Ivry Gitlis.

"That was a condition," the composer later recalled. The music publishers, who were paying for the London sessions, balked at the cost of engaging the well-known Israeli soloist. "Listen carefully," the composer insisted, "if I don't have Ivry Gitlis, I have no score." Gitlis was hired. "He plays with a tone like a real authentic, extraordinary gypsy," Legrand explained. The result was an impressive display of the composer's inspiration and some of the most exquisite violin sounds ever heard in a television score. Legrand's main theme—written for solo violin, flamenco guitar, strings, and harp—captured the romantic soul of the hero. Together with his love theme for Dulcinea (Rosemary Leach) and his brass fanfares for the "tilting at windmills" sequences, it elevated the film to unexpected heights.

For "Casanova," a three-hour biography of the legendary lover, Legrand was reteamed with several of the same collaborators who had made the big-screen adaptation of *The Three Musketeers* (1973) such an enjoyable romp: stars Richard Chamberlain and Faye Dunaway, supporting players Frank Finlay and Jean-Pierre Cassel, and writer George MacDonald Fraser. European film stars Ornella Muti, Sylvia Kristel, and Hanna Schygulla were also in the cast, and the lush settings in Spain and Italy enhanced its look (but not its ratings, which were disappointing despite the film's many assets).

Stylistically similar to his *Musketeers* score, Legrand's "Casanova" music was variously swashbuckling, romantic, and comedic, achieving what the composer called "an eighteenth-century flavor" appropriate to the time and the European locales. He composed in Paris over a three-to-four-week period, but flew to Los Angeles for three days of recording with an ensemble of fifty musicians.

Legrand's more than two hours of music included several major themes—a signature of pomp and grandeur for Casanova; a tender love theme (that later became a bittersweet reminder of Casanova's reckless past); a "traveling" motif of lighthearted adventure; classically styled music for swordplay—and many incidental pieces ranging from chamber music for the salons of Europe to choral music for young Casanova's brief stint as a novice priest. Several period instruments, including harpsichord and crumhorn, helped achieve an authentic sound.

Laurence Rosenthal has always been one of the finest composers active in films. His detailed knowledge of all facets of music coupled with an unerring dramatic instinct set him apart from the vast majority of composers in the Hollywood musical community. It took the development of the miniseries, particularly those of a historical nature, to properly showcase Rosenthal's talents. For the eight-hour "George Washington" (1984, CBS), he suggested the late eighteenth century with music evocative of early America. For the seven-hour "Mussolini: The Untold Story" (1985, NBC), he created music of a "dark character" to reflect the Italian dictator. He won Emmy Awards for his music for "Anastasia: The Mystery of Anna" (1986, NBC) and the Robert Ludlum thriller "The Bourne Identity" (1988, ABC).

Rosenthal's score for "Peter the Great" (1986, NBC) may have been his masterpiece. The eight-hour, $29 million production itself, the first to be made on location in the Soviet Union (under particularly arduous conditions), won the Emmy as Outstanding Miniseries. The all-star cast included Maximilian Schell as Peter, Vanessa Redgrave, Omar Sharif, Hanna Schygulla, and, more briefly, Laurence Olivier, Trevor Howard, and Mel Ferrer.

Much of the composer's homework was already done, by virtue of a film he had scored more than thirty years earlier. Attached to a documentary-film squadron during his Air Force service in 1952, he was assigned to score a ninety-minute history of Russia (a Cold War "know-your-enemy" exercise). "I went to the New York Public Library," he recalled, "and spent three weeks in the music department going through every volume of Russian folk songs they had, and they had many. I copied out hundreds of songs, whichever appealed to me. There were no Xerox machines in those days, and it all had to be done by hand. So I came away with a huge collection of Russian folklore. These songs have a kind of universal beauty. They can touch anyone. Many of them found their way into my score, often transmogrified or improvised upon. In any case, I had received a monumental dose of Russian music.

"Curiously, when I sat down in the screening room for my first look at the rough cut of 'Peter the Great,' I suddenly began hearing in my head those great folk songs I had collected for the Air Force film on Russia." That, plus his already thorough knowledge of Russian composers from Glinka and Tchaikovsky to Prokofiev and Shostakovich, had prepared him well for the story of the seventeenth-century czar who ushered his country out of the Dark Ages.

More than any other element, it was the cinematography of Vittorio Storaro (*Reds*), shooting on historical Russian locations, and the authentic music of Rosenthal that, one critic wrote, "dynamically captured czarist Russia's mood and majesty."

Explained the composer: "I wanted it to be drenched in Russian feeling.

Not only in the folk songs but also in the choral litury of the Orthodox Church. All of this music has enormous richness and power, and its many emotional facets seem to reflect different aspects of the Russian soul." Adopting the leit-motif approach, he composed individual themes for Peter and many of the characters in the epic.

As Rosenthal wrote in his notes for the soundtrack: "Peter has his theme—triumphal, exuberant and full of energy. Other themes are associated with various key elements in the story: Peter's group of supporters, especially Alexander Menshikov. The severe, almost Byzantine, theme of his two enemies: the religious establishment and his half-sister Sophia, which opens the film. The theme of Moscow's foreign colony and of Peter's great friend, the Scottish General Patrick Gordon—a West-European contrast. A winsome Russian folk-song to reflect the short-lived affection between Peter and his wife Eudoxia. Two original quasi-folk melodies, one for Peter's mother, the other for his ill-fated son Alexis, and so on and on. Mingled with these are fragments of pseudo-Baroque German court dances, and strains of the balalaika music of the peasants and Cossacks, with the charming triadic primitivity which so enchanted the young Stravinsky."

For the music of the many scenes set in the Russian Orthodox Church—coronations, weddings, funerals—Rosenthal realized: "there is no way I could hope to improve on that profoundly moving liturgy. So to score the church sequences, we went to Paris, where we recorded the extraordinary male choir of L'Eglise Russe de Saint-Serge. There were only fourteen men, standing directly under the dome of the Russian Cathedral. The sound was unbelievable. We had shown them the specific ceremonies that had been filmed and they knew exactly, for example, which particular chants would be sung for the coronation of the czar, or for the funeral service of his mother." Overall, Rosenthal composed more than three hours of music, recorded by the Bavarian State Orchestra in Munich. "Peter the Great" brought its composer another Emmy for original music.

Composer Allyn Ferguson's ongoing professional relationship with producer Norman Rosemont produced a series of impeccably scored remakes of literary classics, including "The Count of Monte Cristo" (1975, NBC) and "The Man in the Iron Mask" (1977, NBC), both with Richard Chamberlain, "The Four Feathers" (1978, NBC) with Beau Bridges, and "Ivanhoe" (1982, CBS) with Anthony Andrews.

For the lavish, three-hour "Les Miserables" (1978, CBS)—which starred Richard Jordan as Victor Hugo's hero Jean Valjean and Anthony Perkins as the police inspector Javert—the time frame of the picture suggested the approach to Ferguson. "It should probably be Berlioz," he told Rosemont, who promptly asked the composer to send over some musical examples. "I had at hand, for no particular reason, *Harold in Italy,* so I sent him a tape of it," Ferguson said. Rosemont's enthusiasm for the viola-and-orchestra form of *Harold* led the composer to utilize solo viola throughout his "Les Miserables" score. Interpreting Valjean as "a very strong but tender kind of guy," Ferguson found similar qualities in the sound of the viola: the instrument became Valjean's musical voice.

Ferguson won an Emmy for his score for "Camille" (1984, CBS), with Greta Scacchi as the doomed heroine of Alexandre Dumas fils's tragedy. Rosemont's original inclination was to have Ferguson adapt *La Traviata,* since Verdi's opera was based on the same novel. He had even told CBS executives to expect *Traviata* as the score. Although skeptical of the notion, Ferguson delved into the Verdi score. "It turned out that the preludes to act one and three are about the only musical [excerpts] that could have been used," he said. "The arias, after all, are vocal music. I finally had to confront Norman," he said, with the impossibility of adapting the opera into a cohesive dramatic score.

Rosemont was disappointed. But Ferguson had, as a backup plan, been developing thematic ideas along the lines of "the great romantic music of Ravel. I wanted that feeling about it, without actually imitating Ravel," he explained. His theme for lovers Marguerite (Scacchi) and Armand (Colin Firth), which featured prominent violin and cello solos, a "death" theme (inspired by the Verdi preludes), and some Offenbach-inspired French party music, formed the basis of much of the "Camille" score.

Also for Rosemont, Ferguson scored "Captains Courageous" (1977, ABC), "A Tale of Two Cities" (1980, CBS), "The Corsican Brothers" (1985, CBS), and, in a very different vein, the six-hour Sidney Sheldon miniseries "Master of the Game" (1984, CBS).

ROMANTIC, CONTEMPORARY, AND THRILLER FILMS

The "Night Gallery" pilot called attention to the talents of Steven Spielberg, but "Duel" (1971, ABC) established him as a first-class filmmaker. A seventy-three-minute exercise in terror, "Duel" was a man-versus-machine thriller about a traveling salesman (Dennis Weaver) who, for reasons that he cannot understand, becomes the target of an apparently crazed, anonymous tanker-truck driver on deserted mountain roads.

"ABC had been very low in the ratings, and they had to get something out really quickly to goose up their ratings," composer Billy Goldenberg recalled. "They were going into [November] sweeps, one of those times when it was important that they have something that was dynamite. They really felt that this was it."

Goldenberg, who had worked with Spielberg on "Night Gallery," "Name of the Game," and "Columbo," and become one of his best friends at Universal, was signed to score the picture. "I don't remember the exact time frame," he said, "but it was really short, either two or three weeks to shoot, score, and dub the [entire] show." Producer George Eckstein and Spielberg informed Goldenberg that he would have to write the music while the film was still being shot.

"I said, how can I do that? I don't have any edited film," Goldenberg pointed out. Spielberg had a partial solution: invite the composer to the Soledad Canyon shooting location to give him a sense of the picture. When he arrived, Spielberg told Goldenberg that he wanted the composer to ride in the ten-ton tanker truck that veteran stunt driver Cary Loftin was piloting down steep hills at high rates of speed. "Oh my God, what are you talking about?" was the composer's initial reaction. Spielberg introduced him to Loftin, who was "this big red-faced man who looked like he'd just gotten out of a bar or something," Goldenberg recalled. "He slapped me on the back—he was like a sea captain—and said, 'Lad, I hear you're going to do the music.'" Spielberg reminded the composer, who was to be in the passenger side of the cab, to duck before approaching the cameras.

"So we're at the top of this hill, and the camera's at the bottom of the curve," Goldbenberg said. "We started down, and [the truck] is going like seventy miles an hour. I'm screaming, and the whole time Cary Loftin is telling dirty jokes and asking me about myself. I said, 'How can I think? I'm going to die in a minute!'" They did this several times over the course of the next few days. "It was terrifying," Goldenberg said, "although I got kind of used to doing it. And I met Dennis [Weaver] and watched a lot of the shoot." He began watching dailies as well and then spent about a week writing the score.

"I knew I was going to have to have music for the truck running, some slow music for the times that there was suspense, and then there would be music for the truck going over precipices. I wanted to write a Bernard Herrmann sort of score, but I wanted it to be a little metallic, rough-sounding, scraping. I recorded lots of different percussion sounds. I did very little with timing—I didn't have anything to time to." Goldenberg recorded about two hours of music—"more music than we ever needed"—so that, with only a few days left before air to mix all of the sound effects, music, and what little dialogue there was, "I would go in with the music editors and we would just pick from all the pieces we had and cut it together."

The film's only Emmy went to its film sound-editing team, including sound effects editor James Troutman. Troutman and Goldenberg, working separately to devise a sound "for the final demise of the truck at the very end," the composer recalled, coincidentally came up with the same idea: a dying dinosaur—Goldenberg's created with percussion instruments, Troutman's from an old monster movie. Spielberg loved them and combined the two.

Goldenberg later won Emmys for "Benjamin Franklin" (1974, CBS), the six-hour "King" (1978, NBC), the four-hour "Rage of Angels" (1983, NBC), and his undisputed masterpiece, the made-for-TV musical "Queen of the Stardust Ballroom" (1975, CBS), written with lyricists Alan and Marilyn Bergman.

A handful of miniseries had preceded "Rich Man, Poor Man" (1976, ABC), but none had met with the kind of ratings success that would ensure the future of the genre. Based on an Irwin Shaw book, this twelve-hour "novel for television" made stars of Peter Strauss, Nick Nolte, and Susan Blakely as the key protagonists of a twenty-year saga about three postwar teenagers whose lives took dramatic turns yet remained intertwined. Undeniably melodramatic yet thoroughly involving, "Rich Man, Poor Man" won four Emmys, including one for the music of Alex North.

"Rich Man, Poor Man" was North's longest score, written during one of the most difficult periods in his life. After he began the project in late 1975, he was diagnosed with prostate cancer. "He decided that he was going to continue working as long as he could," his wife Anne-Marie recalled. "We then moved from here [Pacific Palisades, California] to Palo Alto, where he had all the radiation treatments. . . . He wrote several episodes up there." She would often rush his sketches from Palo Alto to the airport at San Jose, where they were pouch-mailed to orchestrator Gus Levene back in Los Angeles. "And the irony of this," she added, "is that Alex survived the cancer and Gus contracted it a couple of years later and died of it." North conducted the early sessions, but his illness prevented him from conducting all of the score; Universal music supervisor Hal Mooney completed the task.

As North explained in his liner notes to the soundtrack LP, "the treatment of the score called for a virtual musical anthology spanning 20 years in the lives of the Jordache family." Because the film was so long and encompassed so many characters, he wrote individual themes for several and described them this way: for Rudy (Strauss), "a rather sophisticated waltz"; for Tom (Nolte), "bluesy, virile and jazz-oriented 'carnal' music"; for Julie (Blakely), "a thematic portrait of a lovely adolescent girl, her desires and sensual curiosity . . . both naive and at times richly textured"; for Rudy and Tom's father Axel (Edward Asner), a German folk tune suggestive of his heritage.

The main title was a "slightly flavored Americana theme," he explained, designed to reflect Axel, "as the hard-working German emigré striving to fulfill the American dream for his wife and two sons." Apart from accompanying the main title of each part, it did not appear in the score until the two-hour conclusion, when it became the recurring motif for Tom's newfound happiness as a yacht skipper in the south of France.

North didn't simply repeat themes: he developed, interwove, and modified them throughout the course of the miniseries, often creating new material for specific scenes in the drama: a bittersweet melody for Julie's affair with Boylan (Robert Reed); a love theme for Tom's brief fling with Clothilde (Fionnuala Flanagan); a "light, somewhat elusive piece" for Rudy's flirtation with Ginny (Kim Darby); "heavy, forceful and dramatic" music when Tom beats up a boxer (George Maharis); a theme of "vivid tones and strong orchestral colors" for the brutal Falconetti (William Smith); and a poignant finale for Tom's death and the scattering of his ashes at sea.

North returned to the miniseries genre with a superb score for "The Word" (1978, CBS), an eight-hour adaptation of Irving Wallace's novel about the discovery of an ancient manuscript that may be an eyewitness account of the life of Jesus. North's six-minute main-title music, set to a fascinating visual journey deep into the archaeological dig where the papyrus was found, explored the complex intellectual territory: hints of the purely religious aspects and the dark political undercurrents beneath the discovery haunt the piece. North's Emmy nomination was the miniseries' only one.

After the success of "Rich Man, Poor Man," NBC commissioned several miniseries from romantic novels and aired them on consecutive Thursday nights under the umbrella title of "Best Sellers." The first, and best, was "Captains and the Kings" (1976), which composer Elmer Bernstein ranked as his "all-time favorite" among thirty years of television projects. It was based on the Taylor Caldwell novel about an Irish immigrant who arrived in America in the 1850s, became a self-made millionaire, and established a family dynasty with political as well as financial goals. The nine-hour series was popular as much for the story's obvious parallels to the Kennedy family as for its romantic, melodramatic saga of money, sex, and power. Richard Jordan became a star as a result of his Emmy-nominated leading role as the ambitious Joseph Armagh; the supporting cast was a TV who's-who including Charles Durning, Patty Duke Astin, Jane Seymour, Blair Brown, Perry King, Barbara Parkins, and even Henry Fonda.

Bernstein's "Best Sellers" theme incorporated a fanfare and sweeping melody (somewhat reminiscent of his "Hollywood and the Stars" music from the early 1960s) to which a fast-moving montage of images from the miniseries was cut. For "Captains and the Kings," he created a rich musical tapestry based on Irish folk music.

"I love Ireland," the composer said. "I've spent a lot of time there, and I loved the idea of being able to do anything that had the character of Irish music in it." From a tender lullaby as the orphaned Joseph and his brother and sister arrived in New York to a sweet love theme for solo violin, and from music of dramatic urgency for the Spanish-American War to a lighthearted turn-of-the-century tune for an Armagh son's aerial adventures, Bernstein's Emmy-nominated "Captains and the Kings" score fairly brimmed with Irish flavor.

Henry Mancini composed a compelling score for the six-and-a-half-hour adaptation of Arthur Hailey's "The Moneychangers" (1976, NBC). But the crowning triumph of his television career was his quintessentially romantic score for "The Thorn Birds" (1983, ABC). Running ten hours over four nights, the David Wolper-Stan Margulies production was a superbly realized adaptation of Colleen McCullough's best-seller, winning six Emmys and capturing the biggest audience for any miniseries since "Roots."

Richard Chamberlain, in his third great miniseries role (after "Centennial" and "Shogun"), was the tormented priest Ralph de Bricassart, whose lifelong passions for the Catholic Church and the beautiful Meggie Cleary (Rachel

Ward) played themselves out over four decades in the Australian outback. Barbara Stanwyck, Richard Kiley, and Jean Simmons won Emmys for their supporting roles; Bryan Brown and Christopher Plummer were also featured.

Mancini composed four hours of music for "The Thorn Birds," the most ever for a single project in his career. In fact, he was hired months before shooting began because of the source-music requirements that ranged from traditional Australian folk tunes to choral music for the several church sequences. "I tried to find church music that would fit the period we were depicting," the composer said at the time. "The best-known piece is [César Franck's] *Panis Angelicus,* which opens part two. We found a terrific boys' choir to sing it. The arrival of the roving band of sheep shearers at Drogheda also required something traditional. I found a wonderful Australian folk song called 'The Springtime It Brings on the Shearing,' which fits the scene perfectly."

During the preproduction phase, Mancini did extensive research into Australian ethnic music. But, in searching for a main theme that would introduce Australia at the start of part one, he later recalled: "I couldn't find anything that didn't sound like it came out of early Nashville or the country gardens in England or the hills of Scotland. It was all very simple folk music." He came up with the "Thorn Birds" theme but initially discarded it as "too simple." A lilting piece with folk overtones reflective of the Clearys' Irish roots, he "kept coming back to it because it seemed to be the only thing. I finally played it for Stan and David and they loved it. I was never sure that someone hadn't written it before; it was so simple."

Adding to the Irish flavor was Mancini's use of a dulcimer in the main title, as Father Ralph is driving through the outback en route to the Drogheda ranch. He had heard a dulcimer—an instrument he had never used before in any of his many film scores—in a record of Australian folk music. "I used it for the first notes in the main theme and I think it sets the Australian tone of the piece," he explained at the time.

Meggie's theme, the other major theme in the "Thorn Birds" score, was one of Mancini's most romantic compositions ever. In addition, he wrote two major set pieces that became a part of his concert suite from the score: a rousing four-and-a-half-minute cue for the sheep-shearing contest in part two ("It's Shearing You're Hearing") and a grand orchestral fanfare for the arrival of Father Ralph at the Vatican that was heard at the end of the same night.

There was also a theme for Meggie's marriage to Luke O'Neill and their life in Queensland, music of high drama for the fire that devastated Drogheda in part two, and a Greek-flavored theme for Meggie's children Dane and Justine frolicking on the beach during what becomes a tragic incident in part four. Mancini's arrangement of Meggie's theme for her holiday on secluded Matlock Island (with piano and organ embellishment) and his lush string arrangement for Ralph's arrival made those already romantic moments at the end of part three even more memorable. And his music for the final moments of part four—as Meggie cradles her head in the lap of the dead Father Ralph, while a plane carrying Justine flies off into the distance—turned a sad finale into one of shattering proportions. Henry Mancini's score—nominated, but shockingly not a winner, for an Emmy—elevated "The Thorn Birds" to all-time classic status.

Eventually, the television film became the medium for dramatization of fact-based contemporary stories, often involving complex psychological cases and sensational murder stories.

"Sybil" (1976, NBC), a four-hour story of a young woman with multiple personalities, and the psychiatrist who attempts to unravel the cause and help her cope, posed an intriguing challenge for composer Leonard Rosenman. At the time, Rosenman had been commissioned to write a double-bass concerto, and he had been considering writing it for two double basses and four string quartets "which would be used in a very microtonal way." He saw "Sybil" as a laboratory to experiment with this sort of advanced composition.

"For any composer to write 'crazy music' is a cinch. I wasn't interested in that," Rosenman explained. "I was interested in something more dramatically basic." The score, as written, consisted of "this pure childlike tune, a waltz that could be played with one finger, which was distorted by microtonal aspects. The orchestra consisted of strings only; two harps that were tuned a quarter-tone apart; percussion; two pianos that were tuned a quarter-tone apart; four children's voices, and electronics."

Lyricists Alan and Marilyn Bergman wrote a lyric for a song that was used over the end titles ("Mirror, mirror, in my mind, there's so much to see. . . .") that Rosenman then used as a dramatic device throughout the score: at first "in a noncommunicative fashion," the composer said, then gradually, bit by bit, until the entire song was heard in the finale. "Sybil" won four Emmys, including one for the score, awarded to both composer Rosenman and the Bergmans.

"Fatal Vision" (1984, NBC) and "The Deliberate Stranger" (1986, NBC) posed a very different, even disturbing, challenge for composer Gil Mellé. Both were grim chronicles of multiple murder: "Fatal Vision," based on the Joe McGinniss book about Green Beret Dr. Jeffrey MacDonald, accused of murdering his wife and children in 1970; "The Deliberate Stranger," the story of convicted mass killer Ted Bundy. "In order to do justice to the picture," Mellé said, "to really capture the horror of what these people were, you have to get inside of those characters. You have to see the world through their eyes, and then step outside and look closely at them, almost under a microscope. And it's a painful experience working on a picture like that."

Mellé's electronic palette was appropriate in each case. "Fatal Vision" and "The Deliberate Stranger" utilized unique, often eerie sounds and textures— sometimes in tonal, sometimes atonal, ways—to paint musical portraits of deranged men. The main title of "Fatal Vision," for example, "starts off with a hurdy-gurdy kind of theme at the beginning," Mellé observed, "then this vast swooping of colors, like a watercolor painting somebody doused with water, everything melting one into the other."

Miniseries based on Stephen King's best-selling horror novels became a cottage industry in the nineties. Richard Bellis's harrowing score for the four-hour "It" (1990, ABC), which included a calliope theme for the demonic clown Pennywise, won an Emmy.

The eight-hour "The Stand" (1994, ABC) was King's own adaptation of his apocalyptic 1978 novel about a plague that wipes out much of the American population, and the good-versus-evil struggle among the survivors starting anew. The cast included Gary Sinise, Molly Ringwald, Rob Lowe, Laura San Giacomo, and Ruby Dee. King became personally involved with the music, which was composed by W. G. Snuffy Walden. "We asked Snuffy to provide us with a mostly acoustic soundtrack, which I described as 'blue-jeans music,'" King explained in a letter to members of the Television Academy music branch. "I wanted music that would reflect the decency and growing spiritual commitment of the men and women."

Recalled Walden: "One time, he told me, 'The only strings I want to hear on this score are guitar strings.' I couldn't take that literally," he said, "because I knew we had too much scope to try and score with a solo acoustic guitar. But in only a couple of instances did I let the orchestra step forward. . . . I did about forty minutes of orchestral music out of the four-and-a-half hours [of score]." In fact, Walden was King's self-described "biggest fan" and *The Stand* his favorite book. "I'd read the unabridged version twice and the original three times. I knew this book backwards and forwards," the composer said. Searching for an approach, he decided: "It was all about the spiritual battle between good and evil. It wasn't about people dying, about people turning into goblins, it was about these human beings having a devastating experience that changed their lives, wiped the slate clean, and they had to go forward from there."

From the slide guitar sounds that opened part one (a last-minute inspiration), Walden created multiple themes for characters and situations, altering the sound of each episode and adding a new theme before the ". . . to be continued" signoff. "Each night I would add a color change as well as a major theme," he explained. "And I did that by design, because I wanted it to flow. I wanted us to feel that we were growing and moving, with a purpose, towards something. Rather than just scoring every cue, I wanted to have a thematic build.

"The fourth night was the most orchestral," Walden said, "and also used the most varied instrumentation: soprano sax, hammer dulcimer, solo fiddle, solo guitar, solo piano, recorders, voices, thirty-five-piece orchestra, as well as all the Synclavier colors that I'd used at the beginning." The composer himself played acoustic and electric slide guitar on much of the score.

Steeped in Americana, finally more uplifting than frightening, Walden's

Emmy-nominated score was his most massive project—and one realized in just eight weeks. Wrote King: "Snuffy responded with a soundtrack which is both spiritual and beautiful. It is the best musical accompaniment I have ever had for a show, either on TV or for a theatrical [film]."

There have been other notable scores for TV movies and miniseries: Hugo Friedhofer's lighthearted western score for "The Over-the-Hill Gang" (1969, ABC); Jerry Fielding's brass-choir opening for the Emmy-winning drama of the conflict in Northern Ireland, "A War of Children" (1972, CBS), and his elegiac theme for the David Carradine-Richard Widmark western "Mr. Horn" (1979, CBS); the primitive-sounding music of Mikis Theodorakis (Z) for "The Story of Jacob and Joseph" (1974, ABC); Richard Rodney Bennett's delightful nineteenth-century melodrama approach to "Sherlock Holmes in New York" (1976, NBC); and Charles Gross's colorful, Gershwinesque Jazz Age score for "The Dain Curse" (1978, CBS).

Also: Jerry Goldsmith's inventive baroque, jazz, and avant-garde combination for "Brotherhood of the Bell" (1970, CBS), his initial collaboration with writer-director Michael Crichton on the political thriller "Pursuit" (1972, ABC), and his lonely trombone melody for Frank Sinatra's detective character in "Contract on Cherry Street" (1977, NBC).

And, later: Gil Mellé's futuristic electronic score for "World War III" (1982, NBC); David Raksin's adaptation of Virgil Thomson's music for the nuclear holocaust film "The Day After" (1983, ABC); John Barry's song score for the Jodie Foster drama "Svengali" (1983, CBS); Charles Bernstein's noble theme for "Sadat" (1983, syndicated); Ernest Gold's period music for the World War II docudrama "Wallenberg: A Hero's Story" (1985, NBC); Elizabeth Swados's piano score for the six-hour "A Year in the Life" (1986, NBC); Georges Delerue's touching music for the five-hour "Queenie" (1987, ABC) and his heroic orchestral and choral finale for the concentration camp drama "Escape from Sobibor" (1987, CBS); Stan Get's tenor-sax improvisations for "In Defense of a Married Man" (1990, ABC); Craig Safan's haunting music for the George Armstrong Custer biography "Son of the Morning Star" (1991, ABC); James DiPasquale's tender touch on "In the Best Interest of the Children" (1992, NBC); and John Debney's powerful score for the Civil War pilot "Class of '61" (1993, ABC).

Not one of these memorable scores received an Emmy nomination, yet each was among the best of its television season. Like all great film scores, they moved us emotionally. And for just a moment, like all great music regardless of the medium for which it was composed, they enriched our lives.

Afterword

In the mid-1990s, television has lost its innocence. The once-adventurous new medium is now middle-aged, cynical, and far less willing to take chances. Much of prime time is inane and banal. The television film, once home to serious examinations of relevant social issues, is reduced to retelling sordid true-crime tales ripped from the tabloids. The chase for an increasingly hard-won ratings point in an era of multiplying networks and cable services has caused a perhaps inevitable decline in standards virtually everywhere on the tube.

Inexperienced producers and network executives are a part of the problem: people who think that music is some kind of necessary evil of postproduction, not an integral element in the collaborative process. People who don't understand that the right score can make the difference between a film that moves a viewer and one that simply tells a story.

This is reflected in shrinking budgets for music that rarely allow for an acoustic ensemble, forcing many composers to fall back on electronic sounds and musical samples. Only a handful of shows still rely on orchestral scores, enabling a few composers to regularly surprise listeners with their creative approaches to scoring for television. Even more rare is the composer who manages to find innovative solutions working in the all-synthesizer milieu.

Apart from these exceptions to the general rule, most music for television these days sounds like it was created in someone's garage. It often is. That's why this history of American television scoring stops short of most TV in the 1990s. Little of the flavor, the bounce, the fun, the dynamic qualities that composers of taste and talent—backed by studio executives and savvy network bosses who valued and appreciated music—brought to TV in the sixties, seventies, and eighties, can be heard today.

But all things in life are cyclical. Perhaps after an extended down period, the glory days of television will return, and with them the understanding that music is a vital element of the filmmaking process: the melodies and harmonies without which no audience can truly be touched.

Sources

The vast majority of this book is the product of personal interviews and primary research. Unfortunately, many of the available books on television's past are filled with factual inaccuracies, and what little published information exists on music (based mostly on screen credits) is often highly suspect. Whenever possible, screen credits were checked against studio music logs, cue sheets, Composers and Lyricists Guild of America records, and/or information provided by ASCAP, BMI, or the composers themselves. All interviews were conducted by the author unless otherwise noted.

A number of reliable reference works on television, music, and films were consulted constantly throughout the writing of this book. They are:

Total Television, third edition, by Alex McNeil. Penguin Books, 1991.

The Complete Directory to Prime Time Network TV Shows, 1946–Present, fifth edition, by Tim Brooks and Earle Marsh. Ballantine Books, 1992.

The *Television Drama Series Programming: A Comprehensive Chronicle* books by Larry James Gianakos. Scarecrow Press: *1947–1959* (1980); *1959–1975* (1978); *1975–1980* (1981); *1980–1982* (1983); *1982–1984* (1987).

Movies Made for Television: The Telefeature and the Mini-Series 1964–1986 by Alvin H. Marill. New York Zoetrope, 1987.

Variety Television Reviews 1946–1988, compiled by Howard H. Prouty. Garland Publishing, 1991.

Classic Sitcoms by Vince Waldron. Collier Books, 1987.

Special Edition: A Guide to Network Television Documentary Series and Special News Reports, 1955–1979 by Daniel Einstein. Scarecrow Press, 1987.

Syndicated Television: The First Forty Years, 1947–1987 by Hal Erickson. McFarland & Company, 1989.

The Soap Opera Encyclopedia by Christopher Schemering. Ballantine Books, 1985.

Variety's Directory of Major U.S. Show Business Awards. R. R. Bowker, 1989.

The Emmys by Thomas O'Neil. Penguin Books, 1992.

Les Brown's Encyclopedia of Television, third edition, by Les Brown. Visible Ink Press, 1992.

The Big Broadcast, 1920–1950 by Frank Buxton and Bill Owen. Viking Press, 1972.

The Norton/Grove Concise Encyclopedia of Music, edited by Stanley Sadie. W. W. Norton & Company, 1988.

New Grove Dictionary of American Music, edited by H. Wiley Hitchcock and Stanley Sadie. Macmillan Press Limited, 1986.

ASCAP Biographical Dictionary. R. R. Bowker Company, 1980.

Variety Obituaries 1905–1986 (plus supplements to 1992). Garland Publishing, 1988.

The Complete Encyclopedia of Popular Music and Jazz, 1900–1950 by Roger D. Kinkle. Arlington House, 1974.

On the Track: A Guide to Contemporary Film Scoring by Fred Karlin and Rayburn Wright. Schirmer Books, 1990.

Listening to Movies: The Film Lover's Guide to Film Music by Fred Karlin. Schirmer Books, 1994.

Music for the Movies by Tony Thomas. A. S. Barnes & Co., 1973.

Film Score: The Art and Craft of Movie Music by Tony Thomas. Riverwood Press, 1991.

The Faber Companion to 20th-Century Popular Music by Phil Hardy and Dave Laing. Faber and Faber, 1990.

Leonard Maltin's Movie and Video Guide, 1995 edition, edited by Leonard Maltin. Signet, 1994.

The Motion Picture Guide 1927–1983 by Jay Robert Nash and Stanley Ralph Ross. Cinebooks Inc., 1985.

Film Composers Guide, second edition. Compiled and edited by Vincent J. Francillon and Steven C. Smith. Lone Eagle, 1994.

Film, Television, and Stage Music on Phonograph Records: A Discography by Steve Harris. McFarland & Company, 1988.

Television Theme Records: An Illustrated Discography, 1951–1994 by Steve Gelfand. Popular Culture Ink, 1994.

Academy Awards, second edition. Compiled and introduced by Richard Shale. Frederick Ungar Publishing Company, 1982.

Joel Whitburn's Top Pop Albums, 1955–1985. Record Research Inc., 1985.

Notes

Chapter 1: The Birth of TV Music

"The Lone Ranger": Interview with Byron Chudnow 2/23/95. *The Mystery of the Masked Man's Music* by Reginald M. Jones Jr., Scarecrow Press, 1987. *Who Was That Masked Man?* by David Rothel, A. S. Barnes and Company, 1976. Interviews with film-music archivist Graham Newton 7/10/95 and Reginald Jones 7/16/95.

Petrillo and AFM issues: *Weekly Variety* 8/9/50, 3/21/51, 6/11/52, 8/12/53. *Los Angeles Times* 3/25/56. Gluskin and AFM: *Weekly Variety* 5/21/56, *Los Angeles Times* 5/22/56. *American Popular Music Business in the 20th Century* by Russell Sanjek and David Sanjek, Oxford University Press, 1991.

"The Adventures of Superman": "Superman's Music of Adventure" by Paul Mandell, *Starlog* March 1992. Interviews with David Chudnow 3/21/95, Herschel Burke Gilbert 7/4/92. Gilbert's detailed documentation of series episodes.

Klatzkin/Laszlo: Robert Raff interview 1/9/95. Glasser: interview 7/30/94, plus excerpts from his unpublished 1992 autobiography, *I Did It!* (used by permission). "Cisco Kid": *Saturday Afternoon at the Bijou* by David Zinman, Arlington House, 1973. Kraushaar: interview 2/20/95 plus MGM music files at USC.

Kahn: interview 8/21/93. Gounod theme on "Alfred Hitchcock Presents": *The Dark Side of Genius: The Life of Alfred Hitchcock* by Donald Spoto, Ballantine Books, 1983. David Gordon library: interview with grandson Jeff Gordon 8/27/95.

Rose and Ziv: interviews with widow Betty Rose 12/3/91, Milton Lustig 1/7/95, Nicholas Carras 7/25/95. Capitol library: interviews with Jack Cookerly 4/11/95, Raff 1/9/95; William Loose CLGA file and obituaries.

"Danger": Tony Mottola interview 8/11/94 plus letter 8/19/94. Guitar "Danger" folio published by George Paxton 1951.

"Dragnet": *Time* 3/15/54, *Saturday Evening Post* 9/26/53. *Television's Greatest Year: 1954* by R. D. Heldenfels, Continuum Publishing, 1994. Nathan Scott interview 2/15/94. Walter Schumann obituary, *Los Angeles Times* 8/22/58. Rózsa/Schumann lawsuit: summary in *Pro Musica Sana* no. 14, publication of the Miklós Rózsa Society, 1975, plus letter from Rózsa to editor John Fitzpatrick 7/19/75.

"Medic": *Playing Doctor: Television, Storytelling and Medical Power* by Joseph Turow, Oxford University Press, 1989. Interviews with Victor Young's niece Bobbie Fromberg 8/18/93, Sidney Fine 9/18/93.

Disney and "Davy Crockett": *The Musical World of Walt Disney* by David Tietyen, Hal Leonard Publishing Corporation, 1990; *The Disney Films* by Leonard Maltin, Bonanza Books, 1973. George Bruns interviews 7/23/68 (by Richard Hubler) and 9/5/78 (interviewer unidentified) in the Disney archives. "Davy Crockett's Songsmith" in *Portland Oregonian* 12/4/55. Interview with Richard and Robert Sherman 5/10/93; interview with Buddy Baker 2/19/93.

Warner Bros. and ABC: *Tube of Plenty: The Evolution of American Television* by Erik Barnouw, second revised edition, Oxford University Press, 1990. *Warner Bros. Television* by Lynn Woolley, Robert W. Malsbary, and Robert G. Strange Jr., McFarland & Company, 1985. Music files in Warner Bros. archives at USC.

Lubin: Byron Chudnow interview 2/23/95. Notes for Lubin LPs *Music for Loretta, The World of Sight and Sound,* and *One Step Beyond*. Selinsky: notes for *Kraft Television Theatre* LP. Copland: *Copland Since 1943* by Aaron Copland and Vivian Perlis, St. Martin's Press, 1989. "Studio One" scores: *The New York Times* 5/2/54.

CBS and Gluskin: Don B. Ray interview 6/21/94. *Down Beat* 4/12/62. Jerry Goldsmith interviews 2/27/87, 5/1/92, 1/16/95. Goldsmith profile by Leonard Feather in *International Musician* December 1970. Goldsmith profile by Derek Elley in *Films & Filming* May 1979. Norman Felton interview 2/4/91.

Chapter 2: Cop and Detective Shows

TV Detectives by Richard Meyers, A. S. Barnes & Company, 1981.

Henry Mancini, "Peter Gunn" and "Mr. Lucky": interviews with Mancini 1/27/87, 1/27/92. *Did They Mention the Music?* by Henry Mancini with Gene Lees, Contemporary Books, 1989. Hal Humphrey column, *Los Angeles Mirror News* 10/27/58; *Newsweek* 12/29/58. Alan Livingston interview 9/14/95.

"M Squad": *TV Guide* 6/13/59. Universal music logs. Benny Carter interview 10/15/93. *Benny Carter: A Life in American Music* by Morroe Berger, Edward Berger, and James Patrick, Scarecrow Press, 1982.

"Richard Diamond": Interviews with Frank DeVol 2/8/95, Pete Rugolo 12/6/91, Richard Shores 6/28/91. Rugolo profile, *International Musician* March 1969. "Staccato": Elmer Bernstein liner notes for *Movie and TV Themes* LP, 1962, and *Staccato* LP notes, 1960. "Checkmate": Eric Ambler liner notes for LP, 1961. John Williams profile, *International Musician* April 1969. Williams interview 4/7/92.

"The Untouchables": Jack Hunsaker interview 6/28/93; Cookerly interview. "Mike Hammer": Kahn interview 8/21/93; Spillane liner notes, 1959 LP.

Warner Bros. detective series: *Warner Bros. Television;* music files in Warner archives at USC; Mack David Collection at USC. Erma Levin interview 3/2/95. Excerpts from Max Steiner's unpublished autobiography, *Notes to You,* in Steiner collection at Brigham Young University.

"Asphalt Jungle": MGM music logs; MGM music files at USC. Harry Lojewski interviews 2/25/92, 10/11/94. Score analysis by R. J. DeLuke 8/19/95. "Burke's Law": Gilbert interview.

"Mr. Broadway": Brubeck liner notes from *Jazz Impressions of New York* LP, 1965. R. A. Israel interviews 8/10/94, 10/21/94. Oliver Nelson profile in *International Musician* July 1968.

"Ironside": Quincy Jones interview 10/4/93. *International Musician* profile June 1968. "Quincy Jones: The Man Behind the Music" by Louie Robinson, *Ebony* June 1972. Marty Paich interview 4/5/95. "Hawaii Five-0": Morton Stevens interview 9/25/91; Leonard Freeman notes for 1969 LP.

"Arrest and Trial": Universal music logs; John Waxman interview 8/15/94. Quinn Martin series: interviews with John Elizalde 7/19/94, Pat Williams 7/14/92, Goldsmith 5/1/92.

"Mystery Movie" series: interviews with Mancini 1/27/92, keyboard player Clare Fischer 3/8/95, Billy Goldenberg 7/23/94, David Shire 1/31/92. *The Columbo Phile: A Casebook* by Mark Dawidziak, The Mysterious Press, 1989. "The Mod Squad": Earle Hagen interview 3/26/92.

"Charlie's Angels": interviews with Allyn Ferguson 6/16/93, Jack Elliott 1/26/95, Scott Smalley 10/10/92. "Baretta": interviews with Dave Grusin 1/16/92, Morgan Ames 6/12/95.

"Rockford Files," "Magnum, p.i.," "Hill Street Blues," "NYPD Blue": Mike Post interviews 10/5/89, 4/5/94. "Miami Vice": Jan Hammer interview 8/10/94, *Rolling Stone* 10/24/85, *Los Angeles Times* 10/27/85, *USA Today* 11/1/85.

"Cagney and Lacey": Bill Conti interview 11/21/94. "Murder, She Wrote": John Addison interview 7/15/93. "Moonlighting": interviews with Lee Holdridge 6/12/89 and 9/23/94, Alf Clausen 3/19/93.

Chapter 3: The Westerns

"Gunsmoke" and the CBS music library: interviews with Don Ray 6/21/94, Lud Gluskin (by Steven Smith) 3/11/84, Herrmann collection and CBS music logs at UCLA. *A Heart at Fire's Center: The Life and Music of Bernard Herrmann* by Steven C. Smith, University of California Press, 1991. "Have Gun—Will Travel": Johnny Western interview 3/7/95.

"The Life and Legend of Wyatt Earp": *The Hollywood Musical: The Saga of Songwriter Harry Warren* by Tony Thomas, Citadel Press, 1987. Interview with Kate Edelman 6/7/94. Ken Darby 1974 biography in files at Margaret Herrick Library of Academy of Motion Picture Arts and Sciences. "Hum Sweet Hum" in *TV Guide* 5/3/58.

Warner Bros. westerns: Correspondence in music files in Warner Bros. Archives at USC. Erma Levin interview 3/2/95. Bert Shefter music collection at UCLA.

Stanley Wilson and "Wagon Train": Wilson profile in *International Musician* August 1970. Logs in Universal music library. Jerome Moross interview (by John Caps) 8/31/79.

"Rawhide": "Eerie Blue Notes in TV Theme Songs" by Herschell Hart, *Detroit News* 4/27/59. Interviews with Frankie Laine 3/8/95, Russell Garcia 8/30/95.

"The Rifleman": Herschel Burke Gilbert interview 7/4/92. "Black Saddle": interviews with Jerry Goldsmith 5/1/92, Arthur Morton 7/13/93.

"Bonanza": interviews with Jay Livingston and Ray Evans 7/24/92, Alan Livingston 9/13/95, David Dortort 6/17/92, Betty Rose 12/3/91. NBC publicity materials for "Bonanza: The Return" October 1993. David Rose interviews in *Daily Variety* 2/7/62, 12/13/74. Harry Sukman collection at Margaret Herrick Library; David Rose collection at USC.

"Riverboat" and "Shotgun Slade": Elmer Bernstein interview 12/1/94. Gerald Fried interviews 5/7/91 and 6/10/91. *Shotgun Slade* album notes by Stanley Wilson. "The Tall Man" and Juan Esquivel: "Viva Esquivel!" notes by Irwin Chusid for *Space Age Bachelor Pad Music* CD 1994.

"Wichita Town": Hans J. Salter interview 8/25/93. "Outlaws": letter from Hugo Friedhofer to film-music critic Page Cook 11/2/75 in Friedhofer collection at Brigham Young University.

"The Virginian": interviews with Sandy DeCrescent 11/23/93, Percy Faith's daughter Marilyn Leonard 9/30/93; correspondence with Bill Halvorsen (the Percy Faith Society) November 1993. Pat Williams interview 7/14/92.

"The Rebel" and "The Wild Wild West": interviews with Richard Markowitz 2/11/92, Andrew Fenady 8/28/95, Herschel Burke Gilbert 7/4/92; CBS music logs at UCLA. "The Big Valley": George Duning interview 7/1/92; Duning collection at USC.

"Branded": Dominic Frontiere interview 9/1/95. "The Loner": Goldsmith interviews 5/1/92, 1/16/95; *Variety* 7/30/65. "Cimarron Strip": Bruce Broughton interview 8/11/92. "Kung Fu": Alex Beaton interview 6/7/95.

Chapter 4: Fantasy and Sci-Fi

Fantastic Television by Gary Gerani with Paul H. Schulman, Harmony Books, 1977.

"The Twilight Zone": *The Twilight Zone Companion* by Marc Scott Zicree, Bantam Books, 1982. *A Heart at Fire's Center: The Life and Music of Bernard Herrmann* by Steven C. Smith. Interviews with Buck Houghton 9/13/93, Don B. Ray 6/21/94 and 3/30/95, Goldsmith 2/27/87 and 5/1/92, Fred Steiner 2/6/92 (plus Steiner lecture at Society for the Preservation of Film Music conference 10/21/94), music editor Bob Takagi 8/27/93. *Musique Fantastique: A Survey of Film Music in the Fantastic Cinema* by Randall D. Larson, Scarecrow Press, 1985. CBS music logs and Herrmann collection at UCLA. John Vonde liner notes for five "Twilight Zone" score albums, 1983–85 on Varèse Sarabande.

"Thriller": interviews with Goldsmith 2/27/87, Pete Rugolo 12/6/91, Douglas Benton 8/19/93; letter from Caesar Giovannini 5/29/93.

"Alfred Hitchcock Presents/Alfred Hitchcock Hour": *Musician: A Hollywood Journal* by Lyn Murray, Lyle Stuart Inc., 1987. *A Heart at Fire's Center: The Life and Music of Bernard Herrmann* by Steven C. Smith. Music logs at MGM and Universal.

"The Outer Limits" and "The Invaders": *The Outer Limits: The Official Companion* by David J. Schow and Jeffrey Frentzen, Ace Science Fiction Books, 1986. Interviews with John Elizalde 7/19/94, copyist Roger Farris 1/4/95, Duane Tatro 3/20/92.

Irwin Allen series: Hugo Friedhofer letters to Page Cook (in Friedhofer collection at Brigham Young University) 3/22/65 and 12/30/76. Interviews with John Williams 4/7/92, Paul Tanner 1/13/94, music editor Ken Wannberg 3/10/95, George Greeley 12/16/93, Herman Stein 7/22/95. Twentieth Century-Fox music logs.

"Star Trek": "Music for 'Star Trek': Scoring a Television Show in the Sixties" by Fred Steiner in *Wonderful Inventions: Motion Pictures, Broadcasting, and Recorded Sound at the Library of Congress,* edited by Iris Newsom, Library of Congress 1985. Interviews with Alexander Courage 7/8/93, Fred Steiner 2/6/92, Robert H. Justman 6/6/94 and 6/29/95, Jack Cookerly 4/11/95 and 8/28/95, Gerald Fried (by D. L. Fuller) 5/19/95, Dennis McCarthy 12/5/94, Goldsmith 1/16/95. Liner notes by Gene Roddenberry and Fred Steiner for two Varèse Sarabande "Star Trek" LPs 1985–86. *Star Trek Creator: The Authorized Biography of Gene Roddenberry* by David Alexander, Roc, 1994. *Gene Roddenberry: The Myth and the Man Behind Star Trek* by Joel Engel, Hyperion, 1994. *The Making of Star Trek* by Stephen E. Whitfield and Gene Roddenbery, Ballantine Books, 1968. Paramount music logs.

"Night Gallery": Interviews with Billy Goldenberg 7/23/94, Gil Mellé 5/14/92. Jack Laird interview by Leonard Feather in *International Musician* November 1972. Correspondence with "Night Gallery" expert Scott Skelton, April to November 1994.

"Kolchak: The Night Stalker": Gil Mellé interview 5/14/92. *Night Stalking: A 20th Anniversary Kolchak Companion* by Mark Dawidziak, Image Publishing 1991. "The Sixth Sense": David Shire interview 1/31/92, Universal music logs.

"Battlestar Galactica": Stu Phillips interview 8/22/95. "Amazing Stories": John Williams interview 4/7/92. New "Twilight Zone": Phil DeGuere press conference 6/6/85, Robert Drasnin interview 8/25/93. "Tales From the Crypt": Danny Elfman interview 8/12/93.

"Beauty and the Beast": Lee Holdridge interviews 6/12/89 and 9/23/94. "Twin Peaks": Angelo Badalamenti interviews 4/27/90 and 7/22/90. "The X-Files": Mark Snow interview 9/22/95.

Chapter 5: Drama

"Route 66" and "Naked City": interviews with Herbert Leonard 5/7/93, Christopher Riddle 3/10/92, Billy May 9/7/93. *Arranged by Nelson Riddle* by Nelson Riddle, Warner Bros. Publications, 1985; Jonathan Schwartz's liner notes for *'Round Midnight* CDs, 1986; profile in *International Musician* June 1973. Riddle comments from *As You Remember Them: Some Notes on the Music* edited by George G. Daniels, Time-Life Records 1972.

"The Fugitive" and "Run for Your Life": interviews with Pete Rugolo 12/6/91 and 4/13/95, John Elizalde 7/19/94, Roy Huggins 2/10/93.

"Dr. Kildare": Jerry Goldsmith interviews 5/1/92 and 1/16/95; MGM music logs. "Ben Casey" and "Breaking Point": David Raksin interview 11/13/91. "Marcus Welby, M.D.": Leonard Rosenman interview 4/21/92; "Could Dr. Welby Practice Without Music?" by Rowland Barber, *TV Guide* 5/19/73. "Medical Center": Lalo Schifrin interview 2/9/87. "St. Elsewhere": Dave Grusin interview 1/16/92.

"Perry Mason": Fred Steiner interviews 2/6/92 and 4/16/95. "The Defenders": Rosenman interview 4/21/92, *Los Angeles Times* profile 6/6/76. "East Side/West Side": Kenyon Hopkins profile in *International Musician* September 1971; R. A. Israel interview 8/10/94.

"L.A. Law": interviews with Mike Post 4/5/94 and Steven Bochco 4/19/94. "Shannon's Deal": interviews with Wynton Marsalis 5/23/89, Stan Rogow 1/11/90.

"Combat!": Rosenman interviews 4/21/92 and 1/17/95. *Unsold Television Pilots, 1955–1988* by Lee Goldberg, McFarland & Company, 1990. "Twelve O'Clock High" and "Rat Patrol": interviews with John Elizalde 7/19/94 and Dominic Frontiere 9/1/95. "M*A*S*H": Johnny Mandel interview 10/10/94. "China Beach": John Rubinstein interview in *Music from the Movies* Winter 1994–95.

"General Electric Theater": interviews with Elmer Bernstein 4/14/92, Morton Stevens 9/25/91. Conrad Salinger profile in Christopher Palmer liner notes for Chandos LP *A Musical Spectacular,* 1990.

"Alcoa Premiere," "Kraft Suspense Theatre": John Williams interview 4/7/92. "Chrysler Theater": interviews with Dick Berg 9/7/94, Lalo Schifrin 10/18/91. "Name of the Game": interviews with Dave Grusin 1/16/92, Billy Goldenberg 7/23/94; Grusin profile in *International Musician* March 1971.

"The Waltons": interviews with Goldsmith 2/27/87 and 5/1/92, Alexander Courage 7/8/93, Earl Hamner Jr. 10/28/93. "Peyton Place" and "Bus Stop": Arthur Morton interview 7/13/93; Hugo Friedhofer letter to Page Cook 3/22/65 (in Friedhofer collection at Brigham Young University). "The Survivors": Universal music logs.

"Dallas" and "Knots Landing": interviews with Jerrold Immel 4/21/95, Bruce Broughton 8/11/92. "Dynasty" and "Falcon Crest": Bill Conti interview 11/21/94. "Lou Grant": Pat Williams interviews 3/11/91 and 6/15/95.

"thirtysomething": interviews with W. G. Snuffy Walden 6/8/94, Stewart Levin 8/30/95.

Chapter 6: The Sitcoms

"I Love Lucy": Eliot Daniel interview 12/17/92; *The I Love Lucy Book* by Bart Andrews, Doubleday 1985. "The Honeymooners": *Jackie Gleason* by W. J. Weatherby, Pharos Books 1992; *How Sweet It Is: The Jackie Gleason Story* by James Bacon, St. Martin's Press, 1985.

"Car 54, Where Are You?": John Strauss interview 7/16/95. "The Beverly Hillbillies" and "Petticoat Junction": interviews with Paul Henning 5/24/93, Jerry Scoggins 7/11/94.

"Gilligan's Island" and "The Brady Bunch": interviews with Sherwood Schwartz 2/27/92, George Wyle 7/17/95, Frank DeVol 2/20/92 and 9/9/95. *Inside Gilligan's Island: From Creation to Syndication* by Sherwood Schwartz, McFarland & Company, 1988. *The Unofficial Gilligan's Island Handbook* by Joey Green, Warner Books, 1988. *The Brady Bunch Book* by Andrew J. Edelstein and Frank Lovece, Warner Books, 1990. DeVol profile in *TV Guide* 3/9/63. CBS and Paramount music logs.

"My Three Sons": DeVol interview 2/20/92. "The Addams Family," "Green Acres": Vic Mizzy interview 10/29/91. "The Addams Family: The Man Behind the Music" by Randall Larson, *Cinefantastique* December 1991.

"Mister Ed": Jay Livingston and Ray Evans interview 7/24/92. "The Danny Thomas Show," "The Andy Griffith Show," "The Dick Van Dyke Show," and other Sheldon Leonard series: Earle Hagen interview 3/26/92; Hagen profile in *International Musician* May 1970. "The Patty Duke Show": Sid Ramin interviews 2/17/94 and 7/28/95.

Jerry Fielding and "Hogan's Heroes": Fielding biography by Nick Redman, *Dictionary of American Biography, Supplement Ten, 1976–1980,* Charles Scribner's Sons, 1995; profile in *International Musician* November 1969. "Bewitched," "Gidget," "Here Come the Brides": interviews with Jack Keller 3/11/95 and Warren Barker 6/19/95. "The Monkees": Ken Barnes liner notes for *The Monkees: Greatest Hits* CD, Rhino 1995; "Monkees" retrospective in *The Television Chronicles* No. 2, 1995.

"The Flying Nun": Dominic Frontiere interview 9/1/95. "Mr. Roberts," "Courtship of Eddie's Father," "Chico and the Man," "Welcome Back Kotter": interviews with James Komack 8/28/95, John Sebastian 9/3/95.

"Love, American Style," "Happy Days," "Laverne & Shirley," "Love Boat": Charles Fox interview 12/21/92. "The Mary Tyler Moore Show," "The Bob Newhart Show," and other MTM comedies: interviews with Sonny Curtis 9/17/95, Pat Williams 7/14/92, James L. Brooks 3/21/92, Allan Burns 6/16/95. "The Days and Nights of Molly Dodd": Jay Tarses interview 4/1/91. Curtis profile in *Entertainment Weekly* 4/12/91.

"All in the Family": Charles Strouse interview 8/11/92. "Maude," "Good Times": interviews with Alan and Marilyn Bergman 3/4/92, Dave Grusin 1/16/92. "Sanford and Son," "The Bill Cosby Show": Quincy Jones interview 10/4/93, *Down Beat* 11/27/69.

"Cheers": Judy Hart Angelo interviews 10/15/92 and 10/21/92. "Roseanne," "Home Improvement": interviews with Dan Foliart 7/31/95, Howard Pearl 8/29/95. "Seinfeld": Jonathan Wolff interview 7/25/95. "Frasier": Bruce Miller interview 9/7/95. "Friends": interviews with Michael Skloff and Allee Willis 7/20/95.

Chapter 7: Action-Adventure

"The Man from U.N.C.L.E.": "Critic's Choice: The Man from U.N.C.L.E." by J.B., *Video Review* January 1986; "Cloak and Swagger: Tracking the Men from U.N.C.L.E." by J.B., *Emmy* July-August 1988; interviews with Norman Felton 7/23/74, Jerry Goldsmith 2/27/87 and 5/1/92, Gerald Fried 7/22/74; MGM music logs.

"I Spy": Earle Hagen interview 3/26/92. "Mission: Impossible," "Mannix": interviews with Lalo Schifrin 2/9/87 and 10/18/91, Robert H. Justman 6/6/94, Jack Hunsaker 6/28/93; Bruce Geller liner notes to *Mission: Impossible* LP, 1967; Schifrin profile in *International Musician* May 1968; Paramount music logs.

"The Saint," "Danger Man," "The Avengers": "The Man with the Baton: Laurie Johnson" by Dave Rogers, "Edwin Astley" by Vanessa Bergman, both in *Music from the Movies* Spring 1995. "Secret Agent": Steve Barri interview 9/20/93. "The Prisoner," "Man in a Suitcase": "The Ron Grainer Story" by Geoff Leonard and Pete Walker in *Doctor Who and Other Classic Ron Grainer Themes* CD, 1994. "The Persuaders!": John Barry interview 3/22/93.

"Batman": interviews with Neal Hefti 3/25/92, Christopher Riddle 3/10/92; "Batmusic" by Bob Garcia in *Cinefantastique* February 1994. "The Green Hornet": Billy May interview 9/7/93. "Wonder Woman": Charles Fox interview 12/21/92.

"The Incredible Hulk": Joe Harnell interview 5/3/94. "The Flash": interviews with Danny Elfman 8/12/93, Shirley Walker 10/7/92.

"Lassie": Nathan Scott interview 2/15/94. "Flipper" and "Daktari": MGM music logs; Shelly Manne profile in *International Musician* November 1970; Leonard Kaufman liner notes for "Daktari" LP 1968.

"Scarecrow and Mrs. King": Arthur B. Rubinstein interview 6/2/94. "The Young Indiana Jones Chronicles": interviews with George Lucas 2/13/92, Laurence Rosenthal 11/30/93 and 12/1/93.

Chapter 8: Documentaries and News Programming

"Victory at Sea": *Musical Stages* by Richard Rodgers, Random House, 1975. "Robert Russell Bennett: A Sound for All Seasons" by Richard Hanser in *Television Quarterly* Winter 1981–82. Liner notes by Hanser for *Victory at Sea, Volume 2* LP 1958 and by Bennett for *Volume 3* 1959. "Man Behind the Tune" in *Newsweek* 7/20/53; reviews in *Time* 11/10/52, *The New Yorker* 4/4/53.

"Project XX": *Documentary in American Television* by A. William Bluem, Hastings House, 1965. Notes for *The Coming of Christ* LP 1961; "He Is Risen" feature in *TV Guide* 4/14/62.

"Wide Wide World": David Broekman essay in *Film and TV Music* Summer 1957; John S. Wilson liner notes for *Wide Wide World* LP 1956.

"Air Power": "TV Music by Contemporary Composers" in *Etude* November 1956. "Twentieth Century": *New York Times* 4/12/59. "Winston Churchill—The Valiant Years": Daniel Melnick interview 8/9/94; liner notes for 1961 soundtrack LP.

Wolper documentaries: interviews with David L. Wolper 2/6/92, Elmer Bernstein 4/14/92, Lalo Schifrin 10/18/91. "Rise and Fall of the Third Reich": *Newsweek* 8/14/67, *Life* 9/29/67, *TV Guide* 3/2/68.

"World War I": Morton Gould interview 6/23/92, liner notes for 1965 LP. "Africa": Anna North interview 9/4/93; liner notes for 1967 LP by Jerry Bredouw; Alex North profile by Christopher Palmer in *Film Music Notebook* Vol. III, No. 1, 1977. "Michelangelo: The Last Giant": Laurence Rosenthal interview 12/1/93.

"National Geographic" and "Jacques Cousteau" specials: interviews with Elmer Bernstein (by *"Geographic"* producer Gail Willumsen) 5/10/94, Walter Scharf 10/14,16/91, Schifrin 10/18/91, Jay Chattaway 6/14/95, John Scott 4/30/95. *Composed and Conducted by Walter Scharf* by Scharf with Michael Freedland, Vallentine, Mitchell & Co., 1988. *TV Guide* 3/2/68.

News and sports themes: interviews with Ray Ellis 5/1/95, Henry Mancini 1/27/92, John Williams 4/7/92, R. A. Israel 8/10/94, Bill Conti 11/21/94.

Chapter 9: Cartoons in Prime Time

Hanna-Barbera cartoons: interviews with Hoyt Curtin 3/22/93, cartoon-music producer Earl Kress 8/3/95; Kress liner notes for *Hanna-Barbera Classics* CD 1995 and *The Flintstones: Modern Stone-Age Melodies* CD 1994. *The Art of Hanna-Barbera* by Ted Sennett, Viking Studio Books 1989.

"The Bugs Bunny Show": *Looney Tunes and Merrie Melodies* by Jerry Beck and Will Friedwald, Henry Holt & Company, 1989; music correspondence in Warner Bros. Archives at USC.

"The Bullwinkle Show": interviews with Fred Steiner 2/6/92 and Frank Comstock 6/13/95; "Inside Story: Rocky and Bullwinkle" by J.B., *TV Update* 9/20/93.

"Charlie Brown" specials: Lee Mendelson interview 10/30/89; Ralph Gleason notes for *Jazz Impressions of a Boy Named Charlie Brown* LP, 1964. *Charlie Brown, A Boy for All Seasons: 20 Years on Television,* Museum of Broadcasting, 1984.

Rankin-Bass specials: Maury Laws interview 8/28/91; *Animated TV Specials* by George W. Woolery, Scarecrow Press, 1989.

"The Simpsons": interviews with Matt Groening 6/23/92, Danny Elfman 8/12/93, Alf Clausen 3/19/93.

Chapter 10: Made-for-TV Movies and Miniseries

THE BEGINNINGS

"Vanity Fair": R. A. Israel interview 8/10/94. "The Power and the Glory": Laurence Rosenthal interview 11/30/93. "The Hanged Man": Benny Carter interview 10/15/93. "CBS Playhouse": *Copland Since 1943* by Aaron Copland and Vivian Perlis.

"Companions in Nightmare": *A Heart at Fire's Center: The Life and Music of Bernard Herrmann* by Steven C. Smith; Norman Lloyd interview 6/18/86.

"Heidi," "Jane Eyre": John Williams interview 4/7/92; liner notes for 1971 "Jane Eyre" LP. "Brian's Song": Michel Legrand interview 9/25/93, *Los Angeles Herald-Examiner* 11/7/71.

"Love Among the Ruins," "The Glass Menagerie," "The Corn Is Green," "Eleanor and Franklin": John Barry interviews 7/29/88, 8/21/90, 3/22/93.

"QB VII": Jerry Goldsmith interview 1/16/95 plus his liner notes for 1974 LP; *TV Guide* 4/27/74. "Holocaust": Morton Gould interview 6/23/92, *Time* 4/17/78 and 5/1/78. "The Winds of War," "War and Remembrance": Bob Cobert interview 8/10/88; Randall Larson interview/analysis in *CinemaScore* No. 11–12, Fall 1983.

AMERICANA

"The Red Pony": Goldsmith interview 5/1/92. "Autobiography of Miss Jane Pittman": Fred Karlin interview 5/7/92.

"Roots": interviews with Quincy Jones 10/4/93, Stan Margulies 1/14/92 (J.B.) and 1994 (D. L. Fuller), Gerald Fried 5/7/91. *Down Beat* 10/23/75, notes and lyrics from *Roots* LP 1977, *Los*

Angeles Times 2/27/77. "The Mystic Warrior": Fried interview 5/7/91; *Mystic Warrior* CD
notes by D. L. Fuller; ABC press releases 1/18/84, 5/7/84; *Newsweek* 5/21/84.

"Centennial": John Addison interview 7/15/93, letter 7/7/95; score analysis by Phil Lehman 9/8/95;
Addison interview by David Kraft in *Soundtrack!* December 1981. "East of Eden": interview
with Lee Holdridge 9/23/94. "Blue and the Gray," "O Pioneers!": Bruce Broughton
interviews 10/30/91, 8/11/92. "North and South": Bill Conti interview 11/21/94.

"Amerika," "Lonesome Dove": interviews with Basil Poledouris 8/12/92 (plus lecture at Society
for the Preservation of Film Music conference 3/19/94), Scott Smalley 10/10/92. *CinemaScore*
No. 15, Winter 1986–Summer 1987; *Variety* 2/18/87, 2/3/89.

HISTORICAL, RELIGIOUS, AND LITERARY SUBJECTS

"Moses," "Marco Polo": Ennio Morricone interviews 3/17/94 (J.B.) and 4/12/94 (by Gary
Crowdus); *Variety* 4/12/82. "Moses" liner notes in 1992 CD; "Marco Polo" score analysis by
Randall Larson in *CinemaScore* No. 10, Fall 1982.

"Jesus of Nazareth": Maurice Jarre interview 7/21/93; interview by Martyn Crosthwaite in *RTS
Music Gazette* August 1977. *Franco Zeffirelli's "Jesus": A Spiritual Diary* by Zeffirelli, Harper
& Row, 1984. "Shogun": Jarre interview 7/21/93; NBC press release June 1980.

"Masada": Goldsmith interviews 2/27/87, 5/1/92; *New York Times* 4/5/81, *Newsweek* 4/6/81. "A.D.":
Lalo Schifrin interview 10/18/91.

"The Adventures of Don Quixote" and "Casanova": Michel Legrand interviews 2/10/87, 9/25/93.
"Peter the Great": Laurence Rosenthal interview 11/30/93; Rosenthal liner notes for 1986
soundtrack LP. "Les Miserables," "Camille": Allyn Ferguson interview 6/16/93.

ROMANTIC, CONTEMPORARY, AND THRILLER FILMS

"Duel": Billy Goldenberg interview 7/23/94. "Rich Man, Poor Man": Anna North interview 9/4/93,
North notes for 1976 soundtrack LP. "Captains and the Kings": Elmer Bernstein interview
4/14/92.

"The Thorn Birds": Henry Mancini interviews 1/27/87 and 1/27/92; profile by Ron Miller in *San
Jose Mercury News* 3/20/83; ABC press release 3/17/83.

"Sybil": interviews with Leonard Rosenman 4/21/92, Alan and Marilyn Bergman 3/4/92. "Fatal
Vision": Gil Mellé interview 5/14/92. "The Stand": W. G. Snuffy Walden interview 6/8/94;
Stephen King letter to music-branch members of the Academy of Television Arts and
Sciences 5/26/94.

Suggested Listening

Most of the television themes discussed in this book have, at one time or another, been commercially recorded. Many are even currently available on compact disc; some, unfortunately, can only be found on out-of-print vinyl LPs or 45 rpm singles.

What follows is an attempt to list the definitive versions of many popular TV scores—that is, those that sound as close as possible to the ones heard on the original television soundtrack. The first choice is often the composer's own recorded arrangement, although that's not always the case (as some artists have strayed too far in misguided attempts to create "pop" versions designed to sell more records). For example, Henry Mancini's own "Peter Gunn" album is the obvious choice for that theme, but Revue music director Stanley Wilson's version of "The Virginian" sounds much more like the TV original than composer Percy Faith's own arrangement.

Some TV theme collections, notably those issued on the TVT and Rhino labels, feature the original TV soundtrack music itself. In most cases, those are the ones I have chosen to list; in a few instances, the sound quality is poor or the expanded version by the composer is actually preferable. All are CDs unless noted otherwise; LPs list the stereo number unless the album was only issued in monaural.

This discography was compiled with the assistance of Steve Harris, the author of *Film, Television and Stage Music on Phonograph Records* and a forthcoming volume, *Music for Television,* that will list more than eight thousand television series, TV movies, miniseries, and specials, and their composers.

Frequently cited compact disc collections are abbreviated:

Television's Greatest Hits volume I, TeeVee Toons, TVT-1100: *TVGH* 1.
Television's Greatest Hits volume II, TeeVee Toons, TVT-1200: *TVGH* 2.
Television's Greatest Hits: The '70s and '80s, TeeVee Toons, TVT-1300: *TVGH* 3.
The Music of Disney: A Legacy in Song, Walt Disney Records 60957–2: *Disney.*
Songs of the West, Volume Four: Movie and Television Themes, Rhino R2–71684: *West.*
Tube Tunes, Volume One: The '70s, Rhino R2–71910: *Tube* 1.
Tube Tunes, Volume Two: The '70s and '80s, Rhino R2–71911: *Tube* 2.
Tube Tunes, Volume Three: The '80s, Rhino R2–71912: *Tube* 3.

Chapter 1: The Birth of TV Music

"The Lone Ranger" (Rossini): soundtrack, *The Music of the Lone Ranger,* Cinedisc CDC 1019.

"The Adventures of Superman" (Leon Klatzkin): *TVGH* 1.

"Waterfront" (Alexander Laszlo): Buddy Morrow, *Impact,* RCA LSP-2042. LP.

"The Cisco Kid" and "Big Town" (Albert Glasser): *The Fantastic Film Music of Albert Glasser,* Starlog SR-1001. LP.

"Alfred Hitchcock Presents" (Gounod): Stanley Wilson, Sunset 2021. Single.

"Leave It to Beaver" (Dave Kahn): *TV Theme Song Sing-Along Album,* Rhino RNLP 703. LP.

"Highway Patrol" (David Rose): Buddy Morrow, *Impact,* RCA LSP-2042. LP.

"Sea Hunt" (David Rose): *TVGH* 2.

"The Donna Reed Show" (William Loose): *TVGH* 1.

"Dennis the Menace" (William Loose): *TVGH* 1.

"Danger" (Tony Mottola): Mottola, *Danger,* MGM E-111. 10–inch LP.

"Dragnet" (Walter Schumann): Frank Chacksfield, *The Great TV Themes,* London SP-44077. LP.

"Medic" (Victor Young): Young, *Forever Young,* Decca DL-8798. LP.

"Davy Crockett" (George Bruns-Tom Blackburn): *Disney.*

"Swamp Fox" (Buddy Baker-Norman Foster): *Disney.*

"Zorro" (George Bruns-Norman Foster): *Disney.*

"The Wonderful World of Color" (Richard and Robert Sherman): *Disney.*

"Cheyenne" (William Lava-Stan Jones): Sons of the Pioneers, *Sunset on the Range,* Pair PDC 2–1156.

"Loretta Young Show" (Harry Lubin): Lubin, *Music for Loretta,* Decca DL7–4124. LP.

"One Step Beyond" (Harry Lubin): Lubin, soundtrack, Decca DL7–8970. LP.

"Kraft Television Theatre" (Wladimir Selinsky): Selinsky, soundtrack, RKO-Unique ULP-127. LP.

"Playhouse 90" (Alex North): North, RCA 47–6896. Single.

Chapter 2: Cop and Detective Shows

"Peter Gunn" (Henry Mancini): Mancini, soundtrack, RCA 1956–2.

"Mr. Lucky" (Henry Mancini): Mancini, soundtrack, RCA 2198–2.

"M Squad" (Count Basie): Basie, Roulette 4109. Single. Score (Benny Carter, Johnny Williams, Stanley Wilson): soundtrack, RCA LSP-2062. LP.

"The Thin Man" (Pete Rugolo): Rugolo, Mercury 71447. Single.

"Richard Diamond" (Pete Rugolo): Rugolo, soundtrack, Mercury SR-80045. LP.

"Staccato" (Elmer Bernstein): Bernstein, soundtrack, Capitol ST-1287. LP.

"Checkmate" (Johnny Williams): Williams, soundtrack, Columbia CS-8391. LP.

"The Untouchables" (Nelson Riddle): Riddle, soundtrack, Capitol ST-1430. LP.

"Mike Hammer" (Dave Kahn): Skip Martin, RCA LSP-2140. LP.

"77 Sunset Strip" (Jerry Livingston-Mack David): *TVGH* 1.

"Hawaiian Eye" (Jerry Livingston-Mack David): *TVGH* 2.

"Surfside 6" (Jerry Livingston-Mack David): *TVGH* 1.

"Bourbon Street Beat" (Jerry Livingston-Mack David): Buddy Morrow, *Double Impact,* RCA LSP-2180. LP.

"The Roaring Twenties" (Jerry Livingston-Mack David): Dorothy Provine with Pinky and Her Playboys, Warner Bros. WS-1394. LP.

"The Asphalt Jungle" (Duke Ellington): Ellington, Columbia 4–42144. Single.

"Burke's Law" (Herschel Burke Gilbert): Gilbert, soundtrack, Liberty LST-7343. LP.

"Honey West" (Joe Mullendore): Mullendore, soundtrack, ABC-Paramount ABCS-532. LP.

"Mr. Broadway" (Dave Brubeck): theme, Brubeck, Columbia 4–43133. Single. Score, Brubeck with quartet, *Jazz Impressions of New York,* Columbia CK 46189.

"Ironside" (Quincy Jones): Jones, *Smackwater Jack,* Mobile Fidelity Sound Lab MFCD-776.

"Hawaii Five-0" (Morton Stevens): Stevens, soundtrack, Capitol ST-410. LP.

"Police Woman" (Morton Stevens): Johnny Gregory, *TV's Greatest Detective Hits,* Mercury SRM 1–1089. LP.

"Arrest and Trial" (Bronislau Kaper): Carl Brandt, *Top TV Themes '64,* Warner Bros. WS-1529. LP.

"The FBI" (Bronislau Kaper): Erich Kunzel/Cincinnati Pops, *Bond and Beyond,* Telarc CD-80251.

"The Streets of San Francisco" (Pat Williams): Pat Williams, Capitol P-4036. Single.

"Barnaby Jones" (Jerry Goldsmith): *TVGH* 3.

"Police Story" (Jerry Goldsmith): Daniel Caine, *Jazz in Prime Time,* Prime Time USA PTD–3008.

"NBC Mystery Movie" (Henry Mancini): Mancini, *Big Screen, Little Screen,* RCA LSP-4630. LP.

"Columbo," "Kojak," "Harry O," and "Banacek" (Billy Goldenberg): Johnny Gregory, *TV's Greatest Detective Hits,* Mercury SRM-1–1089. LP.

"McMillan and Wife" (Jerry Fielding): Johnny Gregory, *TV's Greatest Detective Hits,* Mercury SRM-1–1089. LP.

"McCloud" (David Shire): Johnny Gregory, *TV's Greatest Detective Hits,* Mercury SRM-1–1089. LP.

"The Men" (Isaac Hayes): Hayes, *Tube* 1.

"The Mod Squad" (Earle Hagen): *TVGH* 1.

"Mickey Spillane's Mike Hammer" (Earle Hagen): Daniel Caine, *Cagney and Lacey and Other American Television Themes,* Silva Screen FILMCD 704.

"S.W.A.T." (Barry DeVorzon): DeVorzon, *Nadia's Theme,* Arista AL-4104. LP.

"Charlie's Angels" (Jack Elliott-Allyn Ferguson): Henry Mancini, *Mancini's Angels,* RCA APL1–2290. LP.

"Baretta" (Dave Grusin-Morgan Ames): Sammy Davis Jr., *TVGH* 3.

"The Rockford Files" (Mike Post-Pete Carpenter): Post, *Tube* 1.

"Magnum, p.i." (Mike Post-Pete Carpenter): Post, *Tube* 2.

"The A Team" (Mike Post-Pete Carpenter): *Mike Post,* RCA AFL1–5183. LP.

"The Greatest American Hero" (Mike Post-Stephen Geyer): Joey Scarbury, *Tube* 3.

"Hunter" (Mike Post-Pete Carpenter) and "Wiseguy" (Post): Post, *Music from L.A., Law and Otherwise,* Polydor 422–833–985–2.

"Hill Street Blues" (Mike Post): Post, *Tube* 3.

"NYPD Blue" and "Law and Order" (Mike Post): Post, *Inventions from the Blue Line,* American Gramaphone, AGCD 450.

"Miami Vice" (Jan Hammer): Hammer, *Soundtrack* MCA MCAD 6150.

"The Equalizer" (Stewart Copeland): *Tube* 3.

"Remington Steele" (Henry Mancini): Mancini, *Premier Pops,* Denon CO 2320.

"Cagney and Lacey" (Bill Conti): Daniel Caine, *Cagney and Lacey and Other American Television Themes,* Silva Screen FILMCD 704.

"Murder, She Wrote" (John Addison): Newton Wayland/Houston Symphony, *Prime Time,* Cinedisc CDD-462.

"Moonlighting" (Lee Holdridge-Al Jarreau): Jarreau, soundtrack, MCA MCAD-6214.

Chapter 3: The Westerns

"Gunsmoke" (Rex Koury): soundtrack, *West.*

"Have Gun—Will Travel" (Bernard Herrmann): soundtrack, Cerberus CST-0209. LP. "The Ballad of Paladin" (Johnny Western): *West.*

"The Life and Legend of Wyatt Earp" (Harry Warren-Harold Adamson): Hugh O'Brian with Ken Darby's Orchestra and Chorus, *West.*

"The Californians" (Harry Warren-Harold Adamson): Sons of the Pioneers, *Themes of TV's Greatest Westerns,* RCA Bluebird LBY-1027. LP.

"The Adventures of Jim Bowie" (Ken Darby): Prairie Chiefs, *Wyatt Earp, Cheyenne and Other TV Favorites,* RCA Bluebird LBY-1004. LP.

"Daniel Boone" (Lionel Newman-Vera Matson): *TVGH* 1.

"Sugarfoot" (Max Steiner-Ray Heindorf-Paul Francis Webster): Sons of the Pioneers, *Themes of TV's Greatest Westerns,* RCA Bluebird LBY-1027. LP.

"Maverick" (David Buttolph-Paul Francis Webster): soundtrack, *West.*

"Bronco" (Jerry Livingston-Mack David): Johnny Gregory with Michael Sammes Singers, *Channel West,* Columbia CS-8400. LP.

"Wagon Train" (Henri René): Johnny Gregory with Michael Sammes Singers, *Channel West,* Columbia CS-8400. LP. "Wagon Train" (Jack Brooks-Sammy Fain): Johnny O'Neill, *Themes of TV's Greatest Westerns,* RCA Bluebird LBY-1027. LP. "Wagon Train" (Jerome Moross): Paul Bateman/Prague Philharmonic, *The Classic Film Music of Jerome Moross,* Silva Screen FILMCD 161.

"Rawhide" (Dimitri Tiomkin-Ned Washington): Frankie Laine, *West.*

"Gunslinger" (Dimitri Tiomkin-Ned Washington): Frankie Laine, Columbia 4–41974. Single.

"The Rifleman" (Herschel Burke Gilbert): *TVGH* 1.

"Black Saddle" (Jerry Goldsmith): soundtrack, *Dick Powell Presents Themes from the Original Soundtrack of Four Star Television Productions,* Dot DLP-25421. LP.

"Bonanza" (Jay Livingston-Ray Evans): David Rose, soundtrack, MGM SE-3950. LP.

"The High Chaparral" (David Rose): Rose, Capitol 2094. Single.

"Little House on the Prairie" (David Rose): *TVGH* 3.

"Riverboat" (Elmer Bernstein): Buddy Morrow, *Double Impact,* RCA LSP-2180. LP.

"Shotgun Slade" (Gerald Fried): Stanley Wilson, soundtrack, Mercury SR- 60235. LP.

"Wichita Town" (Hans J. Salter): Salter, soundtrack, Citadel CT-6022. LP.

"The Virginian" (Percy Faith): Stanley Wilson, *Themes to Remember,* Decca DL7–4481. LP.

"The Rebel" (Richard Markowitz-Andrew Fenady): Johnny Cash, *West.*

"The Wild Wild West" (Richard Markowitz): *TVGH* 1.

"The Big Valley" (George Duning): Duning, soundtrack, ABC-Paramount ABCS-527. LP.

"Branded" (Dominic Frontiere-Alan Alch): *TVGH* 1.

"Kung Fu" (Jim Helms): Helms, soundtrack, Warner Bros. BS-2726. LP.

Chapter 4: Fantasy and Sci-Fi

"The Twilight Zone" (Bernard Herrmann): soundtrack, Varèse Sarabande VCD–47247. "Twilight Zone" (Marius Constant): soundtrack, Varèse Sarabande VCD 47233.

"Thriller" (Pete Rugolo): Rugolo, soundtrack, Time 52034. LP. "Teakwood Nocturne" (Caesar Giovannini): Stanley Wilson, *Themes to Remember,* Decca DL7–4481. LP.

"The Alfred Hitchcock Hour" (Gounod): Frank Chacksfield, *The Great TV Themes,* London SP-44077. LP.

"The Outer Limits" (Dominic Frontiere): Frontiere, soundtrack, GNP Crescendo GNPD 8032.

"The Invaders" (Dominic Frontiere): Neil Norman, *Greatest Science Fiction Hits, Volume 3,* GNP Crescendo GNPD 2163.

"Voyage to the Bottom of the Sea" (Paul Sawtell): soundtrack, *The Fantasy Worlds of Irwin Allen,* GNP Crescendo GNPBX 3009.

"Lost in Space," "The Time Tunnel," and "Land of the Giants" (Johnny Williams): soundtrack, *The Fantasy Worlds of Irwin Allen,* GNP Crescendo GNPBX 3009.

"My Favorite Martian" (George Greeley): *TVGH* 2.

"Star Trek" (Alexander Courage): soundtrack, GNP Crescendo GNPD 8006. "Star Trek: The Next Generation" (Courage-Jerry Goldsmith): soundtrack, GNP Crescendo GNPD 8012. "Star Trek: Deep Space Nine" (Dennis McCarthy): soundtrack, GNP Crescendo GNPD 8034. "Star Trek: Voyager" (Jerry Goldsmith): soundtrack, GNP Crescendo GNPD 8041.

"Night Gallery" and "Kolchak: The Night Stalker" (Gil Mellé): Warren Schatz, *Stuck on TV,* MCA 5380. LP.

"Battlestar Galactica" (Stu Phillips-Glen A. Larson): Phillips, soundtrack, MCA 3051. LP.

"Tales from the Crypt" (Danny Elfman): Elfman, *Music for a Darkened Theatre,* MCA MCAD-10065.

"Beauty and the Beast" (Lee Holdridge): soundtrack with poetry, *Beauty and the Beast: Of Love and Hope,* Capitol CDP 7–91583–2.

"Twin Peaks" (Angelo Badalamenti): Badalamenti, soundtrack, Warner Bros. 9–26316–2.

Chapter 5: Drama

"Route 66" (Nelson Riddle): Riddle, Capitol CDP 7–91228.

"Naked City" (George Duning): Buddy Morrow, *Impact,* RCA LSP-2042. LP. "Naked City" (Billy May): Pete Rugolo, *TV's Top Themes,* Mercury SR-60706. LP.

"The Fugitive" (Pete Rugolo): Si Zentner, *From Russia with Love,* Liberty LST-7353. LP.

"Run for Your Life" (Pete Rugolo): Al Hirt, *The Horn Meets the Hornet,* RCA LSP-3716. LP.

"Dr. Kildare" (Jerry Goldsmith): Johnny Spence, *TV Hits of the Sixties,* Watching Music/Moment 105. LP.

"Ben Casey" (David Raksin): William Motzing, *TV Themes, Volume Two,* ABC Festival L-38417. LP.

"Breaking Point" (David Raksin): Carl Brandt, *Top TV Themes '64,* Warner Bros. WS 1529. LP.

"Marcus Welby, M.D." (Leonard Rosenman): *TVGH* 3.

"Medical Center" (Lalo Schifrin): Schifrin, *Medical Center and Other Great Themes,* MGM SE-4742. LP.

"St. Elsewhere" (Dave Grusin): Grusin, *Night-Lines,* GRP GRD-9504.

"Perry Mason" (Fred Steiner): Richard Gleason, *TV Themes,* Tops 9661S. LP.

"East Side/West Side" (Kenyon Hopkins): Hopkins, soundtrack, Columbia CS-8923. LP.

"The Reporter" (Kenyon Hopkins): Hopkins, soundtrack, Columbia CS-9069. LP.

"L.A. Law" (Mike Post): Post, *Music from L.A., Law and Otherwise,* Polydor 422–833–985–2.

"Combat!" (Leonard Rosenman): *TVGH* 1.

"Twelve O'Clock High" and "Rat Patrol" (Dominic Frontiere): *TVGH* 2.

"M*A*S*H" (Johnny Mandel): *TVGH* 3.

"China Beach" (John Rubinstein): soundtrack, *China Beach: Music and Memories,* SBK 2–93744.

"General Electric Theater" (Elmer Bernstein): Bernstein, soundtrack, Columbia CS-8190. LP. "General Electric Theater" (Stanley Wilson): Pete Rugolo, *TV's Top Themes,* Mercury SR-60706. LP.

"Alcoa Premiere" (Johnny Williams): Stanley Wilson, *Themes to Remember,* Decca DL7–4481. LP.

"Richard Boone Show" (Henry Mancini): Mancini, *Dear Heart and Other Songs About Love,* RCA LSP-2990. LP.

"Profiles in Courage" (Nelson Riddle): soundtrack, RCA VDM-103. LP.

"The Name of the Game" (Dave Grusin): *TVGH* 3.

"The Waltons" (Jerry Goldsmith): *TVGH* 3.

"Bus Stop" (Arthur Morton): Jackie Gleason, *Champagne, Candlelight and Kisses,* Capitol SW-1830. LP.

"Peyton Place" (Franz Waxman): Waxman, *The Film Music of Franz Waxman,* RCA 2283–R-2.

"Beacon Hill" (Marvin Hamlisch): Hamlisch, A&M 1775. Single.

"Dallas" (Jerrold Immel): Newton Wayland/Houston Symphony, *Prime Time,* Cinedisc CDD-462.

"Knots Landing" (Jerrold Immel): Frank Barber, *Top BBC TV Themes, Vol. 3,* BBC REH-391. LP.

"Dynasty" (Bill Conti): Newton Wayland/Houston Symphony, *Prime Time,* Cinedisc CDD-462.

"Falcon Crest" (Bill Conti): Conti, Arista AS-1021. Single.

"Lou Grant" (Pat Williams): Williams, *Theme,* Pausa PR 7060. LP.

"thirtysomething" (W. G. Snuffy Walden-Stewart Levin): soundtrack, Geffen GEFD-24413.

Chapter 6: The Sitcoms

"I Love Lucy" (Eliot Daniel): soundtrack, *Babalu Music!,* Columbia CK 48507.

"The Honeymooners" (Jackie Gleason): *TVGH* 2.

"I Married Joan" (Lyn Murray-Richard Mack): *TVGH* 2.

"The Many Loves of Dobie Gillis" (Lionel Newman-Max Shulman): Newman with Jud Conlon's Rhythmaires, *TV Theme Song Sing-Along Album,* Rhino RNLP-703. LP.

"Car 54, Where Are You?" (John Strauss-Nat Hiken): *TVGH* 2.

"The Beverly Hillbillies" (Paul Henning): Jerry Scoggins, *The Beverly Hillbillies* 1993 movie soundtrack, Fox Records 66313-2.

"Petticoat Junction" (Paul Henning-Curt Massey): Massey, Capitol 5135. Single.

"The Real McCoys" (Harry Ruby): Neal Hefti, *Themes from TV's Top 12,* Reprise RS-6018. LP.

"Gilligan's Island" (George Wyle-Sherwood Schwartz): *TVGH* 1.

"The Brady Bunch" (Sherwood Schwartz-Frank DeVol): *TVGH* 2.

"My Three Sons" (Frank DeVol): DeVol, *The Theme from Peyton Place and 11 Other Great Themes,* ABC-Paramount ABCS-513.

"Family Affair" (Frank DeVol): Lawrence Welk, *Winchester Cathedral,* Dot DLP-25774. LP.

"The Addams Family" (Vic Mizzy): Mizzy, soundtrack, RCA 61057-2.

"The Munsters" (Jack Marshall): Marshall, Capitol 5288. Single.

"Green Acres" (Vic Mizzy): *TVGH* 1.

"Mister Ed" (Jay Livingston-Ray Evans): *TVGH* 1.

"The Andy Griffith Show" (Earle Hagen): Hagen, soundtrack, Capitol ST-1611. LP.

"The Dick Van Dyke Show" (Earle Hagen): Pete Rugolo, *TV's Top Themes,* Mercury SR-60706. LP.

"Gomer Pyle, USMC" (Earle Hagen): *TVGH* 2.

"That Girl" (Earle Hagen): *TVGH* 2.

"The Patty Duke Show" (Sid Ramin-Robert Welles): *TVGH* 1.

"The Trials of O'Brien" (Sid Ramin): Al Caiola, UA 932. Single.

"McHale's Navy" (Axel Stordahl): *TVGH* 1.

"Hogan's Heroes" (Jerry Fielding): *TVGH* 2.

"Bewitched" (Howard Greenfield-Jack Keller): *TVGH* 2.

"Gidget" (Howard Greenfield-Jack Keller): Johnny Tillotson, *TVGH* 2.

"Here Come the Brides" (Jack Keller-Ernie Sheldon): New Establishment, Colgems 66–5009. Single.

"The Monkees" (Tommy Boyce-Bobby Hart): *The Monkees' Greatest Hits,* Rhino 72190.

"F Troop" (William Lava-Irving Taylor): *TVGH* 1.

"My Mother the Car" (Paul Hampton): *TVGH* 2.

"The Courtship of Eddie's Father" (Harry Nilsson): Nilsson, *TVGH* 2.

"Chico and the Man" (José Feliciano): Feliciano, *Tube* 1.

"Welcome Back, Kotter" (John Sebastian): Sebastian, *Tube* 2.

"Love, American Style" (Charles Fox-Arnold Margolin): The Cowsills, *Tube* 1.

"Happy Days" (Charles Fox-Norman Gimbel): Pratt & McClain, *Tube* 1.

"Laverne & Shirley" (Charles Fox-Norman Gimbel): Cyndi Grecco, *Tube* 1.

"The Love Boat" (Charles Fox-Paul Williams): Jack Jones, *Tube* 2.

"Angie" (Charles Fox-Norman Gimbel): Maureen McGovern, *Tube* 2.

"The Mary Tyler Moore Show" (Sonny Curtis): Curtis, *Tube* 1.

"The Bob Newhart Show" (Lorenzo and Henrietta Music): Patrick Williams, *Theme,* Pausa PR 7060. LP.

"The Days and Nights of Molly Dodd" (Patrick Williams): Daniel Caine, *Quantum Leap: TV Hits Volume 1,* PrimeTime USA PTD 3001.

"All in the Family" (Charles Strouse-Lee Adams): Carroll O'Connor and Jean Stapleton, *Tube* 1. Closing theme "Remembering You" (Roger Kellaway): Kellaway, A&M 1321. Single.

"Maude" (Dave Grusin-Marilyn and Alan Bergman): Donny Hathaway, *Tube* 1.

"Good Times" (Dave Grusin-Marilyn and Alan Bergman): Jim Gilstrap and Blinky Williams, *Tube* 1.

"Sanford and Son" (Quincy Jones): *Quincy Jones Classics Volume 3,* A&M CD 6550.

"The Bill Cosby Show" (Quincy Jones-Bill Cosby): Jones and Cosby, Uni 55184. Single.

"Cheers" (Gary Portnoy-Judy Hart Angelo): Portnoy, *Tube* 3.

"Roseanne" (Dan Foliart-Howard Pearl): Daniel Caine, *Roseanne: The Sitcom Theme Collection,* PrimeTime USA PTD 3007.

"Friends" (Michael Skloff-Allee Willis): The Rembrandts, soundtrack, Reprise 9 46008–2.

Chapter 7: Action-Adventure

"The Man from U.N.C.L.E." (Jerry Goldsmith): theme, Erich Kunzel/Cincinnati Pops, *Bond and Beyond,* Telarc CD-80251. Score: Hugo Montenegro, *The Man from U.N.C.L.E.,* RCA/BMG 74321241792.

"I Spy" (Earle Hagen): Hagen, soundtrack, Warner Bros. WS-1637. LP.

"Mission: Impossible" (Lalo Schifrin): soundtrack, *The Best of Mission: Impossible,* GNP Crescendo GNPD 8029; Schifrin albums, *Mission: Anthology,* One Way MCAD-22122.

"Mannix" (Lalo Schifrin): Schifrin, soundtrack, Paramount PAS-5004. LP.

"T.H.E. Cat" (Lalo Schifrin): Al Hirt, *The Horn Meets the Hornet,* RCA LSP-3716. LP.

"The Saint" (Edwin Astley): Astley, soundtrack, RCA LSP-3631. LP.

"Secret Agent" (P. F. Sloan-Steve Barri): Johnny Rivers, *Anthology 1964–1977,* Rhino R2–70529. Score (Edwin Astley): Astley, soundtrack, RCA LSP-3630. LP.

"The Baron" (Astley): Astley, Parrot 10816. Single.

"Department S" (Astley): Cyril Stapleton, *The A to Z of British TV Themes from the Sixties and Seventies,* Play It Again PLAY 004.

"The Avengers" (Johnny Dankworth): Dankworth, *Jazz from Abroad,* Roulette Birdland SR-52096. LP. "The Avengers" (Laurie Johnson): Johnson, *The Avengers,* Varèse Sarabande VSD 5501.

"The Prisoner" (Ron Grainer): Grainer, soundtrack, Silva Screen FILMCD 042.

"Man in a Suitcase" (Ron Grainer): Grainer, *Doctor Who and Other Classic Ron Grainer Themes,* Play It Again PLAY 008.

"The Persuaders!" (John Barry): Barry, *Great TV and Film Hits of John Barry,* Columbia 467956 2.

"The Adventurer" and "Orson Welles' Great Mysteries" (John Barry): Barry, *The Best of John Barry,* Polydor 849 095–2.

"Batman" (Neal Hefti): Hefti, *Batman Theme,* RCA 3573–2–R.

"The Green Hornet" (Billy May): Al Hirt, *The Horn Meets the Hornet,* RCA LSP-3716. LP.

"Wonder Woman" (Charles Fox-Norman Gimbel): Fox and New World Symphony, *Tube* 2.

"The Incredible Hulk" and "V" (Joe Harnell): Harnell, *The Film Music of Joe Harnell,* Five Jays Records FJCD 001/002.

"Flipper" (Henry Vars-By Dunham): *TVGH* 1.

"Daktari" (Shelly Manne): Manne, soundtrack, Atlantic SD-8157. LP.

"Tarzan" (Sydney Lee): Al Hirt, *The Horn Meets the Hornet,* RCA LSP–3716. LP. "Tarzan" (Nelson Riddle): Riddle, *The Riddle of Today,* Liberty LST-7532. LP.

"Scarecrow and Mrs. King" (Arthur B. Rubinstein): Power Pack Orchestra, *Crimebusters,* Music for Pleasure/EMI MFP-5768. LP.

"The Young Indiana Jones Chronicles" (Laurence Rosenthal, Joel McNeely): soundtrack, Varèse Sarabande VSD-5381, 5391, 5401, 5421.

Chapter 8: Documentaries and News Programming

"Victory at Sea" (Richard Rodgers): Robert Russell Bennett/NBC Symphony, RCA/BMG 09026–60963–2; (volume two) BMG/RCA 09026–60964–2.

"The Coming of Christ" (Robert Russell Bennett): soundtrack with narration, Decca DL-79093. LP.

"Wide Wide World" (David Broekman): soundtrack, RCA LPM-1280. LP.

"Air Power" (Norman Dello Joio): Eugene Ormandy/Philadelphia Orchestra, Columbia MS-6029. LP.

"Winston Churchill—The Valiant Years" (Richard Rodgers): Robert Emmet Dolan, soundtrack, ABC-Paramount ABCS-387. LP.

"Hollywood and the Stars" (Elmer Bernstein): theme, *Elmer Bernstein by Elmer Bernstein,* Denon CO-75288.

"The Making of the President 1960" (Elmer Bernstein): soundtrack with narration, UA UXS-59. LP.

"The Rise and Fall of the Third Reich" (Lalo Schifrin): cantata adaptation, MGM S1E-12ST. LP.

"World War I" (Morton Gould): Gould, soundtrack, RCA LSC-2791. LP.

"Africa" (Alex North): North, soundtrack, MGM SE-4462. LP.

"Elizabeth Taylor in London" (John Barry): Barry, *The Ember Years, Volume One,* Play It Again PLAY 002.

"Sophia Loren in Rome" (John Barry): Barry, soundtrack, Columbia OS-2710. LP.

"A Look at Monaco" (Percy Faith): Faith, soundtrack, Columbia OS-8819. LP.

"National Geographic" theme (Elmer Bernstein): Harry Rabinowitz/United Kingdom Symphony Orchestra, *Public Television's Greatest Hits,* RCA 60470–2–RC.

"Cousteau/Amazon" (John Scott): soundtrack, JOS JSCD 104 and 105. "Cousteau's Papua New Guinea Journey" (Scott): soundtrack, JOS JSCD 112. "Cape Horn/Channel Islands" (Scott): soundtrack, JOS JSCD 103.

"NBC Nightly News" theme (Henry Mancini): Mancini, *The Theme Scene,* RCA AQL1–3052. LP.

"The Mission" NBC News theme (John Williams): Williams/Boston Pops, Philips 420–178.

Chapter 9: Cartoons in Prime Time

"The Flintstones" (Hoyt Curtin-William Hanna-Joseph Barbera): soundtrack, *The Flintstones: Modern Stone-Age Melodies,* Rhino R2 71648.

"Top Cat" and "The Jetsons" (Hoyt Curtin-William Hanna-Joseph Barbera): *TVGH* 1. "Jonny Quest" (Hoyt Curtin): *TVGH* 2.

"The Bugs Bunny Show" (Jerry Livingston-Mack David): *TVGH* 1.

"The Bullwinkle Show" (Fred Steiner): Steiner, soundtrack, *Jay Ward Music,* cassette issued by Jay Ward Productions.

"Peanuts" music (Vince Guaraldi): Guaraldi, *Oh, Good Grief!,* Warner Bros. 1747–2. Guaraldi, *A Boy Named Charlie Brown,* Fantasy FCD-8430–2. "Joe Cool," "Little Birdie" (Guaraldi): *Happy Anniversary, Charlie Brown!,* GRP GRD-9596.

"Rudolph, the Red-Nosed Reindeer" (Johnny Marks): soundtrack, Decca DL-74815. LP.

"The Hobbit" (Maury Laws): soundtrack with dialogue, Buena Vista 103. LP.

"The Simpsons" (Danny Elfman): Elfman, *Music for a Darkened Theatre,* MCA MCAD-10065.

Chapter 10: Made-for-TV Movies and Miniseries

"The Power and the Glory" (Laurence Rosenthal): soundtrack, Windemere Music 42345.

"The Hanged Man" (Benny Carter): "Only Trust Your Heart," Astrud Gilberto and Stan Getz, *Astrud Gilberto: Compact Jazz,* Verve 831 369–2.

"Carol for Another Christmas" (Henry Mancini): theme, *A Merry Mancini Christmas,* RCA/BMG 3612–2–R.

"Heidi" (John T. Williams): soundtrack, Capitol SKAO-2995. LP. "Jane Eyre" (John T. Williams): soundtrack, Silva FILMCD 031.

"David Copperfield" (Malcolm Arnold): soundtrack, GRT 10008. LP.

"Brian's Song" (Michel Legrand): *Brian's Song, Themes and Variations,* Bell 6071. LP.

"Love Among the Ruins" and "The Glass Menagerie" (John Barry): *The Best of John Barry,* Polydor 849–095–2.

"QB VII" (Jerry Goldsmith): soundtrack, Intrada MAF 7061D.

"Holocaust" (Morton Gould): soundtrack, RCA ARL1–2785. LP.

"The Winds of War" (Bob Cobert): soundtrack, Varèse Sarabande VSD-47180. "War and Remembrance" (Cobert): soundtrack, Mediatrax MT-R0001. LP.

"The Autobiography of Miss Jane Pittman" (Fred Karlin): soundtrack, *The Fred Karlin Collection, Volume 1,* Reel Music RMFK-5701.

"Roots" (Quincy Jones): Jones, *Music from and Inspired by Roots,* A&M SP-4626. LP. "Roots" (Gerald Fried): soundtrack with dialogue, *Roots: The Official Original Television Soundtrack,* Warner Bros. 3WS-3048. LP.

"The Mystic Warrior" (Gerald Fried): soundtrack, Screen Archives GFC-1.

"East of Eden" (Lee Holdridge): suite, *Charles Gerhardt Conducts the Music of Lee Holdridge,* Citadel STC 77103.

"The Blue and the Gray" (Bruce Broughton): theme, William Motzing/Czech Symphony Orchestra, *The Wild Bunch: Best of the West,* Silva Screen FILMCD 136. "O Pioneers!" (Broughton): soundtrack, Intrada MAF 7023D.

"North and South" (Bill Conti): suite, Varèse Sarabande VSD-47250.

"Lonesome Dove" (Basil Poledouris): soundtrack, Cabin Fever CFM 972–2.

"Moses the Lawgiver" (Ennio Morricone): soundtrack, RCA (Italy) OST 113. "Marco Polo" (Morricone): soundtrack, Arista AL 8304. LP.

"Jesus of Nazareth" (Maurice Jarre): soundtrack, Pye NSPH 28504. LP. "Shogun" (Jarre): soundtrack, RSO RX-1–3088. LP.

"Masada" (Jerry Goldsmith): soundtrack, Varèse Sarabande VSD-5249.

"A.D." (Lalo Schifrin): soundtrack, Prometheus PCD–112.

"Peter the Great" (Laurence Rosenthal): soundtrack, Southern Cross SCCD 1011.

"Camille" (Allyn Ferguson): soundtrack, *The Film Music of Allyn Ferguson, Volume 2,* Prometheus PCD 135.

"Rich Man, Poor Man" (Alex North): soundtrack, Varèse Sarabande VSD-5423.

"The Moneychangers" (Henry Mancini): theme, *Mancini's Angels,* RCA APL1–2290. LP. "The Thorn Birds" (Mancini): suite, *Premier Pops,* Denon CO-2320.

"The Stand" (W. G. Snuffy Walden): soundtrack, Varèse Sarabande VSD-5496.

"A War of Children" (Jerry Fielding): suite, *Jerry Fielding: Film Music 2,* Bay Cities BCD-LE 4003. "Mr. Horn" (Fielding): suite, *The Film Music of Jerry Fielding,* Bay Cities BCD-LE 4005.

Index

Numbers in italics refer to photographic inserts.